ZERO-CARBON INDUSTRY

CENTER ON GLOBAL ENERGY POLICY SERIES

CENTER ON GLOBAL ENERGY POLICY SERIES

JASON BORDOFF, SERIES EDITOR

Sustainably meeting the world's energy needs is the defining challenge of the twenty-first century. The Center on Global Energy Policy (CGEP) at Columbia University's School of International and Public Affairs advances actionable solutions to this challenge through research, dialogue, and education. We operate at the intersection of geopolitics, climate, and the economy on the understanding that energy is at the heart of each. The Center on Global Energy Policy book series furthers this mission by offering readers accessible and policy-relevant books, grounded in the highest standards of research and analysis.

Michael D. Tusiani with Anne-Marie Johnson, *From Black Gold to Frozen Gas: How Qatar Became an Energy Superpower*

Mark L. Clifford, *Let There Be Light: How Electricity Made Modern Hong Kong*

Johannes Urpelainen, *Energy and Environment in India: The Politics of a Chronic Crisis*

Agathe Demarais, *Backfire: How Sanctions Reshape the World Against U.S. Interests*

David R. Mares, *Resource Nationalism and Energy Policy: Venezuela in Context*

Ibrahim AlMuhanna, *Oil Leaders: An Insider's Account of Four Decades of Saudi Arabia and OPEC's Global Energy Policy*

Amy Myers Jaffe, *Energy's Digital Future: Harnessing Innovation for American Resilience and National Security*

Jim Krane, *Energy Kingdoms: Oil and Political Survival in the Persian Gulf*

Richard Nephew, *The Art of Sanctions: A View from the Field*

Daniel Raimi, *The Fracking Debate: The Risks, Benefits, and Uncertainties of the Shale Revolution*

Robert McNally, *Crude Volatility: The History and the Future of Boom-Bust Oil Prices*

For a complete list of books in the series,
please see the Columbia University Press website.

ZERO-CARBON INDUSTRY

TRANSFORMATIVE
TECHNOLOGIES AND
POLICIES TO ACHIEVE
SUSTAINABLE PROSPERITY

JEFFREY RISSMAN

Columbia University Press
New York

Columbia University Press
Publishers Since 1893
New York   Chichester, West Sussex
cup.columbia.edu

Library of Congress Cataloging-in-Publication Data
Names: Rissman, Jeffrey, author.
Title: Zero-carbon industry : transformative technologies and policies
to achieve sustainable prosperity / Jeffrey Rissman.
Description: New York : Columbia University Press, [2024] |
Series: Center on global energy policy series | Includes index.
Identifiers: LCCN 2023035821 | ISBN 9780231204200 (hardback) |
ISBN 9780231555425 (ebook)
Subjects: LCSH: Carbon dioxide mitigation—Economic aspects. |
Industries—Environmental aspects. | Pollution prevention. |
Environmental policy.
Classification: LCC HC79.P55 R57 2024 | DDC 363.738/746—dc23/eng/20231004
LC record available at https://lccn.loc.gov/2023035821

Cover design: Jeffrey Rissman
Cover art: Shutterstock

FOR CASSIE

AND OUR CHILDREN'S

CHILDREN'S CHILDREN

CONTENTS

III. POLICIES

ZERO-CARBON INDUSTRY

INTRODUCTION

What Is Zero-Carbon Industry?

Worldwide, there is growing agreement that eliminating human-caused greenhouse gas emissions is essential to securing a livable climate for humanity and can be achieved in the 2050–2070 time frame. China, the world's largest emitter, has committed to achieving net zero by 2060. The European Union, United States, and dozens of other countries have set 2050 targets.[1] There is greater optimism about the possibility of rapid emissions cuts than ever before, driven by plunging prices of clean energy technologies and the identification of policy pathways that will achieve economic growth and create jobs through smart decarbonization investments.

Global industry is at the heart of this transition. Industry is responsible for roughly one-third of human-caused greenhouse gas emissions, including emissions associated with electricity and steam purchased by industry (figure 0.1), so efficiently and cost-effectively reducing industrial emissions is crucial. Though industry is a major emitter, it is also at the core of developing low-carbon solutions: manufacturers produce technologies such as solar panels, wind turbines, clean vehicles, and energy-efficient buildings. Therefore, industry must transition to zero-carbon processes while continuing to supply transformational technologies and infrastructure to all sectors of the economy.

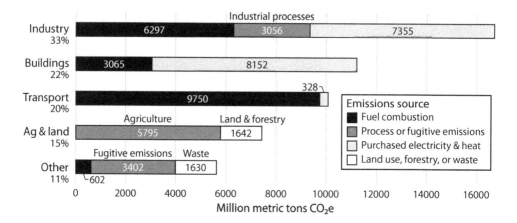

FIGURE 0.1 **Global Greenhouse Gas Emissions by Sector and Emissions Type in 2019** Emissions from generating purchased electricity or heat (i.e., steam) are assigned to the purchasing sector. In this book, the industry sector includes all manufacturing and construction activities. Emissions from transporting input materials or finished products are part of transportation, not industry. Industry does not include agricultural operations or emissions associated with waste (e.g., landfills and water treatment plants). It also excludes fugitive emissions (methane leaks), which predominantly come from wells and natural gas distribution networks.

Sources: Climate Watch, "Historical GHG Emissions," accessed May 22, 2023, https://www .climatewatchdata.org/ghg-emissions; U.S. Energy Information Administration, "International Energy Outlook," September 24, 2019, https://www.eia.gov/outlooks/archive/ie019/.

There is widespread awareness of techniques to eliminate greenhouse gas emissions from most nonindustrial sectors.

- **Transportation:** Electric vehicles and urban planning that facilitates walking, biking, and transit are making great headway in reducing transportation emissions. More than fifty countries have announced plans to ban the sale of new fossil-fuel-powered cars.[2] Worldwide, electric vehicles' share of new sales is expected to exceed 20 percent by 2030, and it will reach 33 percent in that year if countries enact policies to meet their existing pledges.[3]
- **Buildings:** Smart thermostats, improved insulation, LED lighting, heat pumps, and rooftop solar panels are beginning to dramatically

cut energy use and emissions from buildings. For instance, in 2020, California became the first U.S. state to require solar panels on almost all newly built homes. California homes built in 2020 with solar use an average of 53 percent less energy than those built in 2016 without solar.[4]

- **Electricity generation:** Renewable energy, now cheaper than fossil power in much of the world, is helping to decarbonize the electric grid. Renewables made up 82 percent of newly installed capacity worldwide in 2020.[5] Interconnecting larger areas using transmission lines, instituting demand response programs, and deploying energy storage can manage variability and enable renewables to supply a very high share of total electricity.

In contrast, the techniques to decarbonize industry are less well understood, and policies to accelerate industrial decarbonization are not as common or ambitious as policies targeting other sectors. Policy makers are often hesitant to regulate industry for two reasons. First, industry is complex. Industrial firms produce millions of products using a wide variety of production processes. Industrial greenhouse gas emissions are not just from burning fuels but also include "process emissions," by-products of manufacturing processes. This complexity is seen as an impediment to understanding which policies would be effective and avoid unintended consequences. Second, policy makers are cautious about requirements that might have adverse impacts on domestic firms' competitiveness. Industry is a source of high-quality jobs. Policy makers do not wish to cause industries to move to other political jurisdictions to escape regulation, an effect called "leakage" (see chapter 9).

Fortunately, the challenge is not as great as it seems, for three key reasons. First, industrial emissions predominantly come from a few specific industries, so a large share of emissions abatement can be achieved by improving a small subset of all companies and industrial processes. The three highest-emitting industries—iron and steel, chemicals, and nonmetallic minerals (primarily cement)—account for 59 percent of all industrial emissions worldwide, and the top ten industries account for 84 percent (figure 0.2).

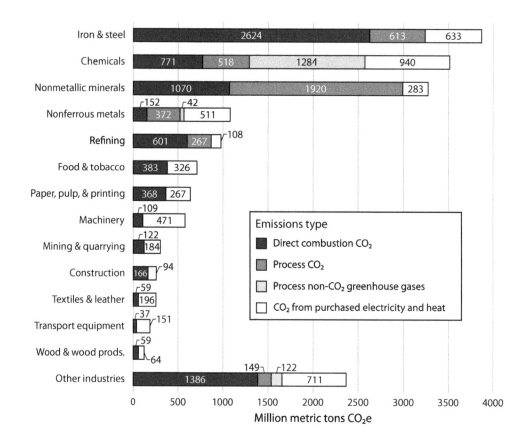

FIGURE 0.2 **Global Greenhouse Gas Emissions by Industry and Emissions Type in 2019** Process emissions (CO_2 and non-CO_2) are greenhouse gases from industrial activities other than burning fuel for energy. "Chemicals" includes basic chemicals and chemical products such as fertilizers, plastic resins, and synthetic fibers. Cement makes up the majority of the "Nonmetallic minerals" category, but this category also includes ceramics (such as brick and tile), lime, glass, and other products. "Food and tobacco" includes the processing, cooking, and packaging of food, beverage, and tobacco products, not agricultural operations. Emissions from agriculture, from waste (landfills, water treatment), and fugitive emissions (methane leakage from oil and gas systems, coal mines, etc.) are not included here but are shown in figure 0.1.

Sources: International Energy Agency, "World Energy Balances Data Service," updated April 2023, https://www.iea.org/data-and-statistics/data-product/world-energy-balances; Johannes Gütschow, Louise Jeffery, Robert Gieseke, and Annika Günther, "The PRIMAP-Hist National Historical Emissions Time Series (1850–2017)," v. 2.1, GFZ Data Services, 2019, https://doi.org /10.5880/PIK.2019.018; U.S. Environmental Protection Agency, *Global Non-CO_2 Greenhouse Gas Emission Projections & Mitigation Potential: 2015–2050* (report no. EPA-430-R-19-010, U.S. Environmental Protection Agency (EPA), Washington, D.C., October 2019), https://www.epa .gov/sites/default/files/2020-05/documents/epa_non-co$_2$_greenhouse_gases_rpt-epa430r19010 .pdf; EPA, "GHG Emission Factors Hub," updated April 3, 2023, https://www.epa.gov /climateleadership/ghg-emission-factors-hub; EPA, "GHGRP Refineries Sector Industrial Pro- file," updated November 18, 2022, https://www.epa.gov/ghgreporting/ghgrp-refineries -sector-industrial-profile; and Joint Global Change Research Institute, "GCAM 5.1.2," October 15, 2018, https://zenodo.org/record/1463256.

Second, industrial emissions are concentrated geographically. China alone accounts for 45 percent of the world's industrial greenhouse gas emissions, while the top ten countries together account for 75 percent (figure 0.3). This means that policy decisions made in just ten countries govern three-quarters of the world's industrial emissions. Even that understates the importance of decisions made in these geographies because policy can help accelerate research and development (R&D) progress and drive down technology costs, benefiting the entire globe. Additionally, if these regions transition to clean manufacturing, they may impose policies requiring that imported materials and products be produced in a sustainable way, to level the playing field for their domestic

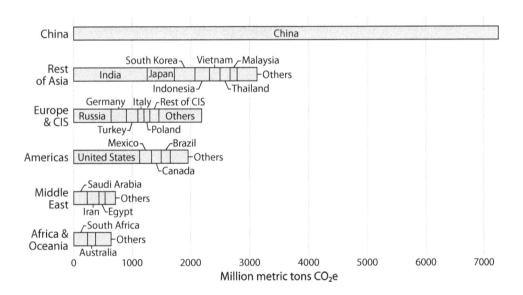

FIGURE 0.3 Industrial Greenhouse Gas Emissions by Country in 2019 Values include direct emissions from fuel combustion by industry, industrial process emissions (of all greenhouse gases), and emissions from generating electricity and heat purchased by industry. CIS = Commonwealth of Independent States.

Sources: Climate Watch, "Historical GHG Emissions," accessed May 22, 2023, https://www .climatewatchdata.org/ghg-emissions; International Energy Agency, "World Energy Balances Data Service," updated April 2023, https://www.iea.org/data-and-statistics/data -product/world-energy-balances.

manufacturers. Improving economics of clean production combined with supply chain requirements can spread decarbonization far beyond the borders of the countries that enact industrial decarbonization policies. Therefore, advocates for industrial decarbonization need not make the case independently in hundreds of countries: helping a few, key countries transition to clean industry will go a long way toward helping the entire world achieve zero-carbon industry.

Third, certain technologies and technical approaches are broadly applicable and can reduce emissions from almost every industry. Energy and carbon management technologies such as energy efficiency, electrification, hydrogen and other renewable fuels, and carbon capture cut across many industries. So do strategies to reduce the need for industrial materials and products while providing equivalent or better services: material efficiency, material substitution, and circular economy measures (such as product longevity, repairability, and recycling). The existence of powerful approaches that work across industry lines helps cut through the complexity of the industry sector and enables policy makers to design supportive policies without possessing deep knowledge of every manufacturing process in every industry.

In short, eliminating greenhouse gases from global industry is very achievable in a time frame compatible with countries' net-zero pledges. Well-designed, ambitious policies and investments in existing and new technologies will be crucial to get there.

WHAT YOU WILL FIND IN THIS BOOK

Zero-Carbon Industry is the definitive guide to understanding emissions from the global industry sector, the technologies that can cost-effectively decarbonize industry, and the policy framework that can commercialize these technologies and deliver them at scale.

Chapters 1 through 3 are devoted to the three highest-emitting industries: iron and steel, chemicals, and cement. They illustrate where and how these industries make their products and why today's manufacturing processes emit greenhouse gases. They also cover exciting new technologies that are poised to transform these industries and enable them to manufacture products in a sustainable way.

Chapters 4 through 8 describe cross-cutting technologies that will be critical for decarbonizing global industry. These include energy and material efficiency; circular economy measures such as product longevity, remanufacturing, and recycling; direct electrification of industrial heat; green hydrogen and other renewable fuels; and carbon capture, use, and storage. These technologies are useful across all industries, including the three profiled in the earlier chapters. Many industries have energy needs that can be met using cross-cutting technologies rather than requiring technology specific to that industry. For instance, 55 percent of global industrial energy use consists of fuels burned inside industrial facilities (figure 0.4), generally to create steam or provide heat to an

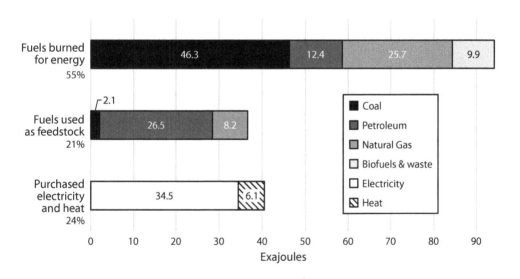

FIGURE 0.4 **Global Industrial Energy Use in 2019** Direct combustion of fuels accounts for over half of industrial energy use. Fossil fuels used as feedstocks (i.e., reactants involved in the production of nonfuel products such as fertilizer, plastics, and asphalt) account for another 21 percent.

Source: International Energy Agency, "World Energy Balances Data Service," updated April 2023, https://www.iea.org/data-and-statistics/data-product/world-energy-balances.

industrial process. Multiple industries can use the same technologies to generate the heat they require.

Technologies are only part of the picture. Enacting the right policies can make investment in cleaner industrial processes more profitable and dramatically accelerate emissions reductions. Chapters 9 through 11 explain how these policies work and highlight critical design considerations that can enable the policies accomplish their goals while avoiding loopholes and pitfalls. Powerful financial policies include carbon pricing, green banks and lending mechanisms, subsidies, tax credits, and equipment fees and rebates. Equally important are nonfinancial policies such as energy efficiency and emissions standards, green public procurement programs, support for R&D, emissions disclosure and labeling, and policies to support circular economy (such as standards governing repairability or recyclability).

Chapter 12 considers how policy makers can ensure that the transition to sustainable, clean industry promotes equity and human development worldwide. Done well, this transition can reduce income inequality, protect public health, strengthen vulnerable communities, and foster a growing economy that minimizes unemployment and inflation.

Finally, the conclusion distills the insights from earlier chapters into a roadmap to clean industry, which divides the industrial transition into three phases and explains the key goals and actions that countries should take in each phase.

There are commercialized technologies that can greatly reduce industrial greenhouse gas emissions, and clear R&D pathways exist to eliminate remaining greenhouse gas emissions and achieve zero-carbon industry in the 2050–2070 time frame. A straightforward set of government policies is necessary to ensure the research gets done and the technologies are deployed at scale. This transition will provide enduring economic strength, secure a livable future climate, and achieve lasting prosperity for generations to come.

I

THE LARGEST GREENHOUSE
GAS-EMITTING INDUSTRIES

1

IRON AND STEEL

S teel is one of the most important manufactured materials, familiar in daily life and used in products such as vehicles, high-rise buildings, wind turbines, and appliances. Annual steel production was 1.87 billion metric tons in 2019, having grown at an average annual rate of 3.6 percent per year from 2015 to 2019.[1] Over half the world's steel production goes into buildings and infrastructure (such as bridges and pipelines), 21 percent goes to equipment and appliances, 17 percent to vehicles, and 10 percent to various other metal products and packaging (figure 1.1).

Steel has many desirable properties, such as an excellent strength-to-weight ratio and low cost due to technologically mature production processes and abundant deposits of iron ore in many parts of the world. Steel is produced in different grades, from corrosion-resistant stainless steels to hardened, high-carbon steels used to make tools. While in some instances steel can be replaced with materials such as timber (discussed in chapter 5), steel is used for so many purposes, in such large quantities, and at such low cost that it will remain a critical material for the production of goods and infrastructure for the foreseeable future.

Iron and steel are closely related materials. Iron is a metallic chemical element (Fe) but can also refer to cast iron, an alloy that contains

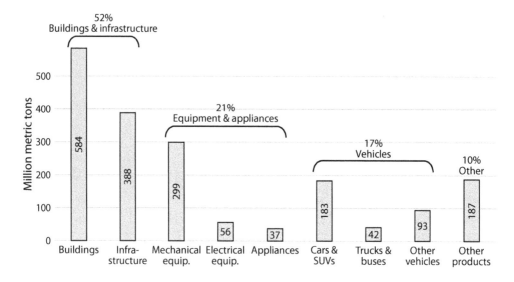

FIGURE 1.1 **Global Steel Production by End Use in 2019** "Other products" includes packaging.

Sources: World Steel Association, "2020 World Steel in Figures" (Brussels, Belgium, April 30, 2020), https://worldsteel.org/wp-content/uploads/2020-World-Steel-in-Figures.pdf; Jonathan M. Cullen, Julian M. Allwood, and Margarita D. Bambach, "Mapping the Global Flow of Steel: From Steelmaking to End-Use Goods," *Environmental Science & Technology* 46, no. 24 (2012): 13048–55, https://doi.org/10.1021/es302433p.

over 2 percent carbon content.[2] Steel consists of iron alloyed with no more than 2 percent carbon (usually 0.25 percent or below) and some-times other metals, depending on the grade of steel. For instance, the most common grade of stainless steel, grade 304, includes 18–20 percent chromium and 8–10.5 percent nickel to confer corrosion resistance.[3]

Iron was commonly used in final products before the advent of inex-pensive steel production processes in the nineteenth century, but today, steel has largely replaced iron in end uses. Of the primary (nonrecycled) iron produced each year, 98 percent is used to make steel, and the rest goes into cast iron products such as cookware and certain machinery components.[4] (Including primary and recycled iron and steel, end prod-ucts consist of 95 percent steel and 5 percent cast iron.)

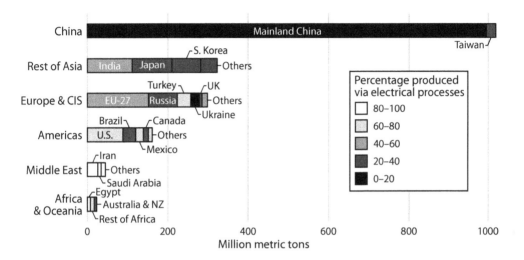

FIGURE 1.2 **Steel Production by Region and Process in 2019** Electrical processes include electric arc furnaces and induction furnaces. Nonelectrical processes include blast furnaces, basic oxygen furnaces, and open-hearth furnaces. CIS = Commonwealth of Independent States.

Source: World Steel Association, "2020 World Steel in Figures" (Brussels, Belgium, April 30, 2020), https://worldsteel.org/wp-content/uploads/2020-World-Steel-in-Figures.pdf.

Steel production is heavily concentrated in mainland China, which is responsible for 53 percent of global production (figure 1.2). Only 10.4 percent of Chinese steel is produced via electrical processes, one of the lowest percentages in the world. Therefore, it is hard to overstate China's importance when considering approaches to decarbonize steelmaking. The next-largest steel producers are the European Union, India, Japan, the United States, and South Korea, which together produce 23 percent of the world's steel.

Steel production is energy-intensive due to the large amount of high-temperature heat required to smelt iron ore and melt metals. Roughly 8 percent of the world's final energy use goes toward making steel.[5] Therefore, understanding current steelmaking processes is important for identifying technological decarbonization opportunities that target the largest drivers of energy use.

CURRENT STEELMAKING PROCESSES

Steel is often divided into two types: primary steel (from iron ore) and secondary steel (from ferrous scrap metal, i.e., recycled steel). In practice, the line between these types is blurry, because sometimes scrap is mixed with primary iron when making primary steel, and sometimes primary iron is mixed with scrap when making secondary steel. However, the overall distinction is useful because different technologies are generally used in primary versus secondary production routes.

Steelmaking processes can be broadly divided into three stages.[6]

- **Creation of input materials**. For primary steel, this includes coke, lime, and iron ore, which is usually sintered (fused) or pelletized. For secondary steel, this includes lime and scrap.
- **Smelting of iron ore** to produce iron (only for primary steel).
- **Creation of steel** from primary iron or scrap.

Different technologies can be used at each stage (figure 1.3).

STEP 1: RAW MATERIAL PREPARATION

The raw materials of steelmaking are processed iron ore, lime, coke, and ferrous scrap.

IRON ORE PROCESSING

All steel initially comes from iron ore, a mixture of minerals including oxidized, iron-containing compounds, the most common of which are magnetite (Fe_3O_4) and hematite (Fe_2O_3).[7] Some mines produce ore with a high concentration of iron oxides. This ore can be crushed and

Step 1: Raw material preparation

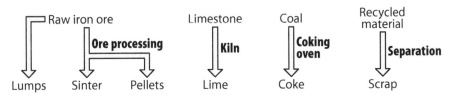

Raw iron ore — **Ore processing**
→ Lumps, Sinter, Pellets

Limestone — **Kiln** → Lime

Coal — **Coking oven** → Coke

Recycled material — **Separation** → Scrap

Step 2: Ironmaking

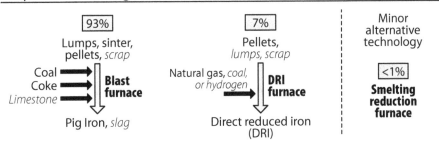

93%
Lumps, sinter, pellets, *scrap*

Coal, Coke, *Limestone* → **Blast furnace** → Pig Iron, *slag*

7%
Pellets, *lumps, scrap*

Natural gas, *coal, or hydrogen* → **DRI furnace** → Direct reduced iron (DRI)

Minor alternative technology

<1%
Smelting reduction furnace

Step 3: Steelmaking

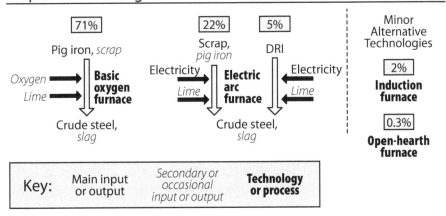

71%
Pig iron, *scrap*

Oxygen, *Lime* → **Basic oxygen furnace** → Crude steel, *slag*

22%
Scrap, *pig iron*

Electricity → **Electric arc furnace** ← Electricity, *Lime*, *Lime*
→ Crude steel, *slag*

5%
DRI

Minor Alternative Technologies

2%
Induction furnace

0.3%
Open-hearth furnace

Key: Main input or output | *Secondary or occasional input or output* | **Technology or process**

FIGURE 1.3 **Processes and Material Flows in Iron and Steelmaking** Energy and flux inputs are shown only for the four main furnace types. Percentages (in gray boxes) indicate the share of iron or steel made via each technological route in 2019.

Sources: World Steel Association, "2020 World Steel in Figures" (Brussels, Belgium, April 30, 2020), https://worldsteel.org/wp-content/uploads/2020-World-Steel-in-Figures.pdf; Jonathan M. Cullen, Julian M. Allwood, and Margarita D. Bambach, "Mapping the Global Flow of Steel: From Steelmaking to End-Use Goods," *Environmental Science & Technology* 46, no. 24 (2012): 13048–55, https://doi.org/10.1021/es302433p; International Energy Agency, *Iron and Steel Technology Roadmap* (technology report, IEA, Paris, October 8, 2020), https://www.iea.org/reports/iron-and-steel-technology-roadmap; Zhiyuan Fan and S. Julio Friedmann, "Low-Carbon Production of Iron and Steel: Technology Options, Economic Assessment, and Policy," *Joule* 5, no. 4 (2021): 829–62, https://doi.org/10.1016/j.joule.2021.02.018; and Lockwood Greene Technologies, *Ironmaking Process Alternatives Screening Study, Volume I: Summary Report* (report, U.S. Department of Energy, October 2000), https://www.energy.gov/sites/prod/files/2013/11/f4/ironmaking_process.pdf.

sintered into small pieces (referred to as "sinter") that are suitable for use in a blast furnace. Other mines produce ore with a lower iron oxide concentration. The iron compounds must be concentrated, such as by grinding them into a fine powder and using density differences or magnets to separate out the iron-containing minerals. The resulting powder is then formed into small, spherical pellets that are suitable for use in a blast furnace.[8] Both sintering and pelletizing involve high temperatures in a furnace, typically fueled by coke or coal.

Some mines produce iron ore "lumps" with high concentrations of iron oxides and physical dimensions that are suitable for use in a blast furnace without sintering or pelletizing.[9]

LIMEMAKING

"Lime" can refer to any of several oxidized calcium compounds. The types of lime used in ironmaking and steelmaking are calcium oxide, or "quicklime" (CaO), and dolomitic quicklime ($CaO \cdot MgO$). Lime is used as a flux, a substance added to furnaces to remove impurities such as silicon, phosphorus, and manganese.[10] The lime and impurities form a byproduct, called *slag*, that is separated from the metal and sold commercially. The main use of slag is as a granular base material or aggregate in construction,[11] though it can also be used as an ingredient in cement-making.

Producing lime involves calcining, or heating limestone (calcium carbonate, $CaCO_3$) to produce carbon dioxide (CO_2) and quicklime (CaO). In a blast furnace, limestone is added along with iron ore and coke, and the heat of the blast furnace converts the limestone to quicklime.[12] In contrast, in basic oxygen and electric arc furnaces, limestone is first heated in a kiln to produce quicklime, and quicklime is added to the furnace.[13] Lime is not used in direct reduced iron furnaces.[14]

The production of lime is central to the cement industry and only a minor contributor to the steel industry's emissions, so the calcining process and technology options for its decarbonization are covered in chapter 3.

COKING

Coke is a porous gray fuel that is composed of mostly pure carbon. It is obtained from specific grades of coal, known as "metallurgical coal" or "coking coal." The coal is heated to 1100°C in a coke oven without oxygen to vaporize volatile impurities (without combusting the coal itself).[15]

Coke is added to a blast furnace to produce carbon monoxide (CO), which chemically reduces (removes oxygen from) iron ore to make pig iron. To a degree, pulverized or granulated coal can be substituted for coke, limited by the need to have sufficiently porous furnace contents to allow hot gases to reach all the materials in the furnace.[16]

Electrical technologies could decarbonize the heat required to produce coke (chapter 6), but the emissions from using coke to make pig iron cannot be avoided except via carbon capture (chapter 8). Therefore, the most promising routes to eliminate greenhouse gas emissions from steelmaking, to be discussed later, involve avoiding the use of coke entirely.

SCRAP SEPARATION

Scrap iron and steel are the main inputs in the production of secondary steel. Some scrap consists of leftover steel from the production of raw steel products, such as steel plates, rods, tubes, and wire—this is called "forming scrap" and "fabrication scrap." The other important source of scrap is "postconsumer scrap" or "end-of-life scrap," which comes from steel-containing products no longer in use, such as old vehicles, machinery, and demolished buildings and infrastructure. Secondary steel scrap inputs are split evenly between these two types of scrap.[17]

Forming and fabrication scrap are relatively pure and require little in the way of separation. However, in postconsumer scrap, steel may be mixed with other materials, such as plastics or copper, requiring separation. Copper can be a particularly difficult contaminant to address, because many grades of steel have little tolerance for copper impurities, and it can be difficult to separate (or even to know) the copper fraction of postconsumer scrap.[18] A variety of techniques are being explored for improving the ability to separate copper from postconsumer steel, such as fine shredding with magnetic separation, reactive gas evaporation, sulfide slagging, ammonium leaching, vacuum distillation, and vacuum arc remelting.[19] In addition to removing contaminants, steelmakers often dilute scrap with virgin pig iron to ensure contaminant percentages are low enough to meet material requirements. Globally, the average ratio of secondary steelmaking inputs is 89 percent scrap to 11 percent pig iron.[20]

STEP 2: IRONMAKING

Chemically extracting metallic iron from iron ore is called "smelting" or "ironmaking." It is a crucial step in making primary steel. It is not involved in secondary steelmaking, except to provide a small quantity of virgin iron to dilute contaminants in scrap steel, as noted earlier.

BLAST FURNACE

Among ironmaking technologies, the blast furnace holds a commanding lead, responsible for 93 percent of all the iron made from ore today (figure 1.3), and the combination of the blast furnace followed by the basic oxygen furnace is responsible for 71 percent of global crude steel production.[21] The blast furnace is responsible for about 70 percent of the CO_2 emissions associated with steel production via the blast furnace–basic oxygen furnace route (figure 1.4), making blast furnaces responsible for about half of all emissions from the iron and steel industry (figure 1.3).

A blast furnace is shaped roughly like a vertical cylinder and produces pig iron continuously rather than in batches. Iron ore, limestone, and coke (collectively called the "charge") are fed into the top of the furnace, while preheated air (known as "hot blast") and pulverized coal are injected near the bottom.[22] The temperature reaches 1400°C–1500°C, around the melting points of iron and steel.

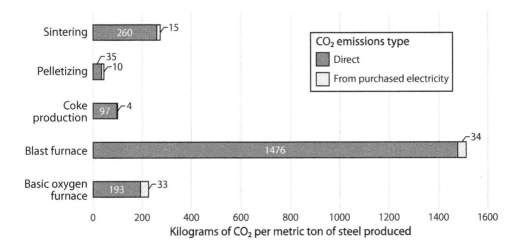

FIGURE 1.4 CO_2 Emissions from Steps in the Blast Furnace–Basic Oxygen Furnace Production Route Values reflect a global average and can be totaled across all five steps, even though an individual blast furnace may use only sinter or only pellets, not both. Emissions from purchased electricity use the 2019 U.S. average emissions intensity of 417 kilograms of CO_2 per megawatt-hour.

Source: Zhiyuan Fan and S. Julio Friedmann, "Low-Carbon Production of Iron and Steel: Technology Options, Economic Assessment, and Policy," *Joule* 5, no. 4 (2021): 829–62, https://doi.org/10.1016/j.joule.2021.02.018.

In the furnace, the oxygen in the hot air reacts with coke to produce carbon monoxide ($O_2 + 2C \rightarrow 2CO$). The carbon monoxide then reduces (takes oxygen atoms from) the iron ore, leaving behind metallic iron and generating carbon dioxide (for hematite ore: $Fe_2O_3 + 3CO \rightarrow Fe + 3CO_2$). Meanwhile, the limestone is converted to quicklime, releasing carbon dioxide ($CaCO_3 \rightarrow CaO + CO_2$), and the quicklime reacts with impurities such as silica to form slag.

Molten pig iron and slag are continuously tapped from the bottom of the furnace. Blast furnace gas (also known as "top gas"), a by-product of the reactions in the furnace, is collected from the top. Blast furnace gas is a mixture of about 55 percent N_2, 20 percent CO_2, 22.5 percent CO, and 2.5 percent H_2.[23] The latter two components are flammable and are typically burned for energy within the steel plant.

Thus, a blast furnace produces CO_2 by three mechanisms: combusting fossil fuels for heat, chemically reducing iron oxides with coke, and calcining limestone. This makes blast furnaces challenging to fully decarbonize. Zero-carbon steel production routes often involve alternatives to the blast furnace.

DIRECT REDUCED IRON

Although the blast furnace is the main source of primary iron today, one other process is used commercially at large scale. Roughly 7 percent of global iron production is "direct reduced iron" (DRI), also known as "sponge iron," made in a DRI furnace (figure 1.3). At least eleven variants of the DRI process exist, the most important of which are MIDREX (with 61 percent of global DRI production), rotary kiln (24 percent), and HYL (13 percent).[24] This section describes a generalized DRI process common across variants.

A DRI furnace takes in iron ore pellets or lumps and may burn either coal or natural gas, bringing the temperature to around 1100°C, well below the melting point of iron or steel. Therefore, the chemical reduction of iron ore to metallic iron happens in the solid phase.[25] A DRI furnace requires iron ore of relatively high purity (and does not utilize lime flux), because impurities cannot be removed in the solid state.[26]

Additional natural gas or coal forms a "syngas," a mixture of primarily CO, H_2, and CO_2. The CO and H_2 play relatively balanced roles in chemically reducing the iron ore to metallic iron.[27] The CO is converted to CO_2, and the hydrogen is converted to water vapor.

The resulting DRI consists of porous gray pellets or ingots similar in chemical composition to pig iron. DRI is structurally weak and prone to rusting or combustion due to its high surface area, so it is not useful without further processing. Almost all DRI produced today is transferred to an electric arc furnace for conversion into steel, although there are occasions when small amounts of DRI may be added to a blast furnace or basic oxygen furnace.[28] DRI furnaces are often part of integrated steel plants, which in some cases move the DRI from the DRI furnace to the electric arc furnace before it has had time to cool, saving energy. In other cases, the DRI may be compacted into high-density briquettes at a temperature over 650°C, producing "hot briquetted iron" (HBI), a form of DRI that is less reactive and more suitable for sale and transport to another site.[29]

Global production of DRI in 2019 was 108 million metric tons (Mt), more than half of which was made in India (34 Mt) and Iran (29 Mt). Other notable producers include Russia (8 Mt), Mexico (6 Mt), and Saudi Arabia (6 Mt).[30] India uses 80 percent coal and 20 percent natural gas in its DRI furnaces, while Iran uses exclusively natural gas.[31] The main costs of DRI are the input materials: high-purity iron ore and natural gas or coal. In the United States, DRI was little used because it was historically one of the highest-cost options for steel-making.[32] This may be changing with lower natural gas prices following the growth of unconventional gas extraction in the 2010s. For example, in 2020, the ore and steel producer Cleveland-Cliffs built a DRI plant with 1.9 Mt per year capacity, the first DRI plant in the U.S. Great Lakes region.[33]

A coal-fired DRI furnace directly emits 1,048 kilograms of CO_2 per metric ton of iron produced (about 70 percent as much as a blast furnace), while a natural gas DRI furnace emits 522 kilograms of CO_2 per metric ton of iron (about 35 percent as much as a blast furnace).[34] While a blast furnace can accept only a low percentage of hydrogen in its syngas mixture, a DRI furnace can accept up to 100 percent hydrogen, avoiding the need for natural gas or coal as a chemical reducing agent.[35] Combined with zero-carbon heating, hydrogen-based DRI (followed by electric arc furnace steelmaking) is one promising pathway to making zero-carbon primary steel, discussed later.

SMELTING REDUCTION

Smelting reduction is a two-stage process whereby iron ore is first reduced in solid state in a prereduction vessel, producing an output similar to DRI. The iron is further reduced in a smelting reduction vessel, producing liquid pig iron, and the resulting hot gases are fed back into the prereduction unit.[36] Smelting reduction is not used commercially to a meaningful degree.

STEP 3: STEELMAKING

Steelmaking is the conversion of primary iron (pig iron or DRI) into steel ("primary steelmaking") or the conversion of scrap into steel ("secondary steelmaking"). Today, the basic oxygen furnace and electric arc furnace are most frequently used, with induction furnaces and open-hearth furnaces playing minor roles.

BASIC OXYGEN FURNACE

The basic oxygen furnace is the most common method of primary steelmaking, responsible for 71 percent of the world's steel (figure 1.3). A basic oxygen furnace is loaded with roughly 20–25 percent scrap and 75–80 percent molten pig iron.[37] The pig iron contains roughly 6 percent impurities, such as carbon, manganese, and silicon.[38] Lime flux is added, and a lance (a long metal tube) rapidly injects pure oxygen into the molten material. Oxygen reacts with the impurities, converting the silicon and manganese to a liquid slag and converting the carbon into carbon monoxide (90 percent) and carbon dioxide (10 percent).[39] These oxidation reactions generate so much heat that no fuel needs to be burned or external heat source used to keep the basic oxygen furnace at the required temperatures.[40] (In fact, scrap is included in a basic oxygen furnace charge to absorb some of the heat and prevent the temperature from becoming too high.[41]) The off-gases are collected, fine dust is removed, and the CO is typically burned for energy within the steel plant, creating more CO_2.

A basic oxygen furnace's CO and CO_2 emissions come from the removal of carbon from pig iron. A typical basic oxygen furnace has direct emissions of 193 kilograms of CO_2 per metric ton of steel, which is only 13 percent as much as from a blast furnace (figure 1.4). However, blast furnaces and basic oxygen furnaces typically form a tightly integrated system, so the basic oxygen furnace can accept hot metal straight from the blast furnace, and the chemical composition of the materials in each furnace can be co-optimized.[42]

Since a basic oxygen furnace does not burn fossil fuels, decarbonizing it requires addressing the emissions from the removal of carbon from pig iron. If the iron ore is of relatively high purity, it can be turned into direct reduced iron, which has lower carbon content and therefore lower process emissions during steelmaking in an electric arc furnace (but not zero; see figure 1.5). To allow for the use of lower-purity ores without CO_2 emissions, a blast furnace or basic oxygen furnace may be equipped with carbon capture (chapter 8). Alternatively, the blast furnace–basic oxygen furnace steelmaking route may be avoided entirely using novel technologies, discussed later in this chapter.

ELECTRIC ARC FURNACE

An electric arc furnace is commonly used to produce new steel from scrap or from direct reduced iron, with some pig iron from a blast furnace added to dilute impurities in scrap and improve steel quality. Globally, 76 percent of the feedstock metal is scrap steel, 14 percent is direct reduced iron, and 10 percent is pig iron.[43]

The material to be melted (the "charge") may be preheated, then it is placed at the bottom of the furnace. One or more holes in the furnace roof allow long graphite electrodes to be lowered into the furnace.[44] A furnace using three-phase alternating current has three graphite electrodes. A furnace using direct current has one graphite electrode, which acts as a cathode, while an anode is incorporated into the bottom of the furnace, beneath the charge. Direct current furnaces are about 5 percent more energy efficient than alternating current furnaces.[45]

The electrodes are lowered via a hydraulic system. At first, a moderate voltage is applied to the cathode(s) until the tips of the electrodes burrow into the scrap. Once the electrodes have done so, there is no risk of electric arcs damaging the walls or roof of the furnace, so the voltage can be increased.[46] The electricity forms arcs, similar to lightning bolts, passing between the electrodes and the scrap (or, in a direct current furnace, from the electrode to the scrap and then to the anode at the bottom of the furnace). The scrap is heated both by radiant energy from the electric arcs and electrical resistance within the scrap itself.[47] The height of the electrodes is frequently adjusted as the height of the scrap or liquid steel changes and as the electrodes are consumed by oxidation or sublimation or worn down through mechanical damage from contact with the scrap.[48]

The electrodes are located near the center of the furnace, so the molten steel temperature is highest in the center and colder near the walls. To help even out the temperature (and to reduce electricity consumption), electric arc furnaces built since the mid-1990s often have natural gas burners and oxygen injectors distributed around the walls of the furnace.[49] On average, producing one metric ton of electric arc furnace steel requires 533 kilowatt-hours (1.9 gigajoules) of electricity and 10.5 cubic meters (0.4 gigajoules) of natural gas (based on 2007 data from Germany),[50] so natural gas makes up 17 percent of the energy inputs.

Electric arc furnaces are not emissions-free. There are three sources of direct CO_2 emissions. First, the charge materials contain some carbon, and additional carbon may be added to the furnace for reaction control purposes, generating about 73 kilograms of CO_2 per metric ton of steel produced.[51] Second, the natural gas burners around the edges of the furnace are responsible for 20 kilograms of CO_2 per metric ton of steel. Third, consumption of the graphite electrodes contributes 11 kilograms of CO_2 per metric ton of steel (figure 1.5). This totals 104 kilograms of direct CO_2 per metric ton of steel produced, roughly 7 percent as much as a blast furnace. There are also indirect emissions associated with the generation of purchased electricity, though these will decline as the power sector becomes increasingly decarbonized or if clean electricity is produced on site.

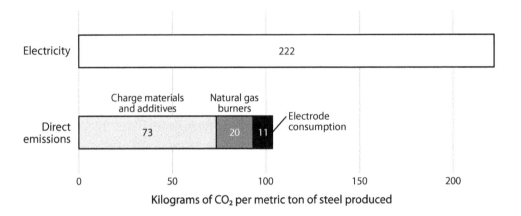

FIGURE 1.5 **Electric Arc Furnace CO$_2$ Emissions by Type** Emissions from purchased electricity use the 2019 U.S. average emissions intensity of 417 kilograms of CO$_2$ per megawatt-hour.

Sources: Marcus Kirschen, Victor Risonarta, and Herbert Pfeifer, "Energy Efficiency and the Influence of Gas Burners to the Energy Related Carbon Dioxide Emissions of Electric Arc Furnaces in Steel Industry," *Energy* 34, no. 9 (September 2009): 1065–72, https://doi.org/10.1016/j.energy.2009.04.015; IPCC, "Industrial Processes and Product Use—Metal Industry Emissions," in *2006 IPCC Guidelines for National Greenhouse Gas Inventories*, chapter 2, vol. 3, 2006, https://www.ipcc-nggip.iges.or.jp/public/2006gl/pdf/3_Volume3/V3_4_Ch4_Metal_Industry.pdf.

Today, almost all alloy steels (such as stainless steel) are produced in electric arc furnaces.[52] The alloying metals (e.g., chromium and nickel, for stainless steel) are included in the charge. However, alloys produced by small manufacturers and specialty alloys demanded in only small quantity may be made in an induction furnace, described later. Prior to the advent of the electric arc furnace in the early twentieth century, some alloy steels were produced in blast furnaces, but blast furnaces cannot produce low-carbon alloys or alloys containing an element with greater affinity for oxygen than iron, such as stainless steel.[53]

Certain steel alloys (including stainless, silicon, tool, and cobalt steels) go through an additional step following the electric arc furnace or induction furnace, called "argon oxygen decarburization," to further reduce carbon content, sulfur, and other impurities.[54]

INDUCTION FURNACE

Like an electric arc furnace, an induction furnace is powered by electricity and produces secondary steel from scrap. Instead of generating electric arcs, induction furnaces use induction coils in the walls of the furnace to heat the charge. (Electromagnetic induction is described in chapter 6.) The electromagnetic forces create a natural stirring effect that helps to evenly mix the metal. Induction furnaces are smaller than electric arc furnaces and have lower equipment costs, so they can be attractive to small-scale producers or for making small batches of specialty steel alloys. For instance, as of 2015, there were more than five hundred stainless steel producers in China, including many small producers using induction furnaces.[55]

For general (nonspecialty alloy) steel production, induction furnaces have three downsides relative to electric arc furnaces:

- Induction furnaces are less energy efficient.[56]
- They have lower annual production capacity (typically 50,000–100,000 metric tons per year, versus over 200,000 metric tons per year for an electric arc furnace).[57]
- Induction furnace steel can be of lower quality. China has found that induction furnaces do not allow for effective control over metal composition, and the firms using these furnaces often do not have satisfactory refining or quality inspection equipment. This can cause safety problems with buildings and steel products, especially if induction furnace steel is branded and sold as quality steel.[58] Therefore, China banned the use of induction furnaces for steel production in 2017, except for steel casting and creating specialty alloys and stainless steel.[59]

Induction furnaces are used in only a handful of countries. Roughly half of India's electrical steelmaking capacity consists of induction furnaces (about 31 million metric tons), representing 1.7 percent of global steel production.[60] Including induction furnace capacity in Iran,

Bangladesh, Vietnam, Pakistan, and Saudi Arabia brings the global share to 2.2 percent.[61]

In China, some induction furnaces operate illegally, and they are estimated to have produced an additional 30–50 million metric tons in 2017.[62] Small amounts of off-the-books induction furnace production may be occurring in Indonesia, Malaysia, the Philippines, and Thailand as well.[63] (Unofficial production is not included in published statistics, so it is not included in the figures in this chapter.)

OPEN-HEARTH FURNACE

The open-hearth furnace is an outdated, less efficient alternative to the basic oxygen furnace. They have largely been phased out, but a few are still used, mostly in Ukraine. Open-hearth furnaces accounted for just 0.3 percent of global steel production in 2019.[64]

INCREMENTAL IMPROVEMENTS TO EXISTING TECHNOLOGIES

There are opportunities for incremental improvements to today's iron-making and steelmaking technologies that can reduce greenhouse gas emissions. Since the abatement potential of these approaches is limited, they cannot by themselves fully decarbonize the iron and steel industry. However, they may help reduce emissions from existing equipment until more transformative technology can be deployed at scale.

ALTERNATIVES TO COKE IN BLAST FURNACES

Coal. A portion of the coke in a blast furnace can be replaced with pulverized or granulated coal, which avoids the energy use, emissions, and cost associated with making coke in a coking oven.[65] However, this does not reduce emissions from the furnace itself.

Hydrogen. In a blast furnace, the main chemical-reducing agent is carbon monoxide (CO), derived from coke. It is possible to inject hydrogen into the furnace along with the heated air. Hydrogen (H_2) can chemically reduce iron ore, reducing the need for coke. Unfortunately, the optimum percentage of H_2 in the CO + H_2 gas mixture is just 5–10 percent. Too much hydrogen causes the reaction to become endothermic and affects the chemistry happening inside the furnace.[66]

The potential CO_2 reduction from injecting hydrogen into a blast furnace is about 21 percent.[67] The steelmaker ThyssenKrupp claimed in 2019 to be the first in the world to test the use of hydrogen in a blast furnace, achieving CO_2 reductions of up to 20 percent.[68] (The hydrogen substitution potential is much better in DRI furnaces, discussed later.)

INCREASED STEEL RECYCLING

Most of the emissions from the iron and steel industry come from producing primary steel (particularly ironmaking in a blast furnace). Producing secondary steel from scrap is done using mostly electricity and requires only 26 percent as much energy as producing primary steel,[69] so it has far lower emissions. However, the extent to which secondary steel can displace primary steel is limited by scrap availability. Steel is used in long-lived products, such as buildings and bridges, and steel demand is higher than it was when steel products now reaching end of life were manufactured, so steel demand far outstrips scrap availability.

The global steel recycling rate is likely around 70–80 percent, while the U.S. rate is 80–90 percent.[70] (These rates include steel in municipal solid waste plus other sources of steel, such as forming and fabrication scrap, demolished buildings, and scrapped vehicles. Recycling rates of steel in municipal solid waste alone are much lower—see figure 5.5.) If the global steel recycling rate were to increase from 75 percent to 100 percent, this would increase recycled steel's market share by only one-third, from 22 percent to 29 percent. Therefore, to eliminate emissions from the steel industry, it is necessary to decarbonize primary steel production.

Aside from scrap availability, there are also challenges regarding scrap quality. See the scrap separation section earlier in this chapter for details.

BIOFUEL USE

Bio-charcoal and torrefied biomass (biomass heated to 250°C–400°C without oxygen) are high-carbon fuels similar to coke or coal and can partially replace these fossil fuels in ironmaking and steelmaking. However, it can be challenging to produce a biofuel with the required physical properties (hardness, purity, reactivity, etc.), which limits the maximum share of biofuels that can be used in a blast furnace without affecting product quality. The maximum biofuel share is not well established; various sources report values ranging from 20 percent to 40 percent, though some small-scale producers in Brazil have operated with 100 percent biofuel.[71] It is easier to substitute biomass for coal in a DRI furnace than in a blast furnace; some DRI producers in India and Indonesia have demonstrated 100 percent substitution, though further testing would be needed to validate this approach for widespread use.[72]

A second concern is that the production of these high-carbon biofuels may not be carbon-neutral on a lifecycle basis, may trigger land use change (such as deforestation), and may not be available in sufficient quantity in some major steel-producing countries (e.g., Japan, South Korea). For more on the availability of sustainably harvested biomass and its carbon neutrality, see chapter 7.

ELECTRIC ARC FURNACE PROCESS IMPROVEMENTS

Replacing natural gas burners. As noted earlier, modern electric arc furnaces use natural gas burners around the perimeter of the furnace to ensure material is evenly heated and reduce electricity consumption. To fully decarbonize them, the gas burners must be omitted or replaced with another technology, such as induction, that heats metal close to the furnace walls.

Inert electrodes. As discussed earlier, electric arc furnaces utilize graphite electrodes to conduct current. During use, the graphite reacts with oxygen in the air to form CO_2, slowly consuming the electrodes. A chemically inert electrode would not break down or create CO_2 emissions. It can be challenging to find a suitable material, which must be conductive, withstand high temperatures, and be resistant to mechanical damage and abrasion. The leader in development of inert electrode materials is the aluminum industry,[73] which makes more extensive use of electrodes than the steel industry.

ZERO-CARBON PRIMARY STEEL PRODUCTION PROCESSES

The preceding section covered process improvements that can achieve only relatively modest reductions in greenhouse gas emissions. This section discusses processes that are different from those in use today but hold the promise of zero-emission primary steel.

HYDROGEN-BASED DRI + ELECTRIC ARC FURNACE

The most technologically mature production route for zero-emissions primary steel relies on a DRI furnace, described earlier. Unlike a blast furnace, a DRI furnace can use hydrogen as a reducing agent and heat source. A natural gas DRI furnace can accept up to 30 percent hydrogen without modification and up to 100 percent hydrogen with minor retrofit.[74] To achieve zero greenhouse gas emissions, this hydrogen must be produced sustainably, such as via electrolysis of water using carbon-free electricity. (Zero-carbon hydrogen production, transport, and storage are covered in chapter 7.) The resulting DRI is then transferred to an electric arc furnace for conversion into steel.

Today, green hydrogen availability is limited. However, DRI furnaces can utilize pure natural gas or any mix of natural gas and hydrogen. Therefore, steelmakers can build natural-gas-fired DRI plants and transition them to green hydrogen as it becomes available. This immediately reduces emissions relative to continuing coal use in blast furnaces, provides a market for green hydrogen, and helps avoid stranded assets (investment in a furnace that needs to be shut down before the end of its service life to achieve climate objectives).

Total energy demand for the electrolytic hydrogen-DRI-electric arc furnace route is 3.5 megawatt-hours per metric ton (12.6 gigajoules per metric ton), roughly two-thirds of which is consumed by the hydrogen electrolyzer, with most of the remainder consumed by the electric arc furnace. This compares with 13.3 gigajoules per metric ton for the traditional blast furnace–basic oxygen furnace route, almost all in the form of coal and coke.[75]

As noted earlier, blast furnaces are tolerant of low-grade ore, but DRI furnaces require higher-grade ore with at least 66 percent iron content.[76] (This implies very few impurities, since pure magnetite and hematite are 72 percent and 70 percent iron, respectively.) While naturally occurring deposits of high-grade ore are limited, ore suppliers can increase the iron content of lower-grade ore (20–40 percent iron) via crushing and magnetic or gravitational separation, producing DR-grade ore.[77] Therefore, the availability of natural, high-grade ore is not a hard constraint on DRI production, but ore suppliers must invest in scaling up their DR-grade ore production capacity to meet growing DRI demand.

A prominent effort to commercialize hydrogen-DRI technology is the HYBRIT initiative, a collaboration of the ore-mining company LKAB, steelmaker SSAB, electric power utility Vattenfall, and the Swedish Energy Agency.[78] The companies completed a pilot plant in Luleå, Sweden, in August 2020 and began small-scale deliveries of zero-carbon steel in 2021.[79] They are planning to construct a full-size demonstration plant in Gällivare, Sweden, to be completed by 2026. It will initially have a capacity of 1.3 million metric tons per year of zero-emissions DRI, which will be expanded to 2.7 million metric tons per year by 2030.[80] SSAB plans to convert all its primary steel production to HYBRIT and phase out other uses of fossil fuels, becoming fossil-free by 2045.[81]

The steelmaker ArcelorMittal is also developing hydrogen-based DRI production. The company is testing the use of 100 percent hydrogen in its existing DRI–electric arc furnace plant in Hamburg, Germany. ArcelorMittal is planning the construction of new hydrogen-ready DRI plants in a half-dozen cities, including Dunkirk, Bremen, and Eisenhüttenstadt.[82] These plants will use natural gas or hydrogen derived from steam methane reforming (potentially with carbon capture) until enough zero-carbon hydrogen is available at competitive prices. The latter two plants will be part of Germany's Clean Hydrogen Coastline project, which aims to provide 400 megawatts of hydrogen electrolyzer capacity and hydrogen storage facilities along the northern German coast by 2026.[83] The company aims to achieve net zero emissions by 2050.[84]

Other companies with hydrogen-DRI projects include China's HBIS Group (in collaboration with the Italian firm Tenova), Salzgitter AG (SALCOS project), and the DRI technology provider MIDREX.[85]

ELECTROLYSIS OF IRON ORE

Electrolysis is the use of an electric current to split a compound into its constituent elements. In nature, metals are often found in the form of mineral ores, with metal atoms bound to other elements, such as oxygen. For some metals (particularly aluminum, lithium, sodium, and magnesium), electrolysis is commonly used to extract the metal atoms from these compounds to produce a pure metal. However, electrolysis has not traditionally been used to obtain iron.

Electrolysis offers a potential alternative to blast and DRI furnaces for producing metallic iron from ore. Two approaches are being developed: "aqueous electrolysis" and "molten oxide electrolysis."

In aqueous electrolysis (also called "electrowinning"), finely ground iron ore is mixed into a water-based alkaline or acidic solution. Electrodes are inserted into the solution, and a current is run between them. Oxygen gas forms near the anode, while metallic iron particles deposit on the cathode.[86] The iron particles are collected and melted down to form high-purity iron ingots.[87] The technology has been demonstrated at laboratory scale, producing iron from bauxite residue, a waste product of the aluminum industry that is 30–45 percent iron by weight.[88]

A prominent effort to commercialize this technology is SIDER-WIN, a consortium of a dozen European companies and universities led by the steelmaker ArcelorMittal.[89] As of 2021, the group was constructing a pilot plant at ArcelorMittal's site in Maizières-lès-Metz, France, which will allow the process to be extrapolated to large-scale production.[90] Another effort is being led by the U.S.-based startup ElectraSteel.[91] Compared with hydrogen-DRI, aqueous electrolysis is less technologically mature but able to accept input materials with much lower iron concentrations and can operate at temperatures as low as 60°C.[92]

In molten oxide electrolysis, iron ore and a mixture of noniron oxides (such as silicon oxide, aluminum oxide, and magnesium oxide) are added to an electrochemical cell. The cell is electrically heated to around 1600°C, turning the noniron oxides into a molten slag electrolyte. A chemically inert anode is inserted into the solution; the floor of the cell is conductive and serves as the cathode. An electrical current is applied, splitting iron ore into oxygen gas (which forms near the anode) and liquid iron (which pools on top of the cathode).[93]

Molten oxide electrolysis was originally investigated by the U.S. National Aeronautics and Space Administration as a means of obtaining oxygen and metal from lunar regolith.[94] For steelmaking, molten oxide electrolysis was independently researched as part of Europe's ultra-low-CO_2 steelmaking (ULCOS) project and at the Massachusetts Institute of Technology.[95] MIT researchers formed a spin-off company, Boston Metal, to commercialize the technology. Its process requires 4 megawatt-hours of electricity per metric ton of steel produced, 14 percent more than the 3.5 megawatt-hours per metric ton required by the hydrogen–DRI–electric arc furnace route.[96] Boston Metal expects to deploy their technology commercially in 2026.[97]

APPROACHES TO OBTAIN CONCENTRATED CO_2 FOR CARBON CAPTURE

The remaining important method of decarbonizing primary steel production is carbon capture and use or storage. Carbon capture is relevant to many industries and is covered in chapter 8. However, there are certain technical approaches particular to the steel industry that can facilitate carbon capture by increasing exhaust CO_2 concentration. They all involve oxy-combustion: reacting fuel with oxygen rather than air to prevent nitrogen from entering the exhaust. Three prominent examples follow.

HIsarna is a modified blast furnace developed by the ULCOS project, the steelmaker Tata Steel, and the mining firm Rio Tinto. Preheated powdered coal is added to the bottom, while powdered iron ore and oxygen are injected into the top of the reactor, forming a turbulent cyclone. The cyclone gives more time for the ore to be exposed to carbon monoxide, beginning its reduction to metallic iron. The ore melts and falls to the bottom of the furnace, where it reacts with the powdered coal and completes its transformation into iron. HIsarna avoids some preprocessing steps (converting coal to coke and sintering/pelletizing iron ore), reducing emissions by about 20 percent relative to the conventional blast furnace–basic oxygen furnace route. As pure oxygen is used for combustion, the exhaust gases contain no nitrogen, facilitating carbon capture, which could bring the CO_2 abatement to 80 percent.[98] A pilot HIsarna plant at Tata Steel's facility in IJmuiden, Netherlands, currently produces 0.06 million metric tons per year of steel. A larger plant (with 1 million metric tons per year capacity) is planned for Jamshedpur, India.[99]

In a top-gas-recycling blast furnace, pure oxygen is injected instead of hot air at the bottom of the furnace (eliminating nitrogen from the top gas stream). The CO_2 in the top gas is captured and removed, leaving CO and H_2, which are fed back into the furnace to reduce iron ore, lessening the demand for coke. Several small-scale versions of this technology have been tested by the ore supplier LKAB since 2007. The recycling of top gas reduced CO_2 emissions by 22–26 percent, while a 76 percent reduction was achieved when also using carbon capture.[100]

The same techniques used in the top-gas-recycling blast furnace (i.e., use of pure oxygen for combustion, CO_2 removal, and reuse of flue gases to reduce iron) have also been employed in DRI furnaces.[101] There exists one full-scale commercial DRI plant with carbon capture: Al Reyadah, in Abu Dhabi, UAE. The plant, which commenced operation in 2016, captures 0.8 million metric tons of CO_2 per year for enhanced oil recovery.[102] Carbon capture has not been applied to blast furnaces commercially, so Al Reyadah is the world's only large-scale (over 0.5 million metric tons of CO_2 per year) carbon capture–equipped steel mill.[103]

ACHIEVING ZERO-CARBON IRON AND STEEL

Using the technologies described in this chapter, it is possible to map out an efficient pathway to zero-carbon steel. Improved iron and steel scrap collection, separation of impurities, and recycling in electric arc furnaces will be important contributors to global zero-carbon steel production, but this method cannot satisfy even half of global steel demand due to a lack of available scrap to recycle. A decarbonized method of producing primary steel is necessary.

The most technologically mature route is hydrogen-direct reduced iron, and this should be one of the highest-priority uses of green hydrogen (chapter 7). Hydrogen-free options involving aqueous electrolysis and molten oxide electrolysis should also be supported and scaled up. New blast furnaces relying on fossil fuels should no longer be constructed, but recently built blast furnaces that are expected to operate for decades are excellent candidates for retrofit with carbon capture equipment (chapter 8). Blast furnaces under seventeen years old represent over 75 percent of global blast furnace capacity,[104] so most existing blast furnaces would qualify for carbon capture retrofits. Blast furnaces without carbon capture should be retired as quickly as clean production capacity can be brought online to replace them.

In a few decades, even carbon capture–equipped blast furnaces will reach the end of their service lives, and they should be replaced with hydrogen-DRI, molten oxide, or aqueous electrolysis. Material efficiency, substitution, and circular economy measures (chapter 5) can reduce primary steel demand and make this entire transition easier. These steps allow for a rapid shift to zero-carbon iron and steel production globally while minimizing early retirement of existing furnaces and avoiding disruptions to global steel supply and prices.

2

CHEMICALS

The chemicals industry is among the most important industries globally, accounting for 10 percent of the world's final energy consumption and producing chemicals that underpin our food supply, our transportation and communication systems, and numerous aspects of daily life.[1] Two of the largest chemical industry products are fertilizers, which represent about one-third of the industry's production by mass, and plastics (used to make everything from packaging to the synthetic fibers in clothing), which make up another 40 percent of output.[2]

Chemical products can be divided in a number of ways, but one categorization (used by the American Chemistry Council) follows.[3]

- **Basic chemicals** are commodity substances produced in large quantities and often used by other industries in the manufacture of products. Basic chemicals can be subdivided into these groups:
    - Ammonia and petrochemicals are chemicals that today generally use fossil fuels as a "feedstock," or chemical precursor. These chemicals are discussed in the next section.
    - Some chemical products derived from petrochemicals also fall within the "basic chemicals" group, such as the resins that make

up plastics and the synthetic fibers used in textiles, including nylon and polyester.

○ Inorganic basic chemicals include compounds such as sulfuric acid, sodium hydroxide, and chlorine, as well as pure gases (known as "industrial gases") such as oxygen and argon. Inorganic chemicals are used to make more complex, downstream chemicals or are sold to industries for use in processes such as steelmaking and electronics manufacturing.

• **Agricultural chemicals** include fertilizers, herbicides, and pesticides.

• **Specialty chemicals** are higher-value chemicals often used by specific industries as, for example, catalysts, adhesives and sealants, coatings (such as enamel), pigments, water treatment chemicals, and fuel additives.

• **Consumer products** include soaps, detergents, cosmetics, perfumes, and deodorants.

Chemicals production is heavily concentrated in Asia (particularly China), Europe, and the United States (figure 2.1). China dominates global chemicals production, accounting for over 40 percent of the world's total output. This may seem surprising, because China does not have abundant deposits of oil or natural gas, key inputs to the chemicals industry. However, China has vast coal deposits, and it demands large quantities of chemicals to sustain its manufacturing-heavy economy. Therefore, with extensive government financial support, China has developed a chemicals industry largely based on coal gasification.[4] Coal gasification is a process whereby coal is converted into "syngas" (synthetic gas), a mixture of compounds—mostly hydrogen and carbon monoxide—which are then converted into a variety of chemicals.[5] This process releases large amounts of CO_2. In 2015, China's coal-to-chemicals industry released 470 million metric tons of CO_2, which is roughly as much as the annual emissions of Mexico, the twelfth-highest-emitting country.[6]

Outside China, chemicals production tends to be highest in countries with good access to oil and gas feedstocks and heavily industrialized economies. The second-largest producer is the United States, where

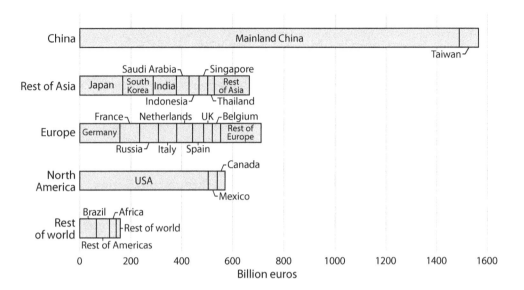

FIGURE 2.1 **Chemicals Production by Region in 2019** Production is measured in sales (billion euros) rather than mass units because chemical products are heterogeneous.

Source: European Chemical Industry Council, "2021 Facts and Figures of the European Chemical Industry," November 20, 2020, https://cefic.org/our-industry/a-pillar-of -the-european-economy/facts-and-figures-of-the-european-chemical-industry/.

unconventional oil and gas production have driven down fossil fuel prices. Brazil, the second-largest chemicals producer in the Americas, is the world's tenth-largest oil producer and has abundant access to bio-mass feedstocks, which are beginning to be used to produce bio-ethylene from sugarcane ethanol.[7]

In Europe, production is highest in Germany. Although Germany is not a significant oil or gas producer, it imports large quantities of oil to feed its refining industry, the largest in the European Union, and has a manufacturing-centered economy. In Asia, after China, production is highest in Japan and South Korea.[8] These countries do not produce significant amounts of oil or gas, but they are the fourth- and fifth-largest oil importers in the world, respectively, and, like Germany, they have highly developed manufacturing sectors.[9]

AMMONIA AND PETROCHEMICALS: KEY CHEMICAL BUILDING BLOCKS

The chemicals industry produces a staggering variety of intermediate and final output chemicals. Regulatory bodies track more than one hundred thousand distinct chemical substances produced or used by the chemicals industry, though only about nine thousand of these compounds are produced in significant quantities and used in commerce.[10] The large number of products and chemical production pathways may make it seem difficult to identify technological strategies that will allow the chemicals industry to reduce its greenhouse gas emissions to zero.

Fortunately, a great many of these output products are made from just a few primary building block chemicals—specifically, ammonia and petrochemicals. The name "petrochemicals" refers to carbon-containing basic chemicals commonly produced from fossil fuels: petroleum, natural gas, and coal (even if they are occasionally produced from other input materials, such as biomass). Downstream products derived from petrochemicals, such as plastics, can be referred to as "petrochemical products" but are not themselves petrochemicals.[11]

Focusing efforts on decarbonizing production of these building blocks can have an outsized impact on greenhouse gas abatement, since their production is responsible for roughly two-thirds of the chemicals industry's total energy consumption, including fuels burned for energy and feedstocks.[12]

The building block chemicals are as follows.

- **Ammonia** (NH_3) is a colorless gas. It is a key precursor to fertilizers, nylon, cleaners, and many other nitrogen-containing compounds. Global production in 2019 was 150 million metric tons.[13] Ammonia is an inorganic (non-carbon-containing) compound, so chemical industry organizations do not consider it a petrochemical, though some publications group it with petrochemicals.[14]

- **Methanol** (CH_3OH) is a nonpotable industrial alcohol that is often converted into intermediate chemicals (40 percent is converted to formaldehyde) and is used to make plastics, plywood, paints, explosives, textiles, antifreeze, and solvents. The 2019 global production was 98 million metric tons.[15]

- **Light olefins** are the colorless gases ethylene (C_2H_4) and propylene (C_3H_6). They are mainly used in the making of plastics. Global production in 2019 was 166 million metric tons of ethylene and 110 million metric tons of propylene.[16]

- **BTX aromatics** are benzene (C_6H_6), toluene (C_7H_8), and xylene (C_8H_{10}). These colorless liquids go into the making of plastics, adhesives, and solvents for use in industries such as health care, hygiene, food production, and electronics. The 2019 production of BTX aromatics was 121 million metric tons.[17]

- **C4 olefins** are butadiene, butene-1, butene-2, and isobutene, known as such because they are hydrocarbon molecules containing four carbon atoms. Butene-1, butene-2, and isobutene all have the same chemical formula (C_4H_8) in different molecular configurations, while butadiene has fewer hydrogen atoms (C_4H_6). They are colorless gases used in the production of rubber, plastics, and octane fuel additives. Global production of C4 olefins in 2019 was around 99 million metric tons.[18]

- **Carbon black** is a dark-colored powder derived from the incomplete combustion of oil. It is less important than the other building block chemicals. Carbon black is used in tires and pigments, with total production of 14 million metric tons in 2019.[19]

The light olefins, BTX aromatics, and C4 olefins are together known as "high-value chemicals" (HVCs), because they are made from oil, which is more expensive than coal and natural gas.[20] They are often produced in a "steam cracker," a machine that breaks, or cracks, large hydrocarbon molecules into smaller units in the presence of steam. In contrast, ammonia and methanol are typically made from natural gas, except in China, where they are made via coal gasification.[21] (Even though carbon black is made from oil, it is not considered an HVC, as it is not produced by steam cracking.)

ENERGY, FEEDSTOCKS, AND
SECONDARY REACTANTS

Most industries use fossil fuels principally for one purpose: the fuels are burned to produce energy. This energy is used to fuel boilers, heat input materials, and power other processes. For example, the cement industry burns fossil fuels to heat precalciners and kilns, which melt input materials and break down limestone to form clinker, the main ingredient in cement.

The chemical industry is unusual in that 70 percent of its fossil fuels are used as feedstocks, while only 30 percent are burned for energy.[22] Feedstocks are fuels that are chemically transformed and become part of the output products. For example, roughly 80 percent of global methanol (CH_3OH) is produced via steam methane reforming, using water (H_2O) and methane (CH_4) as inputs.[23] Most of the carbon in the feedstock methane is included in the product, methanol, so relatively little reaches the atmosphere as CO_2. However, in some cases, the output products contain fewer carbon atoms than the feedstocks. For instance, ammonia (NH_3) is made from fossil fuels and contains no carbon atoms.

Today, some of the excess carbon is used to make a variety of chemical products. For example, 36 percent of the CO_2 from producing ammonia is used to make urea and 9 percent is used to make methanol.[24] The CO_2 not incorporated into products becomes nonenergy CO_2 emissions, known as "process emissions." In 2019, 40 percent of the global chemicals industry's direct CO_2 emissions (0.5 billion metric tons) were process emissions, while the remaining 60 percent (0.8 billion metric tons) were energy-related emissions—that is, emissions from fuel combustion (see figure 0.2 in the introduction). (The chemicals industry also generates process emissions of non-CO_2 greenhouse gases, such as fluorinated gases, discussed later.)

Fossil fuels are important feedstocks for the chemicals industry, but they are not the only chemical input materials. Fossil fuels largely consist of hydrocarbons, but many chemical products include other types of atoms, such as oxygen and nitrogen. "Secondary reactants" are nonfuel chemicals used in chemical reactions. The most common of these are water, oxygen gas, carbon dioxide, and nitrogen gas, which together account for more than 80 percent of all secondary reactants by mass.[25]

Some of these secondary reactants are inorganic, basic products of the chemicals industry (such as pure oxygen and pure nitrogen gases). Similarly, alongside commercially desirable products, the chemicals industry produces various "secondary products," or by-product chemicals—mostly carbon dioxide and water but also more complex molecules. The primary or secondary products of one process may be used as reactants in another process, often within the same facility. This leads to chemical "value chains," sequences of steps that produce desired output molecules.

Figure 2.2 shows how the chemicals industry converts fossil fuel feedstocks into chemical building blocks and how those building blocks are used to make final products.[26] Note that some propylene, BTX aromatics, and C4 olefins are sourced from petroleum refineries rather than produced by the chemicals industry; refinery-sourced chemicals are shown separately in the diagram and discussed later.

For a detailed breakout of plastics (including thermoplastics, thermosets, fiber, and elastomers), see figure 5.6.

PETROCHEMICALS SOURCED FROM REFINERIES

To produce useful output products, the chemicals industry needs large quantities of the chemical building blocks. The majority of these chemicals are produced by the chemicals industry itself using feedstocks derived from oil, natural gas, and coal. However, a significant share of building block chemicals are sourced from petroleum refineries.

Underground, petroleum takes the form of crude oil, a raw mixture of hydrocarbons and other organic molecules whose properties vary from oil deposit to oil deposit. Crude oil is seldom used in engines or equipment directly. Usually, it is first refined into fuels that have consistent and favorable combustion properties, such as motor gasoline or diesel fuel. A petroleum refinery takes in crude oil, separates its various components via distillation, and produces refined fuels. In addition to fuels, refineries produce a variety of other compounds. Some of these compounds are burned within the refinery itself for energy—these are collectively called "refinery fuel gas" (RFG). Other by-products are sold to the chemicals industry.

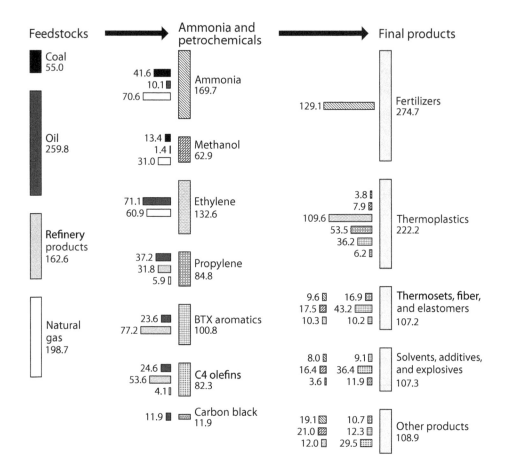

FIGURE 2.2 **Material Flow from Fossil Fuel Feedstocks to Ammonia and Petrochemicals and to Final Products in 2013** Secondary reactants and secondary products are not shown (and are the reason feedstock flows do not sum to the total mass of ammonia and petrochemicals, and their flows do not sum to the total mass of final products). On-purpose technologies, which convert small amounts of natural gas, methanol, ethylene, and C4 olefins into propylene and ethylene, are not shown. Values are in millions of metric tons.

Source: Peter G. Levi and Jonathan M. Cullen, "Mapping Global Flows of Chemicals: From Fossil Fuel Feedstocks to Chemical Products," *Environmental Science & Technology* 52, no. 4 (January 24, 2018): 1725–34, https://doi.org/10.1021/acs.est.7b04573.

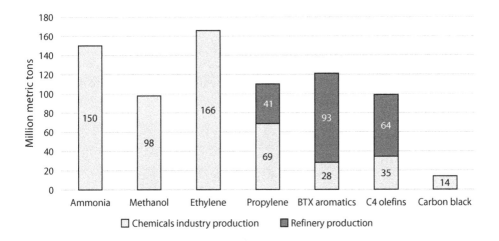

FIGURE 2.3 **Global Ammonia and Petrochemical Production by the Chemicals Industry and Refineries in 2019** Produced quantities are based on 2019 data, while refinery-sourced percentages are based on 2013 data.

Sources: Peter G. Levi and Jonathan M. Cullen, "Mapping Global Flows of Chemicals: From Fossil Fuel Feedstocks to Chemical Products," *Environmental Science & Technology* 52, no. 4 (January 24, 2018): 1725–34, https://doi.org/10.1021/acs.est.7b04573; International Fertilizer Association, "Production and Trade Tables by Region," 2021, https://www.ifastat.org/supply/Nitrogen%20Products /Ammonia; International Renewable Energy Agency and Methanol Institute, *Innovation Outlook: Renewable Methanol* (report, International Renewable Energy Agency, Abu Dhabi, 2021), https:// www.irena.org/-/media/Files/IRENA/Agency/Publication/2021/Jan/IRENA_Innovation _Renewable_Methanol_2021.pdf; Japan's Ministry of Economy, Trade and Industry, "Future Supply and Demand Trends for Petrochemical Products in the World," October 2019, https://warp .da.ndl.go.jp/info:ndljp/pid/12685722/www.meti.go.jp/policy/mono_info_service/mono/chemistry /sekaijukyuudoukou201910.html; Michael Bender, "An Overview of Industrial Processes for the Production of Olefins—C4 Hydrocarbons," *ChemBioEng Reviews* 1, no. 4 (August 2014): 136–47, https://doi.org/10.1002/cben.201400016; and ResearchAndMarkets, "Global Carbon Black Industry Analysis 2017–2020 and Forecast to 2025—Top Companies Focusing on Innovating Carbon Black Production Technologies in an Effort to Comply with Global Sustainability Goals— ResearchAndMarkets.com," January 12, 2022, https://www.businesswire.com/news/home /20220112005648/en/Global-Carbon-Black-Industry-Analysis-2017-2020-and-Forecast-to-2025— Top-Companies-Focusing-on-Innovating-Carbon-Black-Production-Technologies-in-an-Effort -to-Comply-with-Global-Sustainability-Goals—ResearchAndMarkets.com.

Refineries are responsible for producing 38 percent of the propylene, 77 percent of the BTX aromatics, and 65 percent of the C4 olefins used by the global chemicals industry (figure 2.3). However, refineries are optimized to produce fuels, with petrochemical feedstocks typically making up less than 10 percent of their output.[27] Petroleum refining may decline in the future in response to technologies that reduce the demand for liquid hydrocarbon fuels, particularly vehicle electrification. This chapter focuses on technologies to decarbonize the chemicals industry, not refineries. These technologies could be used to supply all the necessary inputs to the chemicals industry, if needed.

MOST CHEMICAL PRODUCTS DO NOT SEQUESTER CARBON LONG TERM

Earlier, it was noted that the difference in carbon content in the fossil feedstocks and in the final output products (plus the mass of oxygen required to form CO_2) represents roughly 0.5 billion metric tons per year of CO_2 process emissions from the chemicals industry. The rest of the carbon inside the feedstocks ends up in the final output products. It may seem that this carbon will not worsen global warming, because it has not entered the atmosphere in the form of carbon dioxide.

Unfortunately, we cannot ignore the carbon locked inside chemical products. Most chemical industry products are not intended to serve as long-term stores of carbon. Some products, such as fertilizers and fuel additives, will release their carbon to the atmosphere very quickly once the products are used. While some chemical products may be in service for decades, such as polyvinyl chloride (PVC) pipes in buildings, the vast majority of plastic products (such as packaging) reach their end of life within a few years.[28] Roughly 24 percent of all discarded plastics are incinerated, immediately releasing the stored carbon, and this share is projected to grow to 50 percent by 2050.[29] Plastic released into the environment can decompose over a period of tens to hundreds of years (a short time from an Earth systems perspective).[30] In the decades since widespread plastics production began, ocean and soil microbe species have collectively evolved more than thirty thousand enzymes capable of breaking down ten plastic types.[31] As more efficient biological pathways for plastic breakdown evolve, decomposition rates could increase.

While a fraction of the carbon in chemical feedstocks may be seques-tered in products for decades, producing chemical products is not a reli-able means of storing carbon long term. Therefore, this book considers technologies to prevent CO_2 emissions from both feedstock and non-feedstock uses of fuels.

ZERO-CARBON CHEMICAL FEEDSTOCKS

To eliminate greenhouse gas emissions caused by the chemicals indus-try (including through the use and disposal of its products), it is nec-essary to switch from fossil to nonfossil feedstocks. The chemicals industry requires carbon-containing feedstocks, as carbon is a necessary ingredient in most of its products. If the carbon is sourced sustainably, it is possible to avoid any net contribution to atmospheric CO_2. Three sources of zero-carbon chemical feedstocks show particular potential: clean hydrogen combined with captured carbon dioxide, biomass, and recycled chemicals.

CHEMICALS PRODUCTION FROM CLEAN HYDROGEN AND CARBON DIOXIDE

Hydrogen gas (H_2) is a high-energy molecule that can serve as a valu-able precursor to the chemical building blocks, replacing fossil fuels. Today, most hydrogen is produced from fossil fuels, but hydrogen can be obtained without greenhouse gas emissions. The only technology in widespread commercial use to create zero-carbon "green" hydrogen is electrolysis: using electricity to split water (H_2O) into hydrogen and oxy-gen gases. Electrolysis and other technological options for creating zero-carbon hydrogen, such as methane pyrolysis, are discussed in chapter 7.

No source of carbon is needed in producing ammonia (NH_3), as ammonia does not contain any carbon atoms. Hydrogen can be com-bined with nitrogen separated from the air. However, the other chemical building blocks do require a source of carbon, such as carbon dioxide. Today, CO_2 can be sourced from fuel combustion or other chemical transformation processes within the chemicals industry, such as recovering the carbon emitted when ammonia is produced from natural gas. CO_2 could also be supplied by a different industry for which it is difficult to eliminate all CO_2 emissions. For example, the cement industry produces large quantities of CO_2 as a by-product of chemically breaking down limestone to form clinker, the main ingredient in cement. Colocating chemicals facilities and cement plants could allow this CO_2 to be used while minimizing transportation costs.

Much of the research and development work to enable hydrogen-to-chemicals pathways has already been done, as indicated by these examples.

- **Ammonia**: Today, ammonia is made via the Haber-Bosch process, wherein hydrogen is reacted with nitrogen gas at high pressures. Green hydrogen is a drop-in substitute for fossil-sourced hydrogen. In fact, ammonia was produced commercially this way during the mid-twentieth century, before declining fossil fuel prices made it cheaper to obtain hydrogen from steam methane reforming.[32] For more details, see the "hydrogen-derived fuels" section of chapter 7.
- **Methanol**: Hydrogen and CO_2 can be converted to methanol. This process offers benefits over traditional methanol production from fossil fuels, such as fewer impurities in the produced methanol, which reduces the need for energy-intensive distillation to remove the impurities.[33] The process is in early commercial stages, with roughly ten plants operating worldwide. For a thorough discussion of hydrogen-derived methanol, see chapter 7.
- **Light olefins, C4 olefins, and BTX aromatics**: To take advantage of abundant coal feedstocks, China has commercialized processes to convert methanol to olefins, now accounting for 21 percent of global methanol production. Methanol-to-aromatics production routes are now in the demonstration stage.[34] These production processes could be supplied with methanol derived from clean hydrogen and CO_2, instead of methanol derived from coal.

CHEMICALS PRODUCTION FROM BIOMASS

In some cases, biomass can be a cost-effective option for the production of chemical building blocks. Biomass such as wood wastes and biofuels such as ethanol provide carbon, and they consist of higher-energy molecules than CO_2, which can reduce the input energy required to transform these molecules into other chemicals.

Sugarcane-derived ethanol is used commercially in Brazil to produce ethylene, one of the light olefins and a precursor to plastics and synthetic fibers.[35] The United States produces about 15 billion gallons of ethanol per year, mostly from corn, accounting for over half of global ethanol production.[36] Today, U.S. ethanol is blended into motor gasoline, but it could instead be used to produce ethylene, which may be increasingly attractive as vehicle electrification lowers gasoline demand in the future.

Methanol can be derived from biomass gasification, and olefins and aromatics can be derived from that methanol using methanol-to-olefins and methanol-to-aromatics processes. Carbon black can be replaced by chemicals made from agricultural or food wastes as a rubber additive and pigment.

While there are potentially important applications for biomass as a chemical feedstock, two challenges exist in supplying the majority of feedstocks for chemicals production via biomass.

- The equipment necessary to process biomass is costly. For example, the equipment to produce ammonia from biomass costs seven times as much as the equipment to produce the same amount of ammonia from natural gas (and 3.5 times as much as the equipment to produce ammonia from coal).[37] Biomass contains more impurities than natural gas or refined petroleum products, necessitating more processing steps and more energy consumption, increasing operating costs as well.
- Biomass supply is limited, and chemicals production must compete with other potential uses of arable land (such as to grow food or for conservation) and of produced biofuels (such as using ethanol as a fuel rather than a chemical feedstock). For example, the U.S.

Department of Energy has estimated the maximum U.S. potential for sustainably harvested biomass (including from forests, agriculture, and wastes) is about 1 billion dry U.S. tons per year, enough to meet roughly 25 percent of the country's energy demand.[38] In 2019, the chemicals industry was responsible for 11 percent of U.S. energy consumption (4 percent for heat/power and 7 percent for feedstocks),[39] so the chemicals industry alone could consume almost half of the United States' biomass potential. The extent to which the chemicals industry uses biomass versus hydrogen-based feedstocks will depend on the relative costs of these options. For more, see the bioenergy section of chapter 7.

It is also possible to use biogenic methane (from landfills, cattle operations, etc.) as a chemical feedstock. Biomethane can be a drop-in replacement for fossil methane, but availability is more limited than for solid biomass (chapter 7).

RECYCLED CHEMICALS

Recycled chemical products can reduce feedstock needs to produce new chemicals. By far the most commonly recycled chemical products are plastics, though certain other chemicals are recycled in smaller quantities, such as fluorinated gases used as refrigerants.

Plastic recycling takes two forms. Today, most plastic recycling is mechanical. Plastic is shredded and melted down, then formed into a new shape. Mechanical plastic recycling often results in a lower-grade material due to impurities and dyes. As a result, not all mechanically recycled plastic can be reused for its original purpose. For instance, plastic food or drink packaging may be recycled into polyester fiber for clothing, a use that can tolerate a higher level of impurities than food packaging. There is no significant market for recycling fibers in clothing, so the plastic is recycled only once, not in a "closed loop."[40] As such, mechanical plastic recycling is not a true replacement for fossil feedstocks.

Alternatively, plastics may be recycled chemically, by breaking them down to their individual monomer molecules. Unlike mechanical recycling, this process can yield plastic material of a quality equivalent to virgin plastics, enabling true displacement of fossil feedstocks and closed-loop recycling. However, chemically breaking down the plastic is more energy- and capital-intensive than mechanical recycling, making this route more costly than using fossil feedstocks. As a result, "back-to-monomer" recycling is not yet used at commercial scale worldwide.[41] It may become a competitive option depending on the costs of alternatives such as hydrogen and CO_2 or biomass feedstocks.

Not all chemical products can be recycled. For example, fertilizers and explosives undergo chemical transformations on use and may be dispersed in the environment. Consumer chemicals such as detergents enter the wastewater system. Thermoset polymers, such as polyurethane foam, vulcanized rubber, and epoxy, undergo a chemical transformation on manufacture or use and cannot be melted down and recast (though in some cases, they can be ground up and used as filler material or burned for energy). Since recycling is not practical for a large fraction of chemical products, even back-to-monomer recycling cannot supply all the chemicals industry's feedstock needs, so the use of zero-carbon hydrogen or biomass feedstocks will be necessary.

NONFEEDSTOCK ENERGY USE

Around 41 percent of the energy (including 30 percent of the fossil fuels) consumed by the global chemicals industry—20 exajoules in 2019—was used to provide heat and power. This nonfeedstock energy consumption helps create the chemical building blocks and other basic chemicals (such as sulfuric acid, sodium hydroxide, and chlorine) and to convert basic chemicals into thousands of downstream chemical products. The largest share of nonfeedstock energy comes from natural gas (33 percent), followed by purchased electricity (24 percent), coal (15 percent), purchased heat or steam (15 percent), and petroleum (13 percent).[42]

A breakdown of energy use by type of chemical product is available for the United States. According to the U.S. Energy Information Administration, in 2018, the American chemicals industry consumed roughly 3,150 petajoules of energy, excluding feedstocks (figure 2.4). (That number also excludes ethanol production, which generally occurs in the United States in ethanol refineries and is not considered part of the chemicals industry.) Ammonia, petrochemicals, plastics, rubber, synthetic fiber, and fertilizer account for slightly over half of that energy use. Other organic chemicals (a category that includes some chemicals derived from plants and some derived from petrochemicals)[43] make up a further 28 percent of the nonfeedstock energy use, with inorganic chemicals representing the last 20 percent.

Over 85 percent of the thermal fuels used by the chemicals industry go toward heating boilers (to produce steam) or to create process heat, which heat fluids and drive chemical reactions. Therefore, many of the techniques to decarbonize thermal fuels used by the chemicals industry can

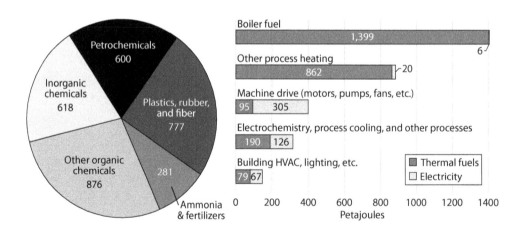

FIGURE 2.4 Nonfeedstock Energy Use by the U.S. Chemicals Industry in 2018 Energy use is disaggregated by chemical product (left) and end use within chemicals industry facilities (right). "Ammonia & fertilizers" includes production of all ammonia and related chemicals (urea, nitric acid), even when not used for fertilizer.

Source: U.S. Energy Information Administration, "2018 Manufacturing Energy Consumption Survey" (Washington, D.C., 2021), https://www.eia.gov/consumption/manufacturing/data/2018/.

decarbonize industrial heat more generally, including waste heat recovery and electric heat pumps for low temperatures, other electrical technologies or renewable fuel combustion for high temperatures, and the capture of emitted carbon. These techniques are discussed in chapters 6–8.

Decarbonization options for certain processes specific to the chemicals industry are highlighted next.

ELECTRIFIED STEAM CRACKING

One of the most important processes in the chemicals industry is the conversion of various hydrocarbon molecules (ethane, propane, butane, naphtha, and gas oil) into high-value chemicals, including light olefins (ethylene, propylene), C4 olefins, and BTX aromatics.[44] The machine used to accomplish this is a steam cracker, which breaks large hydrocarbon molecules into smaller units in the presence of steam. Steam crackers are large and expensive. The chemical company BASF's steam cracker in Ludwigshafen, Germany, covers an area the size of thirteen soccer fields, and a typical machine may cost $2 billion to construct.[45] Steam crackers operate at temperatures around 850°C and must heat nonconductive materials, which makes them challenging to electrify. However, in 2019, several chemical companies formed the Cracker of the Future Consortium to develop steam crackers that generate heat from renewable electricity. (Membership has changed over time. As of 2022, the member companies were Borealis, BP, TotalEnergies, Repsol, and Versalis.)[46] With public support, they believe a demonstration plant could be built in 2023 and a commercial-scale unit delivered by 2026.[47] BASF, Sabic, and Linde have partnered to develop a similar technology.[48]

IMPROVED CATALYSTS AND CATALYTIC CRACKING

A catalyst is a chemical that helps accelerate a reaction by lowering the activation energy barrier that must be overcome for molecules to react. Improved catalysts can allow a reactor to be run at lower temperatures, reducing input energy requirements, and can improve the yield of products.

There are many reactions involved in producing downstream chemical products and, correspondingly, many opportunities for innovation in catalysts. However, in terms of potential energy savings, one of the most promising possibilities is using catalysts to assist in the cracking of hydrocarbons, a process called "catalytic cracking." While catalytic cracking has replaced uncatalyzed cracking for producing fuels in petroleum refineries, uncatalyzed steam cracking remains the standard in the chemicals industry for producing high-value chemicals, particularly the light olefins. Compounds such as zeolites, a type of aluminosilicate mineral, are being studied as a means of saving energy and improving the yields of desirable products. The South Korean firm SK Energy, the U.S. engineering firm KBR, and the Korea Research Institute of Chemical Technology built the first catalytic cracking petrochemical plant, which began operation in Ulsan, South Korea, in late 2017. It operates at a lower reaction temperature (600°C–650°C, versus over 800°C) and achieves a 30 percent increase in light olefin yield relative to conventional steam cracking.[49]

METHANOL FROM PARTIAL OXIDATION OF METHANE

Methanol (CH_3OH) is traditionally produced in a two-step process. First, methane (CH_4) is reacted with steam (H_2O) to produce syngas, a mixture of carbon monoxide, hydrogen, carbon dioxide, and small amounts of unreacted methane and trace chemicals.[50] Then the syngas is pressurized and converted into methanol using catalysts. An alternative route involves reacting methane with oxygen to produce methanol directly. This avoids the need to first produce syngas, the process step responsible for 60 percent of the capital costs and 20–30 percent of the energy inputs (equivalent to 45–70 percent of the net energy consumption, i.e., excluding the energy in the produced methanol).[51]

This process faces significant engineering challenges, such as reducing the cost of obtaining purified oxygen and avoiding oxidation of the produced methanol, which reduces product yield and creates unwanted

CO or CO_2.[52] BASF and the hydrogen company Linde Engineering are working to improve and commercialize the partial oxidation process, aiming to use this methanol production route in a large-scale industrial plant by 2030.[53]

BIOMANUFACTURING

Biomanufacturing is the use of an organism or biological system to produce chemicals or other products. An organism such as a microbe or algae may be genetically engineered to transform a feedstock into a desired substance as a by-product of its metabolism (e.g., via fermentation). Alternatively, enzymes (biological catalysts) can be produced and used in a chemical reactor without the presence of a living organism.[54] These processes require feedstocks—most commonly, biomass feedstocks such as sugar—but organisms can be engineered to utilize other feedstocks, such as methane.[55]

Biomanufacturing can remove steps from the production process and reduce input energy requirements and associated CO_2 emissions. However, it also involves unique complications, such as regulating temperature and nutrients to keep organisms alive and optimize fermentation processes.

Biomanufacturing is best-suited to producing high-value, downstream organic molecules, such as pharmaceuticals, herbicides, adhesives, and coatings.[56] Biomanufacturing will likely have difficulty competing with traditional methods of producing simple, upstream chemicals in extremely large volumes at low cost (such as steam cracking to produce ethylene).

NON-CO_2 PROCESS EMISSIONS

Process emissions are greenhouse gas emissions from industrial activities other than burning fuels for energy. In addition to the CO_2 process emissions discussed earlier, the chemicals industry also creates process emissions of other greenhouse gases, specifically methane (CH_4), nitrous oxide (N_2O), and fluorinated gases (F-gases). According to the U.S. Environmental Protection Agency (EPA), in 2019, the global chemicals industry was responsible for the following emissions (in million metric tons of carbon dioxide equivalent, Mt CO_2e):[57]

- **1,140 Mt CO_2e of F-gases**. This includes
  - 1,016 Mt CO_2e of hydrofluorocarbons (HFCs). Most of these HFCs (768 Mt) are used as a refrigerant—that is, the working fluid in refrigerators, freezers, air conditioners, and heat pumps, which absorbs heat from one area and releases it in another area. HFCs are also used for a variety of purposes in industry, including as an aerosol propellant and foam-blowing agent (95 Mt), in fire suppression chemicals (22 Mt), for cleaning solvents (7 Mt), and in the manufacture of semiconductors and flat-panel displays (2 Mt). The remaining 121 Mt of HFCs are unwanted by-products of producing other F-gases (primarily HCFC-22) for sale.
  - 96 Mt CO_2e of sulfur hexafluoride (SF_6). SF_6 is used as a gaseous electrical insulator in high-voltage electrical systems (63 Mt), to assist in the manufacture of semiconductors and flat-panel displays (28 Mt), and to protect molten magnesium metal from exposure to air during casting (5 Mt).
  - 28 Mt CO_2e of perfluorocarbons (PFCs; 18 Mt) and nitrogen trifluoride (NF_3; 10 Mt). These chemicals are used in the semiconductor, flat-panel display, and photovoltaic cell manufacturing industries. (A further 38 Mt of PFCs are emitted by the aluminum industry, but that industry generates these PFCs rather than purchasing them from the chemicals industry, so they are not included in the chemicals industry's total.)
- **261 Mt CO_2e of nitrous oxide**. Of this total, 75 percent is due to the production of just two chemicals: 114 Mt is emitted during the production of adipic acid ($C_6H_{10}O_4$), and 81 Mt is due to the production of nitric acid (HNO_3).
- **9 Mt CO_2e of methane**, though this may be a serious underestimate. A 2019 study by Cornell University found methane emissions from

six U.S. ammonia-based fertilizer plants were 145 times higher than reported by the EPA. These plants represented over 25 percent of U.S. ammonia-based fertilizer production.[58]

F-GASES

Fluorinated gases are commercial products of the chemicals industry. The most common F-gases, HFCs, were introduced as a replacement for gases that were found to damage the ozone layer (a layer of ozone in Earth's stratosphere that filters out harmful ultraviolet radiation before it reaches the ground). Earlier chemicals used as refrigerants (CFCs and HCFCs) and for fire suppression (halons) were phased out under an international agreement signed in 1987, the Montreal Protocol. HFCs were widely adopted as a replacement. While safe for the ozone layer, HFCs were found to be extremely potent greenhouse gases that remain in the atmosphere for thousands of years.

To mitigate this danger to the climate, the Montreal Protocol was amended in 2016 to gradually phase out the production and use of HFCs. As of June 2023, 150 countries had ratified the Kigali Amendment, including India and China in 2021 and the United States in 2022.[59] The United States enacted legislation that will reduce HFC production and use by 85 percent by 2036, in line with the amendment's targets.[60]

The chemicals industry's process CO_2, methane, and nitrous oxide emissions are due to production processes or leakage from its facilities. In contrast, only about 10 percent of global F-gas emissions come directly from chemical manufacturing facilities (predominantly in the form of HFC-23, a by-product of the manufacture of other F-gases, primarily HCFC-22).[61] About 90 percent of produced F-gases reach the atmosphere only after they are sold—either when the product is used (as with aerosol propellants and foam-blowing agents) or gradually, such as when refrigerants leak from air conditioners and refrigerators—or are released when these products are scrapped at end of life.

Since the F-gases are not emitted directly from chemicals industry facilities, some sources do not ascribe these emissions to the chemicals industry but to the industries that purchase the F-gases. However, the chemicals industry has a key role in reducing F-gas emissions by developing and marketing substitute chemicals that can fulfill customers' needs without harming the climate. (Until safer chemicals are universally adopted, there are also important actions for F-gas buyers to take.) Accordingly, this book discusses F-gases and associated abatement options in this section.

There are two broad strategies to reduce F-gas emissions from industry. First, use less harmful chemicals to fulfill the same needs. The chemicals industry can develop and market chemicals that work effectively as refrigerants, propellants, and insulators while meeting environmental and consumer safety needs. For example, a replacement for HFCs must be safe for the ozone layer and for the climate and must have good heat transfer properties to allow for energy-efficient refrigerators and air conditioners.

Many candidate chemicals have specific limitations or drawbacks. For example, hydrocarbons such as propane and isobutane have low global warming potential and good energy efficiency, but they are highly flammable, limiting the applications in which they can be used. Ammonia has good energy performance, low global warming potential, and is less flammable than hydrocarbons, but it is toxic. CO_2 has low global warming potential and is nonflammable, but it must be used at a very high pressure, under which conditions it exhibits supercritical behavior, posing risks and requiring expensive system redesigns. Also, it is not as efficient as other refrigerants for certain applications, such as air conditioning in hot climates.

The chemicals industry has developed a variety of hydrofluoroolefins (HFOs), which are promising but require more research to bring down costs, and there are often trade-offs between global warming potential, flammability, and energy efficiency.[62]

The second strategy for reducing F-gas emissions from industry is to prevent leakage, then recycle or destroy F-gases at equipment end of life or after use. For refrigerants, industries can carefully monitor their equipment for leaks and respond promptly to any leakage. When a machine containing refrigerants reaches end of life, the industry can have the F-gas carefully extracted and destroyed before the equipment is scrapped. Alternatively, the recovered F-gases can be reused in other equipment (i.e., recycled) if no safer alternative chemicals are available for that specific industrial purpose. Extended producer responsibility policies (chapter 11) can encourage or require manufacturers to offer take-back and recycling programs.

Industries such as semiconductor and flat-panel display manufacturing use HFCs in the fabrication process, not as refrigerants in a closed-loop system. For instance, semiconductor manufacturers use seven different F-gases to clean chemical vapor deposition equipment and to etch microscopic patterns onto silicon wafers.[63] Like refrigerants, the F-gases used in manufacturing processes can often be recovered and destroyed rather than released into the environment. European semiconductor manufacturers achieve a 75 percent destruction rate.[64]

NITROUS OXIDE

Nitrous oxide (N_2O) is primarily emitted by the production of nitric and adipic acids. In 2020, 70 million metric tons of nitric acid were produced from ammonia (one of the main chemical building blocks), oxygen, and water.[65] Roughly 3.5 million metric tons of adipic acid were produced from nitric acid and cyclohexane (C_6H_{12}), itself derived from benzene, one of the BTX aromatics.[66] Most nitric acid is used to produce nitrogen-containing fertilizers, while almost all adipic acid is turned into polymers to produce nylon and polyurethane.[67] N_2O is produced as a by-product of these chemical reactions.

Although methods exist for producing adipic acid without forming N_2O, they have not been commercialized on a large scale.[68] The main technique for reducing N_2O emissions from adipic acid is to capture and convert the N_2O into nitrogen and oxygen gases through catalytic decomposition or thermal destruction.[69] Similarly, the N_2O from nitric acid production can be destroyed, most commonly by adding a catalyst to the reactor in which the nitric acid is produced. Around 95 percent of N_2O emissions can be destroyed at low cost using these commercialized technologies.[70] BASF has achieved an N_2O destruction rate of 99.9 percent without major plant modifications or investments.[71]

METHANE

Methane is the main constituent of natural gas, a key feedstock input to the chemicals industry. Unlike N_2O, which is produced as a by-product of certain chemical reactions, methane emissions are a result of undesired leakage from pipes and equipment. Therefore, the key control strategy for methane is to find and plug methane leaks.

Methane is colorless, but it can be detected with lasers or infrared cameras. Methane leakage is not a problem unique to the chemicals industry. In fact, most methane leakage occurs at the wellhead in oil and gas fields, as well as from natural gas transmission and distribution pipes. Technologies such as sensor networks or drones equipped with infrared cameras are used to identify leaks so the equipment can be serviced.

Leakage rates can be difficult to estimate with precision, but studies find much lower rates from chemicals facilities than from oil and gas operations (0.34 percent leakage from ammonia fertilizer plants versus 3.7 percent leakage from gas extraction in the Permian Basin,[72] a large oil-producing region in the United States).

No new technology is required to reduce the chemicals industry's methane emissions—better leak detection and servicing of equipment could greatly reduce leaks. However, reducing or eliminating the use of methane feedstocks in favor of zero-carbon hydrogen would also help address methane leakage.

ACHIEVING ZERO-CARBON CHEMICALS

There are three aspects to eliminating greenhouse gas emissions from the chemicals industry: decarbonizing the heat that drives chemical reactions, cleaning up the feedstocks that make up chemical products, and avoiding the release of by-product, non-CO_2 greenhouse gases. The most efficient way to decarbonize heat is via direct electrification using technologies such as plasma torches, electric resistance heating, and infrared heating, or sometimes by replacing heat with electrolysis (see chapter 6). Efforts to commercialize electrified chemical manufacturing equipment, such as steam crackers, should be supported and accelerated. Process improvements and better catalysts can reduce energy requirements and ease the load on the electricity grid.

Eliminating fossil feedstocks is necessary to avoid upstream greenhouse gas emissions from fossil fuel extraction and downstream emissions released when chemical products are used or incinerated or when they decay. The chemical industry will demand vast amounts of green hydrogen and sustainably grown bioenergy to replace its oil, gas, and coal feedstocks, which cannot be directly electrified. Chemical feedstocks are one of the highest-priority uses to which green hydrogen and sustainable bioenergy should be directed (chapter 7).

Avoiding non-CO_2 greenhouse gas emissions largely amounts to switching to climate-safe substitutes for F-gases, thermally or catalytically destroying formed N_2O, and avoiding methane leaks. Of these, only F-gases pose a technical challenge. F-gas production should be phased out, which would cause manufacturers to design their products (such as chillers and foams) to be compatible with climate-safe refrigerant and propellant gases.

Though the chemicals industry may at first appear overwhelmingly complex, breaking it down into specific emissions sources makes it easier to identify and prioritize the technologies that can efficiently achieve sustainable, zero-carbon chemicals globally.

3

CEMENT AND CONCRETE

Every year, 32 billion metric tons of concrete are produced globally, making it the most-used human-made material.[1] Concrete's popularity stems from its favorable properties (durability, compressive strength, nonflammability, resistance to pests and flooding) and widespread availability of its constituent materials.[2] Concrete consists of sand and crushed rock, called "aggregate," held together by a binder, called "cement." Aggregate production energy requirements are small and largely in the form of electricity for crushing rock, which can be provided by zero-carbon electricity sources (chapter 6). Cement accounts for the vast majority of greenhouse gas emissions from concrete production.[3]

In 2019, 4.1 billion metric tons of cement were produced worldwide. Production was essentially flat from 2014 to 2019, after having grown at an average rate of 6.4 percent per year from 2000 to 2014.[4] China produces 55 percent of the world's cement, while India is second, with 7.5 percent. No other country is responsible for more than roughly 2 percent (figure 3.1). Cement production is projected to rise to 4.6 billion metric tons per year by 2050, with production in India and Africa more than tripling (and non-China, non-India Asia more than doubling), more than compensating for anticipated declines in Chinese output.[5]

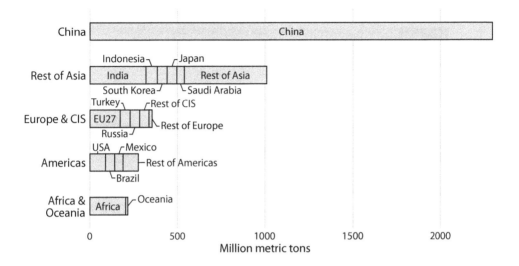

FIGURE 3.1 **Cement Production by Region in 2019** CIS = Commonwealth of Independent States.

Source: European Cement Association, *2020 Activity Report* (report, CEMBUREAU, Brussels, May 2021), https://www.cembureau.eu/media/1sjf4sk4/cembureau-activity-report-2020.pdf.

CEMENT COMPOSITION AND TYPES

Today's cement consists primarily of "clinker," a mixture of minerals containing calcium oxide and silicon dioxide, primarily alite ($3CaO \cdot SiO_2$) and belite ($2CaO \cdot SiO_2$). Other oxides, particularly aluminum, iron, and sulfur oxides, also make up a small percentage of clinker (figure 3.2).

The fraction of cement that consists of clinker varies by region and cement type. Globally, clinker makes up 66 percent of cement, while the remainder consists of slag (a by-product of ironmaking), limestone, fly ash (a by-product of coal combustion), gypsum, and natural pozzolana (volcanic ash) (figure 3.2).

Cement composition can vary to optimize its performance under different conditions. Cement can be classified in several ways.

- The standards organization ASTM International divides cement into ten classes. Six classes encompass normal cement (also called

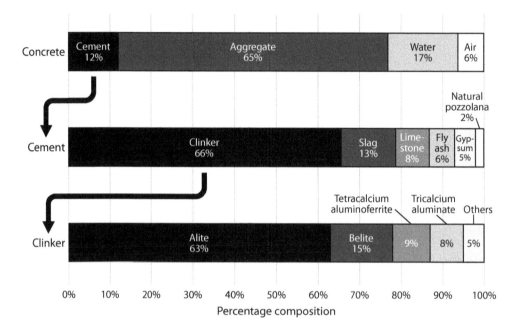

FIGURE 3.2 **Global Average Concrete, Cement, and Clinker Composition in 2014**
Concrete composition shares are by volume. Cement and clinker composition shares are by
mass. In cement, "8 percent limestone" refers to uncalcined limestone, while the "66 percent
clinker" is largely derived from calcined limestone, described later in the chapter.

Sources: International Energy Agency and Cement Sustainability Initiative, *Technology Roadmap:
   Low-Carbon Transition in the Cement Industry* (technology report, Paris, April 6, 2018), https://
   www.iea.org/publications/freepublications/publication/TechnologyRoadmapLowCarbonTransition
   intheCementIndustry.pdf; Portland Cement Association, "Cast-In-Place (CIP) Concrete," accessed
   July 1, 2023, https://www.cement.org/cement-concrete/cement-specific-materials/how-concrete-is-made.

"ordinary Portland cement" or "OPC") and variants that offer benefits such as increased sulfate resistance, low heat of hydration, or rapid
hardening. The remaining four classes refer to blended cements, such
as those that use larger shares of limestone, slag, or pozzolana.[6]

- Almost all cement used today is "hydraulic cement," which hardens when mixed with water. Older "nonhydraulic cements" are
rarely used because they must be kept dry while they slowly harden
by reaction with atmospheric CO_2. Some new, alternative clinker
cements, discussed later in this chapter, are nonhydraulic cements
that are cured using high concentrations of CO_2 rather than water.

- Around 99 percent of cement is "gray cement." Approximately 1 percent is "white cement," which is light in color and has a smooth surface texture.[7] White cement requires higher kiln temperatures and therefore more energy to produce. It has the same physical strength as gray cement and is used for aesthetic reasons.

USES OF CEMENT

Cement powder is mixed with water and aggregate to form concrete, either as ready-mix concrete (a pourable product mixed at a concrete plant and delivered to a building site in a truck with a rotating drum), as a dry bagged product that is mixed on site by the builder, or inside a factory producing precast products (such as pavers) that are delivered once hardened.[8] Concrete typically is 10–15 percent cement, 60–75 percent aggregate, 15–20 percent water, and 5–8 percent entrained air by volume.[9] Once mixed with water, hydraulic cement undergoes chemical reactions called "hydration," which causes cement to harden, binding the aggregate. The resulting concrete is strong against compressive forces but weak in tension. For this reason, concrete is often poured around steel reinforcements, which add tensile strength.

In 2022, 33 percent of global ready-mix concrete consumption was for residential buildings, 28 percent for infrastructure, 22 percent for commercial buildings, and 17 percent for other uses.[10] Nonconcrete applications of cement (representing 10 percent of U.S. cement consumption) include grouting oil and gas wells, stabilizing soils, and making building materials such as stucco.[11]

CEMENT PRODUCTION

Cement production involves essentially three steps: grinding and mixing the raw materials, heating the materials in a kiln (and often a precalciner) to form clinker, and, finally, grinding and mixing the clinker with other minerals to produce powdered cement.

Limestone, clay, and marl (a carbonate-rich mineral) are quarried and crushed, forming pieces under 5 cm in diameter.[12] These may be mixed with a small quantity of other materials that contribute iron oxide, alumina, and silica to the clinker.[13] Two methods of processing these raw materials are in use today. The "dry process," the more common and efficient method, involves drying the raw materials to about 0.5 percent moisture content and grinding them to form a powder. An older approach, the "wet process," involves grinding and mixing the raw materials with around 36 percent water to form a slurry, though semi-wet variants with moisture content as low as 17 percent exist.[14] The wet process greatly increases the kiln's energy consumption, as additional heat must be used to evaporate the water. Global Cement and Concrete Association data representing 22 percent of 2019 global capacity show that dry processes are used for 88 percent of clinker production, semi-wet or mixed processes for 10 percent, and wet processes for 2 percent.[15] (The share of wet and semiwet processes would be higher if data from all cement producers were available, as less efficient producers are less likely to be association members.)

In a modern dry process system, the ground raw materials are fed into a preheater, raising their temperature. Most dry process plants also include a precalciner, a system that uses waste heat from the kiln and additional heat from fuel combustion to further increase the materials' temperature and begin the process of "calcination," chemically transforming the materials into clinker.[16] A precalciner contains between three and six stages in which heated exhaust gas rises from below and powdered inputs descend from above. In each stage, powdered inputs are blown in a cyclone, ensuring the materials are uniformly mixed and that heat is efficiently transferred from the gas to the materials. (The earliest dry process systems, as well as semiwet and wet process systems, pass raw materials to the kiln without preheating.)[17]

The kiln is a large cylinder, up to 5 meters in diameter and 75 meters in length for dry process plants and up to 8 meters in diameter and 230 meters in length for wet process plants.[18] It is tilted three to four degrees from horizontal and rotates one to three times per minute.[19] The raw materials are fed into the higher end.[20] Fuel is burned to add heat at the lower end of the kiln, raising its temperature to 1450°C.[21] Globally, coal is the most common fuel, comprising 70 percent of thermal fuel use, while oil accounts for 15 percent, natural gas 10 percent, waste 3 percent, and biomass 2 percent (figure 3.3). The most efficient dry process kilns have six-stage precalciners and consume 3.0–3.4 gigajoules of fuel per metric ton of clinker produced.[22] Typical wet process kilns use 5.3–7.1 gigajoules per metric ton.[23]

In the kiln, the materials finish calcining, and calcium carbonate breaks down to form calcium oxide ($CaCO_3 \rightarrow CaO + CO_2$). The CaO combines with other materials, such as silicates, to form clinker (primarily alite and belite; see figure 3.2). The CO_2 is released to the atmosphere.

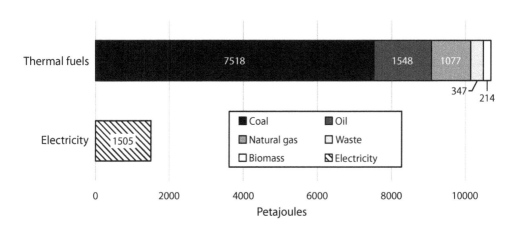

FIGURE 3.3 **Global Cement Industry Energy Use in 2019** Thermal fuels are used to heat the kiln and precalciner, while most electricity is used to grind input materials and cement.

Sources: International Energy Agency and Cement Sustainability Initiative, *Technology Roadmap: Low-Carbon Transition in the Cement Industry* (technology report, Paris, April 6, 2018), https://www.iea.org/publications/freepublications/publication/TechnologyRoadmap LowCarbonTransitionintheCementIndustry.pdf; European Cement Association, *2020 Activity Report* (report, CEMBUREAU, Brussels, May 2021), https://www.cembureau.eu/media /1sjf4sk4/cembureau-activity-report-2020.pdf; and Global Cement and Concrete Association, "GNR 2.0—GCCA in Numbers," accessed May 22, 2023, https://gccassociation.org /sustainability-innovation/gnr-gcca-in-numbers/.

On exiting the kiln, clinker consists of small gray pellets about the size of marbles. Modern plants cool the clinker using a grate cooler, which can recover 0.1–0.3 gigajoules of heat per metric ton of clinker to use in the preheater or precalciner.[24] Older kilns may be equipped with planetary or rotary coolers that do not recover heat.

Finally, the clinker is mixed with additives such as blast furnace slag, limestone, and fly ash (see figure 3.2) and ground to a fine powder. Grinding consumes electricity and is most efficient in a high-pressure, horizontal, or vertical roller mill, all of which are more efficient than ball or tube mills.[25] The ground cement is packaged and shipped to buyers.

GREENHOUSE GAS EMISSIONS

Cement-making represents roughly 7 percent of global CO_2 emissions.[26] The cement industry produces greenhouse gas emissions through three mechanisms (table 3.1).

The largest emissions sources are calcination of the raw materials and combustion of fuels to provide heat, which together account for over 90 percent of cement-making's greenhouse gas emissions. Direct CO_2 emissions per unit of cement can vary significantly depending on the

TABLE 3.1 Breakdown of Greenhouse Gas Emissions from Cement-Making

Emissions type	Emissions source	Share of total
Direct process emissions	Calcination of minerals	58%
Direct energy-related emissions	Combustion of fuels for heat	33%
Indirect emissions	Purchased electricity	9%

Note: Emissions share data are from China in 2017 but are similar worldwide.

Source: Zhi Cao, Eric Masanet, Anupam Tiwari, and Sahil Akolawala, "Decarbonizing Concrete: Deep Decarbonization Pathways for the Cement and Concrete Cycle in the United States, India, and China" (report, Industrial Sustainability Analysis Laboratory, Northwestern University, Evanston, IL, March 2021), https://www.climateworks.org/wp-content/uploads/2021/03/Decarbonizing_Concrete.pdf.

type of cement. Typical direct emissions intensity is around 0.54 metric tons of CO_2 per metric ton of cement, but the figure can be as high as 0.93 for cement that consists of 90–100 percent clinker and as low as 0.25 for blended cement with a high share of supplementary cementitious materials and fillers (described in the clinker substitution section later).[27]

Indirect emissions result from electricity use. Around 29 percent of the electricity consumed by a cement plant is for grinding produced cement, 27 percent for grinding raw materials, and 7 percent for grinding fuel, so electricity use is primarily determined by choice of grinding technology. A further 29 percent goes into operating the cement kiln and feeding material between components in the plant. The remaining 7 percent is consumed when packaging and loading produced cement.[28] Efficient grinding technologies are discussed later in this chapter, but the most important mechanism for eliminating indirect emissions is to decarbonize the electric grid (chapter 6).

CARBONATION

After cement is put into service (usually as part of concrete), it gradually absorbs CO_2 from the atmosphere, a process called "carbonation." Over a period of decades, the cement absorbs CO_2 equivalent to almost half of the process emissions (i.e., excluding energy-related emissions) released when the cement was made (figure 3.4). Cement carbonation is significant on a global scale. For instance, in 2013, carbonating cement removed 0.9 billion metric tons of CO_2 from the atmosphere, offsetting 2–3 percent of that year's global CO_2 emissions.[29]

Carbonation is prevented when concrete is coated with a CO_2-impermeable material, such as plaster.[30] Conversely, carbonation proceeds more rapidly after a building is demolished, as breaking up the concrete exposes more surface area, accelerating CO_2 diffusion. However, burying the demolished concrete (e.g., if used as aggregate in a roadbed) slows carbonation.[31]

Freshly made concrete is highly alkaline, which protects steel reinforcements inside the concrete from corrosion. Traditionally, engineers

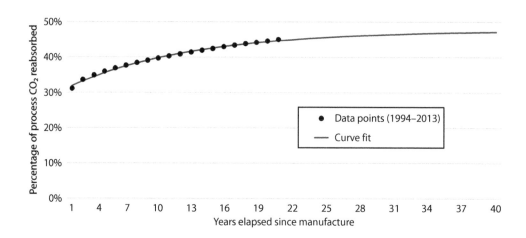

FIGURE 3.4 Share of Cement Process Emissions Reabsorbed via Carbonation The share of emissions reabsorbed refers only to process emissions (CO_2 from limestone calcination), not energy-related emissions from burning fuels for heat or indirect emissions from purchased electricity.

Source: Fengming Xi, Steven J. Davis, Philippe Ciais, Douglas Crawford-Brown, Dabo Guan, Claus Pade, Tiemao Shi, et al., "Substantial Global Carbon Uptake by Cement Carbonation," *Nature Geoscience* 9, no. 12 (December 2016): 880, https://doi.org/10.1038/ngeo2840.

viewed carbonation negatively because it reduces concrete's alkalinity, allowing steel reinforcements to corrode.[32] Techniques for preventing corrosion, such as using galvanized (zinc-plated) or epoxy-coated steel, or making reinforcements from stainless steel or glass-fiber-reinforced polymer, have cost and performance trade-offs and can increase the energy use and emissions from manufacturing the reinforcements.[33]

Since eliminating greenhouse gas emissions has become a pressing issue for industry, carbonation is more often viewed positively. The cement industry highlights carbonation's CO_2 sequestration benefits and credits CO_2 absorbed by carbonation against cement-making's CO_2 emissions in carbon neutrality roadmaps.[34]

Carbonation is relevant to a zero-emissions cement industry, as it can arguably enable the cement industry to achieve carbon neutrality while continuing to emit some CO_2 if the rate of CO_2 emissions is no larger than the rate of carbonation. Carbonation could enable cement makers to achieve net negative emissions if nearly all direct CO_2 emissions from cement-making are eliminated (or captured and permanently stored; see chapter 8). However, some of the innovative cement decarbonization technologies discussed later, particularly CO_2-cured cements, reduce the extent to which cement carbonates during its decades in service. Therefore, carbonation presents a mixture of pluses and minuses that must be considered when evaluating cement decarbonization approaches.

EMISSIONS-REDUCING TECHNOLOGIES

Technological approaches to reducing greenhouse gas emissions from cement-making can be sorted into several broad categories: reducing the percentage of clinker in cement, alternative clinker chemistries, CO_2 curing and injection, material efficiency, energy efficiency, alternative fuels and electrification, recycling, and carbon capture. Some approaches aim to address only one type of emissions, such as energy-related emissions, while others target emissions of multiple types.

CLINKER SUBSTITUTION

Most direct cement industry emissions result from making clinker. Therefore, technologies that replace some clinker with materials that require less energy to make and do not require the breakdown of calcium carbonate can reduce both energy-related and process CO_2 emissions.

Cement's clinker content affects its physical properties, so cement used for different applications may have lower or higher clinker content. In 2014, the global average clinker content of cement was 65 percent, though this varies by world region due to differences in available raw materials and construction standards, from a high of 87 percent in Central Asia to a low of around 57 percent in China.[35] Accounting for regional availability of materials to replace clinker, a global average target of 60 percent clinker is achievable by 2050.[36] Specific cement technologies can achieve lower percentages.[37]

Clinker can be replaced with "supplementary cementitious materials," substances that behave like and contribute to the binding ability of cement. Cements with high supplementary cementitious material content are called "blended cements." (These materials can also be added during concrete mixing rather than during cement-making.) The most common supplementary cementitious materials are blast furnace slag, a by-product of primary steelmaking, and fly ash. However, these substances may be in short supply in a decarbonized industry sector after blast furnaces and coal-burning equipment have been replaced by cleaner alternatives. Where available, natural pozzolana can be used, but availability is limited in many regions. Some of the most promising supplementary cementitious materials are the following.

- **Calcined clays** are widely available worldwide, and some types of clay (such as kaolin and metakaolin) exhibit cementitious properties after they are calcined. Calcining clay requires temperatures of 750°C–800°C, considerably lower than the 1,450°C required to produce clinker, and the clays contain little carbon, so they do not emit significant amounts of CO_2 when heated.[38] Calcined clays are used commercially in Brazil, where they make up 3 percent of cement content.[39]
- **Silica fume** (SiO_2) is an ultrafine powder by-product of silicon and ferrosilicon production. Silica fume contributes significantly to cement strength, but its use is restricted by limited availability and very high prices.[40]
- **Other** options include biomass ash (from burned agricultural residues and waste), bauxite, finely ground glass, and slag from smelting copper or other nonferrous metals.[41]

Many supplementary cementitious materials (including fly ash, slag, and metakaolin) contain aluminum and silica. They are called "alkali-activated materials," as they become binders on reaction with an alkaline activator, usually sodium hydroxide.[42]

In addition to supplementary cementitious materials, it is possible to replace a share of clinker with fillers, materials that do not exhibit cementitious (binding) activity. Typical fillers are finely ground limestone or quartz.[43] Chemical admixtures, such as dispersants and plasticizers, can help ensure that filler materials are uniformly distributed and reduce the space between solid material grains, contributing to cement strength.

ALTERNATIVE CLINKER CHEMISTRIES

Alternative clinker chemistries are among the most innovative cement decarbonization approaches. Today's clinker is mostly made from limestone and other carbonate-rich minerals. Instead, cement-makers can use minerals that contain less carbon (reducing process emissions) and require lower calcining temperatures (reducing heat demand and energy-related emissions). Many of these technologies are relatively new and are being developed by small companies, sometimes in partnership with large cement makers.[44] Six classes of alternative clinker cements are commercially available or have been demonstrated at small production scale (table 3.2).

Reactive belite cement has a lower share of alite and a higher share of belite than ordinary cement, slightly reducing emissions. Reactive belite cement gains strength more slowly than ordinary cement, limiting its use in construction projects, which generally prioritize short build times.[45]

Belite-yeʼelimite-ferrite cement and calcium sulfoaluminate cement use no alite. Instead, they consist of belite and two calcium aluminate compounds. They offer significant reductions in process and energy-related emissions. They have been used commercially in China for niche applications in which rapid hardening and minimal shrinkage are required. Their widespread adoption is limited by the high cost and limited availability of their aluminous materials.[46]

Carbonatable calcium silicate cement is mostly composed of low-calcium silicates such as wollastonite ($CaO \cdot SiO_2$). It hardens by reaction with CO_2 rather than with water. Relying on atmospheric CO_2 would be far too slow, and the cement would harden unevenly, so it must be mixed

TABLE 3.2 Alternative Clinker Cements

Cement type	Process CO_2 reduction potential	Thermal energy reduction potential
Reactive belite cement (RB)	3.1%	8.2%
Belite-yeʼelimite-ferrite cement (BYF)	29.1%	34.9%
Calcium sulfoaluminate cement (CSA)	42%	46.9%
Carbonatable calcium silicate cement (CCSC)	24.8%	38.9%
Calcium hydrosilicate cement (CHS)	33.2%	50.6%
Magnesium oxides derived from magnesium silicates (MOMS)	100%	46.5%

Note: This table lists the most technologically mature classes of alternative clinker cement and their potential reductions in process and energy-related CO_2 emissions.

Source: Zhi Cao, Eric Masanet, Anupam Tiwari, and Sahil Akolawala, "Decarbonizing Concrete: Deep Decarbonization Pathways for the Cement and Concrete Cycle in the United States, India, and China" (report, Industrial Sustainability Analysis Laboratory, Northwestern University, Evanston, IL, March 2021), https://www.climateworks.org/wp-content/uploads/2021/03/Decarbonizing _Concrete.pdf.

with high-purity CO_2 during the curing process, effectively an accelerated form of carbonation (discussed earlier). Carbonatable calcium silicate cement significantly reduces process emissions and thermal energy requirements, and it can permanently store captured CO_2 (see chapter 8). However, several challenges remain.[47]

- Maintaining a high-CO_2 atmosphere is straightforward in a factory producing small precast products, such as pavers, but is more difficult on a construction site.
- Carbonated cement does not protect steel reinforcements from corrosion. This limits carbonatable calcium silicate cement to nonreinforced applications or necessitates the use of corrosion-resistant reinforcements, which require more energy to produce than regular reinforcements.[48]
- Carbonatable calcium silicate cement is carbonated when put into service, so it is not expected to meaningfully absorb CO_2 from the atmosphere during its service life or after demolition.[49]

Calcium hydrosilicate cement, like carbonatable calcium silicate cement, is produced from low-calcium silicates. The minerals are calcined, and the resulting lime (CaO) is combined with silicon dioxide and hydrogen in an autoclave to form a hydrogenated calcium-silicate compound. This compound is blended with ground quartz filler to form a binder. Calcium hydrosilicate cement has significantly less process and thermal CO_2 emissions than ordinary cement, but its manufacturing process is complex, making it more expensive than ordinary cement.[50]

Magnesium oxides derived from magnesium silicates can form a cement composed of magnesium oxysulfate $(3Mg(OH)_2 \cdot MgSO_4 \cdot 8H_2O)$. Since it is produced from carbon-free magnesium silicate minerals rather than carbonates, it offers the potential to eliminate CO_2 process emissions, and it may reduce energy demand by almost half. Magnesium-oxide-based cement can react with either water or CO_2 to cure and has the potential to provide negative CO_2 emissions, even without carbon capture, if produced with decarbonized heat. Drawbacks include its low level of technological maturity and limited availability of magnesium silicate input minerals in certain regions.[51] Additionally, like fully carbonated cement, magnesium-oxide-based cement does not protect steel reinforcements from corrosion.[52]

Alternative clinker chemistries must come to be accepted by regulators and the construction industry, which are slow to embrace new products out of an abundance of caution regarding safety, performance, and longevity. Therefore, if alternative clinkers are to substantially contribute to achieving net-zero industry by 2050, they must receive necessary approvals and grow their market shares as soon as possible.

CO_2 CURING AND INJECTION

Cement generally reacts with water to cure, or harden. However, as discussed earlier, some alternative cements can be cured with CO_2. The resulting CO_2 sequestration contributes significantly to their process emissions abatement but adversely affects how much CO_2 will be stored via carbonation in the decades after the cement is manufactured.

Alternatively, it is possible to inject CO_2 into a concrete mix involving ordinary cement. The amount of CO_2 added to concrete (0.5 kilograms of CO_2 per cubic meter of concrete, 0.02 percent by mass) is too small for CO_2 sequestration to meaningfully contribute to greenhouse gas abatement.[53] However, CO_2 injection improves the strength of the concrete, allowing for less cement to be used. (One cement maker found that CO_2 injection enabled a 5 percent reduction in cement use.[54]) Therefore, CO_2 injection into concrete mix is essentially a material efficiency strategy, not a CO_2 sequestration strategy.

It is possible to use steel slag as the sole binder (i.e., without cement) in concrete cured in a CO_2 atmosphere. Slag-based, CO_2-cured concrete has been demonstrated in precast products.[55] After curing, net emissions are negative if the emissions associated with slag production are ignored. Being a by-product of CO_2-intensive primary steelmaking (chapter 1), slag may be scarce in a zero-carbon industrial sector.

MATERIAL EFFICIENCY

Material efficiency—using less material to produce a building or product—is covered in chapter 5. However, several strategies specific to concrete are noted here.[56]

- Concrete can be poured into any shape, but molds with right angles are often used for simplicity. Optimized mold geometry (for example, curved fabric molds) can reduce concrete use by up to 40 percent in some applications.
- Prestressing concrete with steel cables can strengthen it, reducing the amount of concrete needed to achieve a required strength.
- Where solid concrete is not needed to resist compressive forces, pockets of air or polystyrene can be used to reduce concrete use and structure weight.
- Higher-strength concrete mixes often have higher cement content. High-strength mixes can be reserved for structural elements requiring more strength, such as support pillars, while mixes with lower

cement content can be used where less strength is required, such as for walkways, stairs, and countertops.

ENERGY EFFICIENCY

There are essentially two areas where cement makers can pursue energy efficiency improvements: thermal efficiency of the kiln and precalciner and electrical efficiency of grinding equipment.

As noted earlier, a state-of-the-art dry process cement plant includes a six-stage precalciner and a grate clinker cooler that recovers heat and uses it to preheat input materials. These plants may consume as little as 3.0–3.4 gigajoules per metric ton of clinker.[57] The theoretical minimum energy requirement is 1.85–2.8 gigajoules per metric ton, varying with the raw materials' moisture content, so the potential for further improvement is limited. One option is to operate the kiln with oxygen-enriched air, which can achieve 5 percent thermal energy savings.[58] Another option is to use solar process heat (see chapter 4) to preheat input materials.

Alternative clinker chemistries that lower the temperature requirements of the calcination reaction (discussed earlier) reduce thermal energy demand per unit of clinker. Additionally, measures that reduce the share of clinker in cement, reduce the share of cement in concrete, or reduce demand for concrete all reduce energy demand per building constructed.

More than 60 percent of cement-making electricity demand is for grinding materials, so electricity efficiency improvements involve new grinding technologies. Current best practice is to use high-pressure grinding rolls and vertical roller mills, which reduce electricity consumption by 50–70 percent relative to ball mills, the most common grinding technology in cement plants.[59] Globally, the tenth percentile most-efficient plants consume 85 kilowatt-hours per metric ton of cement, while the best-performing plants achieve 74 kilowatt-hours per metric ton.[60] Further improvements can be achieved by separately grinding materials of different hardness or different fineness requirements, and by adding grinding aids such as amines or glycols, which help prevent particles from clumping. Futuristic options, far from commercial readiness, include vortex layer grinding (wherein ferromagnetic particles grind cement in a rotating magnetic field), ultrasonic-assisted grinding, high-voltage power pulse grinding, and low-temperature grinding.[61]

ALTERNATIVE FUELS AND ELECTRIFICATION

Today, fossil fuels supply 95 percent of cement-making heat needs, while waste supplies 3 percent and biomass 2 percent (see figure 3.3). Nonfossil fuels are referred to as "alternative fuels." Increasing the use of alternative fuels and electricity for heat is a key technique for reducing energy-related CO_2 emissions.

Waste burned by cement plants largely consists of tires, waste oil and solvents, industrial and domestic waste, plastics, textiles, and wastepaper.[62] Today, the carbon in tires, plastics, and synthetic textiles comes from fossil feedstocks (chapter 2), and most products' manufacture involves energy-related greenhouse gas emissions, so waste fuels are not low-carbon. In a zero-carbon industrial future, waste fuels could become carbon-neutral if industrial energy and feedstocks are decarbonized. Until then, sustainably harvested biomass (see chapter 7), green hydrogen, and carbon-free electricity, which have lower greenhouse gas emissions than waste fuels, can be used.

Wastes and biomass have lower energy density than fossil fuels, but this does not pose serious technical challenges for the cement industry. In Europe, several plants already operate using 100 percent alternative fuels.[63] Some operational changes are required, as well as the installation of a system to reduce chlorine and sulfur impurities in the kiln atmosphere.[64]

Beyond waste and biomass, the main options are hydrogen combustion and electrification. Burning hydrogen (or hydrogen-derived fuels) can be useful for heating nonconductive materials to high temperatures (chapter 7), but the energy penalty involved in producing green hydrogen and heat losses in exhaust gases and formed water vapor make it cheaper to use electricity. In 2018, the Swedish cement maker Cementa and the power utility Vattenfall studied clinker production using electrical plasma heating and found the process to be technically and economically viable. Additionally, since there was no combustion, flue gas consisted of over 99 percent CO_2, facilitating carbon capture. The companies plan further tests and hope to have their first commercial, zero-carbon cement plant built by 2030.[65]

A theoretical alternative to electrified heat is direct electrolytic breakdown of calcium carbonate. This process would be very different from today's cement-making (for instance, utilizing an electrolyzer rather than a kiln). It has been demonstrated at laboratory scale.[66]

RECYCLING AND REUSE

At end of life, concrete can be crushed and used as aggregate in the manufacture of new concrete. However, the emissions benefits are minimal (about 15 kilograms of CO_2 per metric ton of recycled aggregate), because cement, not aggregate, is the emissions-intense component of concrete. (Recycled aggregate is more commonly used as roadbed material.)[67]

In theory, concrete fines (pieces smaller than 4 millimeters in diameter) can be ground and their hydrated cement separated from sand and aggregates. The old cement can be used as a supplementary cementitious material, replacing some clinker in the manufacture of new cement. Once incorporated into new concrete, the old cement can absorb 28 grams of CO_2 per 100 grams of recycled cement. This translates into 30 percent more CO_2 savings than replacing the same amount of clinker with a filler, such as ground limestone.[68]

Alternatively, the separated, old cement can be used as a flux when producing secondary steel in an electric arc furnace. The resulting slag is chemically similar to ordinary cement and could serve as the sole binder in concrete, avoiding the need for new cement. This approach has been demonstrated at laboratory scale at Cambridge University.[69] The potential of these approaches is constrained by the availability of old cement, the need to commercialize technology to separate hydrated cement from other constituents of old concrete, and (for the latter approach) the demand for flux by electric arc furnaces (64 kilograms of flux per metric ton of steel produced).[70]

A small percentage of cement in concrete is not hydrated and, if recovered, can be used in place of new cement without first being processed in an electric arc furnace. In typical five-year-old concrete, just 4 percent of cement remains unhydrated, though that fraction can be higher for newer concrete and for concrete kept in indoor, dry conditions.[71] The low yield and difficulty of separation pose challenges for recycling unhydrated cement.

Greater abatement could be achieved by reusing whole concrete components. One case study found that 60–90 percent of a nine-story building's concrete columns, beams, hollow-core slabs, and core walls could potentially be reused.[72] This strategy works best if components are designed to facilitate reuse (for instance, making components detachable).

More strategies for making the best use of concrete (and other materials) are covered in chapter 5.

CARBON CAPTURE

CO_2 emissions from clinker production can be captured and used or permanently stored. Carbon capture is a good fit for the cement industry because of the difficulty of eliminating CO_2 emissions from limestone breakdown. If heat for cement-making could be provided by electrical plasma torches (discussed earlier), flue gas would consist of nearly pure CO_2, facilitating capture. Without heat electrification, the most promising carbon capture techniques for cement-making are postcombustion capture and oxy-fuel combustion, covered in chapter 8.

No existing cement plants utilize carbon capture, but the Norwegian government is funding the first commercial-scale project at Norcem's cement plant in Brevik, Norway. The system will use postcombustion capture, with heat for regenerating the solvent recovered from the cement plant. It is expected to come online by 2024 and sequester 400,000 metric tons of CO_2 per year, 50 percent of the plant's emissions.[73]

ACHIEVING ZERO-CARBON
CEMENT AND CONCRETE

Concrete is a crucial material for buildings and infrastructure. No substitutes exist at sufficient scale (see chapter 5), and recycling options are limited, so a means of producing zero-carbon concrete is essential. Aggregate represents a small share of concrete's energy use and can be produced using electricity, so the key challenge is to decarbonize concrete's binder material, cement. This requires two things: zero-carbon heat for cement kilns and a means of addressing CO_2 emissions from limestone calcination. The best zero-carbon heat options are sustainably grown bioenergy and direct electrification using plasma torches. Though direct electrification is early in development, it is likely to be the most promising route in the longer term because it is not limited by the availability of sustainable bioenergy, and avoiding fuel combustion reduces heat losses and greatly increases the purity of the CO_2 stream from limestone calcination, facilitating carbon capture. Therefore, cement kiln electrification should be prioritized with additional funding and demonstration projects to accelerate its commercialization.

All existing and new cement-making facilities should be equipped with carbon capture to avoid calcination-related carbon dioxide emissions. (Facilities that are too small, old, or inefficient to be economically retrofitted should be retired or replaced.) Electrified cement kilns with carbon capture could achieve net negative carbon dioxide emissions after accounting for cement carbonation during the years after concrete is put into service. Material efficiency, energy efficiency, alternative cement chemistries, and CO_2-cured concrete should all play supportive roles in this transition. Electrification, carbon capture, and supporting technologies allow for a transition to net-negative-carbon cement production globally over the next several decades, after which the construction of concrete buildings and infrastructure could potentially be used to offset CO_2 emissions elsewhere in the economy or reduce atmospheric CO_2 concentrations.

II

TECHNOLOGIES

4

ENERGY EFFICIENCY

A key technique for reducing industrial greenhouse gas emissions and costs is energy efficiency, using less energy to produce the same products. Until the energy supply is decarbonized, using less energy directly translates into lower emissions. During this century, electrification, renewable fuels, and carbon capture (chapters 6–8) can fully decarbonize industrial energy. The more decarbonized the energy supply, the less greenhouse gas abatement is afforded by energy efficiency. But even with a zero-carbon energy system, energy efficiency remains valuable because it can dramatically lower industrial energy expenditures, making clean production more affordable. (It also saves money outside the industry sector, for instance, by reducing the amount of renewable electricity generation capacity that must be built.) Therefore, energy efficiency is a no-regrets strategy that should be pursued alongside other decarbonization options.

Industrial energy efficiency can encompass improvements to technologies or operations at three scales:

- individual pieces of equipment, such as efficient boilers or electric motors;
- entire manufacturing lines or facilities, such as how different machines are interconnected and how material, energy, and information flow through the system; and

- efficiency beyond the factory, such as supply chain management, product design, and business decision-making that values energy efficiency.

Generally, efficiency measures at the smallest scale are best understood and most commonly implemented today, particularly in countries with relatively new industrial equipment. Some governments have enacted standards mandating minimum energy performance for certain types of industrial equipment. For example, the U.S. Department of Energy (DOE) maintains energy efficiency standards for industrial electric motors that account for motor design, horsepower rating, number of electrical poles, and whether or not the motor is enclosed in a housing.[1] Nonetheless, there remains potential for equipment-level improvements to further improve energy efficiency.[2] Efficiency measures at larger scales are less common today, so even greater cost-effective potential exists.

HISTORICAL AND POTENTIAL ENERGY SAVINGS

In recent years, industrial energy consumption per unit of economic output (revenue) has declined due to a combination of technical energy efficiency improvements and economic structural change—that is, less-energy-intensive industries accounting for a larger share of total output. From 2011 to 2018, industrial energy efficiency improvements averaged 2.5 percent per year, while structural shifts were responsible for an average energy intensity reduction of 0.8 percent per year (figure 4.1). Since 2015, the highest rates of efficiency improvement have been in large, emerging economies, particularly China and India.[3]

Numerous studies have attempted to estimate future energy efficiency potential, but they can be difficult to compare due to differences in the types of measures considered; whether the study estimates technical potential, economic potential, or achievable potential under real-world

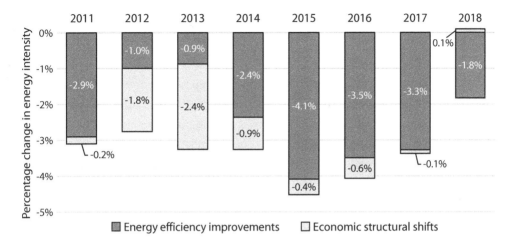

FIGURE 4.1 **Year-Over-Year Change in Global Industrial Energy Intensity** Changes in final energy intensity are due partly to technical energy efficiency improvements and partly to changes in the structure of the global economy; that is, industries with lower energy intensities accounting for a larger share of total industrial economic output (revenue).

Source: International Energy Agency, *Energy Efficiency 2019* (report, International Energy Agency, Paris, revised November 2019), https://iea.blob.core.windows.net/assets /8441ab46-9d86-47eb-b1fc-cb36fc3e7143/Energy_Efficiency_2019.pdf.

conditions; time horizon; and other factors.[4] One estimate by the DOE found that U.S. industrial efficiency through 2030 could improve at 2.4 percent per year, a doubling of the projected business-as-usual improvement rate during that period.[5] The International Energy Agency estimated that using all cost-effective energy efficiency measures (based on energy savings alone, not greenhouse gas abatement) using only read- ily available technology could reduce global industrial energy intensity by 44 percent from 2018 to 2040, an annual average improvement rate of 2.3 percent.[6] Higher improvement rates may be possible with supportive policies (such as carbon pricing and efficiency standards) and increased research and development (R&D) investment in efficient technologies (chapters 9–11).

EQUIPMENT-SCALE EFFICIENCY MEASURES

There is often more than one way to produce a part or product, and different production routes involve different types of equipment. Therefore, it can be useful to think of industrial operations in terms of "unit processes." A unit process is an activity applied to a material, often as a step in a manufacturing process. For example, a metal part may be formed, heat-treated, and then polished; each of these steps is a unit process. More than one hundred unit processes exist, including cutting, griding, casting, forging, welding, annealing, adhesive bonding, laser hardening, polishing, and surface coating.[7] Detailed guidance for optimizing each unit process can be found in engineering texts. This section presents some widely applicable strategies and examples.

- Reduce the number of unit processes required to produce a product. Computer-controlled tools and advanced materials can allow for high morphological accuracy and reduce the need for finishing steps.[8] This approach is called "net shape manufacturing."
- Use remanufactured parts or recycled materials (chapter 5). For example, it requires much less energy to produce steel from scrap than from iron ore (chapter 1).
- For small production runs, it can be expensive and energy-intensive to create custom tooling, such as molds or dies. Flexible techniques such as 3-D printing (also called "additive manufacturing") and incremental forming can create customized parts without custom tooling.[9]
- Use more forming processes (such as casting and forging) and fewer machining processes (such as drilling and grinding). Machining wastes material that required energy to produce and requires further energy to recycle.
- Obtain heat from electricity rather than fuel combustion. Electricity delivers heat to parts and materials more efficiently. For details, see the fossil fuel heating efficiency section of chapter 6.

- Typical electric motors and pumps run at a constant speed and torque determined by the input voltage and frequency, so systems are controlled by mechanically dissipating (wasting) energy. It is often possible to save energy by using "variable-frequency drives" (also called "variable-speed drives"), which adjust their speed and torque to match the load.

- Some unit processes require less energy per unit of material when the material is processed more quickly. Examples include cutting, drilling, abrasion (such as griding or waterjet), and surface coating (chemical or physical vapor deposition).[10]

- Some systems are inherently less efficient than alternatives and should be avoided where feasible. For example, compressed air is among the least-efficient forms of energy used in an industrial plant, with typical efficiencies around 10 percent.[11] Alternatives include fans for cooling; blowers to agitate mixtures or inflate packaging; brushes, blowers, or vacuum pumps to clean parts and remove debris; and electric motors or hydraulics to move machines.[12]

- Optimize moving parts' surface textures. Parts with overly smooth finishes tend to adhere to one another and do not retain lubricant. A surface texture with microscopic bumps and divots can reduce friction and provide reservoirs for lubricant.[13]

- Optimize boiler efficiency. Boilers are among the most common pieces of energy-using industrial equipment, and detailed guidelines exist for improving their operation, involving steps such as installing flue shut-off dampers, regularly removing scale deposits, optimizing blowdown rate, avoiding excess combustion air, and recovering and using condensate.[14] The best boilers can achieve fuel-to-steam efficiencies of 85–90 percent (and 94 percent has been demonstrated).[15] (Boilers that produce hot water rather than steam can achieve even higher efficiencies—up to 98 percent—but industrial processes usually require steam.[16])

- Properly maintain equipment to avoid energy losses from steam, water, and air leaks; friction from poorly lubricated parts; and so on. Predictive maintenance (using sensors or measurements to detect when machines need repair or replacement) is particularly effective at optimizing performance while reducing unnecessary maintenance costs. Preventive maintenance on a fixed schedule is the next best approach. Reactive maintenance (running a machine until it breaks) can result in energy waste going undetected for long periods.[17]

Although many equipment-scale improvements can be achieved using commercialized technology, there are areas where R&D may be particularly helpful in improving existing processes. For example, due to its high heat capacity and high latent heat of evaporation, water removal via boiling requires a large quantity of energy. Membrane technologies (such as electrodialysis, forward and reverse osmosis, and membrane distillation) allow for the nonthermal separation of water, saving significant energy.[18] Other areas with high R&D potential include net shape manufacturing and additive manufacturing.

FACILITY-SCALE EFFICIENCY MEASURES

Facility-scale efficiency refers to improvements that occur within the walls of a single facility but beyond the confines of a single machine or unit process. Cost-effective energy reduction opportunities at this scale are common, but they are more challenging to regulate due to the diversity of manufacturing setups, in contrast to the standardization of machines such as electric motors or industrial boilers. Technology-neutral standards that regulate facility-level energy use for commodity products, such as a particular grade of steel or type of cement, are discussed in chapter 10. The financial benefits of energy savings are currently the main driver of facility-scale efficiency efforts. These benefits can be increased through carbon pricing, subsidies, and other financial policies (chapter 9).

RIGHTSIZING EQUIPMENT AND OPTIMIZING MATERIAL FLOWS

Industrial equipment is most energy-efficient when operating at or slightly under its intended design capacity. Installing high-capacity equipment and operating it far below its optimal rate or idling (waiting for material to process) wastes energy.

Equipment must be sized to handle the maximum load it may encounter. Therefore, one way to reduce required equipment capacity is to even out material flows over time. For example, a nonoptimized industrial process may occasionally pump a large amount of fluid but will usually pump only a small amount. The plant manager must install a pump large enough to handle the peak load, and that pump wastes energy when load is low. If the material flow rate can be evened out, the same amount of fluid can be processed per hour by a smaller pump operating closer to its design capacity.

When material flow variability cannot be reduced, it is possible to save energy by utilizing multiple, smaller machines rather than a single, large machine. For example, the Japanese boilermaker Miura estimates that replacing a large boiler with multiple small boilers whose operation is controlled to match fluctuations in steam demand can reduce energy consumption 10–30 percent.[19]

EFFICIENT FLUID DISTRIBUTION

The way components are connected can have large efficiency implications, particularly when moving steam and other fluids. To reduce pressure drops, pipe runs between machines should be short, pipe diameter should be sufficiently large, and sharp bends should be minimized. However, pipes transporting heated (such as steam) or chilled fluids should not be oversized, as this can lead to increased temperature losses, since fluid moving at a given volumetric flow rate (cubic meters per second) spends more time in a fatter pipe.[20]

Pipes for heated and chilled fluids should be insulated and properly maintained. Case studies of pipe insulation improvement projects have found payback periods of less than one year.[21] A predictive maintenance program (described earlier) can quickly detect and repair leaks.

WASTE HEAT RECOVERY AND COMBINED HEAT AND POWER

Fuel-burning industrial equipment, such as furnaces and boilers, cannot transfer all the energy from the fuel into the material being processed. For instance, in a furnace operating at 1100°C with no excess air, 55 percent of the fuel's energy is lost in hot exhaust gases.[22] "Waste heat recovery" involves extracting some heat that did not go into the product (such as by routing exhaust gases or steam through a heat exchanger) and using it to perform useful work. All commonly used fuels contain hydrogen atoms, which bond with atmospheric oxygen to form water vapor during combustion (for example, for methane: $CH_4 + 2O_2 \rightarrow CO_2 + 2H_2O$). Water vapor contains considerable latent heat, so one key to maximizing heat recovery is to recover both "sensible heat" (lowering the temperature of the exhaust) and "latent heat" (condensing the water vapor).[23]

One technique for extracting more heat from gases is "mechanical vapor compression," which involves pressurizing the gas. Pressurizing a gas increases its temperature, making it easier to extract its heat using a heat exchanger. When the gas is water vapor, pressurization also facilitates condensation and latent heat recovery.[24]

Recovered heat can be used to preheat materials and combustion air before they enter a furnace, so the furnace needs to do less work to bring the material up to the desired temperature. Waste heat can also dry input materials, reducing the energy used to evaporate water. Waste heat can be used by the same machine or by a different machine within the same facility.

Waste heat recovery has the theoretical potential to displace 11–12 percent of industry's nonfeedstock energy use, almost all of which (10–11 percent displacement) is economically achievable today.[25] Improvements in energy efficiency tend to reduce waste heat recovery potential, as more efficient use of energy produces less waste heat. For example, the European Union's waste heat recovery potential declined by around 13 percent from 2012 to 2015, mostly due to improvements in industrial energy efficiency over this period.[26]

"Combined heat and power" (CHP), also known as "cogeneration," involves obtaining electricity and useful heat from the same combustion process. CHP systems typically have efficiencies of 60–80 percent, compared with 50 percent when generating heat and electricity separately.[27] There are two types of CHP.

- In "topping cycle CHP," fuel is first used to generate electricity, with heat recovery afterward. The typical design varies by fuel. Gaseous and liquid fuels are usually burned in an internal combustion engine or gas turbine, which turns a generator to produce electricity. Waste heat is recovered from the exhaust. In contrast, solid fuels are usually combusted in a boiler, and the steam from the boiler is used to turn a steam turbine to produce electricity. Subsequently, heat is recovered from the steam.[28]
- In "bottoming cycle CHP," also called "waste-heat-to-power," fuel is burned primarily to provide high-temperature heat for an industrial process. Afterward, waste heat is recovered and used to raise the temperature of a working fluid in a heat recovery boiler that drives a steam turbine to produce electricity. The most common working fluid is water, which requires waste heat exceeding 260°C to be cost-effective. Newer technologies use an organic working fluid (allowing for use of waste heat as low as 150°C) or a mixture of water and ammonia (100°C). Although less common, it is also possible to use thermoelectric materials (semiconductors that produce electricity when subjected to a temperature differential) to convert waste heat into electricity.[29]

Today, topping cycle CHP is more common than bottoming cycle. For example, in the United States in 2021, 90 percent of industrial CHP capacity was topping cycle and 10 percent was bottoming cycle.[30]

There remains large industrial CHP potential. For instance, in 2016, the DOE estimated that CHP potential at U.S. industrial plants was 162 gigawatts, while the installed capacity was 66 gigawatts (41 percent of potential).[31] The percentage of untapped CHP potential is likely higher in many countries.

In a zero-carbon future, CHP potential might be lower than it is today. Many industrial heat needs will be electrified, and electrical heating does not produce hot exhaust gases (except for off-gassing by-products of the heated material, in some cases) and produces less waste heat due to more efficient transfer of heat to the processed material (chapter 6). However, in some cases, zero-carbon electricity will be used to create steam, and some high-temperature heat needs will be met by burning hydrogen, hydrogen-derived fuels, or bioenergy (chapter 7). In these cases, CHP (particularly bottoming cycle) will remain useful.

SOLAR PROCESS HEAT

"Solar process heat" involves using solar radiation to directly supply heat to industrial processes (i.e., without converting the sunlight into electricity). Three technologies (figure 4.2) are particularly suited to collecting solar heat for industrial use.[32]

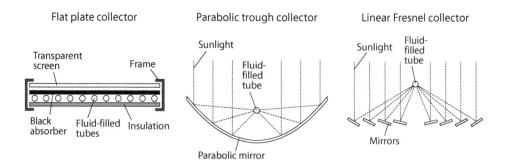

FIGURE 4.2 Solar Collector Designs for Industrial Process Heat

- "Flat plate collectors" are the simplest and lowest-cost type of collector. Sunlight passes through a transparent screen and is absorbed by a black plate. The heat is then transferred to tubes of fluid (often water) in an insulated space behind the plate. Flat plate collectors do not track the sun and can be mounted on roofs, like photovoltaic panels. They typically supply water at up to 90°C, which can serve as preheated boiler feedwater. (When hot water is not demanded, stagnant water in the collector can reach 200°C.)[33] The best commercially available flat plate collectors have efficiencies around 50–65 percent.[34]
- A "parabolic trough collector" consists of a row of parabola-shaped mirrors that focus light into a horizontal line. A fluid-carrying pipe is located along the focal line. Concentrated solar energy heats the fluid in the pipe. Parabolic trough collectors may be oriented north to south and use one-axis tracking to follow the sun as it moves east to west. Some are enclosed in greenhouse-like structures to protect them and improve their efficiency. Parabolic trough collectors can accommodate process heat needs up to 340°C.[35] Their efficiency is typically 65–80 percent.[36]
- "Linear Fresnel collectors" are similar to parabolic trough collectors, except instead of a large, parabolic mirror, they use a series of flat (or slightly curved) mirrors, each at a different angle, to focus light into a line. They achieve efficiencies of 40–65 percent, lower than that of parabolic trough collectors.[37] However, linear Fresnel collectors are cheaper to manufacture due to their simpler mirrors, and tracking the sun involves rotating only the mirrors, whereas for parabolic trough collectors, the entire collector must rotate.[38] Linear Fresnel collectors can accommodate process heat needs up to 212°C.[39]

Solar collectors can be combined with thermal energy storage technologies to extend the hours during which solar heat may be used. A promising method for reducing thermal losses during storage is to change the phase of a material (i.e., solid to liquid or liquid to gas) rather than changing its temperature. More than one hundred phase change materials have been investigated for use in storing solar thermal heat for industrial applications at temperatures from 120°C to 400°C, but none is yet commercialized.[40]

Of the total industrial heat demand, 35–45 percent is at temperatures achievable by solar thermal processes (see figure 6.2), but the ability of solar heat to meet this need varies with geography. The locations with highest potential have intense sunlight and more hours of sunshine per day. Additionally, how well an individual plant's manufacturing schedule aligns with the sunniest months of the year and hours of the day strongly influences solar thermal potential for that business. For example, solar thermal has high potential for facilities processing certain foods (such as tomatoes and nuts) because their work is concentrated in summer and fall, and their working hours include all daylight hours.[41]

Therefore, estimates of solar thermal potential must account not only for technology properties but also for geography and industries within the studied area. A major analysis of the United States at the county level found that the technical potential to reduce industrial nonfeedstock combustible fuel demand (and associated CO_2 emissions) is 3 percent for flat plate collectors, 8 percent for linear Fresnel collectors, 11 percent for parabolic trough collectors, and 15 percent for parabolic trough collectors equipped with thermal energy storage.[42] (These figures are not additive. For instance, the heat needs that could be met by linear Fresnel collectors are a subset of the heat needs that could be met by parabolic trough collectors.)

The land requirements for solar thermal systems can be significant. For example, for the United States to achieve the 15 percent energy savings from parabolic trough collectors with thermal energy storage noted earlier, almost 5,500 square kilometers are needed for a system sized for summertime, or almost 19,000 square kilometers (roughly 0.2 percent of U.S. land area, about the size of New Jersey) for a system sized to deliver similar performance in wintertime, when there are fewer daylight hours and sunlight is less intense.[43] Solar heat systems must be near the industrial facilities demanding heat, so land requirements may pose challenges for facilities located in urbanized areas.

AUTOMATION

Broadly, there are two ways that automation (i.e., robots) can improve industrial energy efficiency. First, robots can apply tools more quickly and with more precision than human workers, minimizing the amount of time the tool is active and consuming energy. For example, today, most oxy-acetylene welding is done by hand, which is relatively slow. A robot can complete a welding task more quickly, so the welding torch is used for a shorter period per product, saving fuel.[44] (Automation can also reduce material use, discussed in chapter 5.)

Second, robots generally do not require light and can tolerate much wider temperature ranges than human workers. This raises the possibility of "lights-out manufacturing," the concept of a factory staffed by robots in which manufacturing occurs in the dark and without heating or air conditioning. Humans would access the factory floor only for troubleshooting or maintenance tasks. This would save on lighting, heating, and air conditioning energy use, which make up 16 percent of electricity consumption and 6 percent of nonfeedstock fossil fuel consumption by U.S. industry.[45]

The technology for lights-out manufacturing exists today, but a long history of attempts by various companies has shown that it is rarely cost-effective.[46] Making a business case for full automation usually requires another reason that human operators should be minimized, such as avoiding contamination during microchip or pharmaceutical manufacturing. It is inordinately costly to make a system that runs without human operators, and the resulting facility is inflexible and therefore poorly equipped for current trends toward increased customizability, frequent product updates, and short production runs.[47]

In practice, even extensive automation usually does not eliminate on-site jobs. For example, the German technology company Bosch opened a state-of-the-art, automated microchip factory in 2021. The factory cost $1.2 billion and employs seven hundred people on site, only 35 percent as many people as is typical for an industrial facility of its size but still enough to require lighting, heating, and air conditioning services.[48]

Automation best contributes to energy efficiency through optimization of production processes, not lights-out operation.

EFFICIENCY BEYOND THE FACTORY

There exist at least three important approaches to improving industrial energy efficiency beyond the walls of any individual industrial facility: supply chain optimization, product design, and corporate decision-making to properly value energy efficiency.

SUPPLY CHAIN

A company's supply chain is the set of businesses that produce the materials and parts that go into making the company's products, from immediate suppliers all the way back to raw material extraction. Supply chain emissions come from the energy used by these suppliers, as well as the transportation of parts and materials between businesses. Supply chain may also include certain downstream companies, such as shipping firms used for order fulfillment.[49]

Companies may desire to reduce the energy consumption and emissions from their supply chain to meet customer demand for sustainable products or in response to regulatory requirements. Carbon pricing with border adjustments (chapter 9) and standards applied to whole-lifecycle emissions (chapter 10) can incentivize companies to decarbonize their supply chains. Companies may seek out suppliers that achieve certain energy efficiency or emissions metrics, or they may help their existing suppliers to implement new, energy-efficient processes. Industrial firms may also locate production in an area with reliable, high-quality transportation links to suppliers (or to their target market), reducing transportation energy use.

Large firms have more sway with their suppliers, so they are best positioned to negotiate for low-carbon inputs or changes to the suppliers' processes. One example is Walmart's sustainability index and "Project Gigaton," which Walmart calculates has reduced emissions from its suppliers by 93 million metric tons of carbon dioxide equivalent from 2017–19 and will avoid one billion metric tons by 2030.[50]

PRODUCT DESIGN

Companies can alter the design of their products in ways that reduce the energy required to produce those products. Design alterations may enable the use of fewer or lower-energy unit processes (covered earlier), or they may overlap with material efficiency measures (see chapter 5), since it takes less energy to process less material. Additionally, design changes may save on transportation energy use, particularly by reducing the volume of the product when shipped (for instance, by shipping unassembled items), so more instances of the product can fit in a shipping container.

CORPORATE DECISION-MAKING

It is sometimes assumed that manufacturers already pursue all cost-effective energy-saving opportunities due to market pressures. In fact, industrial firms routinely forgo cost-effective energy efficiency opportunities. For example, from 2009 to 2013, a program by DOE provided energy efficiency assessments to 2,158 small- and medium-sized manufacturers, identifying unrealized energy savings opportunities of 15 petajoules per year. Subsequently, manufacturers implemented measures to achieve only 33 percent of identified energy savings, investing $172 million (in 2019 dollars), equivalent to $11 per gigajoule per year. At 2019 energy prices (see figure 6.5), this would offer a payback of under one year for electricity, 3.2 years for natural gas, and 4.5 years for coal.[51] An earlier DOE program that focused on larger manufacturers had similar results: 680 energy assessments identified a total of 144 petajoules per year in annual energy savings opportunities, worth $1.3 billion per year (in 2019 dollars), only half of which were ultimately pursued.[52] Companies that do not undertake energy assessments likely have even higher rates of unrealized savings.

There are several reasons that some companies do not pursue cost-effective energy efficiency measures. First, nonfeedstock energy expenditures consume a small share of manufacturers' revenues—1.4 percent in the United States (figure 4.3)—so even a large percentage reduction in energy spending may represent a small savings in absolute

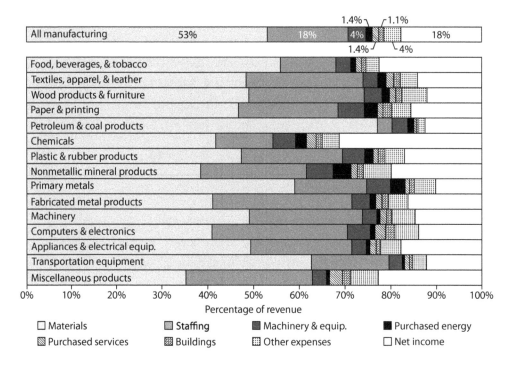

FIGURE 4.3 Uses of Revenue by U.S. Manufacturers in 2019 "Materials" includes fuels used as feedstocks (such as crude oil purchased by refineries and natural gas converted into ammonia). "Staffing" includes employee compensation, benefits, contractors, and temporary workers. "Machinery & equip." includes equipment purchases, leasing, and maintenance. "Purchased energy" includes fuels combusted for energy and electricity.

Source: U.S. Census Bureau, "Annual Survey of Manufactures 2019," June 21, 2021, https://www.census.gov/library/publications/2021/econ/e19-asm.html.

terms. (There are exceptions. For instance, electricity can account for up to 40 percent of primary aluminum production costs, equivalent to around a third of total revenue, depending on profit margin.)[53] Due to limited capacity to take on many projects simultaneously, companies may prioritize investing in product development to grow revenue or reducing their largest cost centers (materials, staffing, and machinery), even if energy efficiency offers a better percentage return. Efficient corporate management and a special emphasis on decarbonization projects, as will be increasingly required of manufacturers this century, can enable energy efficiency to be pursued alongside other business goals.

Second, energy efficiency improvements often have benefits other than fuel savings, which may be overlooked when evaluating projects. For example, a study of the iron and steel industry found that energy efficiency resulted in productivity improvements. Accounting for these improvements doubled the efficiency potential deemed cost-effective.[54] Benefits associated with energy efficiency can include[55]

- increased productivity,
- reduced exposure to energy price volatility,
- reduced electricity capacity charges,
- reduced capital costs and associated insurance premiums,
- reduced maintenance costs,
- reduced need for cooling water and other inputs,
- reduced waste generation and disposal fees,
- reduced cost of compliance with greenhouse gas or conventional pollutant regulations,
- improved workplace health and safety,
- improved ability to sell products to environmentally conscious buyers, and
- improved ability to sell to companies and governments with green procurement policies (chapter 10).

Properly accounting for the full range of benefits can improve corporate decision-making around energy efficiency projects.

Third, manufacturers may feel pressure to take a short-term view to meet quarterly financial targets and investor expectations. This can lead to demands for unreasonably short payback periods and the prioritization of high-risk, short-term projects, forgoing high-quality, longer-term investments. Interviews with seven energy service companies, firms that conduct energy audits and help client businesses save energy, found that commercial clients (such as schools, hospitals, and office buildings) were willing to undertake efficiency measures that offered ten-year payback periods, while manufacturing clients sought payback periods of two to three years or less.[56] A ten-year payback period is far shorter than the typical lifetime of industrial machinery and often would be cost-effective for industry. Management should prioritize the long-term success of the company and communicate this intention to investors and staff, supporting investment in energy efficiency (and other decarbonization technologies) whose greatest gains will manifest over a period of decades. A long-term mindset will also help businesses navigate a pathway to zero greenhouse gas emissions within thirty to fifty years, as is increasingly demanded by governments and society.

Fourth, some businesses (particularly small manufacturers) may lack the money to make up-front investments in more efficient capital equipment. Government can help overcome these barriers via policies including lending mechanisms, subsidies, tax credits, and equipment rebates, covered in chapter 9.

Tools exist to help businesses improve decision-making around energy efficiency. The International Organization for Standardization (ISO) maintains a set of guidelines, ISO 50001, for corporate "energy management systems." In this context, an energy management system is not a piece of technical equipment but, rather, a set of corporate practices. ISO 50001 helps companies develop policies around energy use, set corporate energy efficiency targets, gather energy use data, regularly review performance, and build continuous improvement into energy management practices.[57] Related standards cover specific implementation details, such as how to conduct energy audits (ISO 50002) and how to measure energy performance (ISO 50006).

ENERGY EFFICIENCY'S CONTRIBUTION
TO ZERO-CARBON INDUSTRY

Energy efficiency is a cost-effective way to reduce industrial emissions today, even as it reduces the quantity of zero-carbon energy that industry requires, making the transition to clean industry faster and cheaper. Many efficiency techniques can be implemented at the level of individual pieces of equipment, and these are comparatively well understood and should become the global standard of practice. Efficiency measures that span an entire facility or extend beyond the facility (in supply chains, product design, and corporate decision-making) are potentially even more powerful but less often prioritized. Businesses that understand the full range of benefits from efficiency, rather than looking narrowly at fuel savings, are more likely to make smart investments in energy efficiency.

Most efficiency technologies are already commercialized and ready to be deployed at scale, so standards are a particularly good policy for driving adoption (see chapter 10), potentially accompanied by low-cost financing or retooling grants for smaller manufacturers (chapter 9). As a no-regrets technology, energy efficiency should be part of any industrial decarbonization strategy, with technologies such as electrification, hydrogen, bioenergy, and carbon capture used to meet the remaining energy demand.

5

MATERIAL EFFICIENCY, MATERIAL SUBSTITUTION, AND CIRCULAR ECONOMY

Most industrial energy use and greenhouse gas emissions are associated with the production of materials, especially steel, chemical products (particularly plastics and fertilizers), and cement. While it is possible to produce these materials without greenhouse gas emissions, doing so requires investment in new production processes and innovation to bring down the costs of new technologies. Therefore, reducing the amount of new material required to meet society's needs is a powerful strategy for decreasing required investments and accelerating decarbonization. Broadly speaking, there are three ways to accomplish this: material efficiency, material substitution, and circular economy.

MATERIAL EFFICIENCY

"Material efficiency" refers to making the same products while using less material. Material efficiency does not reduce product quality or functionality, and in some cases, it can improve products (for instance, by making them lightweight and therefore easier to handle or more fuel-efficient).

Like energy efficiency (chapter 4), material efficiency can reduce industrial firms' costs, even in the absence of policy support, since less material needs to be purchased and processed. Nonetheless, there exists considerable untapped material efficiency potential. There are several reasons that firms may use more material than necessary.

- **Complexity of design and assembly**: A product or building may be easier to assemble when parts are more standardized. For instance, a building may place different loads on different steel beams, varying with their placement throughout the building. However, the use of numerous steel beam sizes at different locations, angles, and heights within the building would make engineering and construction more complex and time-consuming. Use of a smaller number of beam sizes allows for simpler design and faster construction.
- **Safety margin**: Where a product's failure could cause harm, such as a building or bridge, engineering firms design the product to withstand greater forces than it is anticipated to encounter during its service life. This often involves using extra material. Some safety margin is necessary, but design firms have incentives to include excessive safety margin, since the firm will be blamed if the structure fails, though the design firm isn't the purchaser of the construction materials.
- **Component cost**: Less material does not always translate into lower-cost components. For example, curved elements can be mechanically strong, but curved steel beams cost more than straight beams, and curved components are less efficiently packed into a small volume for transport.
- **Familiarity**: Creating new, material-efficient designs may require the firm to alter familiar production processes, steps, and tools (such as dies and molds).
- **Market acceptance**: Some buyers may question whether material-efficient products are as durable and functional as material-intensive products.

Several technical strategies can help improve material efficiency, lowering producers' cost and industrial greenhouse gas emissions.

MATERIAL-EFFICIENT COMPONENTS

One of the most straightforward material efficiency techniques is to replace typical components with functional equivalents designed to use less material. For example, based on engineering case studies of common products like cars, structural beams, rebar, and pipelines, Allwood and Cullen found that "we could use 30 percent less metal than we do at present, with no change in the level of material service provided, simply by optimizing product design and controlling the loads that they experience before and during use."[1]

The increased complexity of material-efficient components may be managed through off-site fabrication. For example, less steel rebar can be used in concrete if the diameter and spacing of the rebar rods vary within each concrete component. It would be time-consuming and error-prone to lay out complex rebar patterns on site, but rebar can be welded into a material-optimized mesh in a factory and delivered to a construction site in rolled form, reducing steel consumption by 15–30 percent.[2]

In some cases, components are designed to resist much greater stresses during installation than they will encounter during their service lives. For example, undersea pipe segments are built to support the weight of a 2.5-kilometer length of pipe as it is deployed from a ship onto the seabed. Innovative installation techniques, such as laying pipe in segments and linking them once they are on the seabed, could allow for large reductions in material requirements.[3]

AI-ASSISTED DESIGN AND SIMULATION

"Computer-aided design" (CAD) refers to the use of computers to create technical drawings and designs, often prototyping products in 2-D and 3-D space. CAD is today's standard for product design, but the computer largely acts as a drawing and calculation tool for human engineers.

There is potential for computers to take over more design tasks. Machine learning or artificial intelligence (AI) can devise novel designs and predict their real-world performance through physics- or chemistry-based simulations. The computer can iteratively tweak the designs using evolutionary algorithms (e.g., making small, random changes to the most successful designs while discarding the least-successful designs) and rerun the simulations to home in on promising options. Introducing different, random starting points helps explore a large search space (set of potential designs) without getting stuck at a local maximum (a design whose performance cannot be improved by slightly tweaking its traits) while overlooking a superior design possessing very different traits.[4]

AI-assisted design is most promising for optimizing complex products with a vast search space, such as novel materials, catalysts, biological molecules, and semiconductors. However, it also may be useful for a variety of product types, including 3-D objects.[5] Machine learning can explicitly optimize environmental performance if relevant data are available (for example, the greenhouse gas emissions associated with each material and the energy requirements of different manufacturing processes) and if optimizing greenhouse gas performance is included in the fitness function (goal definition). Optimization of environmental performance can include the product's use phase. For example, machine learning can be used in a building's early design stages to assess how various design decisions will affect the completed building's energy use and emissions.[6]

AUTOMATION

Automation involves using computer-controlled machines, such as robots, to perform production steps. Automation increases the processes' precision, which can improve material efficiency. For example, industrial painting robots can apply paint to surfaces evenly while minimizing paint wastage, and cutting robots can cut closely spaced (sometimes tessellating) parts from sheets of material, enabling more parts to be cut from a single sheet.

ADDITIVE MANUFACTURING (3-D PRINTING)

Additive manufacturing (AM), or 3-D printing, involves using a computer-controlled machine to construct an object by depositing material layer by layer. The earliest 3-D printers, invented in the 1980s, created resin objects via stereolithography (described later).[7] Today, many types of materials can be 3-D printed, including thermoplastics, metals, ceramics, glass, concrete, paper, yarn, and food.[8] There are several common AM technologies.[9]

- **Fused deposition modeling (FDM)** heats feedstock materials (generally thermoplastics) that harden by cooling.
- **Stereolithography (SLA)** uses photopolymer resins that are cured by exposure to ultraviolet light.
- **Selective laser sintering (SLS)** fuses powdered feedstock (primarily nylon) particles using a laser.
- **Selective laser melting (SLM)** melts powdered metal feedstocks with a high-powered laser.

AM places material only where it is needed, reducing the need for machining processes that remove material, such as drilling, milling, and sawing. Additionally, the complex 3-D shapes made possible by AM can in some cases confer extra strength with less material.

Although 3-D printing is material-efficient, it is not waste-free. AM material waste includes support structures (temporary vertical pieces to hold up overhanging elements during the printing process), failed prints, and test prints.[10]

AM on an industrial scale is used primarily for rapid prototyping, to produce customized parts (e.g., in dentistry or prosthetics), and where parts must be lightweight and have complex shapes (as in aerospace applications and high-performance bicycles).[11] AM is slow, and depending on the printing technology, printed parts sometimes require finishing steps to obtain a desired surface texture. Therefore, AM is not well suited to producing many copies of parts with simple shapes, such as beams, rebar, and bolts. A large share of industrial material output is used to produce many copies of products with simple shapes (and most concrete is already poured into custom-shaped molds on site), which may limit AM's potential to reduce industrial greenhouse gas emissions.

DIGITALIZATION

The most extreme form of material efficiency is "digitalization": replacing a physical product with a material-free digital product. Common examples include news articles, e-books, audiobooks, music, and video delivered over the internet. Digital products typically require a material-intensive device to access the content (e.g., a computer or smartphone), so digitalization is most environmentally beneficial if the buyer already owns a suitable device or if a dedicated device, such as an e-reader, replaces a sufficiently large number of print books.

Digitalization of services can indirectly reduce material demand. For example, videoconferencing can lessen travel demand, reducing the need for vehicles and material-intensive infrastructure such as roads, garages, and airport terminals. Online shopping can lessen demand for commercial floor space for physical shops. Digitalization increases demand for other types of infrastructure, particularly data centers, but rapid improvements in computing technology (such as energy efficiency and server virtualization) have enabled data centers to keep pace with rapidly growing demand while limiting energy use and physical server infrastructure growth.[12]

It is difficult to forecast the future opportunities and limits of digitalization. Technologies such as virtual reality, haptic feedback, and others yet unforeseen may make it possible to digitalize products and services that are difficult to digitalize today.

FERTILIZER EFFICIENCY

By mass, fertilizer is the largest output of the chemicals industry (see figure 2.2). Fertilizer provides nutrients, particularly nitrogen, to growing crops. Fertilizer use can be reduced by optimizing plants' ability to absorb nitrogen and preventing nitrogen loss to the groundwater and atmosphere. Specific techniques include the following.[13]

- Plant crop varieties that are tolerant of low-nitrogen conditions.
- Avoid applying more fertilizer than necessary to meet crops' needs. Use a soil probe (a device that reports soil pH and nutrient levels) before applying fertilizer to accurately assess fertilizer needs.[14]
- Time fertilizer application to coincide with crops' nitrogen demand. Demand is greatest a few weeks after planting.
- Place fertilizer near plant roots rather than at ground level.
- Plant winter cover crops to reduce nitrogen losses from leaching and runoff.
- Employ nitrification and urease inhibitors to delay fertilizer breakdown and dissolution. This causes nitrogen to be released more gradually, improving plants' ability to absorb it.
- Similarly, slow-release fertilizer formulations (typically based on urea) can reduce nitrogen losses by 50 percent compared with fertilizers that release nitrogen rapidly (such as anhydrous ammonia, ammonium nitrate, and ammonium sulfate) in some locations.
- Avoid unnecessary irrigation and excessive soil wetness. Underground drip irrigation allows for better control of soil moisture (and is more water-efficient).
- In some cases, long-term reduction of tillage may reduce nitrogen losses.
- Grow perennial crops (plants that produce food for multiple years) instead of annual crops (plants that last one growing season). Perennial crops require less fertilizer, as they improve soil nutrient retention and do not need to regrow the entire plant each year.[15] Although 80 percent of today's food crops are annuals, researchers are developing perennial varieties of common crops, including rice, wheat, and legumes.[16]

Soil microbes convert some of the nitrogen that is not taken up by plants into nitrous oxide, a powerful greenhouse gas. Therefore, the techniques discussed here not only reduce fertilizer demand—they also help avoid agricultural nitrous oxide emissions.

CEMENT

Material efficiency strategies specific to cement and concrete are covered in chapter 3.

MATERIAL SUBSTITUTION

Material substitution involves using low-carbon materials in place of high-carbon materials (particularly steel, plastic, and concrete). Promising replacement materials must have lower manufacturing emissions, satisfactory use-phase performance, and sufficient availability worldwide at reasonable cost. Relatively few materials pass this test. This section will focus on the most promising options.

WOOD

Today, wood framing and sheathing is common for small residential buildings, but large buildings are often built of steel and concrete. Laminated (multilayer) wood building materials can substitute for steel and concrete and have enabled the construction of large wood structures in recent years. There are several varieties of laminated wood materials.[17]

- **Glued laminated timber (glulam)** is made by gluing together multiple layers (laminations) of dried structural timber. The layers are pressed together and heated while the adhesive cures. The wood grains in all laminations run in the same direction, typically along the length of a beam. Like solid wood, glulam expands and shrinks with temperature. It is primarily used for columns, beams, and other load-bearing elements that must be strong along one axis.
- **Cross-laminated timber** is like glulam, but every other layer is rotated 90 degrees, so each layer's wood grain is perpendicular to

the grain of adjacent layers. It is generally used for surfaces, such as walls and floors.

- **Other laminated wood products** include nail-laminated timber, dowel-laminated timber, and laminated veneer lumber.[18] They involve different methods of joining layers or layer thicknesses, but all rely on the fact that multilayered wood materials are stronger than regular lumber.

These innovative materials have enabled wooden skyscrapers to be constructed, including Mjøstårnet (85 meters tall) in Norway, HoHo Wein (84 meters) in Austria, and Sara Kulturhus (75 meters) in Sweden.[19] All were built with laminated timber and completed between 2019 and 2021.

Based on a full-life-cycle analysis for a central European climate (including construction, energy use during the building's lifetime, and demolition waste at end of life), the climate change impact of a wood building is 22–25 percent lower than that of a comparable building made of traditional materials.[20] Additionally, making buildings or other long-lived products out of wood may be an efficient way to store CO_2 captured by forests, although if this approach were to be used at large scale, careful measures would be needed to avoid deforestation and protect biodiversity.[21]

Constraints on global wood availability limit the extent to which wood can replace other building materials. For example, in 2018, total global production of sawnwood (beams, joists, planks, etc.) and wood-based panels (plywood, particleboard, fiberboard, etc.) was 901 million cubic meters, while the volume of concrete produced was fifteen times larger, around 14 billion cubic meters.[22] Even a large percentage increase in structural wood production could displace only a small percentage of concrete use.

ORGANIC FERTILIZER

Today, roughly half of global crop harvests rely on synthetic fertilizer, which is produced by the chemicals industry from fossil fuels (see

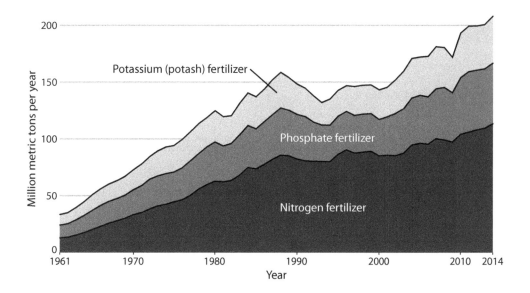

FIGURE 5.1 Global Synthetic Fertilizer Production by Nutrient Type

Source: Nick Primmer and WBA Policy, Innovation and Technical Committee, *Biogas: Pathways to 2030* (report, World Biogas Association, London, March 2021), https://www .worldbiogasassociation.org/biogas-pathways-to-2030-report/.

chapter 2).[23] Remaining crops generally rely on organic fertilizer, a prod-uct of the decomposition of organic matter—particularly animal waste, crop residues, sewage, and food scraps. Organic fertilizer can simply mean the application of animal wastes to agricultural land, a common practice worldwide.[24] However, a better method involves "anaerobic digesters," machines that process organic waste to produce fertilizer (as well as biogas, an energy source discussed in chapter 7).

Synthetic fertilizers primarily deliver three types of nutrients: nitro-gen, phosphate, and potassium (also called "potash"). In 2014, global production was 113 million metric tons of nitrogen fertilizers, 53 million metric tons of phosphate fertilizers, and 42 million metric tons of potas-sium fertilizers (figure 5.1).

Organic fertilizers contain all three of these nutrients, along with oth-ers. Table 5.1 shows the nutrient content of "digestate," the output prod-uct of anaerobic digestion, which can be used as fertilizer.

TABLE 5.1 Nutrient Content of Digestate

Source material	Nitrogen (N)	Phosphate (P_2O_5)	Potassium (K_2O)	Magnesium (MgO)	Sulfur (SO_3)
Farm-sourced wastes	3.6	1.7	4.4	0.6	0.8
Food wastes	4.8	1.1	2.4	0.2	0.7

Note: This table specifies the nutrient content of the output of wet (around 95 percent water content) anaerobic digestion. Values are in kilograms of nutrient per metric ton of digestate.

Source: Sarika Jain, David Newman, Ange Nizhou, Harmen Dekker, Pharoah Le Feuvre, Hannah Richter, et al., *Global Potential of Biogas* (report, World Biogas Association, London, June 2019), https://www.worldbiogasassociation.org/wp-content/uploads/2019/07/WBA-globalreport-56ppa4_digital.pdf.

Using organic fertilizer instead of synthetic fertilizer has two key benefits:

- reduced energy and fossil feedstock needs to produce synthetic fertilizer, and
- improved food security. Mineral production is highly concentrated, making synthetic fertilizers dependent on exports from just a few countries. Phosphate fertilizer is made from phosphate rock, 57 percent of which is mined in China and Morocco, and 67 percent of potash production is in Canada, Russia, and Belarus.[25]

Using anaerobic digesters to produce this organic fertilizer confers additional benefits:

- Avoidance of methane emissions from decomposing waste. Decomposing animal wastes, organic waste in landfills, and sewage emitted 2.2 billion metric tons of carbon dioxide equivalent in 2019, about two-thirds as much as the total greenhouse gas emissions of the European Union.[26]
- Production of useful energy as biogas, which can displace fossil fuel use (see chapter 7).
- Proper disposal of wastes. Improper disposal of agricultural wastes has negative health and environmental consequences. In some countries,

crop residues are burned, resulting in harmful air pollution. In many countries, animal waste is stored in lagoons and then applied to fields, polluting waterways and harming the health of nearby communities. These rural communities are often low-income, so proper processing of animal wastes furthers equity (see chapter 12).

- Anaerobic digestion improves the availability of fertilizer nutrients to plants.[27]

Human activity generates 69 billion metric tons of sewage (wastewater), 33 billion metric tons of animal waste, 2 billion metric tons of crop residues, and 1.3 billion metric tons of food waste per year.[28] Only 2 percent is anaerobically digested.[29] This suggests a large potential for increased organic fertilizer production. However, much of the undigested animal waste is already used as fertilizer, and wastewater has a very high water content (and hence a low nutrient density), so the potential is smaller than it first appears.[30] Additionally, some sewage systems are polluted with toxic chemicals—particularly perfluoroalkyl and polyfluoroalkyl substances (PFAS)—which can make sewage-derived materials unsuitable for use as fertilizer.[31]

The World Biogas Association estimates that anaerobically digesting more sewage and food wastes could displace 5–7 percent of global synthetic fertilizer demand,[32] but this involves conservative estimates and disregards any potential from crop residues, animal wastes not already being used as fertilizer, dedicated bioenergy crops that could be planted, or aquatic biomass sources such as algae. The maximum potential is likely significantly higher, with the specific figure dependent on the range of strategies considered.

STONE

Stone has been used as a building material since antiquity. It has physical properties similar to unreinforced concrete: it is strong against compressive forces but weak in tension.[33] Since stone need only be quarried rather than manufactured, it has comparatively low embodied emissions. A UK study found sandstone's emissions to be 50 percent that of ordinary concrete, while granite is around 70 percent and marble around 86 percent.[34]

Unfortunately, stone is difficult to use. Concrete can be poured into any desired shape or around steel rebar to provide tensile strength, but stone must be carved to the required shape and cannot be reinforced. Additionally, stone costs roughly twice as much as concrete per unit mass, and obtaining quality stone with the right properties may depend on the proximity of a suitable quarry.[35]

BIOPLASTICS

The manufacture of traditional plastic requires fossil feedstocks and results in both energy-related and process emissions (chapter 2). Bioplastics (or bio-based plastics) are plastic materials derived from renewable, biological feedstocks, such as starch, cellulose, or vegetable oils. There are eight main types of bioplastics today, each of which uses different input materials and is made through different processes, such as via thermal processing, in biorefineries, or by the action of fungi, cyanobacteria, or microbes such as *E. coli.*[36] Bioplastics can fill many roles of conventional plastic, such as being used in injection-molded products, transparent food packaging, foams, synthetic rubber, paints, and coatings.[37]

Life cycle analyses find significant greenhouse gas reduction potential from substituting bioplastics for fossil-based plastics. Relative to their fossil equivalents, starch-based thermoplastic (polylactic acid; PLA) can reduce life cycle greenhouse gas emissions by 50–70 percent, while bio-urethanes and polytrimethylene terephthalate (PTT) may reduce emissions by 36 percent and 44 percent, respectively.[38]

One downside to bioplastics is cost. For example, PLA is 20–50 percent more expensive than comparable fossil-derived plastic.[39] Additionally, bioplastic requires suitable organic feedstocks, such as corn or sugarcane for PLA, which competes with other uses of agricultural land (for food and bioenergy) and nonagricultural land uses (habitat, forests for carbon sequestration, etc.). The sustainability of energy and feedstock crops is discussed in the bioenergy section of chapter 7.

PAPER

Paper products can substitute for plastic in certain applications, such as packaging, disposable plates and cups, and shopping bags. Paper has several environmental advantages relative to plastic: it is based on biological rather than fossil fuel feedstocks, it is biodegradable and compostable, and it can be recycled more easily (for instance, many types of plastic are not accepted in curbside recycling programs, and plastic bags can interfere with recycling machinery). Paper can be made from various types of plant fibers, so it has widespread availability.

If paper is landfilled at end of life, it has higher life cycle greenhouse gas emissions than plastic due to CO_2 and methane formed during paper decomposition.[40] Better paper disposal methods include recycling, composting, or incinerating the paper for energy.

Paper may replace plastic only in certain end uses. Plastic has a greater range of potential physical properties. For example, it can be stronger than paper, it is waterproof, it resists decay, it can be transparent, and it can form fabric such as polyester. When paper is used for packaging—particularly food and drink packaging such as milk cartons and juice boxes—it is lined inside and out with polyethylene plastic (and sometimes with an internal aluminum layer as well).

In some cases, replacing disposable plastic with a nondisposable product instead of paper may be the environmentally preferred alternative. For example, reusable shopping bags (which are generally made of polypropylene or polyester) have lower environmental impacts than paper or plastic disposable bags if they are used six to twenty times before disposal (depending on bag material and whether disposable bags are reused as trash can liners).[41]

SUPPLEMENTARY CEMENTITIOUS MATERIALS AND FILLERS

Supplementary cementitious materials and fillers can replace a portion of the clinker in cement. This approach is discussed in chapter 3.

CIRCULAR ECONOMY

Circular economy is the concept of putting products and materials to their highest and best use at each point in their life cycles, minimizing both the demand for virgin materials and unrecoverable waste. From highest to lowest priority, techniques include improved product longevity, intensification of product use, transfer or resale, repair, refurbishment and remanufacturing, and recycling (figure 5.2).

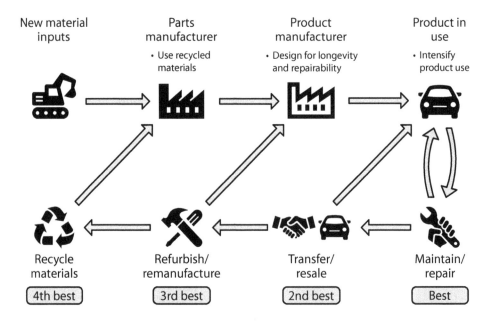

FIGURE 5.2 An Illustrative Diagram of Material Flows in a Circular Economy A circular economy puts a product to its best use at each stage of its life cycle.

LONGEVITY

One of the first ways to reduce demand for new materials is to ensure that existing products and buildings last as long as possible before they must be replaced. This is more complicated than simply making products more physically durable, as there are several reasons that consumers and businesses replace old products.[42]

- A product may break or its performance may diminish over time. For example, many homeowners keep a furnace until it ceases to work well.
- A product may still work as designed, but it is outdated or obsolete compared with new products. This is common for electronics.
- A product may still work as designed, but it no longer suits the needs of the current user. For example, parents may no longer need a stroller when a child grows too large.
- A product may still work as designed, but there is no longer sufficient market demand for that product. For example, as shopping has increasingly moved online, there is less demand for mall and department store buildings (and more need for warehouses).

Therefore, the most appropriate technical approach to increase longevity varies depending on the most common reasons for replacement.

Products that are discarded because they break or wear out should be designed for increased durability and repairability. This may entail only small design changes to some products. For example, refrigerators' most common failure mode occurs when the bearings in the compressor motor wear out. These bearings constitute a tiny share of the material that makes up the refrigerator. Producing longer-lasting bearings or making it easier to replace the compressor motor could extend the lifetime of the entire refrigerator.[43]

Products that become obsolete may sometimes be designed to facilitate component-level upgrades to extend useful life. For example, a computer's graphics card may be user-replaceable rather than soldered to the motherboard. In other cases, the product may still possess useful life in a different market. For example, trade-in cell phones in good condition may be refurbished and sold elsewhere. As of 2020, 70 percent of refurbished iPhones were sent to India, China, and Russia.[44]

Working products that no longer suit the current user should be resold or transferred, an option discussed in more detail later in this chapter.

When there is insufficient market demand for certain products, such as severely outdated electronics or products subject to recall, it is difficult or undesirable to extend that product's life, making recycling the best option. However, it can be financially worthwhile to convert buildings to new uses, a process called "adaptive reuse." The resulting structures are often beautiful and highly functional and possess historic character. Examples of adaptive reuse include converting a warehouse into loft apartments, a church into a performing arts space, or a railway station into a hotel.

In some cases, such as buildings in China, misaligned financial incentives or policy can contribute to poor longevity. Policy-related challenges and solutions are covered in chapter 11.

INTENSIFICATION OF PRODUCT USE

Another method of reducing material demand is to use existing products more intensively. Many products and buildings have low utilization rates. For instance, the typical U.S. car is used just 5 percent of the time to transport an average of 1.67 people, implying an overall capacity utilization rate of 2 percent.[45] Utilization rates for laundry and cooking appliances are similarly low.[46] Commercial buildings are often unused outside business hours. These examples imply a large theoretical potential to use existing products more often instead of manufacturing new products.

Sharing products is the main way by which intensity can be increased. For instance, ride-sharing services and public transit increase the utilization rate of vehicles, laundromats increase laundry appliance use intensity, and coworking spaces reduce the demand for private offices. Products and buildings can generally be used more often without substantially decreasing their service lives.[47]

In practice, it is challenging to increase use intensity because sharing can reduce privacy, availability, or convenience. For example, households generally prefer private laundry equipment rather than a laundromat or shared laundry room because the equipment is always available to that household and laundry may be done in private without risk of theft. Ride-sharing services and public transit increase convenience in some ways (e.g., avoiding the need to find parking), but they involve trade-offs, such as the need to wait for a vehicle to arrive, the lack of privacy during travel, and their inability to accommodate long-distance road trips (e.g., for vacation). Sharing offices complicates their use as secure spaces to keep equipment, possessions, and data.

Nonetheless, there are promising sharing options for certain types of goods. For example, some cities and neighborhoods have established tool lending libraries that loan home and garden tools to community members.[48] Makerspaces provide shared access to machine tools, sewing machines, and similar devices. Digital platforms allow individuals to rent out spare living or storage space, vehicles, musical instruments, tools, camping gear, and even clothing. There may be opportunities to grow the popularity of library-based and peer-to-peer lending models in the future.

TRANSFER OR RESALE

When an item is no longer needed by its owner, the environmentally preferred option is to transfer or sell it to a new owner. This avoids the energy required to remanufacture or recycle the item. If the recipient would otherwise have purchased a new item, transfer or resale also avoids the manufacture of a product from virgin materials. (If the recipient would otherwise have done without any item, transfer does not reduce virgin material demand but improves human well-being.)

Resale is common for buildings and vehicles in good condition but less common for other goods. For example, in 2009, the United States generated 11.3 billion kilograms of unwanted textile products, of which only 15 percent were resold, donated, or recycled. The remaining 85 percent were landfilled or incinerated.[49]

Manufacturers and retailers can take specific steps to increase transfer and resale rates.

- Design products for longevity so they remain in good condition for multiple owners.
- Include end-of-life instructions on packaging and product labels suggesting ways the product may be resold, donated, or recycled.[50]
- Work with reverse logistics firms to better manage returned items and excess inventory. In the United States, 5.1 billion items worth $400 billion were returned to stores in 2019.[51] More than half of retailers send over 25 percent of returned items directly to landfill, typically because it is cheaper to discard the item than inspect it, restore the item and packaging to salable condition, and send it to resale channels, such as thrift and discount sellers.[52] As a result, over 2.3 billion kilograms of returns were sent to U.S. landfills in 2019.[53] Similarly, unsold inventory—especially apparel—is often destroyed.[54] Effective reverse logistics integrated with resale, donation, and recycling channels can reduce the rate of landfilled returns and excess inventory to 4 percent.[55]
- Retailers may participate in the resale market by purchasing their own used merchandise (often for store credit) and reselling it. This can increase brand loyalty and reduce competition from external sellers. Retailers including Patagonia, REI, Lululemon, and IKEA have buyback programs.[56]

REPAIR

Repairing a broken item allows it to continue to be used by its existing owner or transferred to a new owner. However, a product may be easy, difficult, or impossible to repair depending on how it was designed and the availability of replacement parts, software, tools, and manuals. Some straightforward steps that manufacturers can take to increase the repairability of their products include the following.[57]

- Make outer cases easy to open (for example, by using ordinary screws instead of high-security screws or glue).
- Ensure individual parts can be detached and replaced.

- Make spare parts available.
- Do not require special or proprietary tools.
- Label wires and circuit boards.
- Include appropriate documentation, such as parts lists, schematics, and pinout diagrams.
- Make diagnostic software, firmware, and drivers permanently available online.

Unfortunately, some manufacturers intentionally impose repair restrictions, such as designing a product to be physically difficult to repair, using software locks (digital rights management), and making spare parts, manuals, tools, and diagnostic software unavailable.[58] Common reasons include a manufacturer's desire for worn-out items to be replaced to increase new item sales, minimization of manufacturing costs (modularity adds cost), aesthetics (screws are visible; glue is not), a belief that consumers prefer new items over repairing existing items, and concerns over protection of intellectual property, cybersecurity, or liability and reputational harm (if a repaired product does not perform well).[59] As a result, increasing items' repairability might require legislation. Right-to-repair laws are discussed in chapter 11.

REFURBISHMENT AND REMANUFACTURING

"Refurbishment" and "remanufacturing" refer to a manufacturer restoring used products to working, salable condition. There is no standardized definition of these terms, and some companies use them interchangeably or use related terms such as "renewed," "reconditioned," "recertified," "rebuilt," and "restored." Generally, refurbishment involves a surface-level cleaning, inspection, and testing to verify that the product works, but it does not involve full disassembly or replacement of worn parts.

Remanufacturing implies a more thorough process that includes disassembly and replacement of worn components, resulting in a product with like-new performance and quality. In some cases, remanufactured parts may be used in a different final product—remanufactured automotive parts are a common example.

Refurbishment often applies to small, durable consumer goods, such as electronics, power tools, cameras, and small kitchen appliances. Remanufacturing is more cost-effective for vehicle parts, vehicles, and heavy machinery (such as construction equipment), where the higher price of the item justifies the effort involved. Remanufacturing heavy equipment can extend its lifetime by roughly 80 percent.[60] Globally, sales of remanufactured products exceeded $100 billion in 2014, of which only 5–10 percent were consumer-oriented products.[61]

One challenge in expanding the market for refurbished and remanufactured products is overcoming negative consumer perceptions. Consumers may worry that a refurbished or remanufactured product will be unreliable and may irrationally believe it is dirty or contaminated because a previous user has touched the product.[62] Also, consumers often fail to recognize the environmental benefits associated with restored products.[63] Better consumer education regarding rigorous restoration, testing, and cleaning protocols, combined with information on environmental benefits (such as greenhouse gas abatement), may be helpful.

Remanufacturing can apply to building components. Sometimes, adaptive reuse of buildings (discussed earlier) is impractical or economically undesirable (for example, because the land value has increased and higher-density infill development is desired for that site). New technologies such as reversible joints for steel beams allow buildings to be safely and quickly deconstructed rather than conventionally demolished, facilitating reuse of their parts.[64] Opportunities to reuse concrete building components involve incorporating elements of the foundation or structural columns into a new building on the same site, but standardized concrete components with reversible chemical or mechanical connectors are a possibility for the future.[65] Voluntary green building standards, such as the U.S. Green Building Council's LEED system, give builders credit for reuse of old building materials.[66]

RECYCLING

"Recycling" refers to breaking down a product into its constituent materials—such as steel, glass, aluminum, paper, and plastic—for use in new products. ("Composting" organic materials for use as fertilizer is sometimes grouped with recycling.) Recycling may be one of the first strategies consumers think of when considering actions to protect the environment. However, recycling is less environmentally preferred than other circular economy options, such as repair, resale, or refurbishment, because recycling requires more energy and faces challenges related to material contamination, which can lead to material losses or "downcycling" (using recycled materials for a lower-value purpose than their original function). Nonetheless, recycling is frequently the best option for obsolete or heavily damaged products and for packaging materials. Recycling material instead of producing virgin material reduces life cycle greenhouse gas emissions by 35–40 percent for paper products, 45–55 percent for glass and plastics, and 50–85 percent for metals (see figure 5.3).

Globally, just 19 percent of solid waste is managed sustainably: 13.5 percent is recycled and 5.5 percent is composted. A further 11 percent is incinerated, 37 percent is landfilled, and 33 percent is left in open dumps.[67] However, recycling rates vary greatly by country. Within the OECD, South Korea has the highest recycling rate (64 percent) and Slovenia has the highest combined recycling and composting rate (72 percent) (figure 5.4). China, which produces more waste than any other country, issued a 2017 directive requiring its forty-six largest cities to introduce recycling programs by 2020. Estimates of China's nationwide 2019 recycling rate range from 5 percent to 20 percent.[68] Many low- and middle-income countries do not have widespread recycling availability.

Recycling rates also vary by material. In the United States, more than two-thirds of paper and paperboard in municipal solid waste is recycled, but the rate is much lower for other materials: 34 percent of metal, 25 percent of glass, and 8.7 percent of plastic in municipal solid waste are

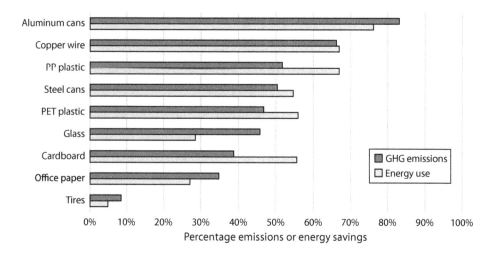

FIGURE 5.3 **Greenhouse Gas and Energy Savings from Recycling** This graph depicts life cycle emissions and energy savings (percentage reduction in emissions and energy use) from producing recycled instead of virgin material. Data exclude any change in emissions or energy use from avoided landfilling of materials (which can be positive or negative, depending on whether or not the material decomposes and whether or not the landfill captures and uses landfill gas for energy). PP = polypropylene; PET = polyethylene terephthalate.

Source: U.S. Environmental Protection Agency, "Versions of the Waste Reduction Model: Current WARM Tool—Version 15," November 2020, https://www.epa.gov/warm /versions-waste-reduction-model-warm#15.

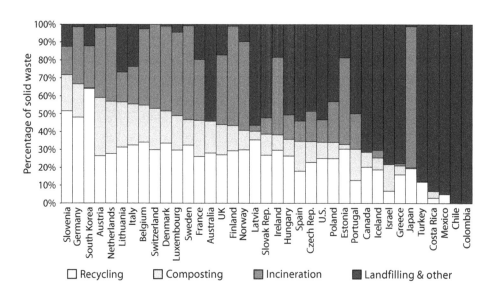

FIGURE 5.4 **Solid Waste Disposal Mechanisms by OECD Country** Data reflect 2019 (for most countries) or latest available data. No data were available for New Zealand, the only OECD country omitted from the figure.

Source: OECD, "OECD Environmental Statistics," 2020, https://stats.oecd.org /viewhtml.aspx?datasetcode=MUNW&lang=en.

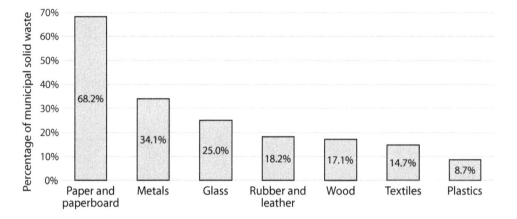

FIGURE 5.5 U.S. Recycling Rates of Materials in Municipal Solid Waste in 2018 Rates include only materials in municipal solid waste. For example, steel from forming and fabrication scrap, demolished buildings, and scrapped vehicles is generally recycled but is not part of municipal solid waste. Therefore, overall U.S. steel recycling rates (see chapter 1) are much higher than the "Metals" rate in this figure.

Source: U.S. Environmental Protection Agency, "Advancing Sustainable Materials Management: 2018 Fact Sheet," December 2020, https://www.epa.gov/sites/default/files /2021-01/documents/2018_ff_fact_sheet_dec_2020_fnl_508.pdf.

recycled (figure 5.5). (The U.S. plastics recycling rate is low for a high-income country. In comparison, Europe's plastic recycling rate is 30 percent and China's is 25 percent.[69])

One reason for low recycling rates is contamination by other materials. Difficulties separating steel from impurities (such as copper) are discussed in chapter 1, and contamination in plastics recycling is covered in chapter 2. Plastic recycling is particularly uneconomical because plastic has low value, and it generally costs less to make new plastic. In the United States, 87 percent of residents have access to a recycling program that accepts plastic bottles and jugs made of polyethylene terephthalate (PET; labeled #1) or high-density polyethylene (HDPE; labeled #2), and 31 percent of residents can recycle tubs made of polypropylene (PP; labeled #5). No more than 7 percent of Americans have access to a program that recycles any other type of plastic.[70] Plastics that recycling centers cannot process are landfilled, incinerated, or exported to countries that recycle, landfill, or incinerate them.[71] In 2015, the most recyclable plastic products—PET, HDPE, and PP packaging—made up less than 25 percent of global plastics production (figure 5.6), and only 18 percent of all plastic waste generated was actually recycled (55 percent entered landfills or open dumps, 24 percent was incinerated, and around 3 percent entered the oceans).[72]

A number of technical approaches can increase materials recycling.

- Researching and deploying improved material separation technologies can reduce the impact of contamination and increase the quality of recycled materials.
- Shifting to a multistream recycling model (whereby consumers sort recyclable waste materials such as glass, paper, and plastics into separate bins) reduces contamination and increases the fraction of materials able to be successfully recycled. For example, only 40 percent of glass placed into single-stream (mixed) recycling bins is ultimately able to be recycled, but 90 percent of glass placed into glass-only bins can be recycled.[73] However, switching to a multistream recycling model requires consumer education and increases collection and handling costs.[74]
- Producers can opt to use materials in products and packaging that are more easily recyclable and design products so materials of different types are easily separated. Policies such as extended producer responsibility (see chapter 11) can incentivize manufacturers to consider recyclability in their product designs and packaging choices.

Ultimately, the cost of recycling certain materials (such as mixed plastics) is likely to remain higher than the cost of landfilling those materials, and recycling may not be possible if no producers wish to use the recovered materials in new products. In these cases, it may be necessary to encourage or require manufacturers to switch to more easily recyclable materials in their products and packaging as a first step toward increasing recycling rates. Relevant policy options are covered in chapter 11.

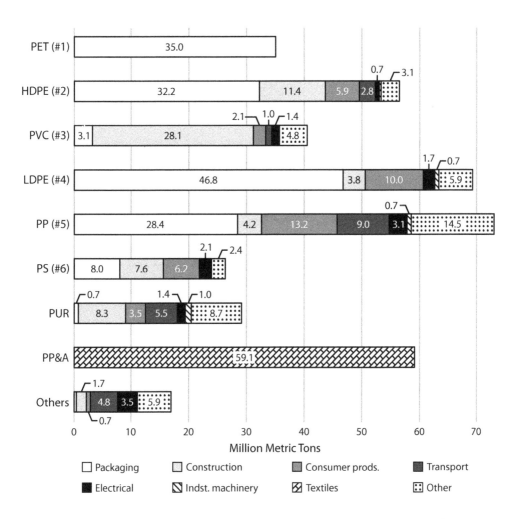

FIGURE 5.6 **Global Plastic Production by Resin Type and End Use in 2015** The designations #1–6 indicate each plastic's resin identification code, which may appear inside a triangle or "chasing arrows" symbol on rigid plastic items. PET = polyethylene terephthalate; HDPE = high-density polyethylene; PVC = polyvinyl chloride; LDPE = low-density polyethylene; PP = polypropylene; PS = polystyrene; PUR = polyurethane; PP&A = polyester, polyamide, and acrylic. "Others" includes polycarbonate (PC), acrylonitrile butadiene styrene (ABS), polymethyl methacrylate (PMMA), polyacrylonitrile (PAN), and polyvinyl acetate (PVA). This figure encompasses thermoplastics, thermosets, fiber, and elastomers from figure 2.2 after differences in year and data source.

Source: Roland Geyer, Jenna R. Jambeck, and Kara Lavender Law, "Production, Use, and Fate of All Plastics Ever Made," *Science Advances* 3, no. 7 (July 19, 2017): e1700782, https://doi.org/10.1126/sciadv.1700782.

MATERIAL EFFICIENCY, SUBSTITUTION, AND CIRCULAR ECONOMY'S CONTRIBUTION TO ZERO-CARBON INDUSTRY

Most industrial greenhouse gas emissions are associated with the production of materials such as metals, cement, and plastics, so reducing the amount of material needed for final products (without compromising on their quality or functionality) is a cost-effective way to reduce industrial emissions. Material efficiency reduces not only combustion-related emissions but also industrial process emissions, the use of fossil feedstocks, emissions from products' incineration or decay at end of life, and even emissions from harvesting and transporting raw materials and finished goods. Smart design of products and computerized manufacturing processes can create high-quality, material-efficient products.

Substituting low-carbon materials for high-carbon materials, such as using wood instead of concrete, can be a useful supplementary strategy. However, land is required to grow materials such as wood and bioplastic inputs; substitute materials will struggle to match the immense scale of demand for conventional materials; and production of some substitute materials, such as bioplastics, still generates greenhouse gas emissions. Material substitution will play a role in a decarbonized industry sector, particularly for fertilizer, but cannot be the central decarbonization mechanism.

Today, without researching new technology, it is possible to implement circular economy measures such as designing products for longevity and repairability, facilitating transfer or resale of products, making products easy to disassemble for remanufacturing, opting for materials that are easy and cost-effective to recycle, and incorporating more recycled materials into products. The important challenges relate not to technology but to companies' financial incentives, logistics of product sharing or resale, and the economics and availability of recycling. Chapter 11 discusses policy tools that can overcome these challenges and achieve a high degree of circularity of products and materials within the economy.

6

ELECTRIFICATION

To reduce industrial emissions to zero, fossil fuels must be replaced with zero-emissions energy sources. Electricity is one of the most important clean energy options for industry. Electricity can be decarbonized as electric power producers and utilities increasingly shift to renewables, such as wind and solar, supported by technologies that improve grid flexibility, such as the interconnection of larger areas with transmission lines, demand response programs, and energy storage (chemical batteries, hydrogen, compressed air, etc.). Industrial electrification would significantly increase electricity demand, but industry can also help decarbonize the grid by providing demand response services. Decarbonizing the electricity sector is outside the scope of this book, so this chapter considers only the demand side of electrification: how industrial firms can cost-effectively replace fuel-using processes with electrified equivalents and the implications for electricity demand.

INDUSTRIAL HEAT DEFINES ELECTRIFICATION POTENTIAL

It is necessary to identify industry's electrification potential—that is, the specific uses of fossil fuels that are amenable to being replaced by electricity. First, we set aside two uses of fossil fuels.

- **Feedstocks** are fuels used as chemical inputs to industrial processes, making up 30 percent of global industrial fossil fuel use and almost half such use in the United States (figure 6.1).[1] Feedstocks contribute mass to industrial products, so they cannot be replaced with electricity directly. However, it is possible to create zero-carbon hydrogen using electricity and use it as a feedstock. Clean hydrogen production is discussed in chapter 7, and the use of hydrogen to replace fossil feedstocks is discussed in chapters 1 (for the steel industry) and 2 (for the chemicals industry, which accounts for about three-quarters of all industrial feedstock use).

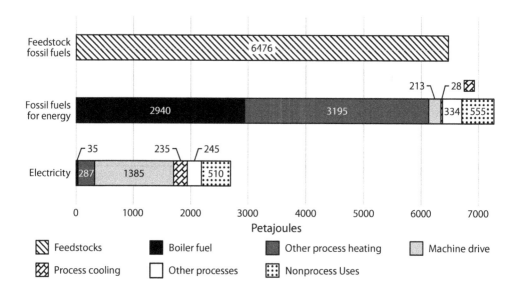

FIGURE 6.1 **Uses of Fossil Fuels and Electricity by U.S. Industry in 2018** "Machine drive" includes pumps, conveyor belts, fans, robots, and other moving elements of production processes. "Other processes" includes electrochemistry and miscellaneous processes. "Nonprocess uses" include heating, cooling, and lighting buildings for the comfort of workers, using vehicles to transport items around an industrial site, and the like. The figure excludes energy whose fuel type and end use were not reported (including biomass and waste, refinery fuel gas, blast furnace gas, and steam purchased from external suppliers, such as district heating plants).

Source: U.S. Energy Information Administration, "2018 Manufacturing Energy Consumption Survey—2018 MECS Survey Data," accessed May 25, 2023, https://www.eia.gov/consumption/manufacturing/data/2018/.

- **Nonprocess uses** are industrial energy uses that are not part of the actual process of manufacturing products. For example, heating, air conditioning, and lighting of factories for the comfort of workers, as well as using forklifts or other vehicles to move items around the site, are nonprocess energy uses. Such uses account for just 8 percent of the nonfeedstock fossil fuels consumed by U.S. industry (figure 6.1). Electrifying these uses is the purview of buildings sector technologies (i.e., electric water heaters and heat pumps for buildings) and transportation technologies (vehicle electrification), so nonprocess uses are not within the scope of this chapter.

PROCESS USES OF FOSSIL FUELS

The remaining uses of fossil fuel by industry are "process uses," fuels burned for energy to heat or drive an industrial process. The main process uses are:

- **Boilers** are large devices that generate hot water or steam. Steam is used in almost every industry. It is a common way to heat materials, distill liquids, preheat air to be used for combustion, and perform other tasks. Heat exchangers are often used, so the steam does not mix with the fluid or product being heated, and the steam can be recovered and reused. Steam also can turn turbines, providing motive force or on-site electricity generation, alone or in combined heat and power boiler systems (chapter 4). Today, boilers almost exclusively use fossil fuels, accounting for 44 percent of U.S. industry's process fossil fuel use.[2]
- **Other process heat** refers to all other uses of heat that are part of the process of producing industrial products, such as heating a kiln to make cement or heating a blast furnace to make steel. Other process heat accounts for 47 percent of process fossil fuel use by U.S. industry.[3]
- **Machine drive** is the operation of moving equipment, such as pumps, fans, conveyor belts, and robots. It accounts for half of U.S. industrial electricity use but only 3 percent of process fossil fuel use.[4]

- **Other process uses** (predominantly adding nonthermal energy to chemical reactions) and a small amount of energy for which the end use was not reported account for the last 6 percent of industrial process fossil fuel use.[5]

In addition to combustible fuels and electricity, industries also purchase "heat," which refers to hot water or steam piped in from a plant that supplies heat to nearby facilities. Purchased heat accounts for 5 percent of industrial energy use worldwide.[6] The hot water or steam is produced by boilers, so the same techniques to decarbonize industrial boilers can be used to decarbonize boilers in heat plants. Alternatively, industries may replace the use of steam with another method of providing heat.

This review of industrial energy use reveals that industries primarily burn fossil fuels to supply heat. Heat accounts for 91 percent of U.S. fuel use for industrial processes, excluding feedstocks.[7] Therefore, how to electrify industry largely boils down to how to produce heat from electricity (or, in very limited cases, how to replace processes that use heat with nonthermal, electrical alternatives).

INDUSTRIAL TEMPERATURE REQUIREMENTS

Industrial processes, such as steelmaking and certain chemical reactions, require input materials to reach a sufficiently high temperature. Temperature can be thought of as the density of heat energy within a material. Heat can be imparted to a material using electricity or by burning fuels, but heat is continuously lost through the walls of the furnace, chemical reactor, or other industrial equipment holding the material. When combustion is used, heat is also lost in the exhaust stream. Heat must be added in sufficient quantity and at the correct temperature to offset heat losses and ensure that industrial production is fast and efficient.

Electrical heating technologies differ in their ability to cost-effectively deliver large quantities of heat at high temperatures. Therefore, it is useful to divide industrial heat demand into temperature categories to better understand the fraction of heat needs that are well suited to particular electrification technologies. Slightly more than half the heat required for industrial processes (including boilers) must be delivered at temperatures greater than 500°C. For example, steam crackers in the chemicals industry operate at around 850°C, cement kilns at 1300°C–1450°C, and steelmaking blast furnaces at 1600°C–1800°C. Only a few industrial processes require temperatures above 2000°C. One example is the manufacture of synthetic graphite, which can require temperatures of 3000°C.[8]

There is also considerable demand for low-temperature heat. For instance, in Europe, 12 percent of industrial heat demand is for temperatures under 100°C and another 26 percent is for temperatures between 100°C and 200°C (figure 6.2). These temperatures are common in processing food and beverages, manufacturing pulp and paper, and fabricating machinery or vehicles from purchased metal and other materials.

Fossil fuels can achieve sufficiently high temperatures for most industrial uses, up to and including steelmaking. However, there is an upper limit to the temperatures they can provide. When organic materials are burned, the flame temperature may exceed 2500°C, but it is not possible to transfer this heat to a furnace without temperature loss, so achievable furnace temperatures are lower (around 1800°C–2000°C).[9] Certain electrical technologies, such as resistance, induction, and electric arc furnaces, can achieve higher temperatures.

ELECTRICAL HEATING TECHNOLOGIES

There are a number of methods by which electricity can be converted into heat for industrial processes. Each has specific advantages and disadvantages in efficiency of heat production, heat delivery to the processed material, achievable temperature, and other considerations.

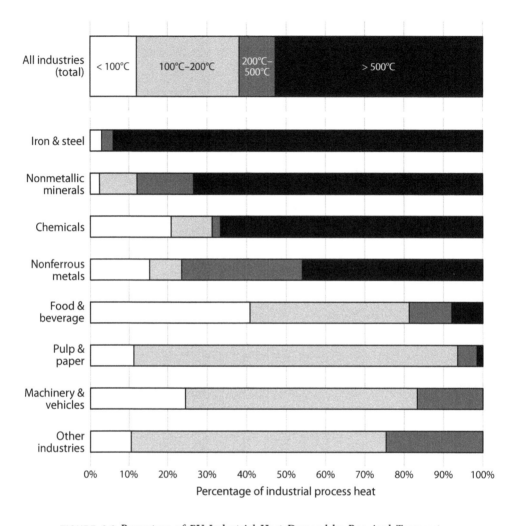

Percentage of industrial process heat

FIGURE 6.2 Percentage of EU Industrial Heat Demand by Required Temperature in 2012 These data refer to heat for industrial processes (including boilers). Nonprocess heating, such as heating air in buildings for the thermal comfort of occupants, is excluded.

Source: European Commission, "Mapping and Analyses of the Current and Future (2020–2030) Heating/Cooling Fuel Deployment (Fossil/Renewables): Work package 1: Final energy consumption for the year 2012," September 2016, https://energy.ec.europa.eu/system /files/2023-04/mapping-hc-final_report_wp1.pdf.

HEAT PUMPS

Heat pumps are unique among electrical heating options. Rather than create heat, a heat pump moves heat from one place to another.

A heat pump operates much like a refrigerator. A refrigerant, or working fluid, is contained within a closed loop of piping that passes through a heat source (such as the air or ground) and a heat sink (the material or equipment to be heated). When in contact with the heat source or sink, the piping is divided into many small tubes, called "coils," to increase the surface area across which heat may be exchanged. Before the fluid enters the heat source, its pressure is lowered by an expansion valve, causing it to cool. The cool fluid absorbs heat from the heat source, causing it to evaporate. Before entering the heat sink, this gas is compressed, causing it to heat up. The gas becomes hotter than the heat sink, so heat is transferred from the gas to the heat sink, and the fluid condenses into a liquid. The liquid is sent back to the expansion valve, and the cycle begins again. (There also exist open-cycle heat pumps employing mechanical vapor compression, a heat recovery technique discussed in chapter 4.)[10]

The main advantage of heat pumps is energy efficiency. While technologies such as electrical resistance may approach "100 percent efficiency," meaning that essentially all the electrical energy is converted into heat, a heat pump may provide several times more heat than the amount of electricity consumed. That is possible because the heat pump does not need to produce new heat—it only needs to move existing heat. A heat pump's efficiency is called its "coefficient of performance" (COP), a ratio of the amount of usable heat it provides to its electricity consumption. For example, a heat pump with a COP of 4 provides four times more heat than an electrical resistance heater would produce using the same amount of electricity.

Unfortunately, heat pumps offer limited maximum temperatures, and their COPs decline as they deliver larger increases in temperature (larger differences between the heat source and the heat sink temperatures). The majority of high-temperature industrial heat pumps on the market deliver heat with a maximum temperature of 90°C, though there are a few with maximum temperatures in the 95°C–150°C range, and one model can achieve 165°C.[11] However, the performance of industrial heat pumps declines at these higher temperatures. The average industrial heat pump delivering a temperature increase of 40°C has a COP of 4, but this drops to 2.5 for an increase of 80°C and just over 1.5 for an increase of 130°C (figure 6.3). As a heat pump's COP approaches 1, the pump's efficiency approaches that of an electrical resistance heater, which has lower capital costs. Therefore, heat pumps have cost and efficiency advantages over other electrical heating technologies only when operating with a COP higher than 1, which today corresponds to output temperatures up to 165°C, covering roughly one-third of industrial heat demand.

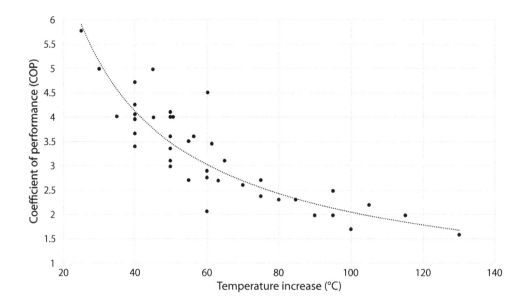

FIGURE 6.3 Industrial Heat Pump Efficiency Versus Delivered Temperature Increase Industrial heat pump efficiency (coefficient of performance, or COP) declines as the increase in temperature provided by the heat pump becomes larger. Each dot is a specific industrial heat pump model configured to deliver a specific temperature increase.

Source: Cordin Arpagaus, Frédéric Bless, Michael Uhlmann, Jürg Schiffmann, and Stefan Bertsch, "High Temperature Heat Pumps: Market Overview, State of the Art, Research Status, Refrigerants, and Application Potentials" (presented at 17th International Refrigeration and Air Conditioning Conference, Purdue University, West Lafayette, IN, 2018), paper 1876, https://docs.lib.purdue.edu/cgi/viewcontent.cgi?article=2875&context=iracc.

ELECTRICAL RESISTANCE HEATING

Electrical resistance may be the most familiar electrical heating technology. Electrical current is run through a resistor, a material that dissipates some of the current's energy in the form of heat. (A small amount of energy is converted into visible light, which is why heating elements glow.) Assuming that sufficient electricity is available, the achievable temperature is limited by the physical and chemical properties of the resistor: the resistor must not melt, oxidize, or chemically break down at operating temperatures.

The most common material for resistance heating elements is nichrome, a nickel-chromium alloy with a melting point of 1400°C. Nichrome is often used in household appliances, such as water heaters and hair dryers, and is also employed in industry for heating metal parts, soldering, and other precision heat applications at temperatures up to 1250°C.[12] At higher temperatures, tungsten is a common material for resistance heating elements. Tungsten has the highest melting point of all pure metals (3422°C) and can provide industrial heat at up to 3000°C when surrounded by an inert gas, such as argon or helium.[13] Tungsten elements are used in specialized, high-temperature furnaces for tasks such as annealing and heat-treating metal parts, vacuum metalizing (depositing vaporized metal onto surfaces), and diffusion bonding or brazing of metals.[14]

Resistors convert nearly 100 percent of electrical energy into heat, but that heat may or may not be efficiently transferred to the target material. If a heating element can be fully immersed in the material to be heated (e.g., water), heat transfer from the heating element to the material may be highly efficient. In other cases, such as heating a furnace, some heat generated by the heating element escapes before it can reach the material to be processed. In contrast, induction can heat suitable materials directly.

INDUCTION

Induction heating relies on a property of physics: a varying magnetic field will create electrical current inside an electrical conductor exposed to the magnetic field. Alternating current provides time-varying electrical energy, so a time-varying magnetic field can be created by running alternating current through an electromagnet (i.e., a coil of wire). If an electrically conductive material, such as most metals, is exposed to the magnetic field, electrical currents will be generated inside the conductive material. These currents, known as "eddy currents," flow in closed loops within the material. A conductive material has a certain degree of electrical resistivity, which converts some of the electrical energy into heat.[15]

This last property, converting electrical current into heat via resistivity, is the same one involved in electrical resistance heating, discussed earlier. The key difference is that resistance heating involves running current through a dedicated heating element, which must transfer its heat to the material to be processed. In induction heating, the material to be processed is exposed to a varying magnetic field, and the heat is generated directly inside that material. This directness offers several benefits, such as reduced heat losses to the surrounding environment and faster heating of the material.

Heat can be controlled with precision by varying the electrical current and the design or positioning of the electromagnet.[16] Another advantage is that the electromagnetic forces create a natural stirring effect that helps evenly mix molten metals.[17]

Modern inductive heating can be over 90 percent efficient in converting electrical energy into heat.[18] This is lower than the nearly 100 percent efficiency of resistance heating, but induction's more efficient heat delivery to the target material (lower heat losses and more precise heat application) can make up for that.

Electrical resistance heating temperatures are limited by the properties of the heating element, which cannot become so hot that it melts or chemically breaks down. Induction has no heating element, so much higher temperatures are achievable. For example, the Joint European Torus experimental fusion reactor uses induction to raise the temperature of a magnetically suspended plasma to 10 million °C, far more than necessary for any industrial process.[19] Induction heating temperatures used by industry range from 100°C to 3000°C.[20]

In industry, induction heating is used for numerous tasks, such as brazing (joining metal parts), hardening metal through rapid heating and cooling cycles, tempering metal parts, welding, annealing (heating a part to relieve internal stresses and improve ductility), forging (heating metal before it is shaped to form a final part), melting metals, and preheating materials before welding or other processes.[21] Induction can heat ferrous or nonferrous metals, though low-resistivity nonferrous metals like aluminum and copper require different operating frequencies.[22]

Induction heats only electrically conductive materials. It is possible to place a susceptor (an object made of an electrically conductive heat-resistant material, such as graphite) in proximity to or in physical contact with the nonconductive material and to heat the susceptor via induction. The heat is then transferred from the susceptor to the material by radiation or conduction, similar to resistance heating.[23] Susceptors have various uses, often related to fine-tuning the geometry of heat application, but they obviate some of the benefits that come from heating a material directly.[24] Induction may not be a good fit for industries such as cement and chemicals manufacturing, where large quantities of high-temperature heat must be applied to nonconductive materials.

ELECTRIC ARCS AND PLASMA TORCHES

An electric arc occurs when high-voltage electricity breaks down a gas to form a plasma (an electrically conductive gas-like state of matter). Arcs emit intense heat and visible light. In nature, a lightning bolt is a familiar example of an electric arc.

Electric arcs are commonly used in furnaces to produce new steel from scrap or from direct reduced iron. In an electric arc furnace, the material to be melted is placed at the bottom of the furnace, and an electric current is applied to graphite electrodes that are lowered through holes in the furnace roof. Arcs form between the electrodes and the metal. The metal is heated both by radiant energy from the electric arcs and electrical resistance within the metal itself.[25] Electric arc furnaces can heat metal to 1800°C.[26] Electric arc furnace steelmaking is described in more detail in chapter 1. These furnaces are also used to make several other materials, such as other metal alloys, calcium carbide, and phosphorus.[27]

Electric arcs are also used in small-scale arc melt furnaces for purposes such as powder melting, annealing, and arc casting. These furnaces, typically employed in industrial research and development but not in full-scale production, can achieve temperatures as high as 3500°C.[28] An important nonfurnace application of electric arcs is arc welding (joining metal pieces by melting portions of the metal).

A "plasma torch" is a tool that uses an electric arc to turn a gas (usually dry air, oxygen, nitrogen, or argon) into a plasma, then emits the plasma from a nozzle. A common application is a "plasma cutter," a tool for cutting metals by shooting a narrow stream of charged plasma from the cutter at the workpiece. Plasma torches are also used in noncutting applications, such as destroying ozone-depleting substances, eliminating organic molecules from industrial gases, and recycling dust and fly ash.[29] The Swedish firm Cementa has found that plasma torches can cost-effectively supply electrical heat for cement-making.[30]

DIELECTRIC HEATING (RADIO WAVES, MICROWAVES)

Dielectric heating involves using radio waves or microwaves to heat dielectric materials (materials containing polar molecules, such as water and some types of plastic). Radio or microwaves create a rapidly oscillating electrical field. The polar molecules in the heated substance attempt to align themselves with the field, rotating back and forth. This causes molecular collisions and friction, raising the temperature of the material.[31] Microwaves can produce temperatures of millions of degrees Celsius (as planned in the ITER fusion reactor), and their highest-temperature industrial applications are in specialized microwave furnaces that reach 2200°C. However, it is far more common for dielectric heating to be used in processes that operate at under 150°C.

Industrial equipment is around 70 percent efficient at converting electrical energy into radio waves or microwaves.[32] Radio and microwave heating are largely similar, but radio waves penetrate more deeply into materials than microwaves, heating them more evenly, while microwaves have higher energy and heat materials more quickly.[33] Dielectric heating is common in the food-processing industry for tasks such as baking, thawing, drying, cooking, and sterilizing food products.[34] These technologies are also used in other industrial processes, such as in the vulcanization of rubber, production of insulation, and drying of paperboard, latex, mineral powders, pharmaceuticals, and construction materials.[35]

INFRARED HEATING

Infrared radiation is sometimes referred to as "radiant heat." All objects warmer than absolute zero ($-273.15°C$) give off infrared radiation, and the intensity of this radiation increases at higher temperatures. Measuring this radiation is how infrared cameras produce false-color images and how contactless thermometers determine temperature. An infrared heater contains an "emitter," a part that is heated (typically via electrical resistance) and gives off infrared radiation, which can be directed out of the heater and toward the target material by a "reflector," most commonly made of anodized aluminum.

Ceramic emitters are 96 percent efficient at converting their heat into infrared radiation, while quartz lamp emitters with a tungsten filament are 85 percent efficient and metal tubular emitters are only 56 percent efficient.[36] Infrared heaters are used in industry for low-temperature applications, such as drying or curing paint and powder coatings, as well as warming heat-sensitive parts (such as plastics and wood) where precision temperature control is needed to avoid damage.[37] Infrared heat losses may be 20–50 percent lower than losses from an electrical or natural gas convection oven, since infrared radiation passes through air with minimal heat loss, whereas a convection oven must heat the air, and only some of this heat is transferred to the material.[38]

Infrared heaters' maximum temperature is limited by the physical properties of the emitter, which must not melt or chemically break down (much like the heating element in a resistance heater). Ceramic emitters can heat materials and parts up to 700°C, while quartz emitters can heat materials to almost 1400°C.[39] (The emitters' own temperatures are higher.)

LASERS (INFRARED, VISIBLE, ULTRAVIOLET LIGHT)

A laser is a device that emits focused, coherent light. In a laser, energy is applied to a lasing medium, boosting the electrons in this material to a high-energy state. When an electron falls to a lower state, it emits a photon of a wavelength determined by the lasing medium. This photon can be absorbed by an atom in a low-energy configuration or can stimulate the emission of an identical photon (i.e., a photon with aligned peaks and troughs, traveling in the same direction) from an atom in a high-energy configuration. If more than half the atoms in the lasing medium are in the excited state, more photons will be emitted than are absorbed, starting a cascade. The lasing medium has a mirror on one side and a parallel, partly transparent mirror on the other side. Some photons will happen to be aligned perpendicular to the mirrors. These photons travel back and forth, causing the emission of many parallel photons.[40] Some emerge from the partly reflecting mirror, where a lens focuses them into a beam or to a point at a specific focal length.

In manufacturing applications, two common lasing mediums are carbon dioxide gas (often used for cutting hard materials) and optical fiber doped with ions of the metal ytterbium. Ytterbium lasers offer the highest efficiencies: a typical industrial ytterbium laser may be 30 percent efficient at converting electricity into light, though efficiencies of up to 50 percent have been achieved by running lasers at lower power.[41] Lasers transmit this light efficiently, with almost no losses in air over short distances, and can treat very specific areas of a material.

Lasers are used for a wide variety of industrial tasks, including cutting, engraving and marking, welding, stripping paint and other coatings, and

drilling. Lasers are also used to sinter materials (to fuse particles into a solid mass), a key technique in additive manufacturing (3-D printing). Due to lasers' emphasis on applying energy to small areas and comparatively low electricity-to-heat conversion efficiencies, they are not well suited to bulk heating applications, such as melting large quantities of material in cement-making and steelmaking.

Lasers can heat materials to temperatures far higher than required for industry. For example, the world's most powerful laser array, in the U.S. National Ignition Facility, is used to heat a target to 100 million °C.[42]

ELECTRON BEAMS

Electron beams are created by applying an electrical current to a filament in a vacuum, so it gives off electrons, which are guided into a beam using electrical and magnetic fields. Like lasers, electron beams can apply energy very precisely. They are used for welding and machining parts. Electron beams can sometimes achieve deeper cutting depth or higher-quality welds than lasers. However, electron beam welding or machining needs to be done in a vacuum (to prevent electrons from striking air molecules), and it emits X-rays, so it must be handled by robots.[43] Electron beams are also used in furnaces under high vacuum for the refining of certain strong and heat-resistant or reactive metals.[44]

Electron beam processes are expensive.[45] Like lasers, electron beams are mostly suited to precision applications rather than bulk heat delivery.

THERMAL BATTERIES

A "thermal battery," also known as a "heat battery," is a device that converts electricity into heat and stores the heat until it is needed for an industrial process. An industrial thermal battery typically consists of a large quantity of heat storage material that will not chemically break down when heated, such as graphite blocks or silica sand, within an insulating enclosure.[46] To charge the battery, electricity is applied to internal resistance heaters, which warm the surrounding storage material. To release the heat, traditionally, a gas is pumped through the battery and then to the industrial equipment requiring heat. Opening shutters in the insulated enclosure to extract heat in the form of visible and infrared light (emitted by the hot storage material) is a newer approach.[47] Thermal batteries can deliver heat at up to 1500°C to 1700°C, hot enough for the vast majority of industrial processes.[48] Round-trip efficiency (conversion of electricity to heat, then extraction of thermal energy from the battery) is around 95 percent.[49]

Many industrial facilities operate twenty-four hours per day to maximize their return on capital and reduce the need for repeated start-up and shut-down procedures. However, wholesale electricity prices vary from hour to hour based on total electricity demand, generation from variable renewables, congestion in electricity transmission lines, and other factors. An industrial facility with a thermal battery can buy extra electricity when it is cheapest, store it as heat, and use the stored heat when buying electricity would be most expensive. This can lower an industrial facility's cost of electrical heat by one half to two thirds, making it competitive with the cost of natural gas heating.[50] Thermal batteries also enable industrial facilities to avoid contributing to peak load, reducing the amount of new generating capacity that must be built to maintain grid reliability.

Facilities with thermal batteries may even provide demand response services for the electrical grid, which can be an additional revenue source for manufacturers. (Many industrial facilities buy electricity at retail, rather than wholesale, rates. Retail rates smooth out some of the hourly fluctuations of wholesale prices, but they are much higher than wholesale rates to cover the costs of maintaining the electrical grid and meeting peak demand. An industrial facility that avoids buying electricity during peak hours puts less strain on the grid and therefore may qualify for a lower retail rate.)

Another application of thermal batteries is for off-grid industrial facilities. A facility that owns or contracts with a power plant to provide electricity specifically for that facility may be able to purchase electricity at lower rates than by buying from the grid. However, due to the need for reliable heat delivery, an industrial firm may be unwilling to rely exclusively on variable renewables (wind and solar) in an off-grid application. Thermal batteries can enable an off-grid facility to continue operating through periods of poor sun and wind conditions, making it more feasible for such facilities to rely exclusively on wind and solar generation.

In theory, chemical batteries that store electricity (such as lithium-ion batteries) provide many of the same benefits as thermal batteries. However, thermal batteries have much lower capital costs because they are made from inexpensive and widely available materials. For example, when manufactured at scale, thermal batteries may cost around $27 per kilowatt-hour capacity (including the battery's electricity input, energy storage, and heat extraction components), while lithium-ion battery packs cost around $150 per kilowatt-hour capacity in 2022.[51] Therefore, thermal batteries can make financial sense even in cases when electrical batteries do not.

Industrial thermal batteries that can reach temperatures up to 1500°C to 1700°C are at an early stage of commercialization. Previous systems capable of storing heat for multiple hours have generally been based on molten salt.[52] Molten salt systems have demonstrated reliability in commercial applications (particularly in concentrating solar power plants), but they have lower maximum temperatures (600°C) and higher capital costs ($15 to $35 per kilowatt-hour capacity) relative to thermal batteries based on noncorrosive, solid materials such as graphite and silica.[53]

HEAT REPLACEMENT

In some cases, nonthermal application of electricity can replace heat in industrial processes.

ELECTROLYSIS

Electrolysis is direct application of an electrical current to chemically break down a substance. In some cases, electrolysis can be an alternative to heat to drive a chemical reaction. Today, electrolysis is common in the smelting of aluminum and in the production of chlorine and sodium hydroxide by the chlor-alkali industry. Electrolysis is the most technologically mature route to produce green hydrogen (chapter 7). It is also being investigated for the smelting of iron ore (chapter 1) and cement production.[54]

ULTRAVIOLET LIGHT

Ultraviolet (UV) light is primarily used in industry for sterilization and for curing some UV-sensitive polymers, such as coatings and adhesives. In some cases where heating is used for sterilization (for instance, in the food industry), it may be possible to substitute UV light, although the opacity of many substances limits UV penetration depth. UV curing of adhesives and coatings can be a low-temperature alternative to heat curing. (Most heat-cured epoxies require temperatures of 100°C–150°C.)[55]

INDUSTRIAL ACTIVITIES, TEMPERATURES, AND TECHNOLOGIES

Table 6.1 summarizes major heat-using activities within various industries and electrical technologies well suited to those activities. Technologies are selected based on the manner in which heat is applied (for instance, welding needs heat applied to precise areas, whereas melting metals does not) and efficiency (for instance, lasers and dielectric heating may not be efficient enough to cost-effectively supply very large quantities of heat).

TABLE 6.1 Industrial Heat Needs and Electrical Technologies

Industrial activity	Temperature range (°C)	Example industries	Electrical technologies
Smelting (extracting metal from ore)	430–1650	Iron and steel, nonferrous metals	Electrolysis, electric resistance, plasma torch
Melting metals	430–1650	Iron and steel, nonferrous metals	Electric arc furnace, induction furnace
Melting nonconductive materials	800–1650	Glass, ceramics	Plasma torch, electric resistance
Calcining	800–1100	Cement, lime	Plasma torch, electric resistance
Producing steam, boiling, distillation	70–540	Chemicals, food processing	Heat pumps, electric resistance
Welding	900–1500	Machinery, vehicles, construction, metal products	Electric arcs, lasers, electron beams
Cutting, drilling/boring	120–3500	Machinery, vehicles, construction, metal products	Electric arcs, lasers, electron beams
Heat treating of metals (annealing, tempering, etc.)	100–800	Metal products, vehicles	Induction, infrared heating
Warming nonconductive, heat-sensitive materials	70–300	Food processing, plastic products, wood products	Dielectric heating, infrared heating
Curing adhesives and coatings	100–150	Vehicles, misc. products	UV light, infrared heating
Molding/forming	120–300	Plastic products	Electric resistance, dielectric heating
Sterilizing/pasteurizing	100–370	Food processing	Heat pumps, UV light, dielectric heating
Baking, thawing, drying	100–370	Food processing, rubber, some mineral and construction materials	Infrared heating, dielectric heating
Exceptionally high-temperature processes	2000–3000	synthetic graphite, specialty metals, vapor deposition coatings	Electric arcs, induction, lasers, electron beams

Note: This table specifies industrial heat-demanding activities, typical temperature ranges, example industries employing each activity, and electrical technologies potentially well suited to provide heat for those activities.

Sources: Jeffrey Rissman, Chris Bataille, Eric Masanet, Nate Aden, William R. Morrow III, Nan Zhou, Neal Elliott, et al., "Technologies and Policies to Decarbonize Global Industry: Review and Assessment of Mitigation Drivers Through 2070," *Applied Energy* 266 (May 15, 2020): 114848, https://doi.org/10.1016/j.apenergy.2020.114848; Permabond Engineering Adhesives, "Heat Cure Epoxy—Making Sure the Adhesive Is Properly Cured," accessed May 24, 2023, https://www.permabond.com/resource-center/heat-cure-epoxy-making-adhesive-properly-cured/; Eco Molding Co., "Injection Molding Temperature" (blog) Ecomolding, accessed May 24, 2023, https://www.injectionmould.org/2019/04/10/injection-molding-temperature/; and Ramūnas Šniaukas and Gediminas Račiukaitis, "Laser Micro-Cutting of Thick Tungsten Sheets" (paper presented at Lasers in Manufacturing Conference 2015, Munich, June 22–25, 2015), https://www.wlt.de/lim/Proceedings2015/Stick/PDF/Contribution287_final.pdf.

ELECTRIFICATION POTENTIAL AND COSTS

An exceptionally wide range of electrical heating (and heat replacement) technologies are available, some of which can reach sufficiently high temperatures to meet any industrial need. Researchers with the Potsdam Institute for Climate Impact Research found that commercialized technologies can directly electrify 78 percent of nonfeedstock European industrial energy demand, while 99 percent could be electrified when including technologies under development, such as electrified steam crackers in the chemicals industry and plasma torch heating for cement kilns (figure 6.4).

The key barrier to electrification of industrial heat is not physics but cost. Per unit of energy, for industrial buyers, electricity is more expensive than natural gas by a factor of 1.7 in India, 2.1 in China, 4.5 in the European Union, and 5.5 in the United States. Relative to coal, electricity's price premium is even larger: 6.9 times higher than natural gas in China, 7.8 times higher in the United States and India, and 9.2 times higher in Europe (figure 6.5). However, coal has many problems not captured in its fuel price, such as requiring more expensive combustion equipment, costly postcombustion exhaust treatment, and siting difficulties due to local air quality impacts. This makes electricity-to-coal price comparisons unduly favor coal.

Nonetheless, electrifying industry often means displacing coal, particularly in China and India, where it is the dominant source of industrial energy. In the United States and Europe, industry uses more natural gas than coal, and stricter air quality standards force companies to bear more of the nonfuel costs of coal combustion, so comparing electricity with natural gas is often more appropriate in those geographies.

In the United States and Europe, part of the price difference between electricity and natural gas is driven by favorable treatment for industrial firms rather than physical properties of the fuels. For example, the average cost of natural gas for U.S. residential buyers is $9.86 per gigajoule, almost three times higher than the $3.41 per gigajoule cost for industrial

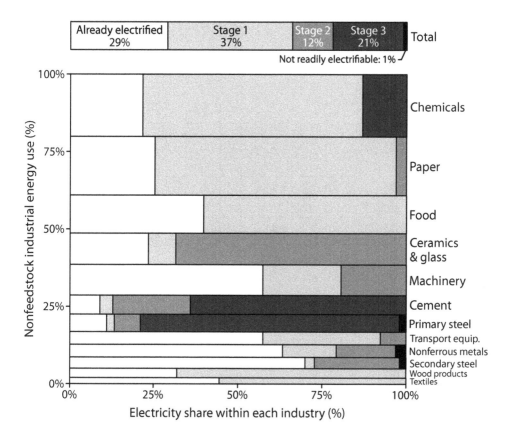

FIGURE 6.4 **Electrification Potential of European Industry** The figure encompasses 2015 nonfeedstock industrial energy use in the European Union. Technologies are divided into three stages of readiness: stage 1 for mature technologies common to many industries, stage 2 for technologies established in some industries that require industry-specific adaptation and know-how to implement more widely, and stage 3 for technologies in research and development.

Source: Silvia Madeddu, Falko Ueckerdt, Michaja Pehl, Juergen Peterseim, Michael Lord, Karthik Ajith Kumar, Christoph Krüger, and Gunnar Luderer, "The CO_2 Reduction Potential for the European Industry via Direct Electrification of Heat Supply (Power-to-Heat)," *Environmental Research Letters* 15, no. 12 (November 2020): 124004, https://doi.org/10.1088/1748-9326/abbd02.

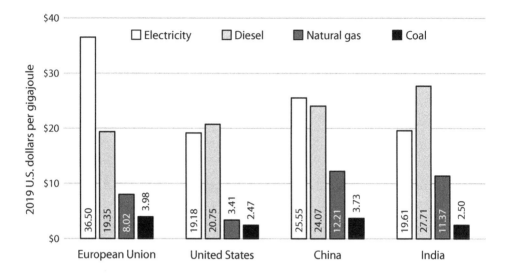

FIGURE 6.5 **Industrial Fuel Prices by Region in 2019** Prices are inclusive of taxes and subsidies. Prices are for industrial energy buyers, which are often different from prices paid by nonindustrial energy buyers. These figures reflect the energy within each fuel or electricity and do not account for differences in how efficiently that energy may be used.

Source: U.S. Energy Information Administration, "Annual Energy Outlook 2020," January 29, 2020, https://www.eia.gov/outlooks/archive/aeo20/; European Commission, "Dashboard for Energy Prices in the EU and Main Trading Partners," accessed May 25, 2023, https://energy .ec.europa.eu/data-and-analysis/energy-prices-and-costs-europe/dashboard-energy-prices-eu -and-main-trading-partners_en; European Commission, "Study of Energy Prices, Costs, and Their Impact on Industry and Households, Final Report," 2020, https://op.europa.eu/en /publication-detail/-/publication/16e7f212-0dc5-11eb-bc07-01aa75ed71a1/; Energy Innovation LLC and World Resources Institute, "India Energy Policy Simulator," accessed June 11, 2023, https://india.energypolicy.solutions/; CEIC Data, "China Diesel Price," accessed June 11, 2023, https://www.ceicdata.com/en/china/diesel-price; State Grid, "Illustrated Electricity Prices" [in Chinese], May 20, 2020, http://www.sasac.gov.cn/n2588025/n13790238/n14546245 /c14637934/content.html; CEIC Data, "China Gas Price: 36 City," accessed June 11, 2023, https:// www.ceicdata.com/en/china/gas-price-36-city; and IHS Markit and Xinhua Infolink, "China Coal Monthly," January 2020, https://www.opisnet.com/wp-content/uploads /2019/04/china-coal-monthly-sample.pdf.

buyers.[56] In Europe, the ratio is similar.[57] Industrial firms receive lower prices by buying in bulk, buying with less seasonal fluctuations, and arguing before regulators that they require lower rates to remain competitive and provide jobs and other economic benefits. (Manufacturers also enjoy lower electricity rates than residential buyers, but the difference is much smaller.) In some other countries, most notably China, industrial buyers pay higher energy prices than residential buyers.

Electricity prices in figure 6.5 reflect purchases of grid electricity, but some large industrial facilities may build or contract for dedicated, off-grid generation, which allows them to purchase electricity at wholesale rates, which are far below retail prices for grid electricity. Also, as discussed earlier, thermal batteries can enable industrial facilities to purchase more electricity in hours when it is cheaper and avoid buying electricity in hours when it is more expensive. (Even if an industrial buyer pays a retail rate that does not fluctuate from hour to hour, if that buyer has a thermal battery, it may enjoy a lower retail rate in return for not buying electricity at peak times or for providing grid flexibility and demand response services.)

While one should be aware of these cost differences, energy prices do not tell the whole story. It is necessary to consider how efficiently each fuel may be converted into heat and how much of that heat can be applied to the material or part being processed by industry. Electricity has efficiency advantages that can partially or fully compensate for higher prices.

FOSSIL FUEL HEATING EFFICIENCY

Burning fossil fuels does not extract 100 percent of their stored energy in useful form. Fossil fuel combustion produces a stream of exhaust gases, and considerable heat can be lost in these exhaust streams rather than be transferred to the equipment or product being heated. (Some of this heat can be recovered and used for lower-temperature processes, but avoiding heat losses in the first place is even better than heat recovery.) Heat is also consumed to evaporate moisture contained within the fuel and, more important, water formed when hydrogen atoms in the fuel bond with oxygen from the air to form H_2O (which cannot be avoided by pre-drying the fuel). In addition, heat is lost through openings in machinery or directly through machinery surfaces.

The theoretical maximum efficiency of an industrial furnace declines with increasing temperature. For a furnace that does not preheat its combustion air (and assuming no heat loss through the furnace's walls or openings), the maximum possible efficiency is 75% at 500°C, 50% at 1000°C, and 23% at 1500°C (though heat losses can be cut by 32–65% by using waste heat to preheat combustion air).[58] In an example furnace with an operating temperature of 1340°C and no combustion air pre-heating, an engineering estimate of the apportionment of the energy in the fuel is as follows:[59]

- 57 percent lost in exhaust gas stream,
- 10 percent to evaporate moisture in fuel (1 percent) and H_2O formed during combustion (9 percent),
- 9 percent lost through furnace openings (6 percent) and furnace skin (3 percent), and
- 24 percent useful heat (i.e., 24 percent efficiency).

Electrical technologies do not produce combustion exhaust gases and do not need to evaporate moisture in or created by fuel, eliminating these major causes of heat loss. Also, some electrical technologies (such as induction) heat materials directly, which may reduce heat losses through furnace openings and skin. For example, in India, new induction furnaces have overall efficiencies of 81–87 percent.[60] Thus, the cost-effectiveness of replacing fossil fuel–powered equipment with electrical equipment depends on the specific application. Replacing a 25 percent–efficient coal furnace with an 85 percent–efficient induction furnace reduces energy demand by 70 percent, which cuts India's electricity price premium from 7.8 to 2.4 times the cost of coal. The remaining gap could be overcome by policies that would place a price tag on coal's air quality and public health harms, policies targeting greenhouse gases, or both. (Note that energy losses due to hot exhaust gases and formed H_2O are not unique to fossil fuel combustion. These loss modes also apply to combustion of hydrogen or other renewable fuels, discussed in chapter 7.)

Combustion can be more efficient than the furnace described here. Boilers may be the most efficient type of industrial equipment commonly used for extracting heat from fossil fuels. Modern industrial steam boilers that recover heat from exhaust, preheat combustion air, and reuse high-temperature condensate can achieve fuel-to-steam energy efficiencies of 85–90 percent (and 94 percent has been demonstrated).[61] (Boilers that produce hot water rather than steam can achieve even higher efficiencies—up to 98 percent—but industrial processes usually require steam.)[62] However, the efficiency of typical industrial steam boilers in China, the largest industrial steam user, is 70–79 percent, and the efficiency of the entire steam system (which includes steam distribution and condensate recovery) is just 61 percent.[63] Additionally, not all the energy in steam is transferred to the materials being heated. If the steam is run through a heat exchanger, no more than 75 percent of the heat can be extracted, implying a fuel-to-heated-product efficiency of up to 46 percent.[64] Injecting steam into a fluid to be heated uses all the steam's heat, but steam injection is not relevant for many use cases and prevents the reuse of condensate water (i.e., if the steam were in a closed loop), so the boiler must instead heat cold feed water, which incurs a 10 percent efficiency penalty.[65]

Thus, overall energy efficiency from natural gas to heated product can vary substantially between various steam systems, but 50 percent may be a reasonable benchmark figure for China. Electric resistance boilers are nearly 100 percent efficient at converting electricity into steam but would still suffer losses in other parts of the steam system. Replacing the entire steam system with an electrical alternative could offer greater efficiency gains.

At temperatures for which industrial heat pumps can be used (encompassing roughly one-third of global industrial heat demand, discussed earlier), electricity may already have a cost advantage. Depending on delivered temperature increase, heat pumps typically have coefficients of performance between 2 and 5 (i.e., 200 percent to 500 percent). A tool for analyzing capital and operational costs of industrial heat pumps developed by Agora Industry, FutureCamp Climate, and Wuppertal Institute can estimate fuel price ranges where industrial heat pumps are more cost-effective than natural gas boilers (figure 6.6).

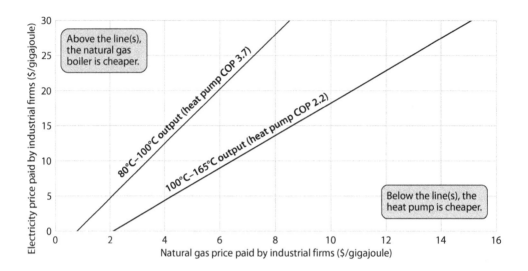

FIGURE 6.6 **Break-Even Fuel Costs for Industrial Heat Pumps Versus Natural Gas Boilers** Each line indicates energy prices at which the total cost per unit of heat output is equal for an industrial heat pump and an industrial natural gas boiler (inclusive of fuel/electricity, capital, staffing, and maintenance costs). The same natural gas boiler is compared with a heat pump with coefficient of performance (COP) of 3.7, corresponding to output temperatures of 80°C–100°C, and with a heat pump with COP of 2.2, corresponding to output of 100°C–165°C. Capital, staffing, and maintenance costs are based on 2019 data from Germany.

Source: Agora Industry, FutureCamp Climate, and Wuppertal Institute, "Power-2-Heat: Direct Electrification of Industrial Process Heat—Calculator for Estimating Transformation Costs" (Berlin, Germany, September 9, 2022).

CAPITAL COSTS

It can be challenging to compare capital costs for electrified technologies with costs for fossil-fired equivalents because of the diversity of electrical technologies and their potential to deliver heat to the target material with lower losses. For example, an electric resistance boiler will typically have lower capital costs than a combustion boiler due to lesser complexity, fewer moving parts, and no need for exhaust pipes.[66] However, such a head-to-head comparison assumes the facility already has sufficient electrical capacity to operate the boiler and overlooks opportunities to replace steam with a more efficient heat delivery mechanism that could offer energy savings. Therefore, capital costs are best assessed by comparing systems that deliver equivalent services rather than equivalent pieces of equipment.

Heating technologies' energy costs are considerably greater than their capital costs over the lifetime of the equipment, particularly for commercialized equipment whose capital costs have been reduced through years of research, development, and refinement. For example, over a typical industrial combustion boiler's lifetime, fuel represents 96 percent of total costs, while capital equipment represents 3 percent and operation and maintenance 1 percent.[67] Usually, the most cost-effective technology choice for industrial heating in a new facility will be the one that delivers the required heat to the processed material or product with the lowest energy costs. In retrofit applications, compatibility with existing equipment, physical plant layout, and the possibility of sparking a cascade of required upgrades must be considered.

REQUIRED ELECTRICITY GENERATION

The amount of additional electricity that would be required to decarbonize industrial nonfeedstock uses of fossil fuels is significant. A purely illustrative estimate can be made using some assumptions. In 2019, global industry burned 94 exajoules of fossil fuels for energy and purchased 6 exajoules of heat (see figure 0.4 in the introduction), for a total of 100 exajoules. Conservatively, industry may be assumed to be 80 percent efficient at temperatures up to 165°C or 60 percent efficient at higher temperatures at converting the fuels' chemical energy into useful heat or work (see the fossil fuel heating efficiency section earlier in this chapter). Assuming that 30 percent of industrial heat demand can be electrified with heat pumps with an average coefficient of performance of 2.5, and the remaining 70 percent can be electrified using technologies such as electric resistance, electric arcs, and induction with an average efficiency of 95 percent, the electricity required to replace these fuels is just under 15,000 terawatt-hours. This is equivalent to 65 percent of global final electricity consumption in 2019.[68] (The amount of electricity required to supply this heat via green hydrogen combustion rather than direct electrification would be more than twice as large, since hydrogen combustion shares the same heat loss modes as fossil fuel combustion, plus losses when converting electricity into hydrogen.)

Decarbonization of feedstocks using green hydrogen would further increase electricity demand. For instance, if 2019's feedstock demand of 37 exajoules (figure 0.4) could be met entirely using hydrogen from 70 percent–efficient alkaline electrolysis (chapter 7), this would require another 14,500 terawatt-hours, or an additional 64 percent of 2019 global electricity demand. Thus, to electrify both energy and feedstock uses of fossil fuels by industry in 2019, an additional 129 percent (a little more than a doubling) of global electricity production would have been required. In the 2050–2070 time frame, the electricity requirement may be larger or smaller, as energy efficiency, material efficiency, and circular economy measures can dramatically reduce energy requirements per unit of industrial production (chapters 4–5), but industrial production must increase to meet the demands of human development (chapter 12).

Discussion of decarbonizing and growing the electricity sector is beyond the scope of this book. However, industry can make the task easier through efficiency and circular economy measures to reduce its own demand and by utilizing bioenergy (chapter 7) and carbon capture (chapter 8) where sufficient zero-carbon electricity is not available. Additionally, some industrial facilities can help balance variable generation resources (wind and solar) on the grid by timing their operations to align with periods when these resources are most productive and/or when total electricity demand is low (demand response). This allows more electricity demand to be met with less capacity.

ELECTRIFICATION'S CONTRIBUTION
TO ZERO-CARBON INDUSTRY

Clean electricity is the most efficient way to provide zero-carbon heat to industrial processes at all temperatures, so it should be prioritized wherever possible (i.e., replacing most industrial fossil fuel uses other than in primary steelmaking, refining, and chemical feedstocks). Using electricity directly is more efficient than forming and combusting green hydrogen (or hydrogen-derived fuels), and electricity can scale up in more places and with less land use impact than bioenergy (chapter 7).

However, even after accounting electricity's efficiency benefits, it is usually cheaper to obtain heat from natural gas or coal for medium to high temperatures (i.e., higher than a heat pump can supply). This gap can be addressed by reducing costs of clean electricity (for instance, through subsidies to industries that adopt modern electrified technologies and accelerated deployment of low-cost wind and solar in the power sector) and imposing a carbon price (chapter 9) that helps level the playing field by making fossil fuel buyers pay for the harms caused by fuel combustion. Electrification can also be driven by nonfinancial policies such as emissions standards (chapter 10). Heat batteries are a technical solution that can reduce a grid-connected firm's electricity costs, or they can enable off-grid facilities to operate reliably while relying on inexpensive renewables.

Due to limited interest by industry in the past, not all industrial fossil technologies have commercialized, electrified equivalents. Research and development efforts are needed to create and improve electrified versions of key industrial technologies. One example is the consortium of chemical companies working to develop electrified steam crackers (see chapter 2). Policies to accelerate industrial technology R&D are discussed in chapter 11.

7

HYDROGEN AND OTHER RENEWABLE FUELS

lectrification provides the most efficient decarbonization pathway for most industrial energy needs. Significant heat losses occur with use of combustible fuels, in the form of hot exhaust gases and water vapor generated by combustion, so electricity tends to be more efficient at delivering heat to processed parts and materials (chapter 6). However, electricity cannot replace chemical feedstocks, which account for 70 percent of the chemicals industry's fossil fuel use (chapter 2), and electrolysis of iron ore is less technologically mature than other zero-carbon ironmaking routes (chapter 1). Therefore, there is a need for zero-carbon fuels that can be used as chemical feedstocks and iron reducing agents. There may also be a role for combustion of renewable fuels, particularly bioenergy, which is not derived from electricity and therefore can help make up for shortfalls in renewable electricity availability.

Renewable fuels for industrial use can be classified into three groups:

- **hydrogen** (H_2) produced from zero-carbon electricity;
- **hydrogen-derived fuels**, primarily ammonia, methanol, and synthetic methane; and
- **bioenergy**, including solid biomass (such as wood), liquid biofuels (such as corn or sugarcane ethanol), and biogas (and its main constituent, biomethane).

Hydrogen's favorable combustion and chemical properties make it promising as an energy carrier and feedstock, but sufficient zero-emissions H_2 must be available to industry at competitive cost. Additionally, challenges relating to storage and distribution of hydrogen (or on-site generation) must be overcome, and industrial equipment must be modified or replaced to accommodate pure hydrogen.

Hydrogen-derived fuels avoid many of the problems with hydrogen storage, distribution, and equipment compatibility, but producers incur an energy penalty when converting hydrogen into these fuels. Additionally, methanol and synthetic methane emit CO_2 when burned, so they are not carbon-neutral unless formed using input CO_2 captured from bioenergy combustion or directly from the atmosphere. This makes hydrogen-derived fuels valuable as transitional fuels, but in the long term, it will be more cost-effective for industry to use hydrogen directly.

Bioenergy production and use is more technologically mature than production and use of hydrogen. However, bioenergy must overcome significant challenges relating to availability of sufficient quantities of sustainably harvested biomass (e.g., avoiding undesirable land use change), water demand, transport and storage costs, equipment costs, food security, and air quality impacts.

HYDROGEN

Hydrogen is a colorless, odorless, flammable gas. It is less dense than air and tends to rise and disperse quickly if released into the atmosphere. Though some naturally occurring hydrogen gas can be found in underground deposits, no strategies currently exist to commercially extract this hydrogen.[1] Therefore, the hydrogen used in the economy is manufactured, making hydrogen an "energy carrier," not a primary energy source.

Hydrogen reacts with oxygen to produce water vapor ($2H_2 + O_2 \rightarrow 2H_2O$). This reaction releases energy, which can be in the form of a flame and heat (if the hydrogen is combusted) or in the form of electricity (if the hydrogen is consumed in a "fuel cell," a device for turning chemical energy into electricity). Hydrogen fuel cells are of particular interest in the transportation sector because a hydrogen tank and fuel cell can substitute for a battery as a means of mobile electricity storage. Industrial facilities have less need for electricity storage, as they can usually obtain electricity from the grid on demand. Though fuel cells can be used for backup power, industry is primarily interested in hydrogen as a source of high-temperature heat and a chemical reactant. Therefore, this chapter discusses hydrogen combustion or use as a feedstock, not hydrogen use in fuel cells. (The same is true for other renewable fuels, such as biomethane.)

Today, hydrogen is used in oil refining to remove sulfur and in various chemical transformations, such as breaking down long-chain hydrocarbons to make gasoline.[2] Hydrogen also plays an important role in the synthesis of ammonia and methanol (see chapter 2). Present-day uses of hydrogen are summarized in figure 7.1. Achieving a zero-emissions global industrial sector will involve expanding hydrogen use beyond these current applications.

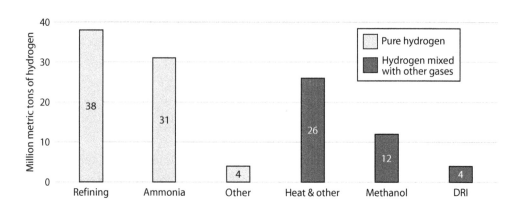

FIGURE 7.1 Global Use of Hydrogen in 2018 "DRI" is direct reduced iron (see chapter 1). "Other" uses of pure hydrogen occur in the chemicals, metals, and electronics industries (and in the transportation sector, which consumed less than 0.01 million metric tons). "Heat & other" uses of hydrogen mixed with other gases are predominantly the combustion of gases from blast furnaces and steam crackers within steelmaking and chemicals facilities.

Source: International Energy Agency, "The Future of Hydrogen: Seizing today's opportunities," (report, Paris, France, June 2019), https://iea.blob.core.windows.net/assets/9e3a3493-b9a6-4b7d-b499-7ca48e357561/The_Future_of_Hydrogen.pdf.

HYDROGEN PRODUCTION TODAY

Unlike fossil fuels and biomass, hydrogen does not contain carbon, so it does not contribute any carbon dioxide to the atmosphere when burned. Therefore, the impact of hydrogen on carbon dioxide emissions depends on how the hydrogen was produced.

Globally, in 2018, 69 million metric tons of hydrogen were produced in dedicated production facilities, while 48 million metric tons were created as a by-product of other industrial processes, such as in top gas recovered from blast furnaces (in the iron and steel industry) or from steam crackers (in the chemicals industry). Dedicated hydrogen production is based primarily on natural gas, except in China, where coal gasification is dominant (figure 7.2). Today, 85 percent of hydrogen is

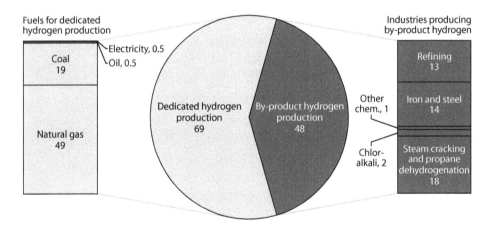

FIGURE 7.2 **Global Hydrogen Production by Source in 2018** All values are in millions of metric tons of hydrogen. By-product hydrogen comes from the chemicals, iron and steel, and refining industries (generally from the fossil fuels used by these industries). The exception is the production of chlor-alkali (chlorine and sodium hydroxide) within the chemicals industry, which involves electrolysis of saltwater. This process was responsible for two million metric tons of hydrogen in 2018 (less than 2 percent of total hydrogen production). This represents around 80 percent of the electrolytic hydrogen produced, with dedicated electrolytic production (0.5 million metric tons) making up the remainder.

Source: International Energy Agency, "The Future of Hydrogen: Seizing today's opportunities," (report, Paris, France, June 2019), https://iea.blob.core.windows.net/assets/9e3a3493-b9a6 -4b7d-b499-7ca48e357561/The_Future_of_Hydrogen.pdf.

consumed at the site where it was produced, while 15 percent is transported by pipeline, ship, or truck.[3]

Colors are sometimes used to distinguish the energy source or production route from which hydrogen was obtained. Sources differ on the number and meanings of colors, but in the simplest, three-color system,

- **gray hydrogen** refers to hydrogen produced from fossil fuels without carbon capture;
- **blue hydrogen** refers to low-emissions hydrogen produced from nonrenewable sources, primarily fossil fuels with carbon capture; and
- **green hydrogen** refers to hydrogen produced from renewable electricity.

However, some sources utilize far more colors (see table 7.1).

TABLE 7.1 Colors Commonly Used to Distinguish Hydrogen Sources

Color	Hydrogen source
Black	Coal (excluding lignite) without carbon capture
Brown	Lignite without carbon capture
Gray	Natural gas without carbon capture
Blue	Any fossil fuel with carbon capture
Turquoise	Natural gas, via methane pyrolysis
Pink, purple, red	Nuclear power (electrolysis or heat)
Yellow	Grid electricity or electricity mix
Green	Renewable electricity
White	Naturally occurring or industrial by-product

Note: Hydrogen from biomass gasification/biofuel reforming has not been assigned a color.

Sources: National Grid PLC, "The Hydrogen Colour Spectrum," accessed May 26, 2023, https://www.nationalgrid.com/stories/energy-explained/hydrogen-colour-spectrum;InternationalEnergy Agency, "The Future of Hydrogen: Seizing today's opportunities," (report, Paris, France, June 2019), https://iea.blob.core.windows.net/assets/9e3a3493-b9a6-4b7d-b499-7ca48e357561/The _Future_of_Hydrogen.pdf; Michael Roeth, "The Many Colors of Hydrogen," *FleetOwner*, January 6, 2021, https://www.fleetowner.com/industry-perspectives/ideaxchange/article/21151562 /the-many-colors-of-hydrogen; Sara Giovannini, "50 Shades of (Grey and Blue and Green) Hydrogen," *Energy Cities*, November 13, 2020, https://energy-cities.eu/50-shades-of-grey-and-blue -and-green-hydrogen/.

Today, most dedicated hydrogen production is "steam methane reforming," a process in which water vapor is heated to 700°C–1000°C and reacted with methane from natural gas in the presence of a catalyst at 300–2500 kilopascals of pressure. This produces a mixture of hydrogen, carbon monoxide, and a small amount of carbon dioxide (primarily $CH_4 + H_2O \rightarrow CO + 3H_2$). Then, in the water-gas shift reaction, the CO is used to extract oxygen from steam, producing more hydrogen and carbon dioxide (CO $+ H_2O \rightarrow CO_2 + H_2$).[4] Subsequently, the hydrogen is isolated from the gas mixture and the CO_2 is vented to the atmosphere. Current steam methane reforming plants have an energy efficiency of 72–82 percent (i.e., energy in the produced hydrogen divided by energy in the methane inputs) and emit 8.3–9.4 metric tons of CO_2 per metric ton of H_2 produced.[5]

The other widely used technology for dedicated hydrogen production is "coal gasification." Coal is reacted with oxygen and steam under high pressure to produce a syngas, a mixture of CO and H_2. Then, as in the case of steam methane reforming, the water-gas shift reaction is used to convert the carbon monoxide to carbon dioxide, producing more hydrogen.[6] Coal gasification has an energy efficiency of 60 percent and emits 19 metric tons of CO_2 per metric ton of H_2 produced.[7] Coal gasification is primarily used in China, which is responsible for 80 percent of the world's dedicated coal-based hydrogen production.[8]

Several other hydrogen production technologies are used for dedicated hydrogen production, but only at small scale: electrolysis (discussed later), partial oxidation (reacting fossil fuels with a limited amount of oxygen), and autothermal reforming (a hybrid of steam methane reforming and partial oxidation).[9] Of these, only electrolysis has potential as a low-carbon production pathway.

ZERO-CARBON HYDROGEN PRODUCTION PATHWAYS

There are several mechanisms for producing hydrogen without greenhouse gas emissions at various stages of technological maturity. They are discussed in order of declining readiness to produce zero-carbon hydrogen at commercial scale.

Electrolysis hydrogen production involves running a current between two electrodes in an aqueous solution to split water into hydrogen and oxygen gases ($2H_2O \rightarrow 2H_2 + O_2$). To be a zero-carbon production route, electrolysis must be done with zero-carbon electricity—for example, produced by renewables or nuclear power. Electrolyzers have three main designs.

- **Alkaline electrolyzers** are the oldest technology, having been the most common method of making hydrogen from the 1920s–60s before being overtaken by steam methane reforming.[10] Alkaline electrolyzers use nickel-based electrodes and a solution of 20–30 percent sodium or potassium hydroxide as the electrolyte.[11] Among electrolyzers, they have the lowest capital cost ($500–$1,400 per kilowatt) and intermediate energy efficiency (63–70 percent of input electricity converted to chemical energy in hydrogen).[12] They have a number of drawbacks, such as a narrow allowable load range, low current density, and low operating pressures.[13] Research into catalysts that reduce electrochemical reaction resistance and electrolytes that improve electron transfer could increase cost-effectiveness.[14]
- **Proton exchange membrane (PEM) electrolyzers**, also called "polymer electrolyte membrane electrolyzers," use a solid polymer membrane separating the two electrodes. When PEM electrolyzers were developed in the 1960–70s, they were considered efficient, but in the years since, alkaline electrolysis efficiency surpassed PEM efficiency. Today's PEM energy efficiency is 56–60 percent.[15] PEM electrolyzers have high capital costs ($1,100–$1,800 per kilowatt) due to the need for expensive, corrosion-resistant materials (platinum, iridium, ruthenium).[16]

  PEM electrolyzers' main advantage is their ability to operate under a wide range of power densities and their tolerance of frequent changes in power input, which makes them useful for balancing an electrical grid containing a high share of variable renewable power sources (solar and wind).[17]
- **Solid oxide electrolysis (SOEC)**, also called "high-temperature electrolysis," is the newest form of electrolysis and is not yet commercialized. SOEC uses a solid ceramic electrolyte that becomes permeable to oxygen

ions at high temperature. The electrolyzer is heated to 700°C–800°C, and an electrical potential is applied. Water is split at the cathode to form hydrogen gas and negatively charged oxygen ions. The ions migrate through the ceramic to the anode, where they form oxygen gas and release their extra electrons to complete the circuit. The high temperatures reduce the electricity required to split water.[18]

SOEC is the most energy-efficient electrolysis technology (74–81 percent), but it has the highest capital cost ($2,800–$5,600 per kilowatt). SOEC electrolyzers are unique in their ability to run in reverse (i.e., convert hydrogen back into electricity, like a fuel cell), so they could provide balancing services to the grid or backup power to an industrial facility. Unfortunately, high temperatures tend to degrade the ceramic materials and shorten the life of SOEC electrolyzers, so improving their durability and longevity is a research focus.[19]

Bioenergy pathways to produce hydrogen include biomass gasification and liquid biofuel or biomethane reforming. These processes are similar to coal gasification and steam methane reforming, respectively, but use bioenergy feedstocks instead of fossil fuels.[20] The carbon in the biomass is released as CO_2, so these processes' CO_2 impact depends on the carbon neutrality of the biomass or biofuel, a topic covered later in this chapter. Biomass routes can be paired with carbon capture and sequestration (chapter 8) to achieve very low or even negative net emissions.

Pyrolysis is a method of converting carbon-based fuels (primarily methane) into hydrogen while producing a solid carbon by-product rather than carbon dioxide gas ($CH_4 \rightarrow 2H_2 + C_{(s)}$). The fuel is heated to around 980°C in an environment without water or air, so there is no source of oxygen that could combine with the produced carbon to form CO_2.[21] Energy efficiency of 59 percent is theoretically achievable, though real-world performance is lower.[22]

Pyrolysis technologies have varying emissions performance. Pyrolysis systems that burn natural gas for their heat do not reduce CO_2 emissions relative to steam methane reforming. Thermal plasma systems that obtain heat from renewable electricity are the lowest-emitting pyrolysis technology, but even these have indirect CO_2 emissions associated with natural gas production, distribution, and leakage (about 28 percent as much as produced in steam methane reforming).[23] Additionally, it is necessary to store the produced, solid carbon and protect it from oxidation. (Some can be used as carbon black [see chapter 2], but large-scale use of pyrolysis would satisfy global demand for carbon black long before meeting global demand for hydrogen.)

Pyrolysis can also use biomass feedstocks, but this introduces challenges relating to impurities in the feedstocks, higher equipment costs, and the production of unwanted tar by-product.[24] A small handful of pyrolysis pilot plants have been built and operated for limited periods, and one company, Monolith Materials, has an operating facility in Nebraska and plans to complete the world's first large-scale hydrogen pyrolysis plant by 2026.[25]

Thermochemical water-splitting pathways use temperatures of 500°C–2000°C to drive a chemical reaction that produces hydrogen from water. More than three hundred thermochemical pathways have been investigated by researchers, but none has yet been commercialized.[26] Generally, these pathways rely on solar heat concentrated by arrays of heliostats (mirrors) or waste heat from fission reactors. Efficiency varies by pathway but is around 20 percent for solar thermal heat and around 45 percent for nuclear heat.[27] Some pathways also involve an electrolysis component.[28]

Photoelectrochemical routes use sunlight and specialized semiconductors to split water into hydrogen and oxygen. These systems come in several physical configurations. The most-studied systems involve panels with electrodes and have similarities to solar photovoltaic panels, but the most cost-effective systems use suspensions of photo-catalyst particles in an electrolyte solution.[29] Photoelectrochemical hydrogen production has been demonstrated only at laboratory scale.[30]

Biological systems use microbes to create hydrogen. In "dark fermentation"–based systems, microbes break down energy-rich organic molecules (such as sugar or plant matter) into simpler molecules, some of which can be converted into hydrogen by enzymes. In "microbial electrolysis cells," the energy released as microbes breaks down biomass, and a small added voltage is used to create hydrogen. In "photobiological" systems, photosynthetic microbes (such as green algae or cyanobacteria) use sunlight to power the metabolic conversion of biomass into hydrogen, either through photo-fermentation or bio-photolysis.[31] Biological systems are being studied at laboratory scale and currently produce hydrogen slowly and with low efficiency, so they are far from commercial viability.

TRANSPORTING HYDROGEN

As a gaseous, combustible fuel, hydrogen is a potential replacement for natural gas in many industrial applications. However, hydrogen has certain physical properties that complicate its transport, storage, and use as a fuel.

Hydrogen has a small molecular diameter. This enables it to diffuse through many materials, including iron and steel pipes commonly used in natural gas distribution networks. It is also more prone to escaping through valves, connectors, and joints. This results in loss of valuable hydrogen and, over time, damages pipes and equipment through a process called "hydrogen embrittlement." Therefore, pipes and tanks that store or transport pure hydrogen must be made of (or lined with) a material resistant to damage from hydrogen, such as polyethylene, nylon, or fiber-reinforced polymer.[32]

Globally, there exist roughly 3 million kilometers of natural gas transmission pipelines and many more kilometers of smaller, distribution pipelines to homes and businesses.[33] Creating a similar transmission and distribution system for hydrogen would be prohibitively expensive and time-consuming. (Though some of these pipes could be converted to transport pure hydrogen, that could be done only once they are no longer used for natural gas, and it would also be expensive.)

Hydrogen can be blended with natural gas in existing pipelines, but tolerances for hydrogen blending vary by component within the natural gas system. Transmission pipelines can accept up to about 20 percent hydrogen, but compressors are limited to 10 percent, and equipment, such as gas turbines and engines, would likely be limited to just 2–5 percent without modifications to seals and control systems.[34] In any case, blending hydrogen into existing natural gas systems implies the continued large-scale use of natural gas, which is incompatible with zero-carbon industry (unless the natural gas consists of synthetic, zero-carbon methane, in which case, hydrogen blending would offer no emissions benefit). Therefore, hydrogen blending is not a reasonable greenhouse gas abatement mechanism.

Hydrogen can be transported long distances by ship, but a different mode is generally needed to transport hydrogen from a ship to an industrial facility. Trucks are sometimes used to transport hydrogen to facilities where it is demanded. However, trucks would not be practical for meeting large, sustained demand for hydrogen, as in hydrogen-direct reduced iron steelworks or chemical plants. Due to these limitations, there are two principal strategies for supplying industrial facilities with pure hydrogen.

First, an industrial facility can produce its own hydrogen, most likely using electricity and a small, modular electrolyzer. Hydrogen is currently produced on site for hydrogen-requiring manufacturing processes such as ultraviolet lithography and chemical vapor deposition, as well as by the chlor-alkali industry. Other industries, such as steel mills, could create their own hydrogen in the future.[35]

Second, industrial facilities may cluster in an industrial park designated for businesses that require hydrogen. Large centralized facilities can produce hydrogen and distribute it to businesses in dedicated hydrogen pipelines. The limited extent of these distribution systems reduces cost and facilitates right-of-way acquisition. For example, the Norwegian utility Statkraft and steelmaker Cesla are planning to develop an electrolysis-based "hydrogen hub" at Mo Industrial Park to supply green hydrogen for high-temperature processes.[36] Northern Germany's clean hydrogen coastline project is an example covering a larger geographic area.[37]

Hydrogen can be transported as a compressed gas, or it can first be bonded to another molecule, a "liquid organic hydrogen carrier" (LOHC) or a "metal hydride." LOHCs have higher energy density per unit volume than compressed hydrogen and physical properties similar to crude oil or gasoline, simplifying transport and storage.[38] At the destination, the reaction is reversed to release hydrogen gas and restore the dehydrogenated LOHC. The LOHC is then returned to the hydrogen source and recharged.

Bonding hydrogen to an LOHC releases energy, whereas heat must be added to extract hydrogen from an LOHC. The energy efficiency of bonding and subsequently releasing hydrogen from an LOHC is 54–74 percent, depending on the specific LOHC. However, if the heat created by hydrogenation is used productively, or if the heat required for dehydrogenation is obtained "for free" as waste heat from another industrial process, the effective efficiency is 72–84 percent. If both are true, the effective efficiency is 84–99 percent.[39] Metal hydrides are similar to LOHCs but less technologically mature.

LOHCs are unlikely to be the most attractive means of hydrogen transport for industry. Their benefits are greatest when large quantities of hydrogen must be transported long distances (e.g., in international hydrogen trade) or stored for long periods (e.g., for seasonal electric grid balancing). LOHCs are also promising for vehicles because their higher energy density allows for longer range and/or a smaller fuel tank. In contrast, industrial facilities do not need to store large quantities of hydrogen for long durations and can be sited near hydrogen production. By using compressed hydrogen, industries achieve better energy efficiency (compressing and decompressing hydrogen for transport is 97.3 percent efficient) and avoid the need to return dehydrogenated LOHC.[40]

HYDROGEN LEAKAGE

Hydrogen is a greenhouse gas with a hundred-year global warming potential of around 11, including hydrogen's effects on stratospheric water vapor and ozone.[41] Researchers have noted that large-scale hydrogen use could cause global warming impacts from hydrogen leakage.[42] Today, the most analogous example of greenhouse gas leakage is methane leaked from natural gas systems, and researchers' assumed hydrogen leakage rates resemble those of methane. However, the climate risk from hydrogen leakage is much smaller, for these reasons.

- Nine tenths of global oil- and gas-related methane leakage come from extraction (wellhead and field operations), while only one tenth comes from gas transmission, storage, and distribution.[43] Hydrogen is manufactured, not extracted from the ground, so it has no analog to the leaky extraction step.
- Natural gas is widely used in buildings, industry, and electricity generation, but hydrogen would be used in much smaller quantities (mostly for certain industries, such as chemicals). Less usage would lead to a lower absolute quantity leaked.
- Rather than transporting hydrogen long distances, electricity can be transported and hydrogen produced on site at industrial facilities or in industrial parks, facilitating leak detection and limiting leakage opportunities.
- Hydrogen's hundred-year global warming potential is 40 percent as large as methane's, so leakage would need to be greater to have a similar climate impact.

Climate impacts of hydrogen leakage need not be among policy makers' top concerns regarding the transition to green industry. Nonetheless, they should set high quality standards for hydrogen pipelines, as leaks can lead to accidental fires as well as climate impacts.

HYDROGEN COMBUSTION EMISSIONS

Burning hydrogen in air is not completely pollution-free, as the heat of combustion causes atmospheric nitrogen and oxygen to react, forming nitrogen oxides (NO_x). NO_x formation increases with higher flame temperatures. Since H_2 burns hotter than methane, its NO_x emissions can be several times higher in typical combustion conditions.[44] However, industrial equipment can be designed to limit the flame temperature (via adjustments to air, fuel, and recirculated flue gas quantities, and ensuring gases are well-mixed so reactions are spread throughout the combustion chamber) to minimize NO_x production. Pure hydrogen burned in such ultra-low NO_x equipment produces 25 percent less NO_x

than methane because H_2 combustion has one fewer chemical pathway by which NO_x is produced (an effect that is outweighed when flame temperatures are different but becomes noticeable when flame temperatures are identical).[45]

HYDROGEN USE IN INDUSTRIAL EQUIPMENT

Industrial equipment designed to use fossil fuels generally cannot burn hydrogen without modification. As noted earlier, equipment may involve materials or seals through which hydrogen can diffuse and escape. Additionally, hydrogen gas has lower density than methane, so a greater volume of gas is required to deliver the same energy content. This affects required gas flow rates.

Hydrogen has a high diffusivity and flame velocity, which can affect the behavior of hydrogen flames. It has a low required ignition energy, so leaks can be a fire hazard. These leaks may be difficult to detect because hydrogen is colorless, so leak detectors may be required. Hydrogen flames primarily give off ultraviolet light, which is invisible to the human eye (and cannot be felt as radiant, or infrared, heat), so UV flame detectors may also be needed.[46]

To ensure the safe handling and use of hydrogen by industry, codes and standards have been developed to certify hydrogen-using industrial equipment.[47] Hydrogen is used safely by many industries today and can be used safely by more industries in the future. However, a switch to hydrogen would require replacement or significant retrofit of existing equipment. Industrial equipment such as blast furnaces and steam crackers are expensive and have useful lifetimes measured in decades, so it can be financially challenging to retire this equipment early.

Therefore, a promising option is to chemically convert green hydrogen into a fuel that is compatible with existing industrial equipment. This allows for immediate progress on decarbonization without stranding capital assets or waiting for commercialization of hydrogen-burning equipment. At the equipment's natural end of life, and once hydrogen-burning models are available, a facility may switch to hydrogen combustion, reducing operating costs by avoiding the energy penalty of converting hydrogen into other fuels. These fuels are discussed in the next section.

HYDROGEN-DERIVED FUELS

Hydrogen can be chemically transformed into other fuels, which can be used as chemical feedstocks (covered in chapter 2) or burned for energy, helping to overcome the challenges of storing and using pure hydrogen. The main candidates for hydrogen-derived chemical fuels are ammonia, methanol, and synthetic hydrocarbons (primarily methane).

AMMONIA

Ammonia (NH_3) is a colorless gas that is easily liquified by moderate chilling or pressure, with storage requirements similar to those for propane or compressed natural gas. Its production from hydrogen is a mature, commercialized process in the chemicals industry (chapter 2). In the Haber-Bosch process, atmospheric nitrogen is reacted with hydrogen to form ammonia at 20–40 megapascals of pressure and temperatures of 400°C–650°C ($N_2 + 3H_2 \rightarrow 2NH_3$).[48] Today's best-practice ammonia production is about 55–60 percent efficient, but most of this energy loss occurs during the creation of hydrogen. Converting hydrogen into ammonia is about 88 percent efficient.[49]

Ammonia's advantages include easier storage and transport compared with hydrogen (though not as easy as methanol or synthetic methane), its ability to be formed without using captured CO_2, and its familiarity due to widespread use in industrial processes for more than one hundred years. Producing ammonia from electricity is roughly half the cost of producing methanol or synthetic hydrocarbons from electricity (per unit energy in the resulting fuel).[50]

However, ammonia has some downsides as a fuel. Ammonia's heat of combustion (megajoules per kilogram) is only 40 percent that of methane, and it has a much narrower flammability range (concentrations at which ammonia burns in air), lower flame velocity, and higher required ignition temperature.[51] Due to its nitrogen content, ammonia combustion tends to produce far more nitrogen oxide (NO_x) pollution than combustion of hydrogen, methanol, or methane (none of which contains nitrogen).[52] Additionally, ammonia is toxic with extended exposure, especially to fish and reptiles, though ammonia is less dense than air, helping to limit potential exposures from leaking tanks or equipment.

Ammonia combustion has primarily been investigated in the context of transportation fuels, where it has been used in a small number of demonstration vehicles. Ammonia combustion is an option for industry, but its difficult combustion characteristics would necessitate changes to equipment.

Alternatively, ammonia can be a means of transporting and storing hydrogen, like liquid organic hydrogen carriers and metal hydrides (discussed earlier), but without any need to return dehydrogenated carrier molecules. (Dehydrogenated ammonia is nitrogen gas, which can be vented to the atmosphere.) This approach allows industries to benefit from ammonia's ease of transport and storage while enjoying the superior combustion characteristics of hydrogen. The efficiency of converting ammonia back into H_2 is 75 percent, which implies roughly 68 percent round-trip efficiency (from hydrogen to ammonia and back to hydrogen), similar to the efficiencies of liquid organic hydrogen carriers.[53]

METHANOL

Methanol (CH_3OH) is a clear, nonpotable alcohol. A liquid at room temperature, methanol requires neither chilling nor pressurization for storage or transport. Today, most methanol goes into making chemicals (chapter 2), but it can also be combusted as a fuel. Of the 98 million metric tons of methanol and methanol derivatives produced in 2019, 31 percent (30 million metric tons) was burned for energy, predominantly in vehicles.[54]

Today, 65 percent of methanol is produced from steam reforming of natural gas, while 35 percent (primarily in China) is produced from coal gasification. In both cases, the fossil fuel is converted into a mixture of hydrogen and carbon monoxide, which are combined to form methanol. On a life cycle basis, natural gas reforming produces about 100 kilograms of CO_2 per gigajoule of methanol, while coal gasification emits over 200.[55]

Methanol can be created by combining green hydrogen with CO_2 captured from other industrial processes or from the atmosphere ($3H_2 + CO_2 \rightarrow CH_3OH + H_2O$). Methanol produced this way is called "e-methanol" (referring to electricity, the energy source used to make green hydrogen). This reaction pathway is also involved in creating methanol from fossil feedstocks, so the necessary technology and catalysts are already commercialized.[56] Therefore, the main challenges of this route are the creation of zero-carbon hydrogen, discussed earlier, and capture of CO_2, discussed in chapter 8. The energy efficiency of the methanol synthesis step is about 80 percent.[57] Roughly ten operating e-methanol plants exist, and more than a dozen are in planning stages.[58]

Methanol can also be created by gasification of biomass (similar to the coal-to-methanol route used in China) or from steam reforming of biomethane. However, for industrial heat needs, it is more cost-effective to simply combust the biomass or biomethane directly, avoiding energy conversion losses. The main purpose of converting bio-feedstocks into methanol is to obtain a liquid fuel suitable for use in vehicles or as a chemical feedstock. Therefore, e-methanol is more promising than bio-methanol as a zero-carbon industrial energy source.

E-methanol has several advantages. It is easy to store and transport, and the same types of equipment used for petroleum products can handle and burn methanol, with minor modifications. Methanol combustion is more technologically mature than combustion of hydrogen or ammonia.

A crucial drawback of e-methanol is the need to obtain input CO_2. Purchasing CO_2 adds cost, and if the CO_2 came from fossil fuel combustion or limestone calcination (for cement-making), the resulting methanol is not low-carbon. (CO_2 from fossil fuels or limestone that is captured, then converted to methanol and combusted, contributes net CO_2 to the atmosphere.) Only CO_2 captured from bioenergy or extracted from the atmosphere ("direct air capture") offers routes to zero-carbon methanol. Availability of CO_2 on the open market from these specific sources is likely to be limited and costly. To overcome that, one option is to colocate biomethanol production with e-methanol production, so that excess CO_2 from biomethanol production can be used in the e-methanol process.[59] (Though e-methanol production could be colocated with any biomass-combusting industry, the fact that e-methanol and biomethanol are chemically identical allows synergies in operations, logistics, and sales.)

SYNTHETIC METHANE AND OTHER HYDROCARBONS

Zero-carbon hydrogen can be converted into familiar hydrocarbon fuels, including methane, diesel, and kerosene. When produced from electrolytic hydrogen and CO_2, these are called "synthetic fuels" or "synfuels." Excluding facilities that produce chemical feedstocks, almost 90 percent of synfuel plants produce methane, which is about 15 percent cheaper to produce per unit energy than liquid synfuels.[60] Liquid synfuels are best suited to vehicles, whereas synthetic methane's lower cost and compatibility with existing natural gas infrastructure make it a better fit for industry.

A variety of electricity-to-methane processes have been investigated, including thermochemical, photocatalytic, electrochemical, and biogenic routes. The most developed of these are thermochemical processes, which combine hydrogen with CO_2 (the Sabatier process) or CO (the Fischer-Tropsch process) at 250°C–350°C and 2.5 megapascals of pressure.[61]

The most important benefit of synthetic methane is its ability to be used in existing natural gas pipelines, tanks, and industrial equipment, either alone or blended with fossil methane. This may be a useful decarbonization pathway for industries that are not ready to modify or replace equipment, and also as a chemical feedstock for production of

BTX aromatics, particularly while methanol-to-aromatics technology remains precommercial (chapter 2).

Synthetic methane's main drawback is the same as that of e-methanol: a zero-carbon source of carbon dioxide (from biomass or direct air capture) is required to produce a zero-carbon fuel. This CO_2 will be limited and costly, so synfuel plants should colocate with industries that combust biomass.

Table 7.2 summarizes key pros and cons of hydrogen and the main hydrogen-derived fuels for providing energy to industry.

TABLE 7.2 Pros and Cons of Hydrogen and Hydrogen-Derived Fuels for Industrial Energy

Fuel	Pros	Cons
Green hydrogen	• Best energy efficiency (no chemical conversion) • Lowest cost to produce • No input carbon required	• Hydrogen embrittlement and leakage require new infrastructure and equipment • Low volumetric energy density • Difficult to transport and store • Higher NO_x emissions than methane unless special combustion equipment is used
Ammonia from green hydrogen	• No input carbon required • Cost to produce is half that of e-methanol or synthetic methane • Easier to store and transport than pure hydrogen (but less easy than e-methanol and synthetic methane) • Can be used as a hydrogen carrier (albeit with significant energy penalty)	• Poor combustion properties • Highest NO_x emissions
E-methanol	• Easy to transport and store	• Requires net-zero input CO_2 • Expensive to produce
Synthetic methane	• Can use existing natural gas infrastructure and equipment	• Requires net-zero input CO_2 • Expensive to produce

No zero-carbon fuel option is better than the others in all circumstances. However, hydrogen-derived fuels will always be more costly to produce than hydrogen (because zero-carbon hydrogen is a required input, and there are energy losses with any chemical transformation). The fuels that are most compatible with existing infrastructure, e-methanol and synthetic methane, are the most expensive to produce and require net-zero input CO_2. In contrast, the downsides of pure hydrogen are solvable through replacement of industrial equipment and deployment of electrolyzers in factories or industrial parks. Therefore, where electrification is not possible, hydrogen-derived fuels may be most useful during a transition period of several decades, during which new industrial equipment is built to use hydrogen.

BIOENERGY

Alongside electricity, hydrogen, and hydrogen-derived fuels, bioenergy has the potential to be a zero-carbon industrial energy source. (For the use of bioenergy as a chemical feedstock or reducing agent, see chapters 1–2.) There are three principal types of bioenergy.

BIOGAS AND BIOMETHANE

Biogas is a mixture of compounds emitted when bacteria break down organic matter without oxygen. It primarily consists of methane and carbon dioxide, with trace amounts of other gases, such as oxygen, nitrogen, and hydrogen sulfide. Biogas is recovered from landfills, anaerobic digesters (machines that manage manure from livestock operations), and wastewater treatment plants. Biogas can be burned directly, or the methane can first be separated. Separated biomethane is essentially identical to its fossil equivalent and can be used interchangeably with natural gas.[62]

Biomethane is easy for industry to utilize, but biogas is produced only from specific sources, so availability is limited. In 2018, global production of biogas was 1.5 exajoules, equivalent to 1.2 percent of the nonfeedstock energy consumed by industry.[63] The estimated maximum potential from currently available feedstocks (without planting energy crops dedicated to biogas production) is 12.5 exajoules from crop residues, 11.5 exajoules from livestock, 3.5 exajoules from food waste, and 1 exajoule from sewage, for a total of 28.5 exajoules, or about 22 percent of nonfeedstock industrial energy use.[64] However, this would require processing nearly all organic wastes globally in anaerobic digesters, which would be very difficult. An ambitious International Energy Agency scenario that achieves net-zero global emissions by 2050 includes 8 exajoules of biogas production in 2050, equivalent to 5 percent of projected industrial energy consumption (though only half is used by industry, with the rest going to other sectors).[65]

A new anaerobic digester produces biogas at a cost of $17–$33 per gigajoule over its lifetime (primarily amortized capital expenses for the plant), higher than industrial natural gas prices of $3.50 per gigajoule in the United States, $8 per gigajoule in Europe, and $12 per gigajoule in China (figure 6.5).[66] However, the digester also provides other important services (waste disposal, organic fertilizer production, and greenhouse gas abatement), the value of which is not captured in this head-to-head price comparison.[67] For more on organic fertilizer, see the material substitution section of chapter 5.

LIQUID BIOFUELS

Liquid biofuels are energy-dense fuels derived from biomass, such as corn or sugarcane ethanol. Liquid biofuels are of greatest value in vehicles, especially difficult-to-electrify vehicles (i.e., aircraft and ships), where limited weight capacity or fuel tank size justifies paying a premium for an energy-dense fuel. Industry is less weight- and space-constrained and need not pay the cost premium (and energy penalty) of converting solid biomass into liquid biofuels. Though liquid biofuels will be an industrial output, they are not projected to play a significant role in providing heat and power for a zero-emissions industry sector.[68]

BIOMASS

Solid biomass consists of materials such as wood pellets, forest residues, and crop wastes. It is the lowest-cost form of bioenergy and has the greatest availability worldwide. In terms of combustion properties, biomass resembles coal, albeit with lower energy density and more impurities. In 2020, global solid biomass production was 22 exajoules (disregarding a further 25 exajoules of "traditional" uses of biomass, such as cooking over open fires, which is inefficient and highly polluting). Industry consumed 9.6 exajoules of solid biomass, accounting for 8 percent of non-feedstock industrial energy use.[69] Biomass is the most promising form of bioenergy for meeting large-scale industrial energy needs, but key challenges remain, including the following.

Availability. Biomass must be produced sustainably while conserving other valuable land uses, such as ensuring sufficient agricultural land for food crops and protecting natural ecosystems. There are wide uncertainty ranges in the literature regarding the quantity of biomass that might be sustainably harvested. Uncertainty sources include land availability, productivity of energy crops per hectare, population growth, diet (meat production requires much more land than vegetable and grain production), and climate impacts (such as water availability). An expert review by the Intergovernmental Panel on Climate Change (IPCC) concluded that the 2050 global potential of biomass for energy is likely between 100 and 300 exajoules.[70] Achieving this potential would require large increases in cultivation of energy crops, sophisticated land and water management, increased productivity per hectare, and other measures.[71]

Industry would receive only a share of this total, as some biomass would be converted to liquid biofuels, used to heat buildings, go toward traditional uses, and so on. Nonetheless, there would be sufficient availability for biomass to play a major role as an industrial fuel. For instance, eighteen IPCC scenarios compatible with 1.5°C warming feature bioenergy production of 118–312 exajoules (median 200 exajoules).[72] If industry were to use 25 percent of the median figure, this would be 50 exajoules, equivalent to 40 percent of present-day industrial nonfeedstock energy demand.

Carbon neutrality. Plants acquire their carbon from the atmosphere, so ideally, biomass combustion simply re-emits this captured CO_2 with no net impact on atmospheric CO_2 concentrations. However, in practice, there are several ways bioenergy use can increase greenhouse gas emissions. The most important of these is land use change. While some biomass can be obtained from existing land uses (e.g., by-products from the agriculture and forestry industries), achieving the bioenergy potentials noted earlier requires significant expansion of dedicated bioenergy crop cultivation. The type of land used for bioenergy crops affects their greenhouse gas performance. If forest is converted to cropland, many years are required for the avoided emissions from bioenergy grown on that land to compensate for the carbon emissions caused by deforestation, a concept known as "carbon payback time." For average bioenergy crops such as sugarcane and cassava, payback time for converting healthy forest is eighty to one hundred fifty years, degraded forest fifty to one hundred years, woody savannah twenty to eighty years, and grassland eight to twenty years; for preexisting croplands or degraded land, the payback time is immediate (no land use change emissions to pay back).[73]

Another source of greenhouse gas emissions is nitrous oxide from nitrogen-based fertilizer use. Techniques to reduce fertilizer use and nitrous oxide emissions are covered in the fertilizer efficiency section of chapter 5. Zero-carbon biomass for industry should come from by-products of preexisting, sustainable agricultural and forestry operations, as well as dedicated bioenergy crops grown on preexisting cropland or degraded land with best practices in fertilizer management.

Logistics. Bioenergy growth potential is unevenly distributed worldwide, with greatest potential in the southeastern United States, central South America, Eastern Europe, equatorial Africa, India's east coast, and Southeast Asia.[74] Biomass must be transported from where it is grown to locations of industrial energy demand. Biomass can be costly to transport because it has low energy density and often requires pretreatment to prepare for shipment. Industrial plants relying solely on biomass may require large storage due to the seasonal availability of bioenergy crops.

Storage, pretreatment, and shipping generally account for 20–50 percent of the price of biomass; for wood pellets, one of the most-traded forms of biomass, the figure is over 50 percent.[75] Therefore, industries with good access to biomass suppliers, and to biomass harvested through-out the year, will find biomass more affordable than will industries located far from biomass production or with only seasonal availability.

Non-greenhouse-gas pollution. Biomass combustion emits conventional (non-greenhouse-gas) air pollutants. When burned in an industrial boiler, wood emits comparatively little sulfur dioxide (SO_2) and nonmethane volatile organic compounds. However, it emits roughly as much nitrogen oxides (NO_x) and more fine particulates than coal (figure 7.3). These pollutants can result in serious health impacts. For instance, in the mid-2010s, after years of declining U.S. coal consumption, biomass surpassed coal as the leading cause of premature deaths from air pollution, with a 39–47 percent share.[76] Therefore, biomass combustion requires pollution control equipment, especially particulate

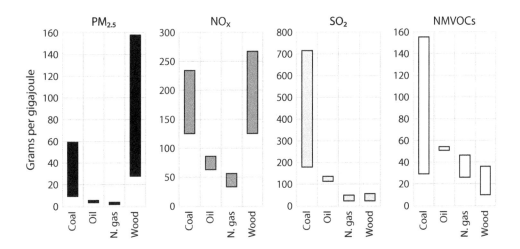

FIGURE 7.3 **Non-Greenhouse-Gas Pollutant Emissions Intensities from Combustible Fuels Used in Industrial Boilers** The range for each fuel and pollutant reflects varying conditions in different countries, such as higher- or lower-sulfur coal, or equipment with varying pollution control measures. $PM_{2.5}$ = fine particulate matter; NO_x = nitrogen oxides; SO_2 = sulfur dioxide; NMVOCs = nonmethane volatile organic compounds.

Source: J. Sathaye, O. Lucon, A. Rahman, J. Christensen, F. Denton, J. Fujino, G. Heath, S. Kadner, M. Mirza, H. Rudnick, A. Schlaepfer, and A. Shmakin, "Renewable Energy in the Context of Sustainable Development," In *IPCC Special Report on Renewable Energy Sources and Climate Change Mitigation*, ed. O. Edenhofer, R. Pichs-Madruga, Y. Sokona, K. Seyboth, P. Matschoss, S. Kadner, T. Zwickel, P. Eickemeier, G. Hansen, S. Schlömer, and C. von Stechow (Cambridge: University Press, 2011).

removal technologies such as cyclone separators, wet scrubbers, electrostatic precipitators, and fabric filters. NO_x emissions can be managed using flue gas recirculation, staged combustion air, and postcombustion catalytic and noncatalytic reduction.[77] In countries with weak or absent emissions standards, companies may underinvest in pollution control equipment, so policies to promote industrial use of biomass should be accompanied by emissions standards sufficient to protect public health.

Other impacts. The following are additional challenges to using biomass for meeting large-scale industrial energy needs.

- Growing more bioenergy crops can increase freshwater demand, and agricultural runoff can contain fertilizers and pesticides that impact aquatic ecosystems.
- Competition between food and bioenergy crops could increase food prices and reduce food security in some regions.[78]
- Industry capital costs may be higher due to the need to handle fuel containing more impurities and lower energy content, and to abate conventional pollutant emissions.

While there is theoretical potential for bioenergy to play a large role in a zero-carbon industrial sector, the forgoing practical considerations should limit bioenergy to a smaller role, primarily for industries located near areas where biomass is produced from waste or grown on marginal lands with appropriate fertilizer management, and where there are strong protections for wildlands, air quality, water, and food security. Even when these conditions are met, biomass will be attractive to industry only when it is the lowest-cost zero-carbon fuel option, after accounting for control equipment to abate conventional pollution. Only a small share of global industry is likely to meet these conditions.

COST COMPARISON

Comparing present-day costs of renewable fuels is challenging because fuel costs depend on many factors. For example, electrolytic hydrogen

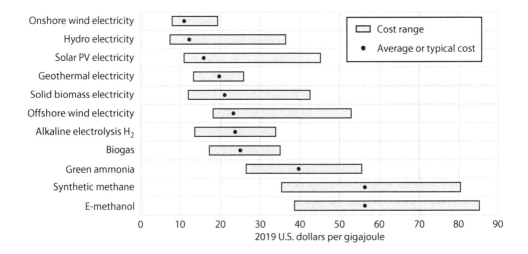

FIGURE 7.4 Renewable Energy Production Costs in 2020 Levelized electricity costs come from utility-scale projects completed in 2020. Biogas's average reflects typical costs from on-farm anaerobic digesters or centralized city wastewater treatment plants. This graph opts to show electricity from solid biomass (rather than the cost of solid biomass fuel, such as wood pellets) because fuel costs make up less than half the cost of delivered energy services from biomass combustion, and heat from biomass combustion is often coproduced with electricity in combined heat and power systems.

Sources: Nick Primmer and WBA Policy, Innovation and Technical Committee, *Biogas: Pathways to 2030* (report, World Biogas Association, London, March 2021), https://www.world biogasassociation.org/biogas-pathways-to-2030-report/; International Energy Agency, "The Future of Hydrogen: Seizing today's opportunities," (report, Paris, France, June 2019), https://iea.blob.core.windows.net/assets/9e3a3493-b9a6-4b7d-b499-7ca48e357561/The_Future_of _Hydrogen.pdf; International Renewable Energy Agency, *Renewable Power Generation Costs in 2020* (report, IRENA, Abu Dhabi, January 2021), https://www.irena.org/-/media/Files/IRENA /Agency/Publication/2021/Jun/IRENA_Power_Generation_Costs_2020.pdf; Richard Michael Nayak-Luke and René Bañares-Alcántara, "Techno-Economic Viability of Islanded Green Ammonia as a Carbon-Free Energy Vector and as a Substitute for Conventional Production," *Energy & Environmental Science* 13, no. 9 (2020): 2957–66, https://doi.org/10.1039/D0EE01707H; and Agora Verkehrswende, Agora Energiewende, and Frontier Economics, "The Future Cost of Electricity-Based Synthetic Fuels," 2018, https://www.agora-energiewende.de/fileadmin /Projekte/2017/SynKost_2050/Agora_SynKost_Study_EN_WEB.pdf.

costs depend on the capital cost and efficiency of the electrolyzer, its annual operating hours, and electricity price, which varies considerably worldwide. Therefore, the global cost estimates presented in figure 7.4 offer a general sense of which energy sources are often cheaper than others, rather than provide specific cost data applicable in particular countries.

Technological advances and returns to scale will reduce future zero-carbon fuel prices. For example, by 2050, the cost of electrolytic hydrogen could reach $6–$10 per gigajoule, and the cost of e-methanol may reach $12–$31 per gigajoule.[79]

Finally, note that cost per unit of energy does not capture the fact that electricity delivers heat to processed parts and materials with lower heat losses than combustion, since electricity has no exhaust gases and no H_2O formation (chapter 6). Accounting for differences in heat losses increases the cost advantage of electricity for applications where direct electrification is possible.

RENEWABLE FUELS' CONTRIBUTION TO ZERO-CARBON INDUSTRY

Green hydrogen will play a necessary role in a decarbonized industrial sector. Two of the highest-priority uses are to produce primary steel (since alternatives based on electrolysis are at an early stage of technological maturity) and to supply chemical feedstocks (where direct electrification is impossible). Replacing just these two fossil fuel uses with an energy-equivalent amount of hydrogen in 2019 would have required 484 million metric tons of additional hydrogen, more than a five-fold increase in global hydrogen production.[80] If these 484 million metric tons of hydrogen were made via 70 percent–efficient electrolysis, the required electricity demand would be 23,000 terawatt-hours, a doubling of global 2019 electricity consumption (across all economic sectors).[81] Thus, even if hydrogen is reserved for the highest-value industrial uses, the required quantity of green hydrogen and associated increase in clean electricity generation would nonetheless be extremely large. Therefore, it is important to directly electrify industrial heating wherever possible (chapter 6), taking advantage of direct electrification's better efficiency (versus forming and burning green hydrogen or hydrogen-derived fuels) to limit the required build-out of renewables. Other measures that reduce energy demand, such as energy efficiency, material efficiency, and circular economy approaches, will also be helpful.

Bioenergy provides another option that avoids increasing renewable electricity demand, and industry is an ideal user of solid biomass and biogas. Bioenergy can relieve pressure on electricity systems and will be the best option in certain regions. Despite the difficulties in ensuring that bioenergy is truly sustainable, efforts to expand bioenergy production are likely to be worthwhile and should be accompanied by careful rules to protect forests, food security, ecosystems, water quality, and air quality.

8

CARBON CAPTURE AND
USE OR STORAGE

ossil fuel combustion and other industrial processes produce carbon dioxide (CO_2). Carbon capture and use or storage (CCUS) aims to permanently prevent this CO_2 from reaching the atmosphere. CCUS technologies can be divided into four categories:

- **capture**: separating CO_2 from mixed gases (or generating CO_2 that is already relatively pure),
- **transport**: compressing and transporting CO_2,
- **storage**: geological storage through underground injection or mineralization, and
- **use**: incorporating CO_2 into commercial materials and products.

CCUS TODAY

CCUS is more technologically mature than certain alternative technologies, such as green hydrogen combustion or hydrogen-derived synfuels. In 2020, there were twenty-six commercial-scale carbon capture facilities operating, with a combined capacity of 38 million metric tons of CO_2 per year.[1] The actual amount of CO_2 captured was less, around 33 million metric tons (figure 8.1), because not all facilities operate at full capacity for the whole year. This is equivalent to 0.3 percent of direct industrial combustion and process CO_2 emissions (see figure 0.2 in the introduction).

Natural gas processing plants accounted for 69 percent of CCUS capacity; they remove CO_2 (and other impurities) to produce pipeline-quality gas. Another 22 percent of capacity was at facilities that produce chemicals, synthetic natural gas, fertilizers, and hydrogen. The remainder was split between oil refining, iron and steel production, and coal power generation.[2]

Of the 33 million metric tons of CO_2 captured, around 25 million were used for "enhanced oil recovery," a technique for extracting oil by injecting CO_2 into underground oil deposits, while the rest was stored underground without associated fuel production (figure 8.1). (Captured

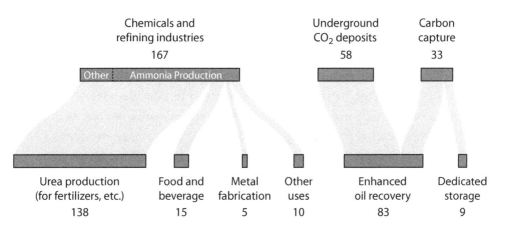

FIGURE 8.1 **Global Sources and Uses of CO_2 in 2020** All values are in millions of metric tons of CO_2. Source quantities do not exactly equal use quantities due to rounding. Calculations assume that carbon-capture-to-dedicated-storage projects had the same capacity factor as carbon-capture-to-enhanced-oil-recovery projects (87 percent, excluding nonoperational plants).

Sources: Global CCS Institute, *Global Status of CCS 2020* (report, Global CCS Institute, Melbourne, Australia, 2020), https://www.globalccsinstitute.com/wp-content/uploads/2020/12/Global-Status-of-CCS-Report-2020_FINAL_December11.pdf; International Energy Agency, *Putting CO_2 to Use: Creating Value from Emissions* (report, International Energy Agency, Paris, September 2019), https://iea.blob.core.windows.net/assets/50652405-26db-4c41-82dc-c23657893059/Putting_CO_2_to_Use.pdf; and International Energy Agency, *CCUS in Clean Energy Transitions* (report, International Energy Agency, Paris, September 2020), https://www.iea.org/reports/ccus-in-clean-energy-transitions.

CO_2 constitutes a minority of the CO_2 used for enhanced oil recovery; around 70 percent is from naturally occurring underground CO_2 deposits.) Enhanced oil recovery is not a climate-safe use of CO_2. For details, see the enhanced oil recovery section later in this chapter.

Enhanced oil recovery is not the only commercial use of CO_2. Purified CO_2 is also used, among other applications, to make urea (over 90 percent of which goes into fertilizers), in the food and beverage industry (for example, to add carbonation to soda), and for cooling (dry ice, or solid CO_2), metal welding, fire suppression, medical sterilization, and in greenhouses to stimulate plant growth.[3] This CO_2 comes from the chemicals and refining industries (around 80 percent is a by-product of ammonia production), where it is produced in relatively pure form, so no CO_2 separation step is needed.[4]

CCUS's NICHE

CCUS has a role to play in achieving zero CO_2 emissions from the global industrial sector, particularly in the next two to three decades. In six use cases, CCUS may compare favorably with alternative options, such as electrification and use of green hydrogen or hydrogen-derived fuels.

First, burning fossil fuels with CCUS may be useful for supplying large quantities of high-temperature heat for nonconductive materials, such as for making cement, glass, and brick. At low and medium temperatures, electrification options are plentiful (heat pumps, dielectric heating, infrared heating, resistance heating, etc.), while electric arc and induction furnaces are efficient at melting metals (chapter 6). However, for large amounts of high-temperature heat for nonmetals, electric technologies are costly or not yet commercial. While direct electrification may provide a better solution after more development and commercialization (chapter 6), CCUS is currently more technologically mature, so it can scale up more quickly.

Second, CCUS is critical for addressing CO_2 process emissions. The largest source of process CO_2 is calcining limestone to produce cement and lime, but other sources include smelting metal ores, producing chemicals, refining petroleum, and making glass and bricks.[5] Non-CCUS technologies can eliminate some of these emissions, such as novel low-carbon cement chemistries (chapter 3) or using electrolytic hydrogen as a chemical feedstock (chapter 2). However, no technology exists that could avert the creation of all process CO_2. Therefore, CCUS is uniquely situated to address these emissions.

Third, CCUS is a good fit for industrial processes that generate high-purity CO_2 streams, because it is cheaper and less energy-intensive to isolate high-concentration CO_2. Industries with the highest-purity CO_2 and the lowest costs include the processing of natural gas, coal-to-chemicals conversion (common in China), and production of ammonia, bioethanol, and ethylene oxide. In contrast, steelmaking, cement-making, and hydrogen production via steam methane reforming all emit CO_2 at concentrations little higher than fossil fuel combustion, so their carbon capture costs are similar to those of fuel combustion (table 8.1). Note that some of these industries (natural gas processing, coal-to-chemicals) are likely to decline or vanish in a zero-carbon future, while others will use alternative production routes that do not involve fossil CO_2 (e.g., ammonia production), so CCUS's biggest opportunities here are in the near term.

Fourth, some CCUS technologies can be retrofit onto newer, efficient industrial facilities, whereas alternatives such as obtaining and burning green hydrogen or replacing fossil heat with electrified heat may require replacement of equipment. While a CCUS retrofit is not cheap, it can be more cost-effective than replacing a plant or machinery that is still relatively new. Retrofits may be particularly relevant in China, because the average age of Chinese iron, cement, and chemicals facilities is just ten to fifteen years, a fraction of their expected lifetimes of thirty to forty years.[6]

In addition to technical considerations, whether or not CCUS retrofitting is a good option for a given facility depends on what the facility would do (e.g., in response to policies, such as carbon pricing or emissions standards) if CCUS retrofits were not an option.

- CCUS retrofits are ideal for facilities that would otherwise continue to operate unabated.

TABLE 8.1 CO_2 Concentrations and Capture Costs for Various CO_2 Sources

CO_2 source	CO_2 concentration (%)	Capture cost (U.S. dollars per metric ton)
Natural gas processing	96–100	15–25
Coal-to-chemicals (gasification)	98–100	15–25
Ammonia	98–100	25–35
Bioethanol	98–100	25–35
Ethylene oxide	98–100	25–35
Iron and steel	21–27	40 (blast furnace only)–100 (whole plant)
Hydrogen (steam methane reforming)	15–20	50–80
Cement	15–30	60 (precalciner only)–120 (whole plant)
Coal combustion (boiler or IGCC*)	12–14	40–100
Natural gas combustion (boiler)	7–10	40–100

*IGCC = integrated gasification combined cycle.

Note: Costs include compression of captured CO_2. Cost ranges in this table reflect the United States and do not include transportation or sequestration costs. Costs vary significantly by country, primarily due to differences in fuel prices.

Sources: International Energy Agency, *Putting CO_2 to Use: Creating Value from Emissions* (report, International Energy Agency, Paris, September 2019), https://iea.blob.core.windows.net/assets /50652405-26db-4c41-82dc-c23657893059/Putting_CO_2_to_Use.pdf; International Energy Agency, *CCUS in Clean Energy Transitions* (report, International Energy Agency, Paris, September 2020), https://www.iea.org/reports/ccus-in-clean-energy-transitions; Adam Baylin-Stern and Niels Berghout, "Is Carbon Capture Too Expensive?," International Energy Agency, February 17, 2021, https://www.iea.org/commentaries/is-carbon-capture-too-expensive; Xiaoxing Wang and Chunshan Song, "Carbon Capture from Flue Gas and the Atmosphere: A Perspective," *Frontiers in Energy Research* 8 (December 15, 2020): 265, https://doi.org/10.3389/fenrg.2020.560849; and Lawrence Irlam, "Global Costs of Carbon Capture and Storage" (summary report, Global CCS Institute, Melbourne, Australia, June 2017), https://www.globalccsinstitute.com/archive/hub /publications/201688/global-ccs-cost-updatev4.pdf.

- Retrofits are not a good option for facilities that would otherwise electrify or switch to green fuels, as CCUS would then be delaying a transition to clean energy.
- For facilities that would otherwise shut down, economic considerations (e.g., loss of jobs and impact on the community) must be weighed against environmental benefits (e.g., elimination of greenhouse gas

and localized air pollution from the facility). This may favor CCUS retrofits for major industrial plants that constitute a large share of the economic activity of a small town or rural area, while it may favor shutting down smaller plants in dense urban areas where many people are exposed to localized pollutant emissions and alternative job opportunities are abundant.

Fifth, where sustainable bioenergy is available (see chapter 7), CCUS can capture CO_2 from bioenergy combustion or gasification. Storing this carbon lowers atmospheric CO_2 concentrations. Alternatively, the CO_2 can be combined with green hydrogen to form chemical products or hydrogen-derived fuels, providing one of the few mechanisms to make these products in a way that avoids net CO_2 emissions when they break down or are combusted.

Sixth, electrification of industrial heat and making chemical feedstocks from electrolytic hydrogen would require large increases in zero-carbon electricity generation (see chapter 6). It may take some time to grow zero-carbon electricity generation to meet those needs (and to displace existing fossil generation). CCUS may be useful for reducing greenhouse gas emissions where clean electricity is in short supply, effectively buying more time for the grid to scale up and decarbonize.

CCUS DRAWBACKS

CCUS has several drawbacks that should limit its use. First, it usually aims to capture carbon from fossil fuels. Producing, processing, and transporting fossil fuels often involve considerable greenhouse gas emissions, which are not affected by CCUS at the industrial plant. In 2020, 77 million metric tons of methane leaked from oil and natural gas operations, and 42 million metric tons leaked from coal mines, together composing nearly a third of human-caused methane emissions (over 5 percent of global greenhouse gas emissions).[7] Methane leakage represents 13–27 percent of natural gas's life cycle emissions (using a hundred-year global warming potential of 28 and leakage rates

ranging from 1.5 to 3.5 percent). Therefore, even CCUS with a 100 percent capture rate would fall far short of achieving zero greenhouse gas
emissions on a life cycle basis. In contrast, techniques such as electrification, use of green hydrogen, or bioenergy can eliminate both fossil
fuel production and use.

Second, energy is required to power the CCUS process; for instance,
to regenerate chemicals that capture carbon and to compress CO_2.
Therefore, CCUS increases fuel consumption by 15–25 percent relative
to an equivalent plant not equipped with CCUS.[8] This increases energy
costs and can increase greenhouse gas and conventional pollutant emissions upstream in the supply chain (i.e., associated with fossil fuel production and distribution).

Third, CCUS captures only CO_2, not conventional pollutants that
harm human health, such as particulates, nitrogen oxides (NO_x), and
ammonia (NH_3). Direct and indirect emissions of NO_x and particulates
grow roughly in proportion to fuel consumption; that is, 15–25 percent.[9] If
amine-based capture technology is used, ammonia emissions may more
than triple due to the breakdown of solvents, but sulfur dioxide (SO_2)
emissions are reduced because SO_2 removal is required for these systems.[10]

Carbon capture equipment also requires improved exhaust treatment
to remove more NO_x and particulates per unit of fuel combusted, but
unlike the case with SO_2, these improvements are small enough to be
offset by the need to burn more fuel to power the carbon capture process, so net NO_x and particulate emissions can increase (figure 8.2).[11]
Since polluting industrial facilities are often located in low-income,
disadvantaged communities, reliance on CCUS can worsen inequitable
health impacts of conventional pollutant emissions. For more on equity,
see chapter 12.

Fourth, today's CCUS systems for exhaust streams with typical CO_2
concentrations (such as from fuel combustion, iron and steelmaking,
or cement-making) capture only 85–90 percent of the CO_2.[12] Capture
rates over 99 percent can be achieved, but that requires larger equipment, more process steps, and more energy consumption per metric ton
of CO_2 captured. The resulting cost increase is on the order of 10 percent
for natural gas–based systems.[13]

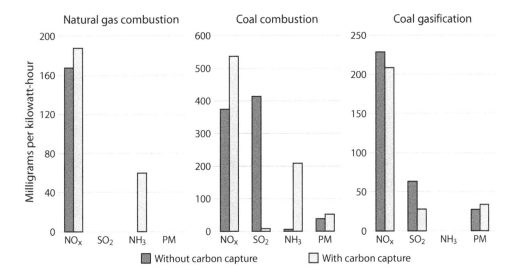

FIGURE 8.2 Conventional Pollutant Emissions With and Without Carbon Capture In this figure, natural gas combustion and coal combustion use postcombustion capture, while coal gasification uses precombustion capture. Carbon capture reduces sulfur dioxide (SO_2) emissions but can sometimes worsen nitrogen oxide (NO_x), ammonia (NH_3), or particulate (PM) emissions.

Sources: European Environment Agency, *Air Pollution Impacts from Carbon Capture and Storage (CCS)* (EEA Technical Report no. 14/2011, Copenhagen, November 17, 2011), https://www.eea.europa.eu/publications/carbon-capture-and-storage/at_download/file.

Fifth, a plant needs to be able to transport CO_2 away for use or storage (or to use CO_2 itself). If there is no viable geological storage or CO_2 user within range of a plant, CCUS may not be a good fit for that plant. An assessment of potential storage sites must consider sites' ability to securely store a sufficient volume of CO_2 and any risks of groundwater contamination or induced seismicity (earthquakes triggered by CO_2 injection).[14]

Sixth, since carbon capture is a relatively mature technology, future cost declines are likely to be smaller than cost declines for less mature technologies such as batteries and green hydrogen. A Global CCS Institute study estimated a future CCUS cost reduction potential of just

8 percent for fertilizer plants, 16 percent for cement plants, and 17 percent for iron and steel plants.[15] Therefore, CCUS will likely be surpassed in cost-effectiveness by other decarbonization technologies.

OTHER CARBON CAPTURE TECHNOLOGIES

Two technologies that may be considered types of carbon capture are not covered in this chapter. One is "methane pyrolysis," which involves converting methane into hydrogen gas and solid carbon. The carbon can be stored or used in products such as tires and pigments. (However, if these products are combusted at end of life, the solid carbon will be converted to CO_2.) As methane pyrolysis is primarily intended for hydrogen production, it is covered in chapter 7.

The second excluded technology is "direct air capture," a process whereby carbon dioxide is separated from other gases in the atmosphere rather than from combustion exhaust or industrial process emissions. Direct air capture has high costs to separate CO_2 ($135–$345 per metric ton), since CO_2 is at much lower concentrations in the atmosphere (0.04 percent) than in exhaust streams.[16] Capturing atmospheric CO_2 does not reduce industrial emissions, so the capture step is outside the scope of this book. Once captured, the CO_2 may be transported, stored, or used in the same manner as any other captured CO_2, and these postcapture steps are covered later.

CO_2 CAPTURE TECHNOLOGIES

Five broad approaches are used for carbon capture in the industrial sector. Three approaches require CO_2 to be separated from gas mixtures.

- **Postcombustion capture** involves burning fuel with air, then extracting CO_2 from the flue gas. CO_2 is primarily separated from nitrogen (which makes up 78 percent of air), water vapor (a combustion by-product), and, to a lesser degree, from argon (1 percent of air) and other gases.

- In **precombustion capture**, fuel feedstocks are converted into a syngas (a mixture of predominantly H_2 and CO) by gasification, steam reforming, autothermal reforming, or partial oxidation.[17] The water–gas shift reaction ($CO + H_2O \rightarrow CO_2 + H_2$) is then used to convert the CO into CO_2 and obtain additional hydrogen.[18] CO_2 is separated, and hydrogen is burned for energy (chapter 7) or used as a chemical feedstock (chapter 2). CO_2 is primarily separated from hydrogen.

- In **natural gas processing**, CO_2 (and other impurities) are separated from raw natural gas to produce pipeline-quality natural gas. CO_2 is primarily separated from methane and, to a lesser degree, from other hydrocarbons (e.g., ethane and propane) and various impurities.

Two approaches aim to burn fuel while producing a relatively pure CO_2 stream, avoiding the need to separate CO_2

- In **oxy-combustion**, fuel is burned with nearly pure oxygen rather than air.
- **Chemical looping combustion** involves delivering oxygen to fuel via metal oxide particles.

Several CO_2 separation technologies exist that can be used with precombustion capture, postcombustion capture, and natural gas processing. Each separation technology is detailed here, followed by a discussion of oxy-combustion and chemical looping combustion.

CHEMICAL ABSORPTION

The most common CO_2 separation technique, particularly for postcombustion capture and natural gas processing, is "chemical absorption." When used with postcombustion capture, the flue gas is cooled by exposure to water, and SO_2 and NO_2 impurities are removed, since these chemicals would interfere with the amine solvent. The gas is routed into an absorber tower (also known as an "amine scrubber"), where it is exposed to a solvent of liquid amines (most commonly ethanolamine), causing CO_2 to chemically bond to the amines.[19] The CO_2-rich solvent is pumped into a stripper tower (also known as a "regenerator"), where it is heated to 100°C–140°C. The heat reverses the reaction, restoring the solvent and releasing pure CO_2.[20] Early amine systems required input energy of 3.7 gigajoules per metric ton of CO_2 to regenerate the solvent, while today's best commercial systems require 2.6 gigajoules per metric ton of CO_2.[21]

Amine-based solvents are the most mature chemical absorption technology and have been used commercially for decades.[22] However, improved solvents are an area of active study; researchers are seeking chemicals that require less energy to regenerate, have fast absorption and desorption rates, can absorb more CO_2 per unit volume, and have better tolerance of contaminants. The main approaches are the use of catalysts (particularly carbonic anhydrase enzymes), multiphase amine mixtures, precipitating solvents, ionic liquids, and sodium hydroxide-based systems. These approaches may reduce solvent regeneration energy requirements to 1.1 gigajoules per metric ton of CO_2 but have been demonstrated only at laboratory scale.[23]

As of 2020, one commercial postcombustion capture facility was in operation (Canada's Boundary Dam 3 project, with total capacity of one million metric tons of CO_2 per year). It uses amine-based chemical absorption. One other completed project, the Petra Nova carbon capture facility in Texas, was shut down in 2020 due to unprofitability. Eleven postcombustion capture facilities with a further 37 million metric tons per year capacity were in planning and design stages, though not all plants at these stages are ultimately built.[24]

Amine-based chemical absorption is much more common in gas-processing plants than in postcombustion capture, as CO_2 must be removed from raw natural gas to produce pipeline-quality gas. Over 95 percent of U.S. gas-processing plants that remove CO_2 use amine-based chemical absorption.[25] (Some of these plants first use membrane separation, discussed later, followed by an amine-based absorption step.[26]) Chemical absorption is also used in other industries, such as an Emirates Steel factory in Abu Dhabi.[27]

PHYSICAL ABSORPTION

In precombustion capture, CO_2 is usually captured using physical absorption rather than chemical absorption.[28] In a physical absorption process, CO_2 dissolves in the solvent without chemically bonding to it. Therefore, much less energy is required to regenerate the solvent. However, the solvent's capacity to absorb CO_2 is linearly correlated with the partial pressure of CO_2, so physical absorption is not effective for separating CO_2 at low pressures. Postcombustion capture produces low-pressure CO_2 (10–20 kilopascals), so chemical absorption is preferred. In contrast, precombustion capture produces CO_2 at pressures suitable for physical absorption (2–7 megapascals). The main physical solvents are propylene carbonate, chilled methanol, and polyethylene glycol.[29]

Physical absorption is used in a number of operating commercial facilities, such as the Great Plains Synfuel Plant in North Dakota, the Coffeyville fertilizer plant in Kansas, and the Quest hydrogen plant in Alberta.

ADSORPTION

Whereas "absorption" refers to a substance mixing throughout the volume of a solvent to form a solution, "adsorption" refers to a substance adhering only to the surface of a material, called a "sorbent." Solvents are usually liquid, while sorbents are usually solid. Like solvents, sorbents can adhere to the separated substance chemically (bonding) or physically (through weaker attractive forces). Sorbents being investigated for CO_2 separation include activated alumina or carbon, ion exchange resins, metal oxides, zeolite minerals, and hydrotalcite clays.[30] At least one commercial-scale plant is operating that uses CO_2 adsorption: Air Products' steam methane reformer in Texas.[31]

MEMBRANE SEPARATION

A membrane is essentially a filter, a material that allows only certain chemicals to penetrate. Some membranes are porous and selectively filter molecules based on differences in molecular weight or size. Membranes can also be nonporous (solid), in which case, one gas may dissolve into the membrane, diffuse through it, and be emitted on the other side. For example, as noted in chapter 7, hydrogen diffuses through metals, which can complicate hydrogen storage and transport. But it is possible to take advantage of this property by using a solid-metal membrane to separate hydrogen from CO_2.[32]

Membranes are designed to maximize the solubility and diffusion rate of the material to be separated while prohibiting other materials from passing. They may involve multiple material layers, including polymers, zeolite minerals, and nanotubes. Membranes may incorporate complicated internal structures, such as transport molecules, molecular gates, or metal oxide lattices, which facilitate the movement of the desired molecules across the membrane while inhibiting other molecules. No heat is needed to regenerate a solvent or sorbent, so membranes have the potential to reduce CCUS energy requirements.

Membrane-based CO_2 capture has been used commercially in natural gas processing since the 1980s, including at a Petrobras-owned gas-processing plant in Brazil, the second-largest operating CCUS project worldwide.[33] Commercialized membranes are effective at bulk separation of CO_2 from methane when input CO_2 concentration is high, but they are not economical at low-input CO_2 concentrations or when the output CO_2 must be high in purity. Therefore, gas-processing plants use membranes only when the CO_2 content at the wellhead is high, and they may follow up the membranes with an amine-based chemical absorption step to remove additional CO_2 and produce pipeline-quality natural gas.[34] Applications of membrane separation outside of gas processing are still at laboratory scale.[35]

CRYOGENIC SEPARATION

At a given pressure, each gas has a boiling point, or temperature below which it condenses (becomes a liquid) or desublimates (becomes a solid). At atmospheric pressure, CO_2's boiling point ($-78.5°C$) is considerably higher than that of other components of air (−183°C for oxygen, −185.9°C for argon, and −195.8°C for nitrogen), except water vapor (100°C). This allows CO_2 to be removed from flue gases by chilling the mixture, first until water solidifies and is removed, then until CO_2 desublimates. The separation is most complete when CO_2 is at higher concentrations and/or when using a temperature significantly below CO_2's boiling point (which can be raised by increasing the pressure of the mixture). The main energy requirement is for refrigeration. Cryogenic separation has been demonstrated for precombustion capture (separating CO_2 from H_2) and for postcombustion capture (separating CO_2 from other flue gases), both at laboratory scale.[36]

OXY-COMBUSTION

Oxy-combustion, also called "oxyfuel combustion," involves burning fuel in the presence of pure oxygen rather than air. When combustion is carefully controlled, essentially all this oxygen can be consumed. Aside from minor impurities such as particulates, oxy-combustion exhaust consists of CO_2 and water vapor. Water vapor is easily removed via condensation, leaving a stream of pure CO_2 suitable for storage or use in products.

While oxy-combustion avoids the need for CO_2 separation, it introduces the need to separate oxygen from other components of air. Commercially, pure oxygen is produced via cryogenic distillation, a process that separates gases based on differences in vapor pressures and boiling points (a form of cryogenic separation, discussed earlier). Currently, the process is energy-intensive and costly.[37] Research efforts focus on developing polymeric membranes or using zeolite or activated carbon adsorption techniques for oxygen separation.[38] Oxy-combustion also requires changes to combustion equipment to accommodate pure oxygen, such as air sealing and alterations of gas flow rates.

Oxy-combustion is widely used in industries such as glassmaking, where it improves furnace energy efficiency, glass quality, and production rate.[39] However, no operating commercial facilities use oxy-combustion for carbon capture, though a number of demonstration projects and pilots have operated successfully. Plans for two commercial facilities have been announced in the United States with total capacity of 1.8 million metric tons of CO_2 per year.[40]

CHEMICAL LOOPING COMBUSTION

Chemical looping combustion is a method of supplying oxygen to a fuel-using process (either combustion or reforming; i.e., to produce hydrogen or chemicals) as a metal oxide rather than a gas.[41] Chemical looping combustion requires two reactors, which are connected in a loop. In the first reactor, called the "air-reactor," metal particles (iron, nickel, barium, manganese, copper, cobalt, or calcium) are oxidized in the presence of air, releasing energy. The metal oxide is then pumped into the second reactor, the "fuel-reactor," where the oxygen is stripped from the metal oxide particles and reacts with the fuel.[42] The reaction in the fuel-reactor can be endothermic (e.g., for iron and nickel carriers) or exothermic (for copper, manganese, and barium carriers).[43]

Chemical looping combustion is more energy-efficient than oxy-combustion because it avoids the costly step of separating oxygen gas from other components of air.[44] However, it has more challenging technical demands. Metal and metal oxide particles must react very quickly and be transferred between the two reactors at a high rate of speed while avoiding gas leakage between the reactors. For example, to sustain a 500-megawatt natural gas power plant, barium oxide must be formed and transported into the fuel-reactor at around 1 metric ton per second.[45] Natural gas must be combusted and the carrier returned to the first reactor at a similar rate. Additionally, particles must not sinter (fuse together).

Chemical looping combustion has been demonstrated only at laboratory scale. Areas of research include improving material handling, using mixes of carrier materials, and embedding carrier nanoparticles in larger nonreactive particles as support or to improve their properties.[46]

CO$_2$ COMPRESSION AND TRANSPORT

In certain cases, the CO$_2$ generated from one process can be consumed by a different process within the same plant. For example, most CO$_2$ from ammonia production goes into making urea (see figure 8.1) in the same facility. In other cases, it is necessary to compress and transport the CO$_2$ to a site where it can be used or stored.

Before CO$_2$ can be transported or stored, it must be compressed, forming a supercritical fluid. Supercritical CO$_2$ behaves more like a liquid than a gas, so more CO$_2$ can be transported per unit volume. CO$_2$ compression is a mature technology, widely used in the fertilizer and petroleum industries, with typical electricity requirements of 80–120 kilowatt-hours per metric ton of CO$_2$.[47] Compression is done in stages. At each stage, a compressor increases the CO$_2$ pressure (causing it to heat up), then the CO$_2$ is cooled, preparing it for the next stage. Individual compressors are generally 80–90 percent efficient, and by optimizing the number of compression stages and the compression ratio used at each stage, it is possible to reduce compression energy requirements by up to 10 percent.[48] Overall, CO$_2$ compression is reasonably well optimized, limiting the potential for future reductions in energy requirements.

Pipelines are the main method of CO$_2$ transport. Over 8,700 kilometers of operating CO$_2$ pipelines exist globally, which together transport roughly 70 million metric tons of CO$_2$ per year. Around 85 percent are in the United States.[49] Most pipelines deliver CO$_2$ to enhanced oil recovery projects. A small pipeline carries about 1 million metric tons of CO$_2$ per year, while a large pipeline may transport 20 million metric tons per year.[50] The cost to transport CO$_2$ by onshore pipeline (excluding costs to construct the pipeline) declines with increasing pipeline capacity, from about $5–$6 per metric ton of CO$_2$ per 250 kilometers in a pipeline with capacity of three million metric tons per year, down to $1.5–$2 per metric ton of CO$_2$ per 250 kilometers in a pipeline with capacity of thirty million metric tons per year.[51]

Pipeline construction costs vary greatly depending on whether the pipeline is onshore or offshore, whether it runs through populated areas, and the type of terrain it traverses. It is possible to repurpose natural gas or oil pipelines to carry CO_2 at roughly 10 percent of the cost of building a new pipeline, although many existing oil and gas pipelines have been in operation for decades and may not have sufficient service life remaining to make conversion worthwhile.[52]

Ships are currently used for CO_2 transport, but only at very small scale. Globally, a total of three million metric tons of CO_2 per year are transported by ship, essentially all for use by the food and beverage industry.[53] Large-scale CO_2 shipping would draw on industries' experience shipping liquified natural gas and liquified petroleum gas, featuring large tanker ships designed to accommodate CO_2, liquefaction and storage facilities at ports, permitting by authorities in various countries, and integration with global maritime operations.[54] Such a system would be expensive, time-consuming to establish, and vulnerable to breakdowns in international shipping logistics. CCUS is best suited to projects located within pipeline range of suitable storage sites, avoiding the need for shipping.

Rail and trucks carry CO_2 at extremely small scale to end user facilities, mostly in the food and beverage industry.[55] Neither truck nor rail is considered capable of shipping CO_2 in sufficient quantities to be practical for CCUS.[56]

GEOLOGICAL CO_2 STORAGE

To effectively mitigate climate change, captured CO_2 must be prevented from reaching the atmosphere for thousands of years. The most-studied and -used mechanism for storing captured CO_2 is injection into underground geological formations. Mineralization (conversion of CO_2 into solid compounds) is an alternative route. (Other proposed mechanisms of carbon storage, such as increasing CO_2 uptake by the oceans, or storing more CO_2 in forests and agricultural lands, generally are not associated with industrial CO_2 capture.)

ENHANCED OIL RECOVERY

Enhanced oil recovery (EOR) is the most technologically mature form of CO_2 storage. EOR has been used for fifty years, and more than one hundred projects currently operate in the United States alone.[57] For EOR, multiple wells are drilled into an oil field. Some are CO_2 injection wells, each of which may be surrounded by three to four production wells, from which oil is extracted. CO_2 is pressurized and pumped into the injection wells, where it enhances oil production through two mechanisms.[58]

- The liquid CO_2 serves as a solvent that is miscible with oil, helping to free oil particles from underground minerals. Additionally, the oil-CO_2 mixture has lower viscosity than pure oil, so it flows more readily.
- The CO_2 increases the pressure underground, driving oil away from the injection wells and toward the production wells.

Some of the injected CO_2 emerges with the produced oil. This CO_2 is separated from the oil and reinjected.[59]

The quantity of carbon that remains underground is roughly comparable to the carbon resulting from the produced oil. For each barrel of oil produced, 300–600 kilograms of CO_2 are injected (varying between EOR projects and over the lifetime of a single project), while a barrel of oil produces 500 kilograms of CO_2 (400 when combusted and a further 100 from its processing and transport).[60] However, this omits upstream greenhouse gas emissions associated with obtaining the injected CO_2, including the energy required for carbon capture and CO_2 compression and transport.

Some studies argue that EOR reduces CO_2 emissions by assuming that demand for oil is fixed and that EOR displaces conventional oil production, and/or by evaluating EOR under narrow system boundaries that omit the upstream energy required for CO_2 capture, compression, and transport (including production of that energy and any associated methane leakage); the downstream emissions from transporting, refining, and using produced oil; or both.[61] Fixed oil demand is a poor assumption, as many energy sources can substitute for oil, and even energy demand is not fixed (as it can be influenced by efficiency technologies and changes in behavior). Studies that use a full-life-cycle analysis find that carbon capture with EOR adds net carbon to the atmosphere.[62] Therefore, to achieve greenhouse gas mitigation, EOR is not a suitable means of carbon storage.

It may be possible to identify specific projects where directing captured carbon toward EOR reduces emissions relative to taking no action, such as by using captured CO_2 in an existing EOR project that otherwise would continue to operate using naturally occurring CO_2 from underground deposits (see figure 8.1). However, there is a risk that CCUS-EOR infrastructure may be forced to retire long before its service life has elapsed if climate policy and clean technology sufficiently reduce oil demand or, conversely, that the existence of CCUS-EOR investments will pressure regulators to delay crucial decarbonization policy steps to avoid inflicting economic losses on energy firms. Given these risks, CCUS-EOR is not an economically or environmentally prudent method for industries to achieve their decarbonization objectives.

Like EOR, enhanced gas recovery (injection of CO_2 into gas fields to increase production) and enhanced coal bed methane recovery (using CO_2 to free methane from coal seams) undermine the greenhouse gas benefits of carbon capture and are incompatible with zero-carbon industry.[63]

DEDICATED GEOLOGICAL STORAGE

Dedicated geological storage refers to underground injection of CO_2 not associated with oil or gas production. Storage must be deep enough to maintain sufficient pressure to keep CO_2 in a liquid state (typically below 800 meters), and the geological formation must include a layer of impermeable rock above the CO_2, called "caprock," to prevent its upward migration.[64] The two main suitable terrain types are depleted oil and gas fields and saline aquifers, porous underground rock formations filled with saltwater. CO_2 has been injected into saline aquifers in six commercial-scale projects and thirteen demonstration projects, whereas depleted oil and gas fields have been used in six demonstration projects. Injection into other geological formations, particularly basalt deposits, is possible but less studied.[65]

Over time frames up to one thousand years, two mechanisms primarily immobilize injected CO_2.

- **Structural trapping**: the caprock and other surrounding formations physically block movement of the dense CO_2 plume.
- **Residual trapping**: any volume of rock through which the CO_2 plume passes retains some CO_2 trapped in the pore space between rock granules.

On longer time scales, other trapping mechanisms become more important, including solubility trapping (CO_2 dissolves into the water in a saline aquifer), ionic trapping (CO_2 is converted into aqueous bicarbonate and carbonate ions), and, finally, mineral trapping (precipitation as a carbonate mineral) (figure 8.3).

Studies broadly support the view that geological storage can securely contain injected CO_2 over long time scales. A 2005 review by the Intergovernmental Panel on Climate Change (IPCC) concluded that if reservoirs are appropriately selected and managed, 99 percent of the CO_2 is likely to remain below ground for over one thousand years.[66] A more recent IPCC review that considered risks of unregulated drilling and limited wellbore integrity found that 70 percent would be retained over a longer, ten-thousand-year time scale.[67] The risk of CO_2 stored in the oceans or biosphere (e.g., in forests) being released is greater than the risk of CO_2 leakage from underground storage.[68]

Estimates of suitable geological storage capacity vary widely (4,000–55,000 billion metric tons), but all estimates vastly exceed the capacity that would be needed to achieve a 1.5°C global warming target.[69] For instance, median estimates of CO_2 storage demand through 2070 for ninety 1.5-degree-compatible scenarios considered by the IPCC ranged from 275–425 billion metric tons. However, storage is not evenly distributed

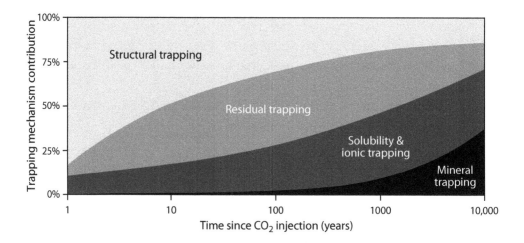

FIGURE 8.3 CO$_2$ Trapping Mechanisms The relative contribution of CO$_2$ trapping mechanisms in geological storage varies with the length of time since CO$_2$ injection.

Source: Stephen A. Rackley, *Carbon Capture and Storage*, 2nd ed. (Oxford, UK: Butterworth-Heinemann, 2017).

worldwide, and in a future with aggressive CCUS deployment, certain regions (such as Japan) could theoretically encounter storage constraints.[70]

MINERALIZATION

Mineralization is the conversion of CO$_2$ into solid carbonate minerals. While this process happens naturally over long time scales (including after underground CO$_2$ injection), it can be accelerated.

CO$_2$ can be combined with calcium oxide (CaO) or magnesium oxide (MgO), but these minerals are reactive and therefore seldom found in nature.[71] (CaO is used for mineralization in the cement industry, where cement takes up CO$_2$ during curing and for decades following manufacture. However, producing cement emits more process CO$_2$ than it sequesters, so this is not a scalable mechanism of carbon storage; see chapter 3.) More abundant, naturally occurring candidate minerals are silicates such as olivine, wollastonite, and serpentine, which react with CO_2 to form ferrous carbonate ($FeCO_3$), calcium carbonate ($CaCO_3$), and magnesium carbonate ($MgCO_3$).[72]

Mineralization is not a commercialized technology. Several routes are being researched, the most mature of which is direct aqueous carbonation. Various indirect chemical pathways are also being studied, including some involving enzymes or cyanobacteria.[73] At least two start-up companies are seeking to commercialize mineralization technology.[74]

CO_2 USE IN PRODUCTS

An alternative to underground geological storage is converting CO_2 into a carbon-containing product. Today, 82 percent of CO_2 used in products goes into making urea (see figure 8.1), 90 percent of which is converted into fertilizer.[75] Other uses include carbonated beverages, use as a shielding gas for welding, and various minor uses. Though a very small portion of these products may retain CO_2 for decades (such as urea-derived melamine resins used in building materials), the vast majority of existing CO_2-using products release the CO_2 shortly after the product is used (e.g., when fertilizer is applied to a field or a carbonated drink is opened). Therefore, the ability to use products as a form of long-term CO_2 storage hinges on the development of a large market for CO_2-derived materials that will not chemically break down over thousands of years.

Very few products pass this test. Chemical products (including plastics) do not have sufficient longevity (see chapter 2). CO_2 can be combined with green hydrogen to make synthetic fuels (chapter 7), but these fuels release CO_2 when combusted. Even if synthetic fuel displaces conventional fuel, this recycles the carbon molecules only once, which is insufficient for climate protection if the captured carbon originally came from a fossil fuel (or from limestone calcination). High-performance materials like carbon fiber and nanotubes may have sufficient longevity (carbon fiber resists oxidation up to 700°C), but their production is energy-intensive (making carbon fiber requires fourteen times as much energy as producing primary steel), and their market size is small, making them impractical for large-scale carbon storage.[76]

Perhaps the only industrial product with sufficient market size and ability to store CO_2 over long periods is limestone aggregate, which can serve as the nonbinder component in concrete, fill material in construction, and similar uses. Aggregate is essentially the output of mineralization (discussed earlier), sold to recoup some costs.

For climate protection, dedicated geological storage remains the most viable option for disposing of captured CO_2, with mineralization playing a supporting role.

CCUS's CONTRIBUTION TO ZERO-CARBON INDUSTRY

To achieve significant economy-wide emissions reductions, CCUS would need to scale up to an economically challenging degree. For example, the International Energy Agency proposes that CCUS provide about 20 percent of total abatement achieved in their net-zero scenario, but this would require a CCUS industry that is roughly four times larger than today's global oil industry (in terms of volume of compressed CO_2 stored versus volume of oil produced).[77] It may be particularly difficult for CCUS to scale so greatly because, unlike oil production, CCUS requires policy interventions (such as carbon pricing) to deliver economic value to CCUS providers.

CCUS is best used to address specific types of industrial emissions, mostly within the next two to three decades. During that time, it may be useful for decarbonizing high-temperature heat for nonmetallic minerals, CO_2 process emissions, and some retrofit applications, such as blast furnaces used for steelmaking. This also buys time for the electricity grid to decarbonize and expand (chapter 6). Beyond twenty to thirty years, industry should shift to electrification for high-temperature heat needs, and fossil-burning plants should have largely retired. Thereafter, CCUS may still be useful to address CO_2 process emissions, such as from calcination of limestone in cement-making.

III

POLICIES

9

CARBON PRICING AND OTHER
FINANCIAL POLICIES

Although cost-effective decarbonization opportunities exist today (particularly in energy and material efficiency), the transition to zero-carbon industry would be slow and incomplete without policy support. Financial policies change the landscape in which firms operate, facilitating and rewarding low-carbon production while making businesses pay for harms caused by their pollution. Well-designed policy produces a competitive landscape in which business decisions that optimize profit also result in lower greenhouse gas emissions, co-benefits such as public health improvements and job creation, and improved social equity.

Financial policies impose monetary costs or provide rewards to firms in response to their emissions, energy or material use, or use of dirty or clean technologies. These policies include carbon pricing (carbon taxes or cap and trade), green banks and lending mechanisms, subsidies and tax credits, fees, rebates, and "feebates." (Green public procurement and financial support for R&D are covered in chapters 10 and 11.)

Financial policies are well suited to influencing industry because, relative to other actors in society, manufacturers face fewer nonprice barriers and more often respond to policy in a profit-optimizing manner. For instance, a residential landlord may decline to invest in cost-effective, energy-efficient appliances because the tenant is responsible for paying the energy bills (a problem known as "split incentives"), whereas industrial firms typically purchase their manufacturing equipment and pay their own energy costs. A consumer purchasing a car may base their decision on up-front price (while disregarding lifetime fuel costs), aesthetics of the vehicle, or emotion. A firm buying an industrial boiler is more likely to choose whichever model generates sufficient steam with high reliability while minimizing lifetime costs. Although industrial firms do encounter market barriers (see chapter 10), can be risk-averse regarding new technologies, and sometimes decline to pursue cost-effective options (for reasons discussed in chapter 4), they generally are policy-responsive and rational, making it easier to use financial policies to achieve a desired outcome.

Financial policies are powerful, but they are not a panacea. They work best in concert with strong standards, policies to promote R&D, and other supporting policies (chapters 10–11).

CARBON PRICING

Carbon pricing policies put a monetary value on the right to emit greenhouse gases. Despite the name, carbon pricing can be applied to all greenhouse gases (converted into CO_2-equivalent; CO_2e), allowing for more ways to reduce emissions and thus a lower cost per metric ton of CO_2e abated than pricing CO_2 alone. There are two general approaches to carbon pricing—carbon taxes and cap and trade—as well as hybrid mechanisms.

A carbon tax is a fee firms must pay for every metric ton of greenhouse gases they emit. The fee should escalate over time (in inflation-adjusted terms) to incentivize stronger emissions reductions until zero emissions are achieved. Fee increases should be specified by formula in the enacted policy (i.e., increases do not require action by politicians or regulators). This provides long-term price certainty (which industries prefer when making investment decisions) and helps insulate the policy from political interference. A carbon tax provides certainty regarding the costs producers incur to emit greenhouse gases, but the resulting level of emissions is uncertain, as it is based on ever-changing factors such as fuel prices and the availability and cost of clean manufacturing technology.

Cap and trade, also known as an "emissions trading system," is a mechanism whereby producers must own permits to emit greenhouse gases. Ideally, permits are auctioned off by the government, so their price is determined by the marketplace. (In practice, many cap-and-trade systems give some free emissions permits to industrial producers, with the quantity of free permits gradually declining over time.) Producers that are able to cheaply reduce emissions will undertake those technical measures rather than buy permits, while producers facing high costs to abate emissions will instead buy permits. Thus, the permit price will settle at the cost of the marginal abatement measure, which can be lowered through advances in clean production technology. A cap-and-trade system should auction fewer and fewer permits every year until zero emissions are achieved, with permit availability specified by formula, similar to formulaic increases in a carbon tax rate.

There are complexities to designing a robust cap-and-trade system, such as whether or not any permits are distributed for free, whether they can be banked, if offsets are permitted, and whether or not to link different jurisdictions, as well as other considerations (discussed later). A cap-and-trade system provides certainty regarding the quantity of greenhouse gases that may be emitted, but the cost to firms is uncertain, as it depends on the market price of permits.

A hybrid system contains features of both carbon tax and cap-and-trade policies. This is usually implemented as a "price collar" in a cap-and-trade system. There is a minimum price below which permits are not sold (i.e., a minimum starting bid in each auction), and if the permit price rises above a specified ceiling, the government creates and auctions off additional permits, keeping the price below the ceiling. (In real-world experience across multiple cap-and-trade systems, permit prices have been lower than regulators expected, so a price floor is far more likely to come into play than a price ceiling, at least in the near term.)[1]

Alternatively, a hybrid system can be designed as a carbon tax with a tax adjustment mechanism, which automatically increases the tax rate if specific emissions targets are not met. Relative to an ordinary carbon tax, a tax adjustment mechanism reduces the odds of extremely high emissions and increases the probability of meeting emissions targets.[2] Hybrid systems balance uncertainty regarding costs and uncertainty regarding total emissions.

Carbon pricing has become common globally. As of 2021, sixty-four carbon-pricing mechanisms were in effect, covering 21.5 percent of global greenhouse gas emissions.[3] Between systems, the emissions price varies widely, as does the share of covered emissions due to exempted industries, fuels, or greenhouse gases (figure 9.1). To date, major carbon pricing systems that cover industry (including those in the European Union, California, Canada, and China) have employed cap and trade with free allocation of some emissions permits to affected industries. Free permit allocation and carbon border adjustments, two methods of limiting carbon pricing impacts on industry, are discussed in the industrial competitiveness, leakage, and border adjustments section later in this chapter.

CARBON PRICING EMISSIONS REDUCTION MECHANISMS

Carbon pricing can reduce emissions through three mechanisms: technology switching, demand reduction, and smart use of tax revenues.

Technology switching involves industries improving their efficiency or substituting low-emissions technologies (such as electrification or green hydrogen) for high-emissions technologies (e.g., fossil fuel combustion). Carbon pricing best incentivizes technology switching when higher- and lower-emissions pathways are commercialized and available to manufacturers, but the low-emissions pathway costs marginally more. A modest carbon tax can shift this balance and favor the cleaner production pathway. For example, low-temperature heat can be delivered by either fossil fuel combustion or industrial heat pumps, and heat pumps may be only slightly more (or less) expensive

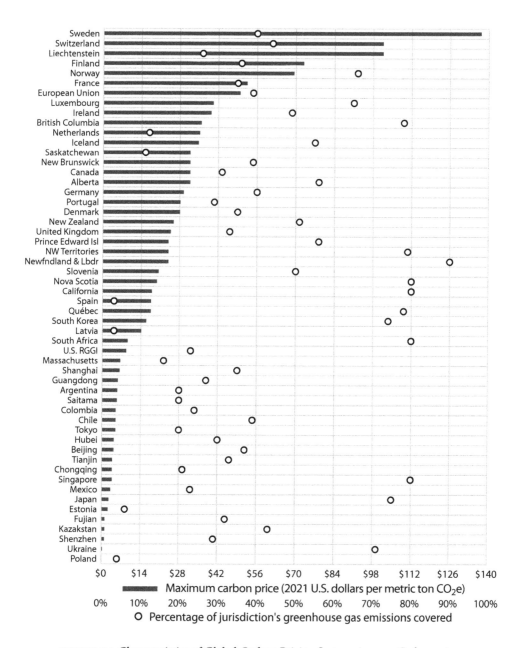

FIGURE 9.1 **Characteristics of Global Carbon Pricing Systems in 2021** Carbon pricing systems for which data are not available (such as China's national emissions trading system, which launched in 2021) are excluded. Some jurisdictions charge different rates on different industries, fuels, or greenhouse gases; the maximum such rate is shown. RGGI = Regional Greenhouse Gas Initiative.

Source: World Bank, "State and Trends of Carbon Pricing 2021," May 25, 2021, https://openknowledge.worldbank.org/handle/10986/35620.

to operate, depending on electricity rates. Therefore, carbon pricing is well suited to incentivize electrification of low-temperature processes, which encompass roughly a third of all industrial heat demand (chapter 6). Similarly, carbon pricing can encourage the use of commercialized, low-cost technologies that reduce non-CO_2 greenhouse gas emissions, such as thermally decomposing by-product nitrous oxide rather than venting it or using methane detectors to locate and plug methane leaks.

Carbon pricing is not effective at incentivizing technology switching when no low-carbon production pathways have been commercialized or where low-carbon pathways are far more expensive than traditional pathways. In these cases, producers will simply pay the fee rather than switch to cleaner technologies.

Demand reduction results from manufacturers paying carbon pricing fees and passing on some or all those costs to consumers by increasing the price of products. Consumers respond by buying fewer goods, so fewer goods need to be manufactured, reducing emissions. For most goods (i.e., products other than fossil fuels and F-gases), demand reduction is not the preferred mechanism by which carbon pricing should operate. That is because demand reduction has a high cost per metric ton of CO_2e abated, resulting in low economic efficiency. Higher prices of goods can be a burden on consumers and may impact economic growth.

When technology switching is expensive or impossible, a carbon price will primarily act through demand reduction. Therefore, carbon pricing is not the best choice when clean production pathways are technologically immature. Other policies, such as R&D support (chapter 11) and financial incentives for demonstration and early commercial plants using clean technologies, can help drive down the cost of new technologies. Once those costs begin to approach the costs of traditional production methods, carbon pricing can be instituted.

Third, carbon pricing revenues can be used to fund programs that reduce emissions, discussed in the carbon pricing revenue use section of this chapter.

WHO SHOULDERS CARBON PRICING COSTS?

Policy makers should understand the dynamics that determine the extent to which carbon pricing's costs are borne by end consumers versus high-emissions manufacturers.

Many industrial products are tradable commodities: they are the same no matter how they were produced and are sold by multiple producers within a geographic area. The price of a traded commodity, like methanol, is set by the market rather than each individual producer. Specifically, the price that competing methanol producers can charge is set by the "marginal producer": the producer with the highest costs of production that is nonetheless able to sell methanol at a price buyers will pay. Low-cost producers pocket the difference between the market price and their own costs, achieving profit. The marginal producer is barely able to cover its costs, so it has near-zero profit.

Without carbon pricing, using today's technology, it is generally more expensive to produce goods cleanly. Producers using cleaner technology tend to be located at or near the margin. When a carbon price is instituted, the costs of dirty plants will increase by more than the costs of the cleaner plants at the margin. This reduces the gap between the market price of methanol and the dirty producers' costs, reducing their profit. This reduction in dirty producers' profit is one source of carbon pricing's revenue.

Cleaner producers at the margin must raise their prices (unless they have zero emissions), passing on most of their increased costs to buyers (with the specific cost pass-through determined by the price elasticity of demand for methanol). This increases the market price of methanol for all buyers, which is the other source of carbon pricing's revenue.

The ratio of the marginal producer's emissions intensity to the emissions intensity of the low-cost producers determines the balance between these two revenue sources.

This can be illustrated by a simplified example. Imagine a market containing two competing methanol plants. One incurs production costs of $400 per ton of methanol and emits 200 kilograms of CO_2e per ton. The other plant incurs production costs of $800 per ton and emits no greenhouse gases. The market price for methanol is $800 per ton, the marginal producer's cost. A carbon price of $1 per kilogram CO_2e will increase the dirty producer's costs to $600 per ton and will not affect the clean producer's costs, so the market price remains $800 per ton. Buyers' costs do not rise. Carbon pricing generates revenue of $200 per ton sold by the dirty producer, all of which comes out of that producer's profits (which have been reduced from $400 to $200 per ton).

In contrast, if both plants have the same emissions intensity (200 kilograms of CO_2e per ton of methanol), the carbon price causes methanol's market price to rise to $1,000 per ton, the new production cost of the marginal producer. The higher market price slightly reduces demand. However, per unit of methanol sold, each producer's profits are unaffected because the increase in market price counteracts the increase in that producer's costs. The carbon tax generates $200 in revenue per ton of methanol sold, all of which is funded by price increases on consumers.

Policy makers may prefer that a carbon price be funded as much as possible out of the profits of dirty producers rather than by imposing higher costs on consumers. That leads to the following implications for policy makers.

- A carbon price is a good policy option when the highest-cost producers of a commodity are using much cleaner production processes than low-cost producers because more of the cost burden will be shouldered by reduction of dirty firms' profits.
- A carbon price is less compelling when all firms have similar emissions because the carbon price will be shouldered by consumers.
- If the marginal-cost producer has higher emissions than low-cost producers, carbon pricing increases the low-cost producers' profits. This profit increase and carbon pricing revenues are both funded by higher costs to consumers. Carbon pricing can impose consumer costs far greater than revenues raised when applied to a market in which marginal-cost producers have much higher emissions than lower-cost producers (e.g., in markets in which marginal producers have high costs not because they use clean processes but because

they use outdated and inefficient fossil-fuel-burning equipment). Other policies, particularly emissions standards (see chapter 10), are more cost-effective than carbon pricing at reducing emissions from these markets.

The discussion in this section applies to commodities. For a differentiated product, such as a patented medicine, there is only one producer. In this case, costs will be borne by consumers, but the policy will not increase the firm's profits.

CARBON PRICING REVENUE USE

The previous section refers to carbon pricing revenues, but not all of this money goes to the government. Some of it funds industries' greenhouse gas mitigation measures. Only when mitigation is more expensive will industries pay the carbon price. Thus, the more effectively a carbon price incentivizes greenhouse gas mitigation, the smaller the government's revenue fraction will be. Unless carbon pricing is heavily funded from dirty producers' profits, the public revenues raised are not sufficient to fully offset increased costs to consumers.

Additionally, carbon pricing revenues are likely to shrink as emissions go down, ultimately reaching zero when the economy is fully decarbonized.

Therefore, carbon pricing cannot be a permanent funding mechanism for government. Rather, policy makers should see carbon pricing revenues as a precious resource, available only for the next three to six decades, to be used strategically to achieve maximum environmental, economic, and social benefits.

Among the best uses of carbon price revenues are programs that reduce industrial greenhouse gas emissions, including R&D funding (see chapter 11), cost-sharing for demonstration and early commercial deployment, and capitalizing green banks (discussed later). Revenues also may fund industrial energy efficiency upgrades, particularly for small manufacturers for whom making the initial capital investment in new equipment is an important barrier to implementing cost-effective efficiency improvements. There also exist projects outside the industry sector where revenues could be spent to achieve environmental and economic benefits. For example, in the United States, every $1 invested in public transit generates between $1.50 and over $3 in economic benefits while lowering greenhouse gas emissions.[4] To support equity goals, some funding can be allocated to disadvantaged communities and to help displaced workers, such as coal miners, navigate the transition to clean industry (chapter 12).

A different approach is to use carbon pricing revenues to lower other tax rates, such as reducing income, payroll, sales, or value-added taxes. This improves economic efficiency by taxing a harmful externality (pollutant emissions) instead of things that contribute positively to the economy (employment, income, and spending). Similarly, carbon pricing revenues can fund a "carbon dividend," a rebate of revenues to the populace. Coupling carbon pricing with tax reductions or a carbon dividend can make the policy revenue-neutral, which can be attractive to lawmakers who do not wish to expand government spending. It also raises the question of how to distribute benefits.

- Equal payments to all eligible individuals, such as all citizens or all adults, would more than offset the increases in prices of energy and goods for lower- and middle-income households, who spend less on energy and energy-intensive goods than high-income households.[5] Such proposals are popular with voters, all of whom would receive payments.[6]
- Tax reductions or dividend payments could be targeted at the lowest-earning members of society. This may do more to increase GDP (since lower-income people spend a greater share of their income) and reduce income inequality than equal payments. However, it narrows political support for the carbon pricing policy, since fewer people would receive payments.[7]
- Tax reductions may be targeted at energy-intensive, trade-exposed industries. Payments linked to production (or other positive traits, such as jobs) can offset any competitive harms those industries

would have suffered from carbon pricing while giving them an incentive to reduce emissions and thereby save money. This is superior to exempting these industries from carbon pricing or granting them free emissions permits, as it protects their financial competitiveness without diluting carbon pricing's incentive to decarbonize. Tax reductions for affected industries can prevent job losses and increase economic growth in communities where these industries are located.

CARBON PRICING DESIGN CONSIDERATIONS

A number of factors must be kept in mind when designing an effective carbon pricing system. Among the first choices is whether to use a carbon tax, cap and trade, or a hybrid system. These are the main advantages of cap and trade.

- **Lower cost to industry**. Trading of permits among covered facilities helps ensure that abatement comes from those facilities facing the lowest costs to cut their emissions, so the market price of tradable emissions permits will generally be lower than the carbon tax rate that would deliver equivalent economy-wide total abatement.
- **Known climate performance**. Greenhouse gas emissions from covered industries cannot legally exceed the quantity of permits issued.
- **Ease of linking to other regions**. Multiple jurisdictions with cap-and-trade systems of similar stringency can agree to mutually recognize emissions permits, facilitating expansion of cap and trade across borders. Jurisdictions with weak cap-and-trade policies may be incentivized to strengthen their policies to link with an interregional cap-and-trade system.

The main advantages of a carbon tax are as follows.

- **Simpler implementation**. There is no need to design tradable permits, run auctions, validate carbon offsets, and so on. The carbon tax may be collected through existing tax collection infrastructure.

- **Resistance to loopholes**. Cap-and-trade systems often come under political pressure to distribute free permits to specific industries, exempt smaller emitters, allow questionable carbon offsets, or create other loopholes. A carbon tax has fewer design complexities and fewer opportunities for loopholes.

- **Known cost of emissions**. The carbon tax rate is set by legislation and does not vary with market demand, providing certainty to manufacturers.

- **Preferred by environmental justice groups**. Facilities that emit greenhouse gases often also emit conventional pollutants, such as particulates, that harm the health of people living nearby. Greenhouse gas abatement strategies, such as switching to more energy-efficient equipment or electrification, can also reduce conventional pollutant emissions. Polluting facilities are disproportionately located in low-income and minority communities. Environmental justice advocates often prefer carbon taxes, as they worry that cap and trade's permit trading and carbon offsets may help companies delay cutting emissions in disadvantaged communities.[8] Real-world evidence regarding the impact of cap- and trade on pollution in disadvantaged communities is mixed and is complicated by the fact that direct emissions standards have sometimes been bartered away when implementing cap and trade.[9]

A hybrid system based on tradable permits with a price collar shares most of the advantages and disadvantages of cap and trade, while a hybrid system based on a carbon tax with a tax adjustment mechanism shares most advantages and disadvantages of the carbon tax. Ultimately, either approach can be designed to function well, so it may be prudent to pursue whichever strategy is more politically achievable.

Several other important carbon pricing design considerations exist.

Scope of coverage. Existing carbon pricing systems generally apply only to the power sector and, sometimes, specific industries. For example, Sweden has the highest carbon tax rate in the world ($126 per metric ton of CO_2e in 2020), but the entire industry sector is exempted.[10] (Some Swedish industries are covered by the EU emissions trading scheme, but it has a lower tax rate and allocates free emissions allowances to industry.) Going upstream and applying carbon pricing to more emitters achieves better environmental performance, sometimes lowers cost per ton abated, and is fairer.

It may be difficult to directly levy a carbon price on numerous small emitters. For energy-related emissions, this can be addressed by levying the carbon price on fuel suppliers (producers and importers) based on the emissions that will result when the fuel they sell is burned. For example, California's cap-and-trade system requires only entities responsible for at least 25,000 metric tons of CO_2e per year to buy emissions permits. This requirement applies not only to electricity generators and industrial facilities but also to fuel suppliers, so emissions from fuel combustion (even from small emitters) are covered by the cap. As a result, the program requires only four hundred fifty entities to buy emissions permits yet covers 85 percent of California's greenhouse gas emissions.[11] (For non-energy-related greenhouse gas emissions, such as nitrous oxide from nitric and adipic acid production, it may be necessary to charge emitters directly.)

Banking. In a cap-and-trade system, permits may expire the year they are issued or may be held to be used in later years. Allowing emitters to bank permits can help prevent shortages and control price swings.[12] However, if the permit price is too low (for example, if emissions drop faster than regulators expected, leading to a surplus of permits), banking exacerbates this issue by allowing emitters to buy large quantities of permits cheaply and use them in future years. Therefore, banking should always be accompanied by a robust price floor.

Offsets. In a carbon pricing system allowing offsets, an emitter may pay another company to reduce emissions or sequester CO_2 in specific ways, rather than reducing its own emissions or buying a permit. Examples of offset activities include protecting forests from logging, providing anaerobic digesters to farms, destroying F-gases, and capturing methane from coal mines.[13] Offsets can reduce costs to industry by broadening compliance options. They can be used to improve environmental justice and equity by prioritizing projects in disadvantaged communities.

However, offsets have drawbacks. First, there is a risk that offsets do not represent additional emissions abatement. For example, a forest owner who sells offsets in exchange for not cutting down trees might have chosen to leave some of those trees standing even in the absence of offset payments. Another risk is that offsets may not represent permanent carbon storage. For example, wildfires have burned at least six forests that are backing carbon offsets in the western United States, releasing carbon that was supposed to remain trapped to compensate for industrial and power sector emissions.[14]

Offsets present difficulties and must be designed carefully to avoid weakening a carbon pricing system. Key design principles include the following.

- The additionality and quantity of abatement should be carefully vetted by an independent, third-party accrediting body.
- Only projects that reliably offer permanent abatement should be eligible to provide offsets.
- Inclusion of equity criteria can enable an offset program to help promote environmental justice and reduce income inequality.
- Offsets should be limited to a small percentage of covered entities' total emissions. This preserves the incentive for industries to reduce their own emissions by shifting to cleaner fuels and production processes.

Linking jurisdictions. Multiple jurisdictions can link their cap-and-trade programs, forming a single pool of emissions allowances. Larger covered areas provide more abatement opportunities, lowering average costs to industry. This may be particularly useful for small jurisdictions that have limited abatement opportunities within their territory. Linked programs need to agree to a common set of rules, which is beneficial when members are required to run stringent, well-designed programs. However, linking to a jurisdiction with abundant low-cost abatement opportunities (for example, a region with many inefficient, coal-burning facilities) may cause abatement projects to cluster in that jurisdiction, stalling progress on decarbonization activities elsewhere.

Generally, linking regions in a well-designed cap-and-trade system is beneficial, but each jurisdiction may wish to require that a certain percentage of abatement come from within its borders, to spread out environmental benefits and ensure each region continues to make progress toward its emissions goals.

INDUSTRIAL COMPETITIVENESS, LEAKAGE, AND BORDER ADJUSTMENTS

A frequent concern is whether industrial carbon pricing will reduce the competitiveness of domestic industries relative to foreign manufacturers or cause "leakage," domestic industries shifting production to countries with weaker environmental rules. Limiting leakage is worthwhile because a high leakage rate negatively affects domestic jobs and production while reducing carbon pricing's emissions abatement.

It is challenging to accurately estimate leakage risk.[15] Study estimates vary widely. Some studies find no evidence that leakage would occur.[16] Others find potential leakage rates ranging as low as 2 percent or as high as 25 percent for all industries, and 5–40 percent for the most energy-intensive industries.[17]

Time frame strongly affects leakage predictions. It is difficult to quickly move production abroad due to the need to acquire or expand foreign facilities, hire local workers, rearrange supply chains, and so on. Therefore, leakage is most relevant over long time frames. With an increasing number of countries setting ambitious emissions targets and enacting climate policy, it is difficult for firms to be confident that carbon pricing or other climate-focused regulation will not be introduced in a given location in the coming years. Therefore, firms may require at least some advantages unrelated to climate policy before choosing to relocate, such as simplification of supply chains, lower labor costs, or lower fuel costs.

Policy makers enacting carbon pricing can limit leakage. To date, the most common mechanism has been to exempt certain industries from carbon pricing or distribute free emissions permits to domestic manufacturers. These techniques may reduce leakage, but they also dampen or eliminate the incentive to decarbonize, reducing the effectiveness of the carbon pricing policy.[18]

A better approach is to ensure that all firms must pay for every unit of greenhouse gases they emit but provide counterbalancing subsidies to domestic manufacturers linked to other positive traits the government wishes to encourage. For example, subsidies may be based on a firm's contribution to GDP or the number of high-quality jobs the firm provides. Firms that perform well on these metrics can receive subsidies sufficient to offset (or more than offset) the carbon price, which protects their competitiveness without dampening the carbon price's incentive to decarbonize. On the other hand, companies that perform poorly on these metrics will not receive subsidies, so the carbon price will increase their net costs.

Another powerful leakage-limiting mechanism is to include "border adjustments" whereby goods imported from jurisdictions with weaker carbon pricing are taxed according to the embodied emissions in the imported goods and the difference in tax rates between the foreign and domestic jurisdictions. This avoids giving advantage to goods imported from places with poor environmental protections. Similarly, domestic firms that export to jurisdictions with weak or absent carbon pricing are given a carbon tax rebate based on the difference in tax rates domestically and in the export market. This prevents carbon pricing from putting domestic manufacturers at a disadvantage when exporting their products.

One of the challenges of implementing border adjustments is knowing the embodied emissions in imported goods. One option is for policy makers to require foreign firms or importers who wish to sell in the domestic, regulated market to monitor and self-report their emissions (following government-specified standards for emissions measurement and reporting), ideally subject to independent third-party verification. Organizations such as CDP and the Science Based Targets initiative help firms accurately report their emissions and identify decarbonization opportunities. (For more on these groups, see chapter 11.) When foreign firms decline to comply, options include barring those products from import or allowing their import but applying a default, unfavorable emissions intensity, so foreign firms do not gain advantage by failing to disclose their goods' embodied emissions.

The European Union is in the process of establishing the world's first carbon border adjustment mechanism.[19] The proposal passed by the European Parliament covers a range of goods, including cement, iron and steel, fertilizers, plastic polymers, organic and inorganic basic chemicals, ammonia, and hydrogen. During a transitional phase from 2023 to 2026, importers will be required to monitor and report embedded emissions. Carbon price payments will begin in 2027.[20]

An international carbon pricing system with border adjustments would not affect all countries equally. Figure 9.2 shows the relative greenhouse gas intensity of industries in specific geographies. Brazil, Canada, the EU, Mexico, and the United States have relatively low emissions intensities, while China, India, and Russia have high emissions intensities. Countries with low emissions intensities stand to gain from the implementation and international expansion of carbon pricing with border adjustments, as this helps improve their products' competitiveness. Manufacturers with high emissions intensities are incentivized to adopt cleaner production technologies no matter where the firms are located. In this way, carbon pricing can reduce emissions even outside the regulated geographical area.

Differences in emissions per unit of economic output (figure 9.2) partly reflect variance in environmental performance, such as differences in fuels used by industry, CO_2 intensity of purchased electricity, use of emissions control technology (for example, thermal or catalytic destruction of nitrous oxide from nitric and adipic acid manufacturing), and production processes (for example, most U.S. steel comes from electric arc furnaces, while most Chinese steel comes from blast furnaces). However, this metric can also be influenced by factors unrelated to environmental performance, such as whether a country tends to produce higher-priced "luxury" or lower-priced "normal" versions of specific goods (since higher sales prices inflate economic output) and types of business activities in each region (for example, in the computer, electronic, and optical products industry, more product design and

	Brazil	Canada	China	EU	India	Mexico	Russia	USA
Agriculture, forestry, & fishing	1.2	1.4	1.2	1.2	0.9	1.6	1.8	1.0
Energy product extraction	0.8	1.2	1.7	0.7	4.5	1.2	1.7	0.8
Nonenergy product extraction	0.4	1.1	1.6	0.6	3.4	0.7	2.3	0.7
Mining support activities	0.9	0.8	2.7	1.0	1.3	0.8	2.2	0.5
Food, beverages, and tobacco	0.9	0.9	1.3	0.7	1.4	0.8	1.6	0.9
Textiles, apparel, and leather	0.5	0.7	1.2	0.5	1.5	0.7	1.3	0.7
Wood and wood products	0.7	0.9	1.3	0.6	2.6	1.2	2.1	0.7
Paper products and printing	0.8	0.8	1.4	0.7	1.9	0.9	2.0	0.8
Refined petroleum and coke	0.7	1.0	1.2	1.0	1.4	1.5	1.3	0.8
Chemicals & pharmaceuticals	0.6	0.9	1.6	0.5	1.3	0.8	3.4	0.6
Rubber and plastic products	0.5	0.5	1.4	0.4	1.1	0.6	1.5	0.5
Nonmetallic mineral products	0.5	0.7	1.2	0.8	1.9	0.7	2.1	0.8
Basic metals	0.9	0.7	1.2	0.6	1.8	0.5	2.5	0.7
Fabricated metal products	0.7	0.5	1.7	0.5	3.4	0.8	2.7	0.6
Computers and electronics	0.6	0.6	1.4	0.5	2.0	0.9	1.9	0.3
Electrical equipment	0.7	0.5	1.4	0.5	1.8	0.6	2.2	0.5
Machinery and equipment	0.6	0.5	1.6	0.4	2.2	0.7	2.5	0.6
Motor vehicles and trailers	0.9	0.7	1.8	0.5	2.7	0.8	2.8	0.8
Other transport equipment	0.9	0.6	1.9	0.5	2.3	0.9	2.1	0.7
Other manufacturing & repair	0.5	0.5	1.5	0.4	2.2	0.9	2.2	0.5
Economy-wide	0.6	0.7	1.8	0.5	2.1	0.8	2.3	0.6

Key to background colors	0.3-0.5	0.6-0.7	0.8-1.0	1.1-1.5	1.6-2.0	2.1-2.5	>2.5

FIGURE 9.2 CO_2 Intensity of Economic Output in Various Regions Relative to the World Average in 2015 Economic output refers to the financial value of produced goods converted into a common currency. Each industry's global average CO_2 intensity is set to 1.0. For example, the value of 0.7 for "Basic metals" in the United States indicates that the U.S. basic metals industry emits 70 percent as much CO_2 as that industry's global average per unit output.

Source: Catrina Rorke and Greg Bertelsen, *America's Carbon Advantage* (report, Climate Leadership Council, Washington, D.C., September 2020), https://clcouncil.org /reports/americas-carbon-advantage.pdf.

marketing work is done in the United States, while more manufacturing is done in China, resulting in a low U.S. CO_2 intensity). To properly emphasize environmental performance, carbon border adjustments should be based on emissions per unit of physical product rather than per unit of economic output where possible.

GREEN BANKS AND LENDING MECHANISMS

The cost to buy new machines and retool factories can be a barrier to industrial uptake of energy efficiency and clean production technologies. One of the most effective mechanisms for government to help businesses upgrade their equipment and facilities is to establish a "green bank," a quasi-governmental or nonprofit institution that helps make low-cost capital available for these projects. Green banks are a relatively recent innovation: in 2010, Malaysia was the first jurisdiction to establish a green bank, followed by Connecticut in 2011.[21] The Coalition for Green Capital, a nonprofit organization, is the leading expert group focused on implementing green banks and has assisted in the establishment of green banks in various U.S. states, South Africa, and Rwanda.[22]

Two key features set green banks apart from other government financial incentives.

- A green bank strives to operate as a "revolving fund," a self-sustaining fund wherein repaid principal and interest on loans are used to finance new loans to other recipients.[23] This allows the green bank to be capitalized once (for instance, from an initial commitment of government revenue) and then to operate in perpetuity. This makes revolving funds more politically durable than programs that require ongoing government appropriations to fund their operations.
- A green bank seeks to partner with private capital, using public money to generate private investment in qualifying green projects. This enables the green bank to direct far more money to qualifying projects than would be possible using government resources alone. For example, from 2012 to 2022, the Connecticut Green Bank mobilized $1.95 billion in private investment using just $322 million in green bank funds, a leverage ratio of 7 to 1.[24]

Green banks aim to support projects that struggle to attract affordable private-sector financing because, for instance, the technology is too new. However, green banks fund only projects that can be accomplished using available technology, because they require a financial return with acceptable risk and in a reasonable time frame to attract private capital and ensure the bank can continue to make new loans. Thus, green banks are best suited to overcoming a gap where clean technology is available but financing or cost barriers hamper its deployment (figure 9.3). To date, funded projects most often pertain to clean energy generation or energy efficiency, but green banks could also be a powerful accelerant for clean manufacturing technologies.

Green banks use several financing mechanisms to provide capital for qualifying projects.

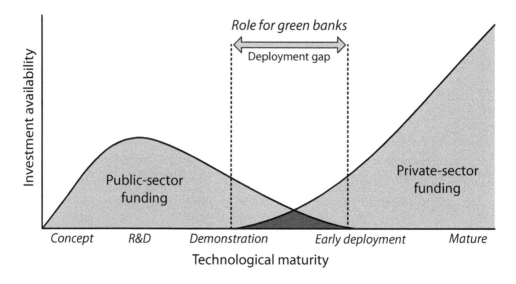

FIGURE 9.3 **Green Banks Help Bridge a Deployment Gap** Green banks are well suited to funding projects that are too technologically mature to receive government research and development (R&D) support but not yet mature enough to secure low-cost funding exclusively from the private sector.

Source: Hallie Kennan, *Working Paper: State Green Banks for Clean Energy* (Energy Innovation LLC, San Francisco, January 2014), https://energyinnovation.org/wp-content /uploads/2014/06/WorkingPaper_StateGreenBanks.pdf.

- **Co-lending**. A green bank can partner with a private financial institution to loan money to a qualifying project. Co-lending allows the green bank and the private lender to share the risks (and rewards) of the loan, which can help private lenders diversify their portfolios and manage risk. Private lenders can also benefit from the green bank's evaluation of borrowers' creditworthiness, as the green bank may have domain-specific expertise in clean energy and industrial technologies.

- **Aggregation**. A green bank can issue loans to many small and diverse projects that are individually unattractive to commercial lenders (due to inefficiencies of scale and difficulty assessing risk on a project-by-project basis). The green bank can bundle these loans to diversify risk and increase scale, then sell the bundled loans to private investors. This replenishes the green bank's public money, allowing it to finance more projects.[25]

- **Loan loss reserves**. The green bank may set aside an amount of money to cover private lenders' losses when they loan money to qualifying projects but are not repaid. This reduces the downside risk to private lenders, increasing their willingness to loan money at favorable interest rates. A green bank should not cover 100 percent of a private lender's losses, so lenders remain motivated to properly evaluate the creditworthiness of applicants and assume their share of the risk. For example, one Connecticut Green Bank program requires private lenders to first absorb losses equal to 1.5 percent of their loans, after which the green bank will cover any additional losses up to a limit of 7.5 percent of the lender's loans.[26] This allows private lenders to tolerate a much higher default rate than they otherwise would.

- **Loan guarantees**. A loan guarantee is similar to loan loss reserves, but the guarantor assumes the remaining debt if the borrower defaults on the loan. Sometimes, a guarantor may assume debt only up to a certain limit. This means that private lenders are not exposed to any risk unless the guarantee is limited and the default is large enough to exceed that limit. In most circumstances, a mechanism that better shares risk with the private lender is more appropriate than a loan guarantee. However, a guarantee may be necessary when the green bank wishes to support a relatively less mature technology, if private lenders are unable to assess creditworthiness and are unwilling to take on any risk.

- **Commercial/Industrial Property Assessed Clean Energy (C-PACE).** In a C-PACE program, a private lender (or the green bank) funds improvements to a commercial property up front, and the property owner pays back the loan via a property tax surcharge. If the property changes hands, the new owner becomes responsible for these payments. Tying repayments to property taxes (which transfer with building ownership) makes it more likely the loan will be repaid, increasing private lenders' willingness to provide funding at affordable interest rates. This financial model is best suited to improvements that increase the value of the property for a new owner, such as improvements to insulation, rooftop solar, heating, air conditioning, and lighting, rather than financing machinery that is useful only to the current owner.
- **On-bill financing**. This is similar to C-PACE, but loan payments are added to a property's utility bills rather than property tax bills.
- **Bond sales**. A green bank can sell bonds to raise capital for qualifying projects. For example, Connecticut Green Bank issued over $80 million in bonds during its first two years of sales (2020–21).[27] While green banks' other financing mechanisms often involve partnering with large corporate lenders, bond sales can obtain capital from individual and institutional bond investors, expanding and diversifying a green bank's funding sources.

Green banks work well alongside other financial policies, such as tax credits or subsidies for clean industrial technology deployment, as many of the private investors that partner with green banks are motivated, in part, by these incentives.[28]

One of the main challenges in setting up a green bank is obtaining initial capital. Public financing is helpful, but many of the key activities undertaken by a green bank do not necessarily require large reserves of cash owned by the green bank itself. Recognizing this, there has been an increase in "lean, origination-focused green banks" that use their expertise to help connect qualifying projects to financing. Additionally, green banks are increasingly working across jurisdiction boundaries and building coalitions to better share expertise, standardize their offerings, and reduce operating expenses.[29]

SUBSIDIES AND TAX CREDITS

Subsidies and tax credits are forms of cost-sharing in which the government provides money (or reduces tax liability) for businesses that undertake specific investments or activities. Unlike loans from a green bank or private lender, a company need not pay back subsidies or tax credits. Therefore, these policies are a good fit for earlier-stage projects and technologies that are unlikely to be able to achieve financial returns and repay loans in a time frame acceptable to a creditor. For example, a first-of-its-kind demonstration plant employing a novel, zero-carbon manufacturing process is a good candidate for subsidies.

Ideally, tax credits are refundable, which means they are paid to qualifying businesses irrespective of those businesses' tax liability. A refundable tax credit is essentially a subsidy or grant. In contrast, a nonrefundable tax credit can be used only to offset taxes. If a business's income tax is less than its tax credit, the remainder of the credit is lost.

Many businesses have little or no net income in particular years, especially newer ones that are working to commercialize innovative technologies—the very businesses that government often wishes to support. Faced with a nonrefundable tax credit, these businesses partner with tax equity investors (large financial firms) that use the tax credit to offset their own income taxes. Financial firms take roughly half the tax credit's value. Therefore, for every dollar of government money spent on the tax credit, only half ends up subsidizing the intended business activity. For example, from 2005 to 2008, the United States spent $10.3 billion on nonrefundable tax credits for wind energy development, but the same results could have been achieved by spending just $5 billion in grants.[30] There is essentially no policy design benefit to making tax credits nonrefundable, but nonrefundable credits are sometimes preferred for political expedience because they are less visible than direct subsidies.

SUBSIDY DESIGN FOR INDUSTRY

There are three broad approaches to subsidizing clean industry. Subsidies may be offered for investment in clean manufacturing equipment, for use of clean energy, or for low- or zero-emission production of output products. Each approach has advantages and disadvantages.

Subsidizing the purchase of green industrial equipment can be the least-expensive approach for government. For example, as noted in chapter 6, over a typical industrial boiler's lifetime, fuel represents 96 percent of total costs, while capital equipment represents 3 percent and operation and maintenance 1 percent.[31] Therefore, a subsidy that helps pay for the boiler may be more cost-effective than subsidizing the use of clean energy, since government is assisting with 3 percent rather than 96 percent of the boiler's costs. Also, subsidizing clean production equipment may expand the market for these machines, helping drive down their costs.

There are several downsides to subsidizing capital equipment. First, there is no guarantee the equipment will be used. If a company buys equipment and receives subsidies, then abandons its clean production plans or goes out of business, the entire value of the subsidy is lost. Second, it is difficult for government to make this policy technology-neutral since it must specify which types of equipment are eligible for subsidies. Third, if electricity is more expensive than fossil fuels even after adjusting for its greater efficiency, subsidizing electrified capital equipment may not be sufficient to sway many industrial buyers.

Subsidizing manufacturers' use of clean energy can help remedy cost discrepancies between clean and dirty energy sources. Like carbon pricing, it helps correct for externalities and thereby puts energy sources on a level playing field. However, a subsidy can be much more targeted than a carbon tax (for example, limited to particular fuels used by specific industries), helping limit its costs, and it may be politically easier to enact.

Unfortunately, subsidizing clean energy fails to incentivize strategies that reduce energy use, particularly energy efficiency, material efficiency, material substitution, and circular economy measures. These are important strategies to promote because they help reduce the need for new clean energy generation, making it faster and cheaper to achieve a net-zero economy.

Subsidizing clean production of output products is the most technology-neutral approach, allowing manufacturers great flexibility in identifying emissions reduction opportunities. For example, energy and material efficiency are viable strategies. (That said, production-linked subsidies are not all-encompassing. They fail to reward circular economy measures that reduce product demand, such as improving product longevity and repairability.) Subsidizing clean production may help increase output and employment in targeted industries, and cost savings may be passed on to consumers. This policy can thereby achieve two policy objectives at once: accelerating the transition to clean production, and supporting specific, domestic industries (such as industries with national strategic importance or those providing jobs in disadvantaged communities).

One mechanism for subsidizing clean production in jurisdictions with a carbon price is a "carbon contract for difference" (CCfD), an agreement between the government and a manufacturer using innovative low- or zero-carbon processes. The government pays the firm the difference between their greenhouse gas abatement costs and the prevailing carbon price (which tends to be lower than the abatement cost). Carbon contracts for difference limit the abatement costs of firms that invest in clean technology to the level of the carbon price, so they are not at a disadvantage relative to firms that use conventional, dirty processes and pay the carbon price.[32] The government's financial liability declines as the carbon price ratchets higher and as the costs of the clean manufacturing technology come down, narrowing the "difference" between these costs.

The main downsides of subsidizing industrial output are the financial cost to government (which grows with increasing production) and the possibility of violating international trade regulations that limit the ways in which countries may subsidize domestic industries, at least for exported products.

PERMANENCE

Subsidies are generally intended to be temporary measures. Subsidies for innovative technologies are best suited for early to middle phases of a technology's life cycle: R&D, demonstration, and early commercial deployment. They may be gradually phased out as a technology achieves maturity and lower costs. Once a technology outgrows subsidies, lending mechanisms that lower the cost of financing for green projects (discussed earlier) may be the next step. Eventually, no government support may be required to sustain a robust and growing market for particular technologies.

Subsidies for clean energy use or clean production might remain justified as long as negative externalities of fossil fuel use (including greenhouse gas and conventional pollution, with associated human health, environmental, and economic damages) are not fully priced into the costs of those fuels. This is because clean energy or production subsidies are helping correct for market distortions, so withdrawing them before correcting the underlying distortions gives unfair competitive advantage to fossil fuels.

AVOID BINS

Subsidies should vary with energy efficiency or emissions performance via a continuous function rather than segmenting products with a range of performance characteristics into large bins (where all products within a bin receive the same subsidy). Bins incentivize equipment manufacturers to improve performance only as much as necessary to reach the bottom of a bin, then to avoid further improvements unless the manufacturer wishes to reach the next bin.

EXAMPLES

One example of subsidies for innovative manufacturing processes is the Swedish Energy Agency's support for hydrogen-based steelmaking via the HYBRIT initiative. In 2018, the agency provided SEK 528 million (equivalent to $61 million 2018 U.S. dollars)—the largest grant in the history of the agency—to help fund two pilot plants. This covered an estimated 38 percent of project costs.[33] For more on HYBRIT, see chapter 1.

Another example is China's Ten Key Energy-Saving Projects initiative, which was initiated in 2004 and continued during the eleventh Five-Year Plan period (2006–10). This program allowed firms to apply for government funding for projects in ten areas related to energy savings, including waste heat recovery, motor system efficiency, and renovation of industrial boilers. Companies applied for funding at twenty government-run technical assistance centers. For successful applicants, the government covered 60 percent of the project's up-front capital costs. The government would reimburse the company's 40 percent contribution after the technology was installed and energy savings confirmed by independent auditors.[34]

An example of a tax credit is the United States' 45Q credit for carbon oxide sequestration. Enacted in 2008 and strengthened in 2018 and 2022, the credit pays facilities up to $85 per metric ton of CO_2 sent to geological storage or $60 per metric ton used for enhanced oil recovery or in certain industrial products. The Global CCS Institute regards it as "the most progressive CCS-specific incentive globally."[35] Prior to 2022, the tax credit was not refundable. The Inflation Reduction Act made the credit refundable for the first five years of a project's lifetime for commercial entities, or for the entire duration of the tax credit for nonprofit and governmental entities.[36]

EQUIPMENT FEES, REBATES, AND FEEBATES

Some industrial needs can be met by equipment from a range of manufacturers, often with different efficiency levels and sometimes using different fuels. For example, a plant manager buying a new boiler may select from a variety of fuel-burning or electrical boilers capable of generating steam at a rate and temperature to meet a facility's needs.

Similarly, a range of manufacturers and technology options are available for furnaces, kilns, and chemical apparatus such as distillation columns, among others.

When various fully commercialized technologies can fulfill a particular function, equipment fees, rebates, and feebates are a powerful policy option to incentivize cleaner choices and drive market improvement.

- A **fee** is a sales tax applied to equipment that fails to meet an efficiency or emissions intensity threshold. The fee should escalate based on the degree to which the equipment falls below the threshold.
- A **rebate** is the opposite of a fee: the government or utilities pay buyers of equipment that exceeds an efficiency or emissions intensity threshold. Rebates should escalate with the degree to which the equipment exceeds the threshold, up to a maximum value for zero-emissions equipment.
- A **feebate** combines a fee and a rebate in a single policy. The level of efficiency or emissions intensity that incurs neither a fee nor a rebate is called the "pivot point." A feebate can be a cost-effective policy for government, as fee revenues can be used to fund rebates.

The threshold or pivot point for these policies should tighten over time to provide incentive for continuous improvement and the development of cleaner industrial technologies. Improvements should be determined by formula and take effect without legislative or regulatory action to make long-term prices more predictable and insulate the policy from political interference. For example, a formula might update the threshold every two years to equal the performance necessary to be in the best-performing quartile of equipment on the market, based on a sales-weighted average during the previous two years. This approach ensures that rebate-qualifying technology exists and is widely available in the market, yet a majority of the market (i.e., 75 percent) will be vying to improve its products and break into the top 25 percent, driving continuous innovation. (A similar principle applies to standards. See chapter 10.)

Since these policies rely on the existence of a range of equipment choices from different manufacturers, they are not well suited to support early-stage technologies or first-of-a-kind demonstration projects. They are ideal for driving improvement of relatively mature technologies.

In practice, rebates have most often been offered for building systems and appliances. For example, more than two hundred rebate programs run by U.S. utilities pay industrial customers that install efficient equipment such as heaters, air conditioners, chillers, lighting, motors, and air compressors.[37] Fees and feebates have more commonly targeted road vehicles. For example, as of 2020, twenty-four EU member states were levying motor vehicle taxes based partly or entirely on vehicle fuel efficiency or CO_2 emissions.[38] The best-known example of a feebate is France's Bonus-Malus system, which contributed to a 25 percent reduction in new vehicles' CO_2 emissions per kilometer between 2007 and 2017.[39] Policy makers who are interested in instituting rebates, fees, and feebates for heavy industrial equipment may learn from the experiences of those who implemented them for these other types of equipment.

FINANCIAL POLICIES FOR ZERO-CARBON INDUSTRY

Financial policies are key to accelerating the deployment of clean industrial technologies, and different policies are effective at supporting these technologies at different points in their life cycles. At its earliest stages, a technology needs research and development support (covered in chapter 11). Once a technology is ready to leave the laboratory, generous subsidies and tax credits are the best tools to help launch demonstration or early commercial projects. At a demonstration or early commercial stage, a technology's financial returns are still too uncertain to be attractive to lenders, and the technologies' small scale helps ensure that the subsidies' cost to government remains affordable.

As a clean technology continues to grow, green banks and lending mechanisms are the next step, helping it to bridge the gap between public and private funding. Industrial firms are now expected to pay back lenders or bondholders, but financing is offered at favorable terms facilitated by government or green banks, since firms commercializing new technologies may otherwise be unable to get private funding at rates as low as those offered to projects involving established technologies. Once a clean technology is competing against dirty technologies in the marketplace, rebates on clean industrial equipment can help overcome price gaps.

Finally, once clean technology is widely available in the marketplace at competitive prices (but not necessarily at lower prices than dirty technology), the time is ripe to use financial policies that penalize dirty technology options. This includes fees on polluting equipment and carbon pricing. Policies that make dirty technologies more expensive are most effective at reducing emissions when there is a clean alternative readily available so firms can switch to clean processes rather than pay the fees or taxes. Fees on polluting equipment can be applied only to specific classes of equipment where clean options are available, making such fees extremely useful when clean versions of some types of equipment can be purchased but other types of equipment lack clean versions. A carbon price applies to all types of equipment used by a particular industry or facility, so carbon pricing is best used once other policies have already helped bring a diverse array of clean equipment options to the market.

Financial policies can dramatically accelerate the commercialization of clean industrial technologies at all stages of development. Applying the right policies in the right order maximizes their effectiveness.

10

STANDARDS AND GREEN
PUBLIC PROCUREMENT

S tandards are policies that require equipment or industrial facilities to achieve specified levels of performance, particularly in energy efficiency or greenhouse gas emissions. Typically, standards determine which products may be sold on the market. Alternatively, a "green public procurement" program can establish standards specifically for materials used in government-funded construction, such as roads and infrastructure. Standards should also specify how emissions or energy use are measured and reported to ensure a fair, consistent accounting basis when comparing firms or products.

ENERGY EFFICIENCY AND EMISSIONS STANDARDS

While financial policies (chapter 9) are powerful, they work best when accompanied by standards. The standards most relevant to industrial decarbonization are for energy efficiency and greenhouse gas emissions. (Material efficiency is best handled with product-specific approaches, such as regulating buildings' whole life cycle emissions, to better account for trade-offs in embodied emissions, product performance, and—for energy-using products—energy efficiency.) It is useful to understand why energy efficiency and emissions standards are important and how they work in concert with financial policies.

OVERCOMING MARKET AND POLITICAL BARRIERS

A modern economy is complex, including actors with varying motivations, information barriers, and time horizons. Financial policies will convince some actors to shift to clean technology quickly, but influencing ever larger shares of the market requires escalating tax or subsidy rates. While financial policies alone can achieve substantial decarbonization, they cannot drive emissions all the way to zero (at least, not at reasonable tax or subsidy levels). Standards help close this gap in a cost-effective way.

Various market barriers and aspects of human psychology can weaken financial policy signals.

- **Split incentives**. These incentives occur when the firm responsible for upgrading a building or equipment would not benefit from the improvement. Although manufacturers generally own their own manufacturing equipment, that is not always true of buildings. U.S. manufacturers lease 43 percent of their industrial space (based on costs).[1] Tenants are typically responsible for paying energy bills, while building owners are responsible for installing more efficient insulation, lighting, heating, and air-conditioning systems. It can be difficult to build the price of such upgrades into commercial rents. Also, an existing tenant who would face high costs to relocate may already be paying the energy bills. Therefore, a building owner may not pursue cost-effective energy-saving upgrades.
- **Short time horizons**. Some firms have trouble justifying long-term investments due to the need to meet quarterly financial targets or satisfy investors. Energy efficiency upgrades and research and development (R&D) projects require up-front investment and may not realize their full potential in a time frame compatible with investor or management expectations.

- **Preference for other projects**. Sometimes efficiency projects are held to higher standards than other projects and may not be pursued even if they have favorable risk-adjusted rates of return. Businesses may not see reducing energy expenditures as worthy of attention or may prioritize revenue-generating activities, such as product development or marketing. (For more on this, see the corporate decision-making section in chapter 4).
- **Familiarity**. Industrial firms are often risk-averse and resistant to changing familiar equipment or processes, which may require staff retraining.
- **Habituation to pricing levels**. Consumers consider things to be cheap or expensive based on mental price anchors.[2] Over the course of years, anchors are adjusted as people habituate to new price levels (and as new consumers enter the market and form up-to-date anchors). Gradually, goods that used to seem unusually expensive or cheap will start to seem normal. Therefore, a financial policy that is effective at reducing emissions by influencing consumer behavior may gradually lose its ability to influence them. In turn, this affects emissions of manufacturers who supply goods to meet consumer demand.
- **Imperfect information**. A firm may not be aware of all available technology options on the market, their costs, and their performance.
- **High transaction costs**. It may be difficult for a firm to adopt cost-effective efficiency or clean production technologies due to ancillary costs, such as the need to pause production for equipment modifications. Additionally, equipment changes may require other equipment to be upgraded to maintain compatibility, sparking a chain of upgrades.
- **Difficulty capturing full benefits**. In some cases, it can be difficult for a business making an investment to capture its full benefits. For example, a firm may decline to invest in R&D—even if the resulting technology would be cost-effective—if some of the results may not be patentable (or copied in a jurisdiction with weak patent protections).

Standards can be more effective than financial policies at overcoming these and other market barriers.

Even if a desired result could be achieved solely through financial policies, it may be politically advantageous to utilize a mixture of standards and financial policies. As noted earlier, it may be difficult to enact a tax or subsidy at the rate required to achieve a particular emissions outcome. Additionally, standards are less visible than taxes. An equipment buyer is more likely to notice a fee on inefficient equipment models than to notice the absence of inefficient models from the marketplace. Policy makers concerned about political opposition may wish to utilize high-visibility policies (well-publicized subsidies) to incentivize clean technology and utilize low-visibility policies (standards), rather than taxes, to remove the worst-performing technologies from the market.

In addition to removing poorly performing products from the market, standards incentivize R&D to reduce the cost of manufacturing standard-compliant products. However, standards do not distinguish between different compliant products, so they are less effective at promoting the development of cutting-edge products that greatly exceed the standard. For example, an emissions standard requiring that primary steel production emit no more than 1.5 tons of CO_2e per ton of steel would block the sale of steel whose production emitted 2 tons of CO_2e, but it would not incentivize zero-carbon production when 1.4 tons of CO_2e per ton of steel would suffice. A subsidy that scales with performance gives larger rewards to better-performing technologies, creating an incentive to produce innovative, top-tier products. Standards and financial policies work best together.

ENERGY EFFICIENCY STANDARDS

Energy efficiency standards require equipment to achieve specific performance levels per unit of energy consumed. For industry, these standards have typically been applied at the component level, such as for pumps and motors. Industrial equipment can be diverse, so equipment standards should be written to account for a range of equipment properties. For example, the U.S. Department of Energy maintains energy efficiency standards for industrial electric motors that account for motor design, horsepower rating, number of electrical poles, and whether the motor is enclosed in a housing.[3]

An important example of energy efficiency standards is the European Union's Ecodesign Directive, which establishes required efficiencies for most nonvehicle energy-using products within the EU. This includes industrial equipment, such as industrial furnaces and ovens, welding equipment, boilers, motors, pumps, and machine tools. Ecodesign's standard-setting process includes a study of market data and technological status, a consultation between member states and stakeholders (industry, nongovernmental organizations, and academia), draft regulations, and final regulations.[4] Stakeholders broadly agree that the Ecodesign Directive is achieving its energy efficiency objectives, though some critique the slow standard-setting process and difficulty ensuring that all noncompliant products are in fact removed from the market.[5] (Ecodesign is not concerned with only energy efficiency. It also includes circular economy policies, discussed in chapter 11.)

Efficiency standards for fuel-burning technologies can reduce the amount of fuel combusted. Policy makers may wonder if reduced fuel use implies reduced emissions of conventional pollutants that harm public health, such as particulates. Unfortunately, tightening fuel efficiency standards may not reduce conventional pollution from facilities already bound by conventional pollutant standards. Conventional pollutants are removed via modifications to combustion processes or postcombustion treatment technologies. These technologies are expensive and often consume energy and/or chemical reagents, so facilities try to remove only enough conventional pollutants to meet relevant air quality standards.

If an efficiency standard causes a facility to reduce its fuel consumption but conventional pollutant standards remain unchanged, the facility manager may install a smaller exhaust treatment system (or throttle down an existing, throttleable system, such as NO_x removal via ammonia injection), so the facility continues to narrowly comply with the conventional pollutant standard. Similarly, new industrial facilities with better energy efficiency can be designed with weaker exhaust treatment systems. Therefore, policy makers should assume that conventional pollutant standards will continue to determine conventional pollution emissions and should not barter them away in return for energy efficiency standards.

EMISSIONS STANDARDS

Emissions standards limit the greenhouse gases (or conventional pollutants) that may be emitted per unit of industrial output. In contrast to energy efficiency standards, emissions standards are typically applied at the facility level and can incentivize a broader range of decarbonization strategies. For example, biomass combustion can reduce life cycle greenhouse gas emissions but is unlikely to improve energy efficiency.

Emissions standards can be set as sector-wide greenhouse gas intensity thresholds (CO_2e per unit of product) for "commodities." (Commodities are products that are identical no matter how they were produced, such as particular grades of steel, types of cement, or bulk chemicals such as ammonia.) Most industrial emissions are associated with commodity production (see figure 0.2 in the introduction), so most industrial emissions can be covered by sector-wide carbon intensity thresholds.

For "differentiated products" (noncommodities), it is difficult to establish carbon intensity thresholds that can be fairly applied to different companies. One approach is to require each facility to report its emissions and establish a plan for improvement relative to its own historical baseline. If historical emissions data are available, the baseline can be based on a period prior to the announcement of standards to prevent gaming (i.e., a firm temporarily increasing its emissions to inflate its baseline).

A real-world example of carbon intensity standards is Canada's Output-Based Pricing System, along with provincial programs that supersede the federal program in specific provinces.[6] For instance, Ontario's Emissions Performance Standard program includes sector-wide emissions intensity thresholds for some commodities, including clinker, cement, refined petroleum products, steel, hydrogen gas, ammonia, urea, and nitric acid. For other products, such as lime, gypsum panels, brick, nylon, ethylene, and glass, it establishes facility-specific performance standards relative to historical baselines.[7] Noncomplying products are not removed from the market, but producers must pay for each metric ton of excess emissions at an escalating rate that will reach C$170 per metric ton in 2030.[8]

Carbon intensity standards have also been used as a component of other policies. For instance, green government procurement policies include carbon intensity thresholds (discussed later in this chapter). Another example is China's national emissions trading system, which proposes to allocate emissions allowances to industries based on their production and a carbon intensity threshold.[9]

DESIGN PRINCIPLES FOR STANDARDS

Policy makers should consider several guidelines to help ensure that standards achieve their goals: to build in continuous improvement, sometimes consider technology-forcing standards, keep standards simple and outcome-focused, encompass the whole market, create tradable and sales-weighted standards, and consider three-scope standards that cover supply chain emissions.

BUILD IN CONTINUOUS IMPROVEMENT

Standards can provide a long-term signal that drives innovation. However, if standards do not become tighter over time, they lose their ability to shift the market toward greener technologies. Therefore, standards should contain a formula that specifies when and how future increases in stringency are calculated. These increases should take effect without requiring legislative or regulatory action. Automatic, built-in improvement provides three benefits.

- **Transparency**. Manufacturers know how the standard is set and can better predict future increases in stringency.

- **Timeliness**. Increases in standards' stringency are not delayed if a regulatory body is distracted by other matters or funding constraints.
- **Resistance to interference**. Future policy makers or regulators cannot undermine the standards program by quietly taking no action. (They may pass legislation repealing the standards, but new legislation is a higher political hurdle and allows space for public debate about the usefulness and value of standards.) Similarly, increases in stringency cannot be influenced by industry lobbying.

Formulas may utilize market data to ensure that heightened standards are achievable with commercially available technology. For example, an energy efficiency standard may specify that it is updated every two years, such that the median efficiency of the products sold during the previous two years (across all manufacturers) becomes the standard for the following two years. This approach ensures that standard-compliant technology exists and is widely available, but manufacturers will be required to improve their worst-performing models, driving continuous innovation.

ENERGY STAR®, a voluntary U.S. program that certifies energy-efficient equipment, illustrates the importance of using formulas to keep standards up to date. Ideally, the market share of ENERGY STAR equipment would remain around 30–50 percent to help steer buyers toward the most efficient products. However, 100 percent of dishwashers, 89 percent of notebook computers, and 88 percent of dehumidifiers sold in 2020 qualified for ENERGY STAR, indicating that the program set standards that were too easy to meet and has failed to keep up with improving technology for these products.[10]

CONSIDER TECHNOLOGY-FORCING STANDARDS

Self-tightening, formula-based standards are essential, but they can emphasize evolutionary improvements while failing to incentivize revolutionary new technology. Regulators may also implement technology-forcing standards that are too stringent to be met without technologies that are not yet commercial. Technology-forcing standards were key to the adoption of fundamental pollution control technologies in the transportation sector, including the catalytic converter in 1975 and three-way catalysts in 1981.[11]

Technology-forcing standards complement formula-based standards. As a revolutionary technology gains market share, its emissions or efficiency impact will automatically be factored into requirements under existing, formula-based standards, so formula-based standards do not need to be explicitly adjusted to account for new, technology-forcing standards.

Setting a technology-forcing standard requires an assessment of the state of research and manufacturability of noncommercial technology options, so it cannot be set via formula. It must be set through agency action based on expert review, with comments from industry and environmental stakeholders.

KEEP STANDARDS SIMPLE AND OUTCOME-FOCUSED

Complicated standards that make many distinctions between different types of technologies and their specific uses are more difficult to write and more prone to loopholes. For example, in 2006, U.S. light-duty vehicle fuel economy standards were updated to consider vehicles' physical footprint when determining required efficiency. This incentivized automakers to manufacture larger vehicles, undermining the goals of the standard.[12]

To the extent possible, policy makers should keep standards simple, technology-neutral, and focused on desired outcomes. For example, an energy efficiency standard for electric motors should not specify how a motor should be constructed or what features it must have but, rather, should simply specify a required percentage efficiency in converting electrical energy into rotational kinetic energy. A standard for a cement precalciner, kiln, or cooler should limit total energy input per unit of ordinary cement produced. Facility-wide standards limiting greenhouse gas emissions per unit of output are even simpler and inherently technology-neutral.

ENCOMPASS THE WHOLE MARKET

Standards must apply to any product sold in the regulated market, whether imported or produced domestically, to avoid giving competitive advantage to foreign producers. For standards set per unit material (such as steel), importers must disclose the embodied carbon in their imports. (This reporting requirement also exists under a carbon pricing system with border adjustments, covered in chapter 9.) For standards governing the performance of imported machinery, such as industrial boilers, the imported products' performance can be directly tested.

Sufficient resources must be devoted to identifying and quickly removing noncomplying products from the market and to impose additional penalties for intentional or negligent noncompliance. Noncomplying products can undermine the incentive to innovate and put manufacturers who comply with the standard at a disadvantage. For example, stakeholders identified inadequate market surveillance as one of the main obstacles to the success of the EU's Ecodesign Directive, as an estimated 10–25 percent of regulated products on the market do not comply with the standard.[13]

CREATE TRADABLE, SALES-WEIGHTED STANDARDS

Traditionally, standards specify the performance that must be achieved by each specific unit of technology, such as individual motors or boilers. However, a standard may instead specify minimum performance of the sales-weighted average of all units sold by a manufacturer. This allows manufacturers to sell some units that fail to meet the standard if they compensate by selling enough units that exceed the standard.

Flexibility may be further increased by making this requirement tradable among manufacturers of the same type of equipment. For example, one manufacturer may sell industrial boilers that greatly exceed the applicable emissions standard, then sell credits to a different boiler manufacturer, enabling that manufacturer to sell more units that do not meet the standard. Thus, the standard governs weighted average performance across all units sold by all manufacturers. This is essentially applying a cap-and-trade approach to standards rather than to carbon pricing. (For more on cap and trade, including design principles and complexities, see chapter 9.)

An example sales-weighted standard is the U.S. corporate average fuel economy (CAFE) standard for light-duty vehicles, which has allowed credit trading among manufacturers since 2011.[14] Another common type of sales-weighted standard, a renewable portfolio standard (RPS), specifies the minimum share of utilities' electricity that must come from qualifying renewable sources. Most RPS programs include tradable renewable energy credits. For example, South Korea has a national RPS with tradable renewable energy credits that requires 12.5 percent renewable generation in 2022, rising to 25 percent in 2026.[15]

To decarbonize industry, sales-weighted tradable standards could be applied to energy-using industrial equipment (akin to CAFE standards) or could require a share of commodity outputs, such as steel or cement, to be made via low- or zero-emissions processes (akin to an RPS). Tradable sales-weighted standards may be applied in addition to or instead of traditional standards that impose firm minimum requirements on specific types of equipment.

CONSIDER THREE-SCOPE STANDARDS TO REDUCE SUPPLY CHAIN EMISSIONS

Greenhouse gas emissions from manufacturing can be divided into three scopes. "Scope 1" refers to direct emissions from the manufacturer's facilities. "Scope 2" refers to emissions associated with purchased electricity and heat. "Scope 3" refers to emissions from the production of purchased parts and raw materials.

Scope 3 emissions are of special concern when the supplier is in a jurisdiction with weak or nonexistent industrial emissions regulations. This can create a loophole that allows domestic firms to sell products with high greenhouse gas intensities, even if the domestic firm's own operations are clean. This loophole can be significant for some countries.

For example, in 2015, the United Kingdom had 258 million metric tons net embodied CO_2 imports, equivalent to 66 percent of the UK's 2015 CO_2 emissions.[16]

Scope 3 emissions have been largely overlooked by policy makers. The most relevant effort is the EU's carbon border adjustment mechanism, highlighted in chapter 9. While it directly regulates only scope 1 and 2 emissions, many of the covered products (such as steel) are inputs to other industries, so it effectively covers some scope 3 emissions of industries that purchase these products.

Carbon pricing is not the only policy that can target embodied emissions. A three-scope emissions standard can reduce emissions from domestic manufacturers and their suppliers. Such a standard requires manufacturers to reduce total emissions from the production of their goods, including embodied emissions in imported parts and materials. Domestic firms may pressure suppliers to reduce their greenhouse gas emissions, or they can switch to suppliers already using cleaner processes, to comply with the standard. Suppliers wishing to sell into the regulated market may choose to adopt cleaner production processes.

Like a carbon border adjustment mechanism, a three-scope standard relies on data on foreign producers' carbon intensities. Therefore, it will be easier to implement once carbon intensity data from the EU carbon border adjustment mechanism are widely available. Labeling and disclosure policies (see chapter 11) may also help establish data sets and reporting systems that facilitate the implementation of a three-scope standard.

GREEN PUBLIC PROCUREMENT

A green public procurement (GPP) program establishes an emissions intensity standard for goods purchased or funded by the government. Effectively, a GPP program segments the market, with a weaker standard (or no standard) determining which products may be sold to private-sector buyers and a more stringent standard for products sold to government. A GPP program can be politically easier to enact than a standard governing access to the market, for the following reasons.

- Manufacturers' participation in GPP is voluntary, since they may decline to meet the standard and continue selling their products to nongovernment buyers.
- Any increased costs for green products are borne by government rather than private-sector buyers.
- Often, which products government should buy is decided administratively, so a GPP may not require authorizing legislation. (However, if politically feasible, legislation requiring agencies to participate can be helpful for achieving buy-in across government.)[17]
- National, state or provincial, and local governments, as well as special agencies (like regional transit authorities), procure products, so a GPP program can be implemented by any interested government. In contrast, standards regulating access to the market may need to be uniform throughout a larger jurisdiction, so those standards are often best suited to national government or large states and provinces.

Governments are major buyers of industrial products. Government pays for roads, bridges, civic buildings, and other infrastructure, demanding large quantities of steel, concrete, brick, and glass. Additionally, government purchases finished products such as military equipment, public transit vehicles, medical and laboratory equipment, computers, and office supplies. Public procurement accounts for an average of 12 percent of GDP in OECD countries and up to 30 percent in many low- and middle-income countries.[18] Therefore, government procurement represents a large and lucrative market that is attractive to many suppliers.

If government is willing to pay more for low-emissions products, public procurement can serve as a lead market that allows novel, clean manufacturing processes to scale up. This enables manufacturers to drive down their costs through returns to scale and learning by doing, helping clean products subsequently break into the private-sector market. Also, a GPP program can have positive spillover effects when a manufacturer does not want to divide its supply chains and production processes into making GPP-compliant and noncompliant products, so they opt to meet the GPP standard with all their products.

GPP programs need not be limited to government-owned facilities. They may also encompass projects that accept government money or subsidies. For example, from 2000 to 2014, forty-five U.S. professional sports stadiums were built or substantially renovated at a cost of $27.8 billion, of which $13 billion (47 percent) was funded by tax-exempt municipal bonds.[19] Similarly, U.S. states and cities routinely offer private firms subsidies worth hundreds of millions or billions of dollars in return for new capital investment.[20] GPP-compliant procurement may be required of a private firm as a condition of accepting government money or tax incentives that exceed a specified percentage (say, 20 percent) of a project's capital costs.

GPP PROGRAM COVERAGE

As of 2017, at least forty-one countries had national public procurement programs, but these programs' social objectives and scope of covered products varied widely. Of these programs, 66 percent included a climate change mitigation objective. (Other goals include support of small and medium businesses, water conservation, biodiversity preservation, and support of military veterans.)[21] Only about half of the GPP programs covered building materials (figure 10.1), even though building materials (particularly steel and concrete) are the most important products for accelerating industrial decarbonization due to their 40 percent share of industrial greenhouse gas emissions (see figure 0.2).

It may not be practical for a GPP program to cover every possible type of product. Policy makers should prioritize coverage of products

- whose production or use generates significant greenhouse gas emissions;
- whose scope 1, 2, and 3 emissions are reported by manufacturers or can be readily determined;

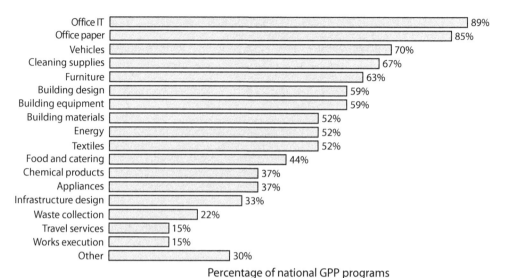

Percentage of national GPP programs

FIGURE 10.1 **Share of National GPP Programs Covering Specific Products and Services in 2017** Regulations for covered products may govern emissions during the product's manufacture (e.g., building materials) or use (e.g., vehicles, appliances), or they may emphasize sustainable harvesting or recycled content (e.g., office paper, food and catering). "Building design" and "Infrastructure design" include engineering design elements affecting in-use performance plus construction impacts. "Building equipment" includes space heating, air conditioning, lighting, and water heating, while "Appliances" includes ovens, dishwashers, clothes washers, and the like.

Source: UN Environment Programme, *Global Review of Sustainable Public Procurement 2017* (report, United Nations Environment Programme, Nairobi 2017), https://wedocs .unep.org/bitstream/handle/20.500.11822/20919/GlobalReview_Sust_Procurement .pdf?sequence=1&isAllowed=y.

- for which commercialized, green alternatives offer large abatement potential;
- for which public procurement represents a large market, making the GPP a stronger incentive for manufacturers;
- where green options provide co-benefits, such as jobs in low-income communities, reduction of conventional pollutants, and the like;

- where green alternatives are available at an acceptable cost to government; and
- where green options have large potential for cost improvement through returns to scale.

CARVE-OUTS

Products and materials made via the most innovative, zero-emissions processes will initially be available in limited quantities. Therefore, it may not be possible for government to satisfy its demand by sourcing these products exclusively. However, a weaker standard that is achievable by more manufacturers might not provide a market for the very cleanest technologies.

To remedy this issue, a GPP may include carve-outs for products that achieve exceptionally high performance (i.e., near-zero emissions) and have limited market availability or high costs. Examples include zero-emissions primary steel made from green hydrogen–direct reduced iron or iron electrolysis (chapter 1) and cements using novel clinker chemistries (chapter 3). Like other standards, a carve-out should be technology-neutral and performance-based. For instance, a carve-out should call for zero-carbon primary steel, not steel produced specifically from iron electrolysis.

A GPP program with a carve-out has two thresholds: an upper tier for zero (or near-zero) emissions and a lower tier for moderate emissions. (Even the lower tier is more stringent than the standard required to sell to private-sector buyers.) Government must satisfy a certain percentage of its demand with products that achieve the upper tier, and the remainder must achieve the lower tier. Over time, as zero-emissions products' prices come down and availability increases, government can increase the percentage it procures from the upper tier without increasing its costs.

A carve-out is not a replacement for tightening a standard over time. The lower tier should gradually become more stringent, driving incremental improvements among moderate-emissions technologies or pushing suppliers to switch to zero-emissions technologies. Eventually, the two tiers may converge, effectively ending the carve-out.

ADVANCE MARKET COMMITMENTS

An advance market commitment is a policy mechanism whereby government agrees to buy a certain quantity of a product that is not yet on the market if it can be commercialized and meet government-set technical benchmarks. For instance, a government may agree to purchase a specific quantity of zero-carbon primary steel at a particular price if manufacturers hit certain carbon or energy targets. Like a carve-out, an advance market commitment aims to spur the development of truly revolutionary, not-yet-commercial technologies like molten iron electrolysis, hydrogen–direct reduced iron, and novel cement chemistries.

The key difference between a carve-out and an advance market commitment is that the advance market commitment involves negotiating a price and quantity of product that the government will buy from specific manufacturers at one point in time, while a carve-out is a standard that applies to all manufacturers, does not guarantee a specific purchase price, and may endure for many years.

Advance market commitments were an important tool in governments' response to the COVID-19 pandemic. Governments agreed to buy billions of COVID-19 vaccine doses from manufacturers at specific prices, conditioned on the vaccines' meeting safety and efficacy benchmarks and receiving approval from health authorities.

REVERSE AUCTION

Government may solicit bids for GPP-compliant materials and accept the lowest bid. This process, called a "reverse auction," can save public money and incentivize firms to reduce the costs of their low- and zero-carbon production processes. Government may give additional credit to proposals in proportion to their emissions' distance below the GPP compliance threshold, thereby valuing a mixture of cost efficiency and superior environmental performance.

CASE STUDY

Researchers Ali Hasanbeigi, Renilde Becqué, and Cecilia Springer published detailed case studies of GPP programs of twenty-two nations, five cities or regions, and three multinational organizations.[22] They find that the Netherlands' program exemplifies best practices, particularly concerning construction materials. The Netherlands' first GPP criteria and targets were established in 2005 and became law in 2012. The program aims to cover 7,500 public entities, including the central government, provinces, municipalities, and district water boards. Criteria exist for forty-five product groups. Criteria are reviewed annually and updated as needed. As of 2013, 59 percent of surveyed government entities reported that they always utilized GPP criteria in procurement, 31 percent sometimes did, and 10 percent never did (with most instances of noncompliance involving purchases under €50,000; compliance was 94 percent for purchases worth at least €50,000).[23]

Two features of the Netherlands' program are particularly notable. First, the government created a software tool, DuboCalc, that evaluates bids for infrastructure against a range of environmental criteria, including climate change impact, and assigns each bid a numerical score. This allows government officials to easily compare the environmental performance of various bids. The software is available to private firms, who use it to help understand how to improve their bids.[24]

Second, in addition to a minimum performance threshold, the GPP program provides credits to projects that exceed this standard, effectively reducing the price of their bid according to their environmental performance. Governments select the bid that has the lowest after-credit price, which allows selection of a project that is slightly more expensive but has better environmental performance ahead of a bid that is cheaper but has worse environmental performance. This provides an incentive for firms to innovate and exceed the standard while limiting costs.[25]

STANDARDS AND GREEN PUBLIC PROCUREMENT
FOR ZERO-CARBON INDUSTRY

Standards are a crucial complement to financial policies. Standards overcome market barriers that hinder financial policies' effectiveness, and the fact that they are relatively invisible to consumers can make them politically easier to enact. Standards can drive continuous innovation (improved performance, lower pollution, lower energy use) without the government paying subsidies or rebates for better-performing equipment and without it levying fees or taxes on industrial firms.

Standards should be designed to automatically tighten based on a publicly known formula, giving manufacturers transparency regarding future requirements and insulating the standards from political meddling. Making standards tradable and sales-weighted can make compliance easier at the cost of slightly increased administrative complexity—a worthwhile trade-off when there are a limited number of manufacturers to monitor, as is the case for manufacturers of industrial equipment and makers of steel, cement, and chemicals.

Green public procurement policies are standards that apply only to government-funded purchases. Through their purchasing decisions, governments can drive the commercialization and scale-up of clean technologies that are not yet price-competitive with products made via established, polluting processes. Compared with standards that regulate access to the market, a green public procurement program can be used much earlier in a technology's life cycle and be tailored to support multiple performance levels through carve-outs and advance market commitments.

Both financial policies (chapter 9) and standards (chapter 10) tend to focus on commercializing clean technology and influencing which technologies are sold and at what prices in the marketplace. While these issues are central to the transition to clean industry, they must not be policy makers' only considerations. Policy makers must also foster the research and refinement of new technologies in the laboratory, address what happens to products at the end of their lives, and ensure that it is possible to assess companies' environmental performance and compliance with other policies. Mechanisms to fill these gaps are the topic of the next chapter.

11

R&D, DISCLOSURE, LABELING, AND CIRCULAR ECONOMY POLICIES

F inancial policies (chapter 9) and standards (chapter 10) are not the only ways government can hasten the transition to zero-carbon industry. Government can also support private or public research and development (R&D), mandate greenhouse gas emissions monitoring and disclosure, establish mandatory or voluntary green product labeling, and enable a more circular economy through measures such as right to repair and extended producer responsibility legislation.

R&D SUPPORT

It is difficult to overstate the importance of government support in developing many of the technologies that underpin today's economy. Government-funded research (whether in government-run or private labs) was integral to the development of the internet, the global positioning system (GPS), touch screens, artificial intelligence and speech recognition, hydraulic fracturing (for natural gas extraction), light-emitting diodes (LEDs), genetic sequencing, numerous vaccines, the first antiretroviral drugs, accelerometers, weather radar, and technologies behind nuclear, wind, and solar electricity generation (among other advances).[1]

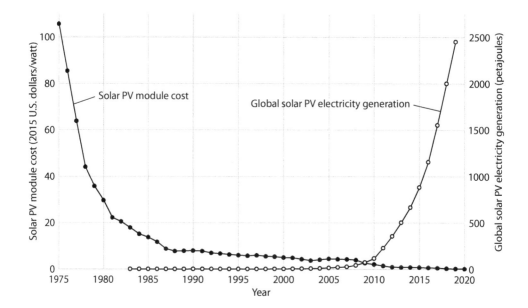

FIGURE 11.1 **Solar Photovoltaic Module Cost and Electricity Generation from 1975 to 2020** Decades of government R&D support brought down the cost of solar panels before they began attracting significant private-sector investment. PV = photovoltaic.

Sources: International Energy Agency, "World Energy Balances Data Service," updated April 2023, https://www.iea.org/data-and-statistics/data-product/world-energy-balances; International Energy Agency, "Evolution of Solar PV Module Cost by Data Source, 1970–2020," July 2, 2020, https://www.iea.org/data-and-statistics/charts/evolution-of-solar-pv-module-cost-by-data-source-1970-2020.

Often, government support was sustained over many years early in a technology's life cycle, before it could attract private funding, as private investors often demand financial returns within a small number of years. For example, solar panels, also known as "solar photovoltaic systems," underwent decades of cost declines, supported by government funding, before they started to become commercially important in the late 2000s (figure 11.1). Without government R&D support, it is unclear if or when solar photovoltaic systems would have evolved from a niche technology into a cost-competitive system installed on millions of homes.

Government R&D support will be no less crucial in the development and commercialization of clean manufacturing technologies. Key techniques include financial support (via direct research, public-private partnerships, grants, etc.); coordination of various research efforts; facilitation of access to science, technology, engineering, and mathematics talent; and thoughtful design of patent protections.

Individual countries' R&D investments can achieve technological progress that benefits the entire world. For example, in the 1970s, solar photovoltaic research was concentrated in the United States due to supportive government programs and the establishment of the Solar Energy Research Institute (later renamed the National Renewable Energy Laboratory).[2] While this gave the United States an early lead (it had an 85 percent share of the global solar market by the early 1980s), these R&D investments produced cost declines that ultimately enabled the solar industry in other countries to flourish.[3] Similarly, in 2000, Germany established a generous feed-in tariff for solar energy that spurred technological progress and global cost declines.

Thanks to global technology diffusion, it is not necessary that every country adopt all the R&D policy recommendations in this section, most of which are geared toward countries possessing substantial R&D infrastructure.

GOVERNMENT LABORATORIES

Governments that own national labs or similar laboratory facilities can research societally important technologies directly. Government labs often have limited capacity and pursue technologies serving societal goals other than climate change mitigation (such as public health or defense), so government must choose carefully which clean manufacturing technologies should be targets for direct government research. Generally, this approach is best suited to technologies that

- could deliver large greenhouse gas emissions reductions;
- are too far from commercialization to attract private investment;
- show promise for eventual commercial competitiveness;

- would be of interest to many private firms, especially firms in different industries; and
- require large or highly specialized lab facilities beyond the scope of private firms' R&D departments.

The U.S. Advanced Manufacturing Office produced sixteen "bandwidth studies" identifying potential energy savings (but, unfortunately, not greenhouse gas emissions abatement) from R&D pathways in manufacturing industries, including iron and steel, chemicals, cement, aluminum, petroleum refining, and glass.[4] Studies like these provide useful input to government laboratories' project selection.

Government can push promising technologies along their learning curves, potentially for many years, and license the resulting intellectual property at low cost. As the technology becomes competitive, private firms gradually take over, building on the foundation the government established and taking a technology in new directions.

Examples of government-run laboratories include the U.S. Department of Energy's national labs, France's National Center for Scientific Research (CNRS) institutes, and labs operated by the Chinese Academy of Sciences. Each of these laboratory networks conducts research at multiple levels of technological maturity, including basic science, early-stage technology, and evolutionary improvements to already commercialized technology (the latter often in partnership with private firms).

RESEARCH PARTNERSHIPS

Once a technology is mature enough to be of interest to industry, a public-private research partnership is a powerful mechanism for commercializing the innovation and helping it to begin capturing market share. Partnerships can involve government labs, private firms, and/or academia. Each partner brings specific advantages.

- Government labs bring a high degree of science knowledge, specialized staff, and expensive equipment. Government may also provide financing (see the grants and contract research section later), de-risking the project for private partners.

- Manufacturers possess deep knowledge of the market, their product needs, and the practical realities of how to cost-effectively manufacture a technology.
- Academia is more diverse than government labs and, collectively, has more capacity, enabling research on a broader array of topics, often at lower cost. Additionally, partnering with universities helps develop students' skills and improves firms' ability to hire talented graduates in relevant fields.[5]

R&D leaders at private firms speak highly of their experiences in partnering with national labs. For example, John Wall, former chief technology officer of the engine manufacturer Cummins, described partnering with Sandia National Laboratories. Wall found Sandia's combustion research facility to be a tremendous asset for engine research and design, but Cummins could not have justified the expense to build, staff, and operate such a facility by itself. The company engages in cooperative R&D agreements that involve 50–50 cost sharing, clarify intellectual property ownership, and forge a collaborative environment that leverages both organizations' strengths.[6]

Research partnerships involve agreements on cost-sharing and intellectual property ownership. If a firm requires exclusive use of the resulting intellectual property, it may shoulder more of the up-front R&D investment. However, if the intellectual property can be licensed widely, the participating firm may receive a no-cost license and pay lower up-front costs, since some R&D expenses can be recovered by licensing the technology to other firms.

INDEPENDENT RESEARCH ORGANIZATIONS

Government may create or fund independent or quasi-independent research organizations that perform contract research for the government and partner with private firms. An independent research organization may be broadly similar to a network of government-owned labs, except it possesses a higher degree of political independence and may derive much of its budget from research partnerships and technology licensing fees rather than government appropriations.

The best-known example is Fraunhofer-Gesellschaft, a network of seventy-six applied research institutes within Germany (and about a dozen in other countries) with 29,000 employees and an annual budget of €2.9 billion. Fraunhofer receives roughly 30 percent of its revenue as "base funding" from the German federal and state governments, while the remaining 70 percent is derived from contract research.[7] A wide variety of technologies have been developed by Fraunhofer, including many relevant to manufacturing, such as systems to produce and use green hydrogen, efficient voltage converters, bioplastics, and green methanol.[8]

Another quasi-independent research organization is Manufacturing USA, a network of sixteen institutes that engage in research partnerships with 1,920 member organizations (61 percent manufacturers, 24 percent academic institutions, and 15 percent government labs or nonprofit organizations). Each institute is sponsored by a federal government department. Manufacturing USA has an annual budget of roughly $500 million, consisting of government and private funding.[9] Other research organizations that receive a mix of government and private-sector support include Research Triangle Institute and Southwest Research Institute.

GRANTS AND CONTRACT RESEARCH

In addition to operating labs or running partnerships, government can pay private firms or academia to conduct research on specific topics. For example, in 2019, U.S. federal and state governments provided $139 billion in R&D funding (21 percent of total R&D investment), covering 44 percent of basic research, 33 percent of applied research, and 12 percent of development expenses (figure 11.2).

Even though government directly funds only a small portion of business's R&D expenses (under 5 percent in the United States), research

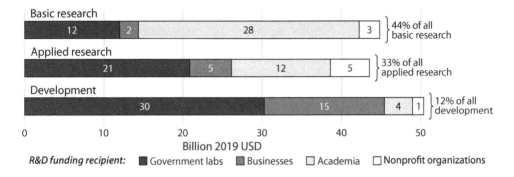

FIGURE 11.2 U.S. Government R&D Funding by Research Type and Performing Entity in 2019 Data include funding from the federal government and state governments.

Source: U.S. National Science Foundation, "National Patterns of R&D Resources: 2019–20 Data Update," February 22, 2022, https://ncses.nsf.gov/pubs/nsf22320.

heads at private firms nonetheless indicated that grants and contract research are among the most important policy tools government has for stimulating private R&D.[10] This may reflect the fact that research forms an ecosystem in which commercial firms benefit from precommercial R&D done in government labs and academia.

Unfortunately, only a tiny share of public funding is directed toward clean manufacturing technologies. The Advanced Manufacturing Office, the only U.S. federal entity focused on innovative manufacturing technology until October 2022, had an annual budget of around $0.4 billion in fiscal years 2020–22.[11] For scale, if annual federal expenditures were equivalent to the average U.S. household's annual spending ($63,000 in 2019), the amount spent on advanced manufacturing would be $3.84, less than the cost of a sandwich.[12] (As part of a new focus on improving U.S. industry, in October 2022, the Advanced Manufacturing Office was split into two successor offices: one focused on industrial efficiency and decarbonization and the other focused on advanced materials and manufacturing technologies.[13]) A few countries spend more—for example, in 2020, Germany's federal government spent about €1.66 billion on industrial technologies such as novel materials and production processes.[14]

Clean industrial technology R&D may also be supported by climate, energy, or cleantech funding agencies, such as Sustainable Development Technology Canada (SDTC), the European Commission's EU Innovation Fund, or the U.S. Advanced Research Projects Agency–Energy (ARPA-E). For example, in the fiscal year ending March 2021, SDTC disbursed C$146 million to around one hundred Canadian companies, many pursuing technologies that reduce industrial firms' emissions.[15]

Nonetheless, direct government support for clean manufacturing technologies is small relative to the importance of decarbonizing industry. Policy makers should greatly increase this funding, learning from the successes of existing programs.

COORDINATION OF RESEARCH EFFORTS

In addition to funding R&D, government can serve as a coordinator, helping connect different teams working on the same challenge so they can share findings and reduce duplication of effort. To encourage participation, government financial support can be made available within a collaborative structure. For example, the U.S. Department of Energy's Innovation Hubs were temporary programs that brought together government, industry, and university researchers to work on specific, difficult technical problems. Steven Chu, the Secretary of Energy when the hubs were established in 2010, compared them to miniature versions of the Manhattan Project, the World War II–era effort to develop atomic weapons. But the hubs' goals were peaceful and mostly related to decarbonization. For instance, one hub aimed to develop a cost-effective method of converting sunlight into hydrogen and hydrocarbon fuels, while another sought to dramatically increase chemical batteries' energy density and drive down their costs. The hubs had varying degrees of success, but by the time the program was winding down in the early 2020s, most hubs had largely achieved their goals and produced useful technical advances. The department decided to launch a series of new research centers based on the hub concept.[16]

Although these Innovation Hubs were in just one country, research can also be coordinated internationally. A prominent example is the European Organization for Nuclear Research (CERN), with twenty-three member states.

Avoiding duplication of effort does not mean constraining R&D to a single path to each technology or scientific goal. It is often desirable for researchers to pursue different strategies, since it may not be clear up front which strategy will reach the goal more quickly or which strategy might ultimately achieve lower costs or better performance characteristics. Robust coordination and knowledge sharing can enable research teams to avoid duplication where it would not add value and pursue different approaches when both show promise.

ACCESS TO SCIENCE, TECHNOLOGY, ENGINEERING, AND MATHEMATICS TALENT

R&D success requires skilled scientists and engineers. In today's increasingly innovation- and technology-driven economy, competition for technical talent can be fierce. In a series of interviews, U.S. corporate R&D heads' most commonly cited obstacle to greater R&D success is a lack of access to strong science, technology, engineering, and mathematics (STEM) talent.[17] They flagged shortcomings in science and math education, as well as an immigration system that makes it difficult or impossible to hire skilled individuals who are not U.S. citizens or permanent residents (even if they graduated from U.S. universities).[18] These issues are not specific to the United States—many countries face challenges in cultivating a skilled workforce.[19]

There are several ways policy makers can help facilitate the development of STEM talent via education.

- Provide strong science and math education in primary, middle, and secondary schools. This requires generous, equitable funding for public schools; high standards and pay for teachers; programs to help struggling students succeed; and programs to help top-performing students continue to be challenged and engaged. Programs can promote equity (see chapter 12) by ensuring that historically underrepresented groups benefit from high-quality STEM education and opportunities.

- Support technical vocational training and apprenticeships. These programs, which are popular and successful in Germany, are discussed in chapter 12.

- Develop stellar research universities. This requires not just STEM instruction but also funding for research performed in academic laboratories and collaboration with industry. Many countries are successfully creating and growing top universities. For example, universities in Saudi Arabia, Egypt, China, Malaysia, and Pakistan are among the fastest rising in international rankings (based on universities' teaching, research, citations, ability to attract international students and faculty, and level of industry collaboration).[20]

- Foreign students who graduate from a domestic university, particularly at the master's or doctoral level, can be offered permanent residency, possibly contingent on having a job offer and/or being in STEM or another in-demand field. It is self-defeating for a country to spend years training a new scientist or engineer, then force that person to leave the country.[21]

Regarding immigration, a country can use a points-based system that facilitates immigration by people who are able to contribute to industry. For example, Canada's Federal Skilled Worker Program gives points to applicants based on their English and French language skills, educational background, work experience, being of working age, and whether the applicant already has a job offer in Canada.[22]

Such a system, which is optimized around the needs of employers, must not be the only immigration mechanism. Other mechanisms to qualify for immigration should be designed to address other needs, such as family-based immigration and refugees and asylum seekers. Canada illustrates that these objectives need not be in conflict; the country is seen as a leader in welcoming diverse people and providing a haven for refugees while also meeting the needs of employers who wish to bring STEM talent into Canada.[23]

PATENT PROTECTIONS

An individual or firm that invents a new technology or method may apply for a patent, a government-granted legal right to exclusively use and license the invention for a given period (at least twenty years in World Trade Organization member countries).[24] Without patent protections, any business could use the innovation in its products, undermining the incentive for firms to invest in R&D. Therefore, the value of a robust and well-enforced patent system, coordinated across national borders, seems obvious.

Less obvious is the fact that patents can themselves stifle innovation. Patent examiners, often with a heavy workload and little time to spend on each patent application, are charged with an impossible task: ensuring that every application describes a novel, unique, and patentable innovation.[25] Existing patents are so numerous (figure 11.3) and sometimes so

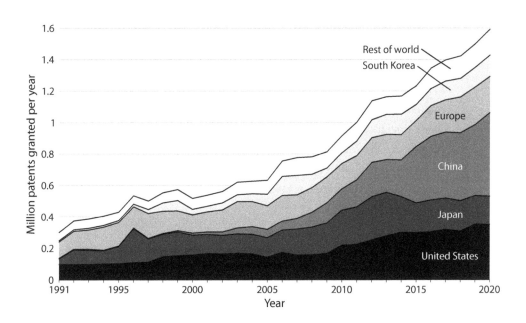

FIGURE 11.3 **Patents Granted per Year by Region** This figure depicts the number of newly granted patents each year. Most patents last around twenty years, so the total number of patents in force is much higher (globally, almost sixteen million in 2020).

Source: World Intellectual Property Organization, "WIPO Statistics Database," updated February 2023, https://www3.wipo.int/ipstats/keyindex.htm.

broad or vague that it is impossible for any person to know which claims are made in existing patents, and with enough effort, it is often possible to find examples of prior art that limit the validity or scope of a patent application.[26] This has led to a number of problems.

First, in some fields, a firm's cost to discover whether a new idea is already covered by any existing patent is prohibitively high. Therefore, in practice, firms check for infringement to only a limited extent, balancing the risks of litigation against the costs of patent discovery.[27]

Second, patents have been weaponized by firms, called "patent assertion entities" (PAEs), also known as "patent trolls." These firms' business model was described by an executive from software-maker SAS:

> A patent troll sets up shop in a jurisdiction known to be support-ive of patent plaintiffs. . . . It buys patents from defunct companies or patents that companies no longer want to keep. It does not hire employees; it does not engage in research; it does not even practice the invention—nor does it ever intend to practice it. The patent troll then either serves a demand letter on the victims or effects legal ser-vice of a complaint. The troll then pursues settlement by threatening massive and costly discovery . . . of every electronic document that might touch upon the alleged claims, by any person inside the defen-dant's operations. . . . [In one recent case], the number of electronic documents that we had to collect exceeded 10 million. . . . SAS won summary judgment in this case and it is now on appeal to the Federal Circuit. So far, this case has cost us in excess of $8 million [in legal fees alone].[28]

While some PAEs pursue large companies, most pursue small compa-nies. A single PAE may make demands of hundreds of firms that work in an area related to the patent without specific knowledge of those firms' products. PAEs know that most threatened companies (95–97 percent) will settle because the costs of not doing so are very high: a victim who fights the case in court must pay considerable legal fees, commit staff time, and may be blocked from innovating on challenged products while legal action is pending (typically for one to three years) because this could be viewed by a court as "willful infringement" and increase the firm's damages if the patent is upheld.[29] Among the very small number of cases that do reach a trial verdict, PAEs have a dismal record: they win only 9 percent of their suits, reflecting the fact that most PAE lawsuits are frivolous.[30]

Problems with patent litigation are not limited to PAEs. Due to the abundance of patents and the need to achieve interoperability with existing software and equipment, it is nearly impossible for firms to innovate in some fields without infringement. Large firms have learned to defend themselves by acquiring portfolios of thousands of patents and threatening to countersue any business that sues them for patent infringement. This often deters non-PAE businesses from filing patent infringement lawsuits, as they would incur large legal expenses and risk to their own products from the resulting countersuit. However, small, new companies do not own large patent portfolios that would offer a credible deterrent, so they may be forced to pay licensing fees, defend lawsuits, or be acquired by a larger firm.

The statistics in this section reflect the United States, but the issues described are not particular to that country. For example, China recently revised its patent laws to combat a rise in Chinese PAEs and other forms of patent system abuse.[31]

There are tools policy makers and firms may use to ensure that patents achieve their intended purpose of fostering and rewarding innovation.

- Patent offices should grant patents only for specific implementations rather than ideas or general methods. For example, a patent should cover a specific way to use electricity to make zero-carbon steel, not the concept of using electricity to make zero-carbon steel.
- Policy makers should establish a streamlined procedure under which defendants in patent infringement lawsuits may request that the patent office reexamine the patents at issue to ensure they are valid. This focuses patent examiners' limited attention on patents whose validity is important to a litigation outcome and provides an affordable way for innovative firms to protect themselves from PAEs asserting improperly granted patents.[32] Policy makers should

consider limiting who may file patent reexamination requests (e.g., to lawsuit defendants) to prevent the rise of "reverse patent trolls," entities that blackmail companies with threats to file requests to invalidate those companies' patents, a problem China is working to address.[33]

- The U.S. Federal Trade Commission recommended revisions to legal processes in patent disputes. These include alterations to the rules and timing regarding discovery of evidence, requiring that infringement charges be resolved against the manufacturer of a product before customers or users may be sued, and requiring plaintiffs to provide clear notice of which products are purported to be infringing which patent claims.[34]

- The nonprofit Electronic Frontier Foundation's (EFF's) recommendations go further. EFF suggests that plaintiffs be required to post a bond when bringing a patent infringement suit and be responsible for the defendant's legal fees if the plaintiff loses. EFF also suggests immunity for end users: only entities producing the relevant products or services could be sued for infringement. They also recommend prohibiting the use of shell companies to hide the beneficiaries of PAE activities.[35]

- Firms may join patent-sharing groups. One popular group is the License on Transfer Network. Members agree to automatically grant all other members a license to any of their patents that is later acquired by a PAE, making their patents worthless to PAEs but otherwise protecting members' full patent rights.[36] There also exist patent pools in which a third party obtains a large number of patents and makes them available to member companies to use for defensive purposes, including countersuits against nonmembers who sue a member firm.[37]

It is possible to design a patent system that provides strong patent protections and is resistant to abuse. Policy makers should keep both goals in mind, seeking win-win solutions that selectively inhibit abusive activities while ensuring that companies have robust tools to prevent bona fide patent infringement.

EMISSIONS DISCLOSURE AND LABELING

Firms may be required to determine the amount of greenhouse gas emissions produced by their activities and publicly report those emissions. Disclosure requirements can accelerate industrial decarbonization via several mechanisms.

First, a company facing a disclosure requirement must understand where its emissions are coming from, which often involves an audit of energy-consuming equipment and industrial process steps. Such audits often identify cost-effective ways for firms to save energy. A disclosure requirement may provide the impetus for a company to conduct an audit that it otherwise would not have prioritized (see chapter 4). This is one way in which greenhouse gas–reporting requirements can benefit firms.

Second, accurately reporting emissions is an enabler of other policies. For instance, it helps the government determine a firm's liabilities under carbon pricing, whether the firm is complying with greenhouse gas emissions standards, and whether its products qualify for green public procurement programs (chapters 9–10). Making these disclosures public (rather than revealing them only to government regulators) helps the public verify that businesses are complying with the law and can lead to pressure for enforcement action targeting noncompliant firms.

Third, reliance on high-emissions processes is a financial liability due to growing public and government recognition of the need for industries to decarbonize (and, ultimately, climate damages to businesses and the economy). Investors are entitled to full and accurate risk disclosures from public companies. Emissions disclosure requirements give investors data they need to make informed decisions. This helps align companies' objective to increase shareholder value with the need to preserve a livable climate.

Fourth, environmentally conscious buyers (including consumers and businesses) may use the disclosed information to direct their spending toward companies with lower emissions impacts.

Fifth, requirements for complete and accurate environmental disclosures can combat "greenwashing," the practice of presenting business operations or products as environmentally friendly (for example, by using terms such as "green," "eco-friendly," "natural," or "sustainable") without delivering corresponding environmental benefits. The media can call attention to instances when marketing claims are contradicted by disclosed data, so companies may need to back up their claims with actual environmental performance.

DISCLOSURE ORGANIZATIONS

To ensure accuracy and comparability across companies in different industries and countries, it is important that greenhouse gas measurement and reporting comply with an international standard. The leading entity managing environmental disclosures is CDP (formerly Carbon Disclosure Project), a nonprofit founded in 2000 with offices worldwide. CDP works with companies to help them accurately disclose emissions from their own facilities (scope 1 emissions), purchased electricity and heat (scope 2), and their supply chains—that is, purchased parts and materials—and the use of their products by purchasers (scope 3). CDP's scoring methodology shows where the largest impacts are, assigns letter grades to indicate performance, and clarifies what can be done to improve.[38] More than thirteen thousand companies disclose data through CDP.[39]

CDP is the principal data clearinghouse for disclosed information, but it is not the only organization setting standards governing what climate-related information should be reported. Other disclosure standard-setting organizations include the Task Force on Climate-Related Financial Disclosures (TCFD), the International Sustainability Standards Board, and the Global Reporting Initiative. For example, TCFD's recommendations include disclosure of scope 1, 2, and 3 emissions; how a company plans to respond to climate-related risks; its climate-related targets; and its performance against those targets.[40]

A related organization is the Science-Based Targets initiative (SBTi). While CDP helps companies disclose their current emissions and understand their performance relative to objective benchmarks, SBTi helps companies set verifiable targets for future emissions abatement. It requires that targets be compatible with a trajectory limiting global temperature rise to 1.5°C. (SBTi previously accepted targets up to 2°C.) All participating firms must set scope 1–2 emissions targets, and firms whose scope 3 emissions are at least 40 percent of their aggregate scope 1–3 emissions must set scope 3 targets. SBTi staff review companies' targets against detailed technical criteria to ensure validity and methodological robustness, including customized industry-specific criteria for a dozen industries.[41] As of early 2022, more than thirteen hundred companies had targets approved by SBTi, and more than fifteen hundred others had publicly committed to setting a target and getting SBTi approval within two years.[42]

VOLUNTARY AND MANDATORY DISCLOSURE

Until recently, most firms that disclosed their emissions did so because they were proud of their environmental record or in response to pressure from stakeholders: more than six hundred eighty large investors (with over $130 trillion in assets under management) and more than two hundred large purchasers (with $5.5 trillion in combined purchasing power) urge companies to disclose their emissions.[43] However, governments are increasingly mandating that companies disclose their emissions and climate-related risks. Mandatory reporting is fairer, as it imposes similar reporting costs (and opportunities) on all firms, gives complete information to investors and customers, rewards clean technology leaders, and prevents highly polluting firms from hiding their environmental impacts.

In April 2022, the UK became the first G20 country to begin enforcing a reporting requirement. UK-registered businesses with more than five hundred employees and £500 million in revenue (more than thirteen hundred firms) are required to report on their climate impacts in accordance with TCFD recommendations.[44] New Zealand enacted a reporting requirement in 2021, which is being phased in from 2023–24.[45] Japan will require large businesses to begin reporting their emissions after the 2023 fiscal year.[46] A European Union reporting requirement will be phased in from 2024–28.[47]

The U.S. Securities and Exchange Commission proposed a rule in 2022 that would require all publicly traded companies to disclose their climate-related risks and their scope 1–2 emissions (plus scope 3 reporting if those emissions are "material" or if the firm has set a scope 3 emissions target). Other countries with forthcoming greenhouse gas–reporting requirements include Brazil, Singapore, and Switzerland.[48]

LABELING

Labeling involves putting notices on a product's packaging and digital store listings indicating its environmental performance. Labels disclosing the energy efficiency of energy-consuming products, such as automobiles and appliances, are common globally. Examples include the China Energy Label, U.S. EnergyGuide, and EU Energy Label. (Certification programs for top-performing devices, such as ENERGY STAR, may also include a label.) However, these labels do not disclose the emissions that occurred during the manufacture of a product. Labels must disclose these "embodied emissions" if they are to be helpful in decarbonizing industry. Embodied emissions labels are relevant to many industrial products, not just energy-consuming devices.

Often, the bulk of the emissions involved in making a product occur during the production of its constituent materials. The finishing steps (e.g., final assembly) often require relatively little energy and produce few emissions. Therefore, labels disclosing only scope 1–2 emissions are not very useful, since companies that manufacture and sell final products usually do not produce those products' materials. A labeling program must require the disclosure of all emissions—that is, scopes 1–3—if labels are to provide useful guidance. If each company in a supply chain is required to label its products, this makes it easier for the next company in the chain to do so, as each company can use the label data from its suppliers in its own calculations. For example, a vehicle manufacturer could use data from the label on the steel it purchases when calculating the vehicles' scope 3 emissions.

Labeling should use a uniform, scientifically sound, and government-mandated emissions accounting methodology, ideally based on international standards and compatible with reporting through CDP. Labels and claims that do not comply with these standards should be prohibited. Today, there are more than four hundred fifty types of eco-labels on consumer products, most of which provide no meaningful guidance, as there are no standards for or verification of the claims being made.[49] Some labels are established by industry groups and have weak standards that can be met via conventional business practices. A profusion of labels making similar-sounding claims can facilitate greenwashing and prevent companies from getting credit for taking genuine steps to decarbonize.

A robust government labeling system helps highlight top performers, steers corporate and household purchasers toward more environmentally friendly options, and makes it easier for businesses and local governments to implement green procurement policies.

CIRCULAR ECONOMY POLICIES

Circular economy involves putting products to their highest and best use at each stage of their life cycle, such as extending product life spans, product-sharing systems, facilitating transfers to new users, refurbishing and remanufacturing products, and recycling. Specific policies can help with each stage.

RIGHT TO REPAIR

One aspect of product longevity is designing products to be repairable. Chapter 5 discusses how and why manufacturers sometimes make their products difficult or impossible to repair. In response, there is growing interest in right-to-repair laws, which regulate the ways in which companies may restrict owners' ability to repair their products. Right-to-repair legislation requires equipment manufacturers to make documentation, parts, and tools (including diagnostic software and firmware) available to product owners and independent repair shops at fair and reasonable terms. It also requires manufacturers to provide any information or tools necessary to disable (and reset) any security locks or functions.

The law specifies the period during which a manufacturer must provide parts and software. For instance, EU regulations specify ten years for appliances and seven years for electronic displays, while California specifies three years for electronics and appliances with a wholesale price of $50.00–$99.99 and seven years for $100 or more.[50] Right-to-repair legislation can also require that disassembly and reassembly require only standard, nonproprietary tools and that, where possible, parts be joined reversibly rather than soldered or glued together. (This also facilitates remanufacturing and recycling.)

The EU and several U.S. states have enacted right-to-repair legislation, the most comprehensive of which is in Rhode Island.[51] Following an executive order in 2021, the U.S. Federal Trade Commission began considering nationwide right-to-repair rules covering farm equipment and electronics.[52] France's 2020 circular economy law requires certain products to be labeled with 0–10 scores on a five-part "repairability index" covering documentation, disassembly, spare part availability, and other details (and will be extended to incorporate durability metrics in 2024).[53]

EXTENDED PRODUCER RESPONSIBILITY

Extended producer responsibility laws make manufacturers partly or wholly responsible for the reuse or disposal of their products at the postconsumer stage. By shifting responsibility from consumers to manufacturers, extended producer responsibility laws can incentivize manufacturers to design products to last longer and be easier to reuse, encourage a secondary market for their products, and design products to be more recyclable by making it easier to separate different materials and using materials that are easier to recycle. Key approaches include the following.[54]

- **Take-back programs**. The manufacturer (or a consortium of manufacturers) collects postconsumer products for reuse, recycling, or appropriate disposal. Take-back programs should be simple and convenient for consumers; product packaging (or products themselves) should indicate that the product must not be placed in household waste and provide instructions on how to return the product to a collection site. Take-back programs are most common for hazardous waste, such as batteries and electronics. However, they can also cover other products, especially those involving large quantities of valuable material, such as vehicles and appliances.
- **Advance disposal fees**. A fee to cover the costs of disposal is added to the product's purchase price if it contains hazardous or hard-to-recycle material or is designed in a way that makes it difficult to disassemble and recycle. Manufacturers are incentivized to make products easy to recycle to avoid the fee. Fees must be highly visible to consumers to influence behavior, so they should be incorporated into products' advertised prices, not added at checkout.
- **Deposit/refund systems**. Most common for beverage containers, a deposit/refund system is an advance disposal fee that is rebated to consumers who return containers to a collection point, such as a grocery store. The store is an intermediary: deposit fees charged by stores are passed on to manufacturers, which in turn reimburse stores for refunds paid to consumers returning empty containers. (For containers placed in curbside recycling, a refund is paid to waste management companies, which can pass on the savings to consumers via lower monthly waste collection charges. To avoid the need to separate refund-eligible containers from other containers of similar materials, refunds can be paid at a lower, "commingled" rate per unit weight.)[55] Deposit/refund systems have been shown to dramatically increase recycling rates of beverage containers, for example, achieving rates of 70–90 percent in eight U.S. states.[56] However, they can

result in windfall profits for manufacturers when containers are not returned, so some jurisdictions require manufacturers to turn over unclaimed deposits to fund government programs.[57]

- **Leasing**. Manufacturers can be encouraged to lease products rather than sell them, so the user has a legal duty to return the product to the manufacturer. For example, some chemical companies lease solvents to metal parts manufacturers and charge based on the period of time the solvent is used or the number of parts cleaned.[58] Governments can facilitate consumer product lending by establishing libraries for tools, gardening equipment, and the like (or expanding the mandate of existing public libraries to encompass these items).

INCREASE DEMAND FOR RECYCLED MATERIALS

Supply-side efforts to increase recycling are constrained by the demand for recycled materials. Therefore, it is crucial to accompany supply-side extended producer responsibility programs with policies that increase recycled material demand.[59]

- **Virgin material taxes**. A tax on virgin materials, such as plastic derived from petroleum, can encourage manufacturers to use recycled materials and to consider material efficiency in product design. These fees can be differentiated based on how easy a material is to recycle. For example, most U.S. residents only have access to recycling for PET and HDPE plastics (chapter 5), so fees on PET and HDPE should be lower than fees on other types of plastic.
- **Recycled content standards**. Standards may specify a minimum percentage of recycled, post-consumer content to be used in specific types of paper, glass, and plastic products and packaging. For example, in 2022, California implemented a requirement that 15 percent of the plastic in beverage containers must come from post-consumer sources, increasing to 25 percent by 2025 and 50 percent by 2030.[60]

- **Green public procurement programs**. Government may incorporate postconsumer recycled content guidelines into green public procurement programs (covered in chapter 10).

PROHIBIT DESTROYING EXCESS INVENTORY AND RETURNED ITEMS

A large share of unsold and returned items are destroyed or incinerated, even if the products are in good condition (see chapter 5). In 2020, France became the first country to adopt a law requiring companies to donate new, unsold goods (except those posing a risk to health or safety) rather than destroy them.[61]

Policy makers may require merchants to inspect and grade returns (rather than destroying them uninspected) and resell or donate items still in new condition. Returns in used condition should be donated or recycled where possible, but some returned items may need to be discarded (e.g., unrecyclable, broken items).

DISPOSABLE ITEM AND PACKAGING RESTRICTIONS AND FEES

Governments may ban certain disposable items or require they be made of easy-to-recycle materials. For example, many municipal governments have banned disposable plastic shopping bags and require stores to charge shoppers for paper bags. France's 2020 circular economy law outlaws disposable straws and stirrers, cutlery, tableware, polystyrene food containers, freely distributed plastic water bottles, and plastic packaging for fruit and vegetables.[62]

Fees can be an alternative to a ban on disposable items and packaging. For example, in 2021, Maine passed a law that imposes fees on corporations based on the type and quantity of packaging they use, its recycled content, and whether the packaging is reusable.[63]

RECYCLING AVAILABILITY AND REQUIREMENTS

Low availability and usage rates are a key barrier to recycling in many nations. As noted in chapter 5, only 13.5 percent of solid waste is recycled globally, and many countries lack widespread access to recycling services. Even in the United States, a high-income country, only 60 percent of the population had access to curbside recycling services in 2021.[64] Therefore, a key aspect of boosting recycling rates is to ensure that residents have access to convenient curbside recycling. More attention is particularly needed for multifamily dwellings, because they have much poorer recycling access than single-family dwellings yet are located in population centers with extensive waste collection infrastructure.[65]

Access to convenient curbside recycling is only half the picture. In some communities, subscribing to recycling is optional, and just 30 percent of these residents subscribe.[66] Low subscription rates not only harm material reuse goals—they also undermine the economics of providing recycling services to a town or community. Enrollment in recycling services should be automatic for all residences within a recycling firm's service area.

Finally, even residents who receive recycling services do not recycle all their recyclable materials. Rates vary by material, ranging from 33 to 79 percent.[67] Among households with curbside recycling, material capture rates can be increased through improved consumer education and prohibitions on including recyclable materials in the landfill bin.

BUILDING LONGEVITY

A critical aspect of circular economy is making buildings last longer. To achieve this, developers' and local governments' financial incentives must align with building longevity. Misaligned incentives are most notably an issue in China, although lessons from that country may be useful elsewhere.

In China, the average service life of buildings is twenty-five to thirty-five years, less than half that of buildings in the United States and

Europe.[68] There is no technical reason that this must be so: China has the capacity for high-quality, long-lived construction. For example, the World Economic Forum ranks China's transport infrastructure in the top 20 percent globally, and the Chinese government has punished construction firms that did not meet its quality benchmarks for public infrastructure.[69] In contrast, many buildings (especially housing) have been built to relatively poor quality standards because developers and local governments gain financially when buildings do not last long.

In China, the government owns essentially all urban land. Individuals and businesses may own apartments or buildings but not the land those buildings sit on. In many countries, governments levy a property tax: an annual fee on building owners that funds government services, such as schooling, police, and fire protection. In China, there is no annual property tax. Rather, a local government receives a lump sum by selling land use rights to a developer, who builds on that land and sells the resulting homes, offices, and so on. These land use rights nominally last forty to seventy years, depending on the intended use, and China is considering allowing these leases to be automatically or cheaply renewed at the end of the lease term.[70]

However, a local government may deem that redevelopment is in the public interest, order buildings demolished (even prior to the expiration of the lease term), and again sell the land use rights to a developer. Homeowners who are required to surrender their property are given financial compensation and/or alternative accommodations, but the government earns far more by reselling development rights than it pays in compensation. This process is easier and cheaper for the government if the condemned building was built to low quality standards and is unsafe or falling apart, as the building's market value will then have depreciated, so the government owes displaced residents less money (while the state owns the land and therefore captures any increase in land value). Developers earn money by constructing and selling buildings, so they also benefit when a structure is demolished and replaced. Close ties between local governments and developers, as well as government's desire to provide jobs and income for construction workers, further enhance the incentives for unending demolition and construction.[71]

(It also incentivizes conversion of rural land to urban land, displacing farmers and contributing to urban sprawl.)

In addition to financial incentives, there are other reasons for early demolition of buildings in China. These include poor architectural designs commonly used prior to the 1980s, lack of building maintenance, and rapid changes in China's urban fabric that rendered some buildings a poor fit for their location within one to two decades.[72]

The solution to poor building longevity in China begins with the implementation of an annual property tax to fund local government operations, coupled with restrictions on local governments' power to condemn buildings that are safe and structurally sound. This should be accompanied by building codes that mandate high-quality construction and regulations governing building operation and maintenance. Chinese developers are capable of building to high standards, though this may involve retraining workers and procuring higher-quality materials in some cases. Improved building quality coupled with modern architectural designs and smart urban planning can ensure that buildings remain desirable and useful for many decades. These reforms would bring several benefits to China: avoiding the costs to frequently replace its building stock, lower greenhouse gas and conventional pollutant emissions, and improved social harmony (as evictions and demolitions are an important source of public anger and unrest).[73]

R&D, EMISSIONS DISCLOSURE, AND CIRCULAR ECONOMY POLICIES FOR ZERO-CARBON INDUSTRY

Government's role in facilitating the transition to clean industry begins years before a technology reaches the market and extends through the end of a manufactured product's service life. Government has long supported science and technology development in the laboratory, and it should direct this support toward clean industrial technologies in its own labs and through research grants, partnerships, and contract research.

Policy makers can create an environment favorable to research success by coordinating public and private research efforts; fostering science, technology, engineering, and mathematics talent; and ensuring that the patent system protects genuine discoveries but cannot be weaponized to harm innovative companies and stymie future research.

Emissions disclosure policies and labeling can be powerful informational awareness tools that can help firms identify energy-saving opportunities, shift consumer purchasing behavior, and increase firms' incentives to adopt cleaner processes. Moreover, industrial emissions and energy use must be monitored so almost any policy can be enforced (for instance, to determine if a firm is complying with standards or how much it owes or is owed due to subsidies or carbon pricing). Since a monitoring framework is necessary in any event, public disclosure and product labeling requirements incur little cost while bringing additional benefits.

Circular economy policies regulate what happens to products at the end of their lives, but some of their most important effects occur at the product design stage, when they encourage or require manufacturers to use more recycled content, choose materials that are easier to recycle, and design their products for longevity, repairability, and ease of disassembly. More durable, high-quality products and buildings improve consumer experience and can save consumers money.

The last three chapters provide a comprehensive set of policy tools with which a country or region can decarbonize its industrial sector. However, it is important that all countries benefit from sustainable industry, and policies must be implemented in a way that protects vulnerable communities and makes certain that jobs and prosperity are broadly shared. How to ensure that the transition to clean industry furthers human development and makes the world more equitable and prosperous is the topic of the next chapter.

12

EQUITY AND HUMAN DEVELOPMENT

The shift to clean industry will have profound effects on the wealth, health, and livelihoods of people worldwide, especially in low- and middle-income countries (LMICs) with growing manufacturing sectors. To secure a livable climate, the transformation of industry must be global, and this cannot be achieved unless clean manufacturing technologies are accessible to LMICs.

Resource disparities also exist at smaller scales: individual towns and neighborhoods have differing financial resources and exposure to pollutants. Some communities may be dependent on industrial facilities for their economic livelihoods even as they suffer health impacts from pollution. Done right, a transition to clean industry can redress inequities and improve the lives of people in industrial and in disadvantaged communities, but this requires policy makers to consider economic and public health impacts when deciding how and where to implement policies to promote clean industry.

This chapter considers equity and human development implications of a move to zero-carbon industry from two angles: ensuring that clean industry furthers economic and human development of LMICs and that industrial and disadvantaged communities reap the economic and public health benefits of clean industry.

TECHNOLOGY ACCESS AND
DEVELOPMENT IN LMICS

In recent decades, the world has made progress on improving human living conditions. From 1990 to 2021, global per-capita GDP (adjusted for inflation and purchasing power parity) more than tripled, from $5,559 to $18,781, and life expectancy rose from sixty-five to seventy-one years. The share of the global population living on less than $3.65 per day, the median poverty line of lower-middle-income countries, plunged from 56 percent in 1990 to 24 percent in 2019. The share of the global population with access to electricity rose from 73 to over 91 percent from 1998 to 2021, and safe drinking water access increased from 62 to 74 percent between 2000 and 2020.[1]

Despite this progress, the world is far from offering a reasonable standard of living to everyone. As noted earlier, about a quarter of people live on less than $3.65 per day, and roughly the same proportion lack safe drinking water. Global resource inequality is high: the top 10 percent of the population possesses 52 percent of global income and 76 percent of global wealth, while the bottom 50 percent possesses just 9 percent of the world's income and 2 percent of its wealth (figure 12.1). The UN Universal Declaration of Human Rights affirms the right to adequate food, clothing, shelter, medical care, education, and financial security in sickness and old age.[2] For this vision to become a reality for all, it will be necessary to substantially increase the production of industrial goods, infrastructure, and buildings.

Past increases in economic output have come at an environmental cost. Regions that industrialized early are responsible for the largest share of cumulative CO_2 emitted to date, notably Europe (including Russia; 33 percent) and the United States plus Canada (27 percent).[3] Since 1990, the largest increases in per-capita emissions occurred in countries that experienced rapid industrialization and fossil fuel development, particularly China and countries in the Middle East. Countries on lower-carbon development pathways, such as Ghana and Costa Rica, relied

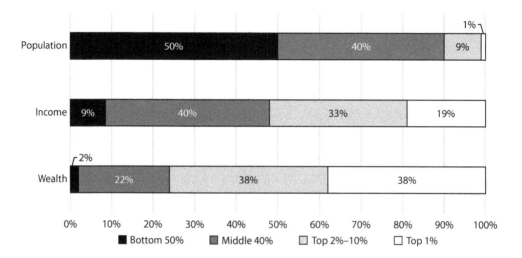

FIGURE 12.1 Global Income and Wealth Inequality in 2021

Source: Lucas Chancel, Thomas Piketty, Emmanuel Saez, and Gabriel Zucman, *World Inequality Report 2022* (report, World Inequality Lab, Paris, 2022), https://wir2022.wid.world/www-site /uploads/2022/03/0098-21_WIL_RIM_RAPPORT_A4.pdf.

more on nonmanufacturing activities, such as corporate services, agriculture, and tourism (figure 12.2).

However, 20–30 percent of global greenhouse gas emissions are embedded in internationally traded goods and services, so purchasing nations also share responsibility for these emissions.[4] All countries must eliminate their industrial emissions, but countries that industrialized early and are now major consumers of high-carbon products manufactured abroad have a special responsibility to take a leadership role in decarbonizing their own economies and helping less wealthy countries pursue sustainable, clean development.

To reduce the carbon intensity of economic development, quick deployment and scale-up of clean industrial technologies is crucial. Affording basic human rights to lower-resource members of the global community is urgent. LMICs will not (and should not) wait: their per-capita wealth is growing steadily, and they will continue to invest in their economies and people. If clean industrial technology is not available and cost-effective, LMICs will purchase conventional industrial

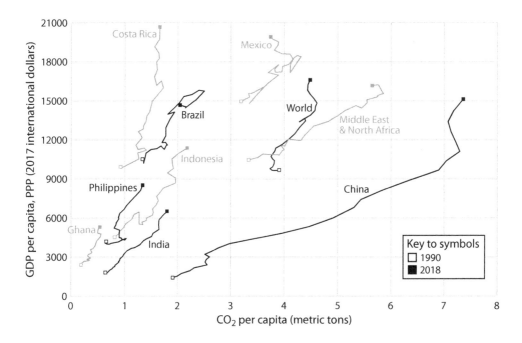

FIGURE 12.2 CO$_2$ and GDP per Capita in Select Geographies (1990–2018) Line shades vary to aid in differentiating overlapping lines. PPP = purchasing power parity.

Source: World Bank, "World Development Indicators," updated May 12, 2023, https://datacatalog.worldbank.org/search/dataset/0037712.

technology, locking in fossil fuel emissions for decades to come. That would be disastrous for the Earth's climate and the future of humanity. Therefore, it is in the interests of all countries to ensure that LMICs have access to clean industrial technology, have the financial resources to make necessary capital investments, and achieve ongoing financial returns (making their commitment to green industry sustainable).

It is in LMICs' interests to leapfrog over dirty industry and develop efficient economies supported by clean manufacturing for three reasons. First, conventional manufacturing results in air pollution that harms public health. For example, because China pursued a high-emissions industrial development pathway (figure 12.2), population-weighted mean exposure to fine particulates climbed to a high of 71 micrograms per cubic meter in 2011, over fourteen times the World Health

Organization's 5 micrograms per cubic meter guideline.[5] In that year, fine particulates caused 59 deaths per 100,000 people in China (around 790,000 deaths).[6] (China has begun taking strong steps to clean up, so fine particulate exposure and the air-pollution-related death rate have fallen in subsequent years.[7]) LMICs that skip over dirty industry can avoid incurring large health and mortality costs.

Second, major importers are increasingly moving toward policies that penalize or prohibit imported goods with high embedded emissions. The most prominent effort is the EU's carbon border adjustment mechanism (discussed in chapter 9). The United States announced in 2021 that it intends to align trade policy with that of the EU and exclude dirty industrial products, beginning with steel and aluminum.[8] Dirty production processes are a growing liability for manufacturers, as governments and consumers increasingly demand clean products and require decarbonization in a time frame compatible with a livable climate.

Third, all countries have a shared interest in protecting Earth's climate, but LMICs have fewer resources than high-income countries with which to adapt to changes in precipitation, temperature, sea level rise, and the like. Preventing climate change through investments in green industry (and similar measures in other economic sectors) affords the best chance of avoiding destabilizing impacts. Without sufficient global action, climate change could inhibit the future improvement of living standards and economic growth in LMICs and even reverse previous gains.

Given their shared interests, technology-providing countries and LMICs should partner to ensure a rapid global transition to zero-carbon industry. Several principles can guide this cooperation and make clean industrial development more successful.

LOCAL LEADERSHIP

Any government effort or program to develop industry in an LMIC should be led by that country and integrated into its national or regional plans. This allows local policy makers to adapt the program to fit the local context, build domestic political support, and find synergies with other, country-specific objectives (such as electricity access and job creation).[9]

INSTITUTIONAL CAPACITY

It is difficult for a country to implement policy or make efficient use of international support if it lacks sufficient "institutional capacity," a term that encompasses the rule of law (whether contracts can be enforced, crime prevented, etc.), stability of the government, reliability of public services, availability of accurate information, and, broadly, the capabilities and willingness of public institutions to fulfill their roles in service to society. To grow clean industry, capacity is needed in relevant specialties like energy, transport, manufacturing, finance, and trade.[10] In some cases, it may be necessary to improve institutional capacity in advance of, or simultaneously with, programs to promote clean industry.

Capacity-building approaches are beyond the scope of this book, but organizations providing guidance include the World Bank, International Monetary Fund, United Nations, Brookings Institution, OECD, and U.S. Agency for International Development.

INTELLECTUAL PROPERTY LICENSING

Decarbonizing industry requires technologies developed by private firms, academia, and government laboratories, any of which may secure patents to guarantee their intellectual property (IP) rights. Rightsholders should widely license their technology to LMIC firms at prices they can afford, with an urgency befitting the fact that climate change is an emergency. Lessons can be drawn from experience with COVID-19 vaccine IP. During the COVID-19 pandemic, vaccine makers rapidly scaled up production capacity by issuing licenses and contracting with facilities worldwide. Nearly two hundred facilities in forty countries were producing vaccines by the end of 2021.[11] (Given time, more capacity could be brought online, including up to one hundred twenty firms in LMICs that meet the technical requirements and quality standards to produce mRNA-based vaccines.[12])

IP owners opposed a global push to temporarily exempt COVID-19 vaccines from IP protections.[13] A government-imposed waiver might not have increased vaccine access in a relevant time frame because production was limited by the availability of suitable manufacturing facilities and raw materials, firms would have faced difficulties setting up complex manufacturing lines for novel technologies without the practical know-how and cooperation of IP owners, and manufacturers may have been reluctant to make long-term investments in new production processes on the basis of a temporary waiver.[14]

Policy makers should consider the following strategies to improve IP licensing in LMICs.

- Rightsholders should be encouraged to license clean industrial technology widely and offer discounted pricing to LMICs based on ability to pay.
- Government can fund R&D efforts aimed at decarbonizing the same industrial processes via multiple technologies to create competition between private firms that can drive down technology costs and encourage widespread IP licensing.
- Government can generously fund R&D efforts on the condition that the resulting technology be licensed broadly on prearranged terms that ensure access for LMICs.
- Governments that develop technology alone or in a public-private partnership may have some IP ownership rights and can insist on generous licensing terms.
- Government may subsidize licensing fees and/or purchase green manufacturing equipment for LMIC firms.
- Government-imposed, temporary IP waivers are unlikely to be effective due to industry opposition, manufacturers' reluctance to make long-term investments backed by a temporary waiver, and difficulties that firms would face in building, deploying, and using technology without rightsholder cooperation.

EDUCATION AND ACCESS TO TALENT

Successful growth of zero-carbon industry relies on industrial engineers, skilled technicians, and factory workers to design and operate plants. Countries may need to increase the resources devoted to education to ensure that firms have access to the talent they need.[15] Improved science, technology, engineering, and mathematics (STEM) education is important in countries of all income levels (see chapter 11), but the need to invest in education can be acute in some LMICs. For example, only 27 percent of students in sub-Saharan Africa complete secondary school (high school).[16]

A promising approach is to support apprenticeship or "dual training" programs that split classroom time with on-the-job training. In Germany, a world leader in this area, nearly 60 percent of youth participate in apprenticeships.[17] The government covers the cost of school tuition and establishes standardized curricula for occupational profiles, so apprentices who train with one firm learn transferable skills and earn a certificate that will be recognized by other firms in Germany and internationally.[18] It is a respected career path and has helped Germany maintain high-quality industrial jobs. Manufacturing accounts for 18 percent of Germany's GDP, significantly higher than other western nations such as France (9 percent), the United States (11 percent), the UK (9 percent), Spain (11 percent), and Canada (10 percent).[19]

Another step policy makers must take to help firms access talent is to ensure equal rights and opportunities for women. This includes providing high-quality STEM education, making financing available for entrepreneurs, and ending cultural stigmas against women working outside the household (and at industrial firms in particular). Equality for women is not only fundamental to human rights; it also accelerates GDP growth and economic development.[20] One example program is Egypt's El Maadi STEM School for Girls, a public high school that uses a project-based curriculum to help girls develop skills in areas such as physics, robotics, and nanotechnology. El Maadi students have won international science competitions, and the school has served as a model for STEM schools elsewhere in Egypt and the Middle East.[21]

FINANCING AND INVESTMENT

Development of new industrial facilities and supporting infrastructure requires significant capital investment. Industries in LMICs can look to governments or private investors for support, and support may be domestic or international in origin.

LMIC governments may directly support domestic industries using cost-sharing, tax credits, and subsidies, or they may provide low-cost loans or use other lending mechanisms. These approaches are covered in chapter 9. However, LMICs may have limited funds available to divide among numerous high-value projects (e.g., transportation infrastructure, health care, education, security, utilities, and internet access), only some of which are of interest to profit-seeking investors. Therefore, LMIC policy makers may wish to reserve public funding for projects that are unable to obtain private funding and, where possible, to leverage foreign capital via "international project finance" (a cost-sharing mechanism to fund revenue-generating infrastructure, typically in telecommunications, energy, and transportation).[22]

Policy makers can prioritize projects that contribute to a business environment that helps domestic industry attract private financing. For example, an educational system that produces a skilled workforce, a judicial system that impartially enforces laws and contracts, transportation systems that allow for efficient movement of workers and goods, and public health systems to prevent and treat disease all lower investment risk and facilitate private investment.

Foreign governments and international finance institutions (such as the World Bank, International Monetary Fund, and Asian Development Bank) are another source of capital for industrial development, but historically, their contribution to decarbonizing industry has been small. International public climate finance totals $227 billion (2019–20 annual average), of which only $9 billion (4 percent) went to industry, the smallest share among recipient sectors.[23] Even that overstates climate funding available to industry in LMICs, since less than 75 percent of international climate finance flows to LMICs.[24] A single large industrial facility can cost over $1 billion, so existing flows to industry are too small to be a promising funding source for zero-carbon industrial development. Other social objectives receive more international public funding, including disaster relief, food security, and health, all of which stand to become much worse if climate change is not adequately mitigated.[25] Therefore, donor countries and international finance institutions should recognize that funding clean industrial development is fundamental to their goals and should dramatically increase their support.

By far, the most promising source of capital for zero-carbon industry in LMICs is private investment. In 2019, total foreign direct investment inflows worldwide were $1.5 trillion, of which $525 billion went to firms in LMICs. This increased the total stock of foreign direct investment to $36 trillion globally, including $7.4 trillion in LMICs.[26] Foreign direct investment flows specifically to manufacturing enterprises were $402 billion for greenfield projects (new capital construction) and a further $243 billion for mergers and acquisitions of existing manufacturing assets.[27]

As these figures include investments only from foreign sources, they don't account for the capital that industries can raise from domestic markets, which can be large in some LMICs. For example, private-sector investment in private, domestic capital assets (machinery, buildings, etc.) represent 15–25 percent of national GDP in most countries and 37 percent in China (though not all of this capital resides within the industrial sector).[28]

The amount of private funding available significantly exceeds direct government financial support to industry. Therefore, policy makers can most efficiently capitalize clean industrial development by helping firms capture a larger share of private investment. Policy makers should take the following actions.

- Create a favorable social and legal climate for international business (discussed earlier).
- Use government funds to leverage private capital for clean industry via mechanisms such as international project finance or the lending mechanisms discussed in chapter 9.
- Be judicious in placing restrictions on foreign ownership of domestic firms and capital, as these restrictions can hinder an important

source of private investment, harming economic growth and clean industrial development. Ownership restrictions are most appropriate for sensitive industries (such as defense) and for investments from countries that are subject to sanctions. To ensure that residents share in the prosperity created by industry, policy makers can generally rely on other policy tools, such as requirements that firms employ a minimum share of residents (including at managerial and executive levels), abide by minimum wage requirements, and ensure that businesses pay their fair share of taxes.

- Consider outreach to "impact investors," asset managers who seek to balance financial returns with positive social and environmental achievements. Supporting clean industry in LMICs delivers greenhouse gas reductions, economic development, and financial returns, so these projects are good fits for impact investors. As of 2020, $2.3 trillion (2 percent of global assets under management) were committed to impact investments, of which 31–43 percent were in emerging markets.[29]
- Package industrial projects into a fund and market the fund to global investors. This facilitates funding for projects that may be too small individually to attract large institutional investors. It helps investors achieve portfolio diversification and reduces risk.[30]

PROSPERITY AND HEALTH FOR ALL COMMUNITIES

A transition to zero-carbon industry presents opportunities and challenges not only at the level of countries but also for specific cities, towns, and neighborhoods within each country. Policy makers can help direct economic and public health benefits to communities where these benefits are most needed. Two types of communities deserve special attention: industrial and disadvantaged communities.

Industrial communities are heavily dependent on industry for their economic livelihoods. Often, jobs there rely, directly or indirectly, on one or a few large employers. For example, in the United States in

2019, there were roughly 2,600 "anchor businesses" (firms employing at least 1,000 people in a city or town with population under 500,000), roughly a quarter of which were manufacturers. The average population of a community with an anchor business was around 64,000, so an anchor business represents a large share of total employment in its community.[31]

Industrial communities may face economic disruptions if existing employers retool or, especially, relocate their facilities. However, these communities may benefit from training opportunities with cutting-edge equipment, improved working conditions, and reduced air pollution. Policy makers should help them navigate this transition, minimizing job disruptions and making industrial communities vibrant and healthy.

Disadvantaged communities are those that have historically experienced low levels of investment and economic opportunity relative to other communities in the same country or region. Disadvantaged communities typically face a range of burdens, including above-average rates of poverty, unemployment, vacant housing, low educational attainment, and low or shrinking numbers of businesses.[32] In the United States, disadvantaged communities are strongly correlated with race: people of minority races make up 56 percent of these communities, compared with 39 percent of the national average and 27 percent of the most prosperous quintile of communities.[33] This is partly a legacy of government policy that explicitly aimed to increase segregation and channel the benefits of homeownership to white Americans.[34]

Policy makers have a responsibility to ensure that a clean industrial transition helps disadvantaged communities, as a matter of fairness, to combat rising wealth inequality, and to right wrongs caused by past policy. Entire cities or regions will benefit, as remedying patterns of disinvestment and segregation brings significant region-wide improvements in GDP, household income, and crime reduction.[35]

Some communities are both industrial and disadvantaged. In the United States, nine of the ten industries most concentrated in disadvantaged communities relate to natural resources or manufacturing (e.g., coal mining, apparel-making, logging, sawmills, and oil and gas extraction).[36] Both industrial and disadvantaged communities frequently suffer public health impacts from industrial and fossil fuel pollution.

Policy makers should consider the following strategies to help direct clean industrial development toward industrial and disadvantaged communities.

CONSULT LOCALLY

Engage with community representatives about their needs, including local elected officials, civic organizations, business and labor leaders, and environmental advocates. Community members have deep insight into problems and may have solutions in mind. Addressing community needs, even if not directly related to industrial development, helps make the community a more attractive place to live and work. This, in turn, helps manufacturers hire and retain talent. Proactive community engagement can also facilitate the construction of new industrial facilities, reducing the odds of community opposition and lawsuits aiming to block development.

INVEST IN INFRASTRUCTURE

Some disadvantaged communities may not possess high-quality infrastructure, which is necessary for workers to get to their jobs and for shipping raw materials and finished products. Industrial communities may have infrastructure suitable for existing businesses, but different kinds of infrastructure may be needed for zero-carbon industry. For example, a factory on a spur rail line may be able to receive coal shipments, but that may not be adequate if the factory switches to electricity for its heat needs. Instead, the factory requires more electricity, which may involve construction of high-voltage electrical cables, towers, and transformers. Targeting communities for new infrastructure investment can help them become—or remain—important industrial employers.[37]

Infrastructure should be designed around the needs of existing communities to help mitigate displacement of residents and destruction of urban fabric. Without smart urban planning, infrastructure can do harm. For instance, construction of some U.S. highways destroyed vast swathes of buildings, bisected neighborhoods, exacerbated inequality, and increased pollution.[38]

OFFER RETOOLING GRANTS

Government may provide subsidies for the conversion of existing manufacturing facilities to new, clean processes.[39] Grants should be targeted at facilities at greatest risk of closure and come with conditions requiring that the facility continue to operate and maintain specific staffing levels for a designated period. For more on grants, see chapter 9.

ENHANCE SUPPLY CHAIN RESILIENCE

Today, supply chains are highly internationalized and vulnerable to disruptions. The Intergovernmental Panel on Climate Change warns that supply chain disruptions may worsen due to climate-related shocks, which can cause shortages and raise goods' prices, setting back equity, human welfare, and development goals.[40] Fragile supply chains not only threaten consumers, they also threaten manufacturers and the economic livelihood of industrial communities. Therefore, policy makers should consider initiatives to enhance supply chain resilience.

Government can reward firms that source a minimum share of their input materials from within the same country or region (e.g., the EU, North America), or they may impose domestic or regional content requirements for government-funded projects. Firms can be encouraged to maintain input reserves (versus "just-in-time" manufacturing). Infrastructure for electricity, transport, coastal defenses, and the like can be hardened against climate change and other disruptions (cyberattacks, for example).[41]

ENSURE BENEFITS REACH COMMUNITIES

Government may use financial incentives to promote clean industry, such as subsidies for clean industrial production, equipment rebates, and low-interest loans (chapter 9). Government can attach conditions to these incentives to ensure that benefits reach community members, such as community benefit agreements, commitments to provide training to local residents, and local hire agreements.[42]

Similarly, requirements to protect workers and promote equity can be incorporated into green public procurement programs (chapter 10). For instance, policy makers may require that a share of qualifying products be produced in disadvantaged communities or be made by companies that achieve high labor standards, pay fair wages, and provide community benefits.

PROTECT PUBLIC HEALTH

Generally, a transition to zero-carbon industry will also reduce conventional pollutants that damage human health, such as particulates. However, there may be exceptions. For instance, carbon capture increases fuel consumption and captures only CO_2, so particulate emissions can increase without improved filtration technology (chapter 8). Another example is the possibility that carbon cap-and-trade systems with offsets might allow harmful emissions to persist longer in disadvantaged communities than other decarbonization policy tools (chapter 9). Accordingly, policy makers should take the following actions to protect public health.

- Consider conventional pollutant impacts on communities near industrial facilities when evaluating technology or policy options.
- Enact or strengthen conventional pollutant standards, including limits on particulates, nitrogen oxides, and sulfur oxides. Conventional pollutant standards are a necessary complement to decarbonization policies. They ensure that greenhouse gas reductions are accompanied by public health benefits and reward technical approaches that reduce all pollutants rather than just greenhouse gases.

- Protect the health of workers on the job. Ensure that strong occupational health and safety regulations are in place and that employees can report violations without fear of retaliation.[43]

SUPPORT DISPLACED WORKERS

Most industries can transition to cleaner processes, but a rare few—such as coal mining—will need to wind down or pivot into a different industry. In these cases, government should provide support to affected workers, primarily by ensuring that high-quality, well-paid jobs with benefits replace lost jobs in those communities. This may lessen affected communities' opposition to the clean energy transition, or in some cases, it might even garner their support. For example, in 2022, the largest U.S. coal miners' union endorsed a bill that would hasten the phase-out of coal because it provided generous incentives for manufacturers to open factories in coal-mining communities (among other provisions), giving those communities a lifeline in a post-coal future. (Unlike workers, coal mine owners, who have fixed assets and cannot simply switch to a different industry, opposed the bill.)[44]

Other forms of worker support include unemployment insurance (cash payments to support unemployed workers while they train and look for work) and uninterrupted health care access. Training (via apprenticeships, community colleges, and other training programs) is also valuable.[45]

Failure to achieve a just transition can have political repercussions. Declining former coal-mining communities in democratic nations have shown increased support for right-wing authoritarian populism and decreased belief in the effectiveness of democracy.[46]

Far-sighted policy makers can ease this transition by helping vulnerable communities start diversifying their economies and retrain workers even before coal mines close. For example, Colorado's Just Transition Office, the first program of its kind, assists workers via individual transition plans, job training, relocation support, temporary income, and benefits. It helps communities through local transition planning, infrastructure funding, an investment fund to finance business development, lending mechanisms, and tax incentives.[47]

BALANCE POLICIES TO MINIMIZE JOB DISRUPTIONS AND INFLATION

Jobs are linked to the level of inflation-adjusted spending in the economy. Policies that increase spending tend to create jobs, while policies that reduce spending tend to cost jobs. However, more spending is not always better: too much spending can trigger inflation or a bubble (unrealistically high valuations for goods or firms that subsequently crash), causing hardship. Therefore, monetary policy typically aims to create a stable and growing economy that balances low unemployment and low inflation.[48]

Some industrial decarbonization policies promote additional spending by making more money available or making things cheaper, while others reduce spending by making things more expensive or otherwise reducing demand. Others have mixed or minimal effects on spending. Table 12.1 categorizes the policies discussed in this book by their effects on economy-wide spending.

TABLE 12.1 Typical Effects of Decarbonization Policies on Economy-Wide Spending

Increases spending	Decreases spending	Mixed or minimal effects
Subsidies and tax credits	Carbon pricing	Energy efficiency and greenhouse gas emissions standards
Equipment rebates	Fees on inefficient equipment	Equipment feebates
R&D support	Product longevity/right to repair	Emissions disclosure and labeling requirements
Green public procurement	Product-sharing systems	Extended producer responsibility and recycling requirements

Note: This table considers only the effects of the policies themselves, not how they are paid for or how revenues they generate are used. For example, subsidies normally increase economy-wide spending, but they could instead decrease spending if the government pays for the subsidies via a new, highly regressive tax.

Utilizing all these policies is ideal for rapid industrial decarbonization, but when choices must be made, policy makers can emphasize policies that increase spending in industrial and disadvantaged communities, where stimulating growth is a primary concern. They may also use general monetary policy to compensate for the spending effects of decarbonization policies, such as a central bank lowering interest rates to compensate for carbon pricing.

SUSTAINABLE PROSPERITY FOR ALL

The transition to clean industry must be global; no one should be left behind. This is a moral imperative and also a practical one: if countries or communities feel they are being harmed, they will oppose this transition, slowing its pace and increasing the risk that it will fail. Sustainable industry can improve the lives of billions of people by creating manufacturing jobs, reducing harmful pollution, protecting ecosystems, and boosting economy-wide growth through investments in clean energy and industrial technologies. If this prosperity is broadly shared, it can reduce today's staggering wealth inequality and raise global living standards, further strengthening the global economy.

Policy makers must resist the temptation to restrict the international flow of clean industrial technology and understand that while individual firms may primarily seek to enrich their shareholders, the goal of public policy should be to grow the wealth, health, and sustainability of all communities, especially those that are furthest behind. Done right, the coming transformation of global industry is an opportunity to usher in a new era of human and environmental well-being.

CONCLUSION

A Roadmap to Clean Industry

E liminating industrial greenhouse gas emissions is crucial for the future of humanity and is achievable in the 2050–2070 time frame. This book provides a comprehensive guide to the technologies and policies that can reduce industrial emissions to zero. However, it may not yet be clear which technologies or policies to prioritize in different years, in different geographies, and at different stages of technological maturity. This section looks across all preceding chapters and assembles their findings into a clear and actionable roadmap to a clean industrial future.

A region's experience transitioning to clean industry will depend on its wealth, the fuels and technologies currently used by its industry, the availability of zero-carbon energy resources (such as wind, solar, and bioenergy potential), and the composition of its economy. Therefore, it is not possible to assign globally applicable date ranges to specific technologies or policies. Some regions will be able to move faster than others, and some technology or policy tools will be more applicable to specific countries or subnational regions. Therefore, this roadmap defines phases that indicate the steps a region should take based on where it is in its industrial decarbonization journey.

PHASE 1

Phase 1 broadly represents the present day. In this phase, heavy industry (making materials such as steel, cement, chemicals, brick, and glass) relies on the use of coal, natural gas, and petroleum. Light industry (assembly of final goods from materials, food processing, and the like) is partly electrified but still derives some heat from fossil fuel combustion.

In phase 1, the top priorities are to stop investing in new fossil-fuel-using industrial equipment, begin a transition to electrified processes, and secure a sufficient clean energy supply. Energy efficiency and material efficiency measures are crucial in reducing energy demand, making the build-out of adequate renewable electricity capacity quicker and cheaper. Efficiency also reduces emissions, since industry is not yet decarbonized. Energy efficiency standards, emissions standards, and circular economy support policies are particularly useful at incentivizing efficiency.

Regions must aggressively invest in zero-carbon electricity generation resources to meet demand for industrial electrification, green hydrogen, and hydrogen-derived fuels (as well as the needs of nonindustrial sectors). This requires large increases in onshore wind, offshore wind, solar photovoltaic, and hydroelectric capacity (allocated based on resource potential), with geothermal and nuclear generation playing a supplementary role. Electricity can be moved from areas of high potential using transmission lines, but the falling costs of solar and wind capacity make long-distance transmission less necessary than in the past, as it can now be cost-effective to build capacity in less windy and less sunny areas close to electricity load centers.

Policy makers must accelerate deployment of already commercialized clean industrial technologies. The first priority is industrial heat pumps, which can supply heat at temperatures up to around 165°C (covering about 30 percent of industrial heat demand) and are often cost-competitive with fossil fuels due to their exceptional efficiency. Financial policies (such as subsidies and lending mechanisms) can make these technologies definitively cheaper than their fossil counterparts and ensure that small manufacturers can afford to upgrade.

Electrified technologies for medium- to high-temperature heat have larger cost and commercialization gaps. Governments need to support the spread of electrified heat technologies across industries (for instance, expanding the use of plasma torches beyond plasma cutting and arc welding to become a general-purpose heating technology), so equipment is available commercially for all industries and temperature ranges. A green public procurement program would enable the government to pay above-market prices for materials produced via clean, medium- to high-temperature processes but would contain total costs to government (whereas making that same level of subsidy available for all buyers in the market might be too expensive).

For earlier-stage technologies, such as electrolysis of iron ore and novel cement chemistries, research and development (R&D) support policies and cost-sharing for demonstration or first-of-a-kind commercial pilot plants can help accelerate commercialization. R&D investment in improving electrolyzer performance is also worthwhile, as green hydrogen will be needed to decarbonize chemical feedstocks and make primary steel in phases 2–3.

Carbon capture and use or storage (CCUS) is not an ideal decarbonization route because it preserves fossil fuel production (with associated upstream emissions) and has conventional air quality impacts. However, in phase 1, CCUS can be the best option in specific situations: where there is difficulty providing sufficient zero-carbon electricity, where electrified technologies are not yet commercially available at scale (for example, primary steelmaking), and for addressing nonenergy CO_2 emissions from cement kilns. Regions with abundant, low-cost fossil resources and suitable geological storage sites can consider CCUS investment as a means of rapidly reducing industrial emissions until better options become available. CCUS should be targeted predominantly at retrofitting existing, relatively new facilities with decades of service life remaining (to avoid extending the life of fossil-using facilities close to retirement), especially cement kilns and blast furnaces. CO_2 should be sent to dedicated underground storage or mineralized, not used for enhanced oil recovery or incorporated into nonmineral products.

Phase 1 is the ideal time to get supporting policies right, to create a favorable business environment for rapid innovation and deployment of clean technologies. To support R&D, policy makers should improve access to science, technology, engineering, and mathematics talent through education, apprenticeships, and immigration; fix issues in the patent system; and establish R&D partnerships and research consortia. Phase 1 is also the time to implement emissions disclosure and labeling requirements because they clarify the existing emissions landscape, help businesses and consumers choose greener options, cause some companies to voluntarily clean up their operations, and lay the groundwork (i.e., emissions monitoring and data reporting systems) necessary to implement other policies.

PHASE 2

Phase 2 represents a time when industrial low-temperature heat has largely been electrified, medium- to high-temperature electric technologies are widely commercialized (but not yet universally adopted), and technologies at early stages today (such as alternative cement chemistries and iron ore electrolysis) are starting to reach commercial viability. *Phase 2's main objectives are to finish the transition to clean industrial heat and begin decarbonizing chemical feedstocks and primary steelmaking at commercial scale.*

Decarbonizing the electric grid is a prerequisite for zero-carbon industry, and the technologies necessary to achieve a clean grid are mature and well understood. Therefore, the electricity sector is on a faster decarbonization timeline than industry and reaches near-zero emissions in phase 2. This requires continued, large investments in zero-carbon generation to keep up with increasing demand from industry, buildings, and vehicles. Mechanisms to address the variability of renewables, such as energy storage (chemical batteries, pumped hydro, etc.), demand response programs, and interlinking larger balancing areas become very important as renewables start to account for over 80–90 percent of generation.

Low-temperature industrial heat needs are largely handled by heat pumps, waste heat recovery, and, occasionally, solar process heat. Widespread deployment of heat pumps has reduced their capital costs, while continued declines in electricity prices (due to cheap wind and solar) make heat pumps affordable to operate, so policy makers may discontinue subsidies for heat pumps. Instead, they should implement standards that prohibit the sale of fossil technologies for low-temperature heat, causing the last stragglers to upgrade during their next equipment replacement cycle.

Medium- and high-temperature electrical technologies are nearing an inflection point, where they are widespread, commercially available for essentially all industries, and roughly competitive with fossil fuels. This is the time when carbon pricing is at its most efficient, able to influence purchase decisions and drive abatement via technology switching rather than demand reduction. Green public procurement and subsidies for clean production remain useful for technologies that need some extra help, but these policies' importance declines as electrified heat becomes cheaper and as standards and carbon pricing reduce the market share of fossil fuel–based heating technologies.

Phase 2 is the time for large investments in green hydrogen. Hydrogen will be needed to create zero-carbon chemical feedstocks (for fertilizers, plastics, etc.) and produce primary steel from hydrogen-direct reduced iron. In phase 1, these technologies were not the lowest-hanging fruit and were primarily relegated to R&D efforts, but in phase 2, they are deployed at commercial scale. Chemicals and steel made with green hydrogen should be the new focus of green public procurement programs and subsidies. Carbon pricing should not yet extend to fossil fuels used as chemical feedstocks, since the alternatives are not mature enough.

In phase 2, the deployment of new CCUS equipment for fossil fuel combustion should be phased out (but it may continue to be deployed to capture CO_2 from bioenergy and limestone calcination). Existing CCUS, deployed in phase 1, can continue to operate until those plants reach the end of their natural life spans in phase 3.

High-income nations and those with more advanced industrial technologies should collaborate with low- and middle-income nations to ensure that as many countries as possible reach phase 2 quickly. Regions that are just beginning industrial development should aim to leapfrog over phase 1 and deploy phase 2 technologies to avoid investing in polluting capital that will quickly become a financial liability and cause public health and climate damages. Policies that seek to decarbonize imported materials, parts, and products—such as three-scope emissions standards and carbon pricing with border adjustments—can provide an economic incentive for suppliers in other jurisdictions to adopt clean manufacturing processes.

PHASE 3

Phase 3 begins when the electric grid, essentially all industrial heat, and a significant share of feedstocks are decarbonized. *The main goals are to finish decarbonizing feedstocks and primary steelmaking and to help lagging regions reach phase 3.*

With most medium- to high-temperature industrial heat decarbonized, governments can withdraw subsidies and incentives for zero-carbon heat and impose ratcheting standards that squeeze the remaining inefficient, dirty technologies off the market. As sufficient zero-carbon electricity capacity comes online, facilities using CCUS with fossil fuel combustion should retire or be upgraded with modern electrical or hydrogen technologies, nudged via policies such as conventional pollutant emissions standards or financial incentives. CCUS may continue to be used for bioenergy and limestone calcination. Additionally, starting in phase 3, deploying CCUS with direct air capture may make sense, either to offset the 1–2 percent most difficult-to-abate emissions economy-wide or to reduce atmospheric CO_2 concentrations to avoid climate damages.

In phase 3, electrified and green hydrogen–based chemical feedstocks and iron smelting gradually increase, ultimately reaching 100 percent market share. Subsidies and green government procurement should gradually give way to tradable, sales-weighted standards limiting the share of chemicals or steel that may be made with fossil fuels.

By phase 3, today's early technologies such as alternative clinker chemistries, iron ore electrolysis, and novel chemical production pathways will either have borne fruit and become commercial or failed to surmount cost and technical feasibility hurdles. Government can identify and support technologies that still have promise for addressing unmet decarbonization needs.

When the first countries reach phase 3, many countries and subnational regions will be significantly behind this timeline. Some may still be in phase 1. Therefore, the most important task for countries in phase 3 is to intensely devote time, effort, and money to helping lagging regions accelerate their own progress. This can be a win-win proposition that achieves economic, public health, and climate benefits for all.

CLOSING THOUGHTS

Decarbonizing human activity is the most consequential challenge of the twenty-first century. Economic development, the fight against poverty, protection of the natural world, and even the preservation of organized human society hinge on its achievement. Industry is the linchpin in this effort. Industry is responsible for a third of human-caused greenhouse gas emissions (including emissions from purchased electricity and heat). Industrial firms supply all the materials and products the world demands, including the technologies that will decarbonize transport, buildings, electricity, and industry itself.

Despite industry's overriding importance, most policy efforts to date have focused on other sectors. Decarbonizing industry is urgent and must not be longer delayed. Technologies we have today, and targeted development and commercialization of new technology, enable industry to adopt clean and sustainable processes. This is necessary for industry to remain the engine of human prosperity in the decades and centuries ahead. Policies can accelerate this transformation, creating a business environment that rewards research and deployment of zero-carbon manufacturing processes.

This book details the technologies that can reduce industrial emissions to zero and the policies that will ensure that those technologies are researched, commercialized, and deployed at scale. All this can be achieved while boosting the economy, creating well-paying jobs, advancing equity, and improving public health. Policy makers and business leaders must seize this opportunity, enacting the policies and making the investments that put us on the path to zero-carbon industry.

LIST OF ABBREVIATIONS

Abbreviations are divided into four categories: technologies and science, policies and economics, organizations, and chemical formulas. They are listed alphabetically within each section.

Some of the items in these lists appear exclusively in their written-out forms in this book as an aid to readability. However, if the abbreviation is commonly used in the field, the item and its abbreviation are included here, so this section may be used to cross-reference this book's terms with other sources that use the same terms in abbreviated form.

TECHNOLOGIES AND SCIENCE

ABS	acrylonitrile butadiene styrene (plastic)
AC	alternating current
AM	additive manufacturing
BF	blast furnace
BOF	basic oxygen furnace
BYF	belite-ye'elimite-ferrite cement
CAD	computer-aided design
CCS	carbon capture and storage

CCSC	carbonatable calcium silicate cement
CCUS	carbon capture and use or storage
CG	coal gasification
CHP	combined heat and power
CHS	calcium hydrosilicate cement
CLC	chemical looping combustion
CLT	cross-laminated timber
COP	coefficient of performance
CSA	calcium sulfoaluminate cement
DAC	direct air capture
DC	direct current
DRI	direct reduced iron
EAF	electric arc furnace
EOR	enhanced oil recovery
EV	electric vehicle
FDM	fused deposition modeling
FPC	flat plate collector
GHG	greenhouse gas
GWP	global warming potential
HDPE	high-density polyethylene (plastic)
HVAC	heating, ventilation, and air conditioning
IF	induction furnace
IGCC	integrated gasification combined cycle
LDPE	low-density polyethylene (plastic)
LFC	linear Fresnel collector
LNG	liquified natural gas
LOHC	liquid organic hydrogen carrier
LPG	liquified petroleum gas
MOE	molten oxide electrolysis
MOMS	magnesium oxides derived from magnesium silicates (cement)
MSW	municipal solid waste
MTA	methanol-to-aromatics
MTO	methanol-to-olefins
OHF	open hearth furnace

OPC	ordinary Portland cement
PAN	polyacrylonitrile (plastic)
PC	polycarbonate (plastic)
PEM	proton exchange membrane
PET	polyethylene terephthalate (plastic)
PLA	polylactic acid (bioplastic)
PM	particulate matter
$PM_{2.5}$	fine particulate matter
PMMA	polymethyl methacrylate (plastic)
post-CC	postcombustion capture
PP	polypropylene (plastic)
PP&A	polyester, polyamide, and acrylic (plastic)
pre-CC	precombustion capture
PS	polystyrene (plastic)
PTC	parabolic trough collector
PTT	polytrimethylene terephthalate (bioplastic)
PUR	polyurethane (plastic)
PV	photovoltaic (solar)
PVA	polyvinyl acetate (plastic)
PVC	polyvinyl chloride (plastic)
RB	reactive belite cement
SCM	supplementary cementitious material
SLA	stereolithography
SLM	selective laser melting
SLS	selective laser sintering
SMR	steam methane reforming
SOEC	solid oxide electrolysis
UV	ultraviolet (light)

POLICIES AND ECONOMICS

AMC	advance market commitment
CAFE	corporate average fuel economy

CBAM	carbon border adjustment mechanism
CCfD	carbon contract for difference
C-PACE	commercial property assessed clean energy
CRADA	cooperative research and development agreement
EJ	environmental justice
EPR	extended producer responsibility
ETS	emissions trading system
FDI	foreign direct investment
GDP	gross domestic product
GPP	green public procurement
IP	intellectual property
LMICs	low- and middle-income countries
PAE	patent assertion entity
PPP	purchasing power parity
R&D	research and development
RECs	renewable energy credits
RPS	renewable portfolio standards
STEM	science, technology, engineering, and mathematics
TAM	tax adjustment mechanism

ORGANIZATIONS

AMO	Advanced Manufacturing Office
CERN	European Organization for Nuclear Research
CNRS	France's National Center for Scientific Research
DOE	U.S. Department of Energy
EIA	U.S. Energy Information Administration
EPA	U.S. Environmental Protection Agency
ESCO	energy service company
GCCA	Global Cement and Concrete Association
GRI	Global Reporting Initiative
IEA	International Energy Agency
IMF	International Monetary Fund

IPCC	Intergovernmental Panel on Climate Change
ISO	International Organization for Standardization
ISSB	International Sustainability Standards Board
NASA	National Aeronautics and Space Administration
RGGI	Regional Greenhouse Gas Initiative
SBTi	Science-Based Targets initiative
SDTC	Sustainable Development Technology Canada
TCFD	Task Force on Climate-Related Financial Disclosures
ULCOS	Ultra-Low CO_2 Steelmaking (European initiative)

CHEMICAL FORMULAS

C_2H_4	ethylene
C_3H_6	propylene
C_4H_6	butadiene
C_4H_8	butene
$C_6H_{10}O_4$	adipic acid
C_6H_{12}	cyclohexane
C_6H_6	benzene
C_7H_8	toluene
C_8H_{10}	xylene
$CaCO_3$	calcium carbonate
CaO	calcium oxide, lime, or quicklime
CFCs	chlorofluorocarbons
CH_3OH	methanol
CH_4	methane
CO	carbon monoxide
CO_2	carbon dioxide
CO_2e	carbon dioxide equivalent
Fe_2O_3	hematite (a form of iron oxide)
Fe_3O_4	magnetite (a form of iron oxide)
$FeCO_3$	ferrous carbonate or iron(II) carbonate
H_2	hydrogen

H_2O	water or steam
HCFCs	hydrochlorofluorocarbons
HFCs	hydrofluorocarbons
HFOs	hydrofluoroolefins
HNO_3	nitric acid
$MgCO_3$	magnesium carbonate
MgO	magnesium oxide
N_2	nitrogen
N_2O	nitrous oxide
NH_3	ammonia
NMVOCs	nonmethane volatile organic compounds
NO_x	nitrogen oxides
O_2	oxygen
PFAS	per- and polyfluoroalkyl substances
PFCs	perfluorocarbons
SF_6	sulfur hexafluoride
SO_x	sulfur oxides

ACKNOWLEDGMENTS

I wish to thank Hal Harvey and Sonia Aggarwal, who perceived the importance of this work at its earliest stages and gave me the time I needed to research and write this book.

Thank you to my editors at Columbia University Press, Caelyn Cobb and Jason Bordoff, for selecting my book proposal and making this book a reality.

Thank you to my brilliant reviewers, whose comments helped strengthen this book in countless ways: Al Armendariz, Sara Baldwin, Chris Busch, Minshu Deng, Jenny Edwards, Dan Esposito, Todd Fincannon, Eric Gimon, Brigitta Huckestein, Hongyou Lu, Silvia Madeddu, Megan Mahajan, Fei Meng, Mike O'Boyle, Robbie Orvis, Lawrence Rissman, Prodipto Roy, Joe Ryan, Aylin Shawkat, Michelle Solomon, Sarah Spengeman, Hadley Tallackson, Lana Vali, Shelley Wenzel, and Wido Witecka.

International Energy Agency (IEA) data are used with permission in figures 0.2, 0.3, 0.4, 3.2, 3.3, 4.1, 7.1, 7.2, 7.4, 8.1, and 11.1 (sometimes in combination with data from other sources), as modified by Jeffrey Rissman. IEA reserves all rights to their data. For attribution information, see the citations indicated in these figures' captions.

NOTES

INTRODUCTION

1. Energy & Climate Intelligence Unit, UNC Data-Driven Envirolab, NewClimate Institute, and University of Oxford, "Net Zero Tracker," accessed May 17, 2023, https://zerotracker .net/.

2. European Council, "Fit for 55 Package: Council Reaches General Approaches Relating to Emissions Reductions and Their Social Impacts," press release, June 29, 2022, https://www.consilium.europa.eu/en/press/press-releases/2022/06/29/fit-for-55 -council-reaches-general-approaches-relating-to-emissions-reductions-and-removals -and-their-social-impacts/; United Kingdom Department for Transport, "COP26 Declaration on Accelerating the Transition to 100 Percent Zero Emission Cars and Vans," policy paper, updated November 17, 2022, https://www.gov.uk/government/publications /cop26-declaration-zero-emission-cars-and-vans/cop26-declaration-on-accelerating -the-transition-to-100-zero-emission-cars-and-vans.

3. International Energy Agency, "Global EV Outlook 2022," May 2022, https://iea.blob .core.windows.net/assets/e0d2081d-487d-4818-8c59-69b638969f9e/GlobalElectric VehicleOutlook2022.pdf.

4. California Energy Commission, "2019 Building Energy Efficiency Standards Frequently Asked Questions," March 2018, https://www.energy.ca.gov/sites/default/files/2020-03 /Title_24_2019_Building_Standards_FAQ_ada.pdf.

5. International Renewable Energy Agency, "Renewable Capacity Highlights 2021," March 31, 2021, https://www.irena.org/-/media/Files/IRENA/Agency/Publication/2021/Apr/IRENA_-RE _Capacity_Highlights_2021.pdf.

1. IRON AND STEEL

1. World Steel Association, "2020 World Steel in Figures" (Brussels, Belgium, April 30, 2020), https://worldsteel.org/wp-content/uploads/2020-World-Steel-in-Figures.pdf.

2. Encyclopedia Britannica, "Cast Iron," updated January 20, 2023, https://www.britannica.com/technology/cast-iron.

3. International Energy Agency, *Iron and Steel Technology Roadmap* (technology report, IEA, Paris, October 8, 2020), https://www.iea.org/reports/iron-and-steel-technology-roadmap; AZO Materials, "Stainless Steel—Grade 304 (UNS S30400)," October 23, 2001, https://www.azom.com/article.aspx?ArticleID=965.

4. Jonathan M. Cullen, Julian M. Allwood, and Margarita D. Bambach, "Mapping the Global Flow of Steel: From Steelmaking to End-Use Goods," *Environmental Science & Technology* 46, no. 24 (2012): 13048–55, https://doi.org/10.1021/es302433p.

5. International Energy Agency, *Iron and Steel Technology Roadmap*.

6. International Energy Agency, *Iron and Steel Technology Roadmap*.

7. Robert Donald Walker, "Iron Processing—Ores" (Encyclopedia Britannica, updated June 16, 2023), https://www.britannica.com/technology/iron-processing.

8. Walker, "Iron Processing—Ores."

9. International Energy Agency, *Iron and Steel Technology Roadmap*.

10. U.S. Department of Transportation, *User Guidelines for Waste and Byproduct Materials in Pavement Construction*, "Steel Slag—Material Description" (Research Publication FHWA-RD-97-148, U.S. Department of Transportation, Federal Highway Administration, April 1998), https://www.fhwa.dot.gov/publications/research/infrastructure/structures/97148/ssa1.cfm.

11. U.S. Department of Transportation, *User Guidelines for Waste and Byproduct Materials in Pavement Construction*, "Steel Slag—Material Description."

12. British Lime Association, "Iron & Steel," accessed May 18, 2023, https://britishlime.org/technical/iron_and_steel.php.

13. National Lime Association, "Iron and Steel," accessed May 18, 2023, https://www.lime.org/lime-basics/uses-of-lime/metallurgical-uses-of-lime/iron-and-steel/.

14. Lockwood Greene Technologies, *Ironmaking Process Alternatives Screening Study, Volume I: Summary Report* (report, U.S. Department of Energy, October 2000), https://www.energy.gov/sites/prod/files/2013/11/f4/ironmaking_process.pdf.

15. International Energy Agency, *Iron and Steel Technology Roadmap*.

16. Mildred B. Perry, "Clean Coal Technology," in *Encyclopedia of Energy* (Amsterdam: Elsevier Science, 2004), 343–57, https://www.sciencedirect.com/science/article/pii/B012176480X002898.

17. Cullen, Allwood, and Bambach, "Mapping the Global Flow of Steel."

18. Katrin E. Daehn, André Cabrera Serrenho, and Julian Allwood, "Finding the Most Efficient Way to Remove Residual Copper from Steel Scrap," *Metallurgical and Materials Transactions B* 50, no. 3 (2019): 1225–40, https://link.springer.com/article/10.1007/s11663-019-01537-9.

19. Daehn, Serrenho, and Allwood, "Finding the Most Efficient Way to Remove Residual Copper from Steel Scrap."

20. Cullen, Allwood, and Bambach, "Mapping the Global Flow of Steel."

21. Zhiyuan Fan and S. Julio Friedmann, "Low-Carbon Production of Iron and Steel: Technology Options, Economic Assessment, and Policy," *Joule* 5, no. 4 (2021): 829–62, https://doi.org/10.1016/j.joule.2021.02.018.

22. Hannu Suopajärvi, Kentaro Umeki, Elsayed Mousa, Ali Hedayati, Henrik Romar, Antti Kemppainen, Chuan Wang, et al., "Use of Biomass in Integrated Steelmaking—Status Quo, Future Needs and Comparison to Other Low-CO_2 Steel Production Technologies," *Applied Energy* 213 (March 1, 2018): 384–407, https://doi.org/10.1016/j.apenergy.2018.01.060.

23. European Commission, Directorate-General for Research and Innovation, W. Adler, M. Dapper, E. Malfa et al., "CO_2 Reduction in Reheating Furnaces (CO_2RED)" (European Commission Publications Office, Brussels, 2012, https://data.europa.eu/doi/10.2777/91701.

24. Lockwood Greene Technologies, *Ironmaking Process Alternatives Screening Study, Volume I: Summary Report*; Midrex Technologies Inc., "2019 World Direct Reduction Statistics," 2020, https://www.midrex.com/wp-content/uploads/Midrex-STATSbook2019Final.pdf.

25. Cullen, Allwood, and Bambach, "Mapping the Global Flow of Steel"; Fan and Friedmann, "Low-Carbon Production of Iron and Steel."

26. Energy Technology Systems Analysis Programme, "Iron and Steel" (International Energy Agency, May 2010), https://iea-etsap.org/E-TechDS/PDF/I02-Iron&Steel-GS-AD-gct.pdf.

27. International Energy Agency, *Iron and Steel Technology Roadmap*.

28. Cullen, Allwood, and Bambach, "Mapping the Global Flow of Steel"; International Iron Metallics Association, "Hot Briquetted Iron (HBI)," accessed May 18, 2023, https://www.metallics.org/hbi.html.

29. International Iron Metallics Association, "Hot Briquetted Iron (HBI)."

30. Midrex Technologies Inc., "2019 World Direct Reduction Statistics," 2020, https://www.midrex.com/wp-content/uploads/Midrex-STATSbook2019Final.pdf.

31. U.S. Energy Information Administration, Today in Energy, "India's Steel Industry, Like America's, Is Dominated by Electric-Based Processes," December 8, 2017, https://www.eia.gov/todayinenergy/detail.php?id=34052; Midrex Technologies Inc., "2019 World Direct Reduction Statistics."

32. Fan and Friedmann, "Low-Carbon Production of Iron and Steel."

33. Cleveland-Cliffs Inc., "Toledo DR Plant," March 2023, https://d1io3yog0oux5.cloudfront.net/_efbb71761bc849e9032a324ad0f9d590/clevelandcliffs/db/1170/10171/fact_sheet/CLF_FactSheet_DRPlant_032023.pdf.

34. Fan and Friedmann, "Low-Carbon Production of Iron and Steel."

35. Fan and Friedmann, "Low-Carbon Production of Iron and Steel."

36. Energy Technology Systems Analysis Programme, "Iron and Steel."

37. Cullen, Allwood, and Bambach, "Mapping the Global Flow of Steel"; Edward F. Wente, Jack Nutting, and E.F. Wondris, "Steel" (Encyclopedia Britannica, updated April 5, 2023), https://www.britannica.com/technology/steel.

38. James A. Charles, Charles B. Gill, Paul G. Shewmon, and Clarence H. Lorig, "Metallurgy—Refining" (Encyclopedia Britannica), accessed May 18, 2023, https://www.britannica.com/science/metallurgy.

39. Wente, Nutting, and Wondris, "Steel."

40. Charles, Gill, Shewmon, and Lorig, "Metallurgy—Refining."

41. Wente, Nutting, and Wondris, "Steel."

42. Wente, Nutting, and Wondris, "Steel."

43. Cullen, Allwood, and Bambach, "Mapping the Global Flow of Steel."

44. Jeremy A. T. Jones, "Electric Arc Furnace Steelmaking" (American Iron and Steel Institute, 2008), https://www3.epa.gov/ttn/chief/old/ap42/ch12/s051/reference/ref_02c02s04_2008.pdf.

45. Ernst Worrell, Paul Blinde, Maarten Neelis, Eliane Blomen, and Eric Masanet, *Energy Efficiency Improvement and Cost Saving Opportunities for the U.S. Iron and Steel Industry: An ENERGY STAR® Guide for Energy and Plant Managers* (technical report, Lawrence Berkeley National Laboratory, Berkeley, CA, October 2010), https://www.osti.gov/servlets/purl/1026806.

46. Jones, "Electric Arc Furnace Steelmaking."

47. *U.S. Steel's Electric Arc Furnace*, video, AL.com, Fairfield, AL, 2020, https://www.youtube.com/watch?v=8J3bMtX9Wq0&t=127s.

48. Jones, "Electric Arc Furnace Steelmaking."

49. Hans-Jürgen Odenthal, Phong Bui, Markus Reifferscheid, Erich Hovestädt, Juliane Nies, Igor Klioutchnikov, and Herbert Olivier, "Advanced Design of Injection/Burner Systems in Electric Arc Furnaces (EAF)" (paper presented at 4th International Conference on Modelling and Simulation of Metallurgical Processes in Steelmaking, Düsseldorf, Germany, 2011), https://www.researchgate.net/publication/279206376_Advanced_design_of_injectionburner_systems_in_electric_arc_furnaces_EAF.

50. Marcus Kirschen, Victor Risonarta, and Herbert Pfeifer, "Energy Efficiency and the Influence of Gas Burners to the Energy Related Carbon Dioxide Emissions of Electric Arc Furnaces in Steel Industry," *Energy* 34, no. 9 (September 2009): 1065–72, https://doi.org/10.1016/j.energy.2009.04.015.

51. IPCC, "Industrial Processes and Product Use—Metal Industry Emissions," in *2006 IPCC Guidelines for National Greenhouse Gas Inventories*, chapter 2, vol. 3, 2006, https://www.ipcc-nggip.iges.or.jp/public/2006gl/pdf/3_Volume3/V3_4_Ch4_Metal_Industry.pdf.

52. Michael M. Gasik, "Chapter 1—Introduction," in *Handbook of Ferroalloys: Theory and Technology* (Oxford: Butterworth-Heinemann, 2013), 3–7, https://doi.org/10.1016/B978-0-08-097753-9.00001-0.

53. Gasik, "Chapter 1—Introduction."

54. David Olsen, "What Is AOD (Argon Oxygen Decarburization)?," blog, MetalTek International, November 30, 2020, https://www.metaltek.com/blog/what-is-aod/; Linde plc, "Argon Oxygen Decarburization," accessed May 18, 2023, https://www.lindeus.com/industries/metal-production/argon-oxygen-decarburization-aod.

55. Kang Ming, "Chinese Private Stainless Steel Mills' Domestic and Overseas Strategy" (10th Asian Stainless Steel Conference, Singapore, June 3, 2015), https://web.archive

.org/web/20180903211834/http://www.metalbulletin.com/events/download.ashx
/document/speaker/7975/a0IDoooooooXokI5MAJ/Presentation.

56. OECD, "Latest Developments in Steelmaking Capacity," June 22, 2020, https://www
.oecd.org/officialdocuments/publicdisplaydocumentpdf/?cote=DSTI/SC(2020)3
/FINAL&docLanguage=En.

57. OECD, "Latest Developments in Steelmaking Capacity."

58. OECD, "Latest Developments in Steelmaking Capacity."

59. OECD, "Latest Developments in Steelmaking Capacity"; Xinhua News Agency, "China
to Cull Shoddy Steel Production by Q2," January 11, 2017, http://www.xinhuanet.com
//english/2017-01/11/c_135973691.htm.

60. World Steel Association, "2020 World Steel in Figures"; U.S. Energy Information
Administration, "India's Steel Industry, Like America's, Is Dominated by Electric-Based
Processes."

61. OECD, "Latest Developments in Steelmaking Capacity."

62. Keith Tan, "Will China's Induction Furnace Steel Whac-a-Mole Finally Come to an
End?," *S&P Global Commodity Insights* (blog), March 6, 2017, https://www.spglobal
.com/platts/en/market-insights/blogs/metals/030617-will-chinas-induction-furnace
-steel-whac-a-mole-finally-come-to-an-end.

63. OECD, "Latest Developments in Steelmaking Capacity."

64. World Steel Association, "2020 World Steel in Figures."

65. Perry, "Clean Coal Technology."

66. Fan and Friedmann, "Low-Carbon Production of Iron and Steel."

67. Fan and Friedmann, "Low-Carbon Production of Iron and Steel."

68. ThyssenKrupp, "World First in Duisburg as NRW Economics Minister Pinkwart Launches
Tests at Thyssenkrupp Into Blast Furnace Use of Hydrogen," press release, November 11, 2019,
https://www.thyssenkrupp.com/en/newsroom/press-releases/world-first-in-duisburg
-as-nrw-economics-minister-pinkwart-launches-tests-at-thyssenkrupp-into-blast
-furnace-use-of-hydrogen-17280.html.

69. U.S. Energy Information Administration, "Recycling Is the Primary Energy Efficiency
Technology for Aluminum and Steel Manufacturing," *Today in Energy* (blog), May 9,
2014, https://www.eia.gov/todayinenergy/detail.php?id=16211.

70. UN Environment Program, *Recycling Rates of Metals: A Status Report* (report, United
Nations Environment Program, 2011), https://www.resourcepanel.org/sites/default
/files/documents/document/media/metals_status_report_full_report_english.pdf;
Christopher Tuck, "Iron and Steel Scrap," in *Mineral Commodity Summaries 2021* (U.S.
Geological Survey, 2021), https://pubs.usgs.gov/periodicals/mcs2021/mcs2021-iron-steel
-scrap.pdf.

71. Suopajärvi, Umeki, Mousa, Hedayati, Romar, Kemppainen, Wang, et al., "Use of Biomass in Integrated Steelmaking"; Fan and Friedmann, "Low-Carbon Production of
Iron and Steel."

72. Fan and Friedmann, "Low-Carbon Production of Iron and Steel."

73. World Economic Forum, *Aluminum for Climate: Exploring Pathways to Decarbonize the
Aluminum Industry* (Community Report, World Economic Forum, Geneva, Switzerland,

November 2020), http://www3.weforum.org/docs/WEF_Aluminium_for_Climate_2020
.pdf.

74. Fan and Friedmann, "Low-Carbon Production of Iron and Steel."

75. Valentin Vogl, Max Åhman, and Lars J. Nilsson, "Assessment of Hydrogen Direct Reduction for Fossil-Free Steelmaking," *Journal of Cleaner Production* 203 (December 1, 2018): 736–45, https://doi.org/10.1016/j.jclepro.2018.08.279.

76. Jane Fan and Peter Hannah, "Understanding the High-Grade Iron Ore Market" (Fastmarkets, March 2021), https://pearlgulliron.com.au/wp-content/uploads/2021/09/Understanding _the_high-grade_iron_ore_market_Fastmarkets.pdf.

77. Fan and Hannah, "Understanding the High-Grade Iron Ore Market."

78. Swedish Energy Agency, "The Swedish Energy Agency Is Investing Heavily in a Carbon-Dioxide-Free Steel Industry," February 27, 2017, https://www.automotiveworld .com/news-releases/swedish-energy-agency-investing-heavily-carbon-dioxide-free -steel-industry/.

79. SSAB, "HYBRIT: SSAB, LKAB and Vattenfall to Begin Industrialization of Future Fossil-Free Steelmaking by Establishing the World's First Production Plant for Fossil-Free Sponge Iron in Gällivare," press release, SSAB, March 24, 2021, https://www.ssab .com/news/2021/03/hybrit-ssab-lkab-and-vattenfall-to-begin-industrialization-of -future-fossilfree-steelmaking-by-estab.

80. SSAB, "HYBRIT."

81. SSAB, "SSAB aims to be fossil-free by 2045," press release, October 25, 2017, https://www .ssab.com/en/news/2017/10/ssab-aims-to-be-fossilfree-by-2045.

82. ArcelorMittal, "ArcelorMittal Europe to Produce 'Green Steel' Starting in 2020," October 13, 2020, https://corporate.arcelormittal.com/media/news-articles/arcelormittal -europe-to-produce-green-steel-starting-in-2020; "ArcelorMittal Plans Major Investment in German Sites, to Accelerate CO_2 Emissions Reduction Strategy and Leverage the Hydrogen Grid," March 29, 2021, https://corporate.arcelormittal.com/media/news -articles/arcelormittal-plans-major-investment-in-german-sites-to-accelerate-co₂ -emissions-reduction-strategy-and-leverage-the-hydrogen-grid.

83. Kerstine Appunn, "Energy and Grid Companies Team Up for Hydrogen Project at German Coast," *Clean Energy Wire*, March 25, 2021, https://www.cleanenergywire.org /news/energy-and-grid-companies-team-hydrogen-project-german-coast.

84. ArcelorMittal, "ArcelorMittal Europe to Produce 'Green Steel' Starting in 2020."

85. Tenova, "First Hydrogen Based ENERGIRON DRI Plant for Tenova in China," November 23, 2020, https://tenova.com/newsroom/press-releases/first-hydrogen-based -energiron-dri-plant-tenova-china; Salzgitter AG, "SALCOS," accessed May 18, 2023, https://salcos.salzgitter-ag.com/en/index.html; and Kobe Steel Ltd., "KOBELCO Group Medium-Term Management Plan," May 11, 2021, https://www.kobelco.co.jp/english /releases/files/20210511_1_02.pdf.

86. Hervé Lavelaine, "Siderwin: Development of New Methodologies for Industrial CO_2-Free Steel Production by Electrowinning," accessed May 18, 2023, https://www .siderwin-spire.eu/sites/siderwin.drupal.pulsartecnalia.com/files/pictures/Rollup -SIDERWIN_final.pdf.

87. Sevasti Koutsoupa, Stavroula Koutalidi, Evangelos Bourbos, Efthymios Balomenos, and Dimitrios Panias, "Electrolytic Iron Production from Alkaline Bauxite Residue Slurries at Low Temperatures," *Johnson Matthey Technology Review* 65, no. 3 (July 2021): 366–74, https://doi.org/10.1595/205651320X15918757312944.
88. Koutsoupa, Koutalidi, Bourbos, Balomenos, and Panias, "Electrolytic Iron Production from Alkaline Bauxite Residue Slurries at Low Temperatures."
89. SIDERWIN Consortium, "Consortium," 2021, https://www.siderwin-spire.eu/consortium.
90. *Awards 2020—Siderwin*, video, 2020, https://www.youtube.com/watch?v=I24DhxzXTjo.
91. Akshat Rathi, "Inside the Bill Gates-Backed Startup Cleaning Up the Steel Industry," *Bloomberg.com*, October 6, 2022, https://www.bloomberg.com/news/features/2022-10-06/how-to-make-emissions-free-iron-at-temperatures-colder-than-coffee.
92. Rathi, "Inside the Bill Gates-Backed Startup Cleaning Up the Steel Industry."
93. A. Keys, M. van Hout, and B. Daniëls, "Decarbonisation Options for the Dutch Steel Industry" (TNO Energy Transition, November 21, 2019), https://www.pbl.nl/sites/default/files/downloads/pbl-2019-decarbonisation-options-for-the-dutch-steel-industry_3723.pdf; European Commission Directorate-General for Research and Innovation, K. Olsen, S. Van der Laan, and H. Lavelaine de Maubeuge, , *Iron Production by Electrochemical Reduction of Its Oxide for High CO$_2$ Mitigation (IERO)—Final Report* (European Commission, October 13, 2016), https://data.europa.eu/doi/10.2777/084034.
94. P. A. Curreri, E. C. Ethridge, S. B. Hudson, T. Y. Miller, et al., *Process Demonstration for Lunar In Situ Resource Utilization: Molten Oxide Electrolysis* (report, NASA Marshall Space Flight Center, AL, August 2006), https://www.nasa.gov/sites/default/files/atoms/files/nasa_tm_06_214600.pdf.
95. Kira West, "High-Temperature Molten Oxide Electrolysis Steelmaking (ULCOLYSIS)" (TNO Energy Transition, July 9, 2020), https://energy.nl/wp-content/uploads/ulcolysis-technology-factsheet_080920-7.pdf.
96. Adam Rauwerdink, "Boston Metal: Steel Production Through Electrolysis: Impacts for Electricity Consumption," (PowerPoint presentation, October 18, 2019), https://iea.blob.core.windows.net/assets/imports/events/288/S5.4_20191010BostonMetalIEADecarbonization2019.pdf; Vogl, Åhman, and Nilsson, "Assessment of Hydrogen Direct Reduction for Fossil-Free Steelmaking."
97. Boston Metal, "Boston Metal Fact Sheet," (January 26, 2023), https://www.bostonmetal.com/wp-content/uploads/2023/01/Boston-Metal-FactSheet-20230126.pdf.
98. Keys, van Hout, and Daniëls, "Decarbonisation Options for the Dutch Steel Industry."
99. Keys, van Hout, and Daniëls, "Decarbonisation Options for the Dutch Steel Industry."
100. Keys, van Hout, and Daniëls, "Decarbonisation Options for the Dutch Steel Industry."
101. Keys, van Hout, and Daniëls, "Decarbonisation Options for the Dutch Steel Industry."
102. Carbon Sequestration Leadership Forum, "Site Visit to the AL Reyadah CCUS Project," 2017, accessed May 18, 2023, https://www.cslforum.org/cslf/sites/default/files/documents/AbuDhabi2017/AbuDhabi17-SiteVisitInformation.pdf.
103. Global CCS Institute, "CCS: A Necessary Technology for Decarbonising the Steel Sector," June 17, 2017, https://www.globalccsinstitute.com/news-media/insights/ccs-a-necessary-technology-for-decarbonising-the-steel-sector/.

104. International Energy Agency, "Age Profile of Global Production Capacity for the Steel Sector (Blast Furnaces and DRI Furnaces)," October 26, 2022, https://www.iea.org/data -and-statistics/charts/age-profile-of-global-production-capacity-for-the-steel-sector -blast-furnaces-and-dri-furnaces.

2. CHEMICALS

1. International Energy Agency, "World Energy Balances Data Service," updated April 2023, https://www.iea.org/data-and-statistics/data-product/world-energy-balances.

2. Peter G. Levi and Jonathan M. Cullen, "Mapping Global Flows of Chemicals: From Fossil Fuel Feedstocks to Chemical Products," *Environmental Science & Technology* 52, no. 4 (January 24, 2018): 1725–34, https://doi.org/10.1021/acs.est.7b04573.

3. American Chemistry Council, *2020 Guide to the Business of Chemistry* (Washington, D.C., December 31, 2020), https://www.americanchemistry.com/chemistry-in-america /data-industry-statistics/resources/2020-guide-to-the-business-of-chemistry.

4. Andrew J. Minchener, Coal-to-Oil, Gas and Chemicals in China (report, IEA Clean Coal Centre, London, February 2011), https://usea.org/sites/default/files/022011_Coal -to-oil,%20gas%20and%20chemicals%20in%20China_ccc181.pdf.

5. National Energy Technology Laboratory, "Syngas Composition," accessed May 20, 2023, https://netl.doe.gov/research/coal/energy-systems/gasification/gasifipedia/syngas -composition.

6. Richard Liu, Zhou Yang, and Zinzhou Qian, "China's Risky Gamble on Coal Conversion," *New Security Beat* (blog), January 9, 2020, https://www.newsecuritybeat.org /2020/01/chinas-risky-gamble-coal-conversion/; Union of Concerned Scientists, "Each Country's Share of CO_2 Emissions," updated January 14, 2022, https://www.ucsusa.org /resources/each-countrys-share-co₂-emissions.

7. Asociacion Petroquimica y Quimica Latinoamericana, *Brazil Petrochemicals and Chemicals 2017*, (report, Asociacion Petroquimica y Quimica Latinoamericana, Buenos Aires, 2017), https://www.gbreports.com/wp-content/uploads/2017/11/Brazil-Chemicals-2017 -Web-Version.pdf.

8. U.S. Energy Information Administration, "International Energy Statistics" (Washington, D.C., 2021), https://www.eia.gov/international/overview/world.

9. U.S. Energy Information Administration, "International Energy Statistics."

10. International Energy Agency, *The Future of Petrochemicals: Towards More Sustainable Plastics and Fertilisers* (report, International Energy Agency, Paris, October 5, 2018), https://www.iea.org/reports/the-future-of-petrochemicals; U.S. Environmental Protection Agency, "2016 Chemical Data Reporting," May 2017, https://www.epa.gov/sites /production/files/2017-09/documents/cdr_basic_information-8.31.17-final.pdf.

11. European Chemical Industry Council, "2023 Facts and Figures of the European Chemical Industry," accessed June 27, 2023, https://cefic.org/our-industry/a-pillar-of-the-european -economy/facts-and-figures-of-the-european-chemical-industry/.

12. International Energy Agency, *The Future of Petrochemicals*.

13. International Fertilizer Association, "Production and Trade Tables by Region," 2021, https://www.ifastat.org/supply/Nitrogen%20Products/Ammonia.

14. American Chemistry Council, "2020 Guide to the Business of Chemistry"; Petrochemicals Europe, "Petrochemicals Flowchart," May 19, 2021, https://www.petrochemistry.eu/wp-content/uploads/2021/05/Petrochemistry-FlowChart_2019MC_V13-13092019-withoutFolds.pdf; International Energy Agency, *The Future of Petrochemicals*.

15. International Energy Agency, *The Future of Petrochemicals*; International Renewable Energy Agency and Methanol Institute, *Innovation Outlook: Renewable Methanol* (report, International Renewable Energy Agency, Abu Dhabi, 2021), https://www.irena.org/-/media/Files/IRENA/Agency/Publication/2021/Jan/IRENA_Innovation_Renewable_Methanol_2021.pdf.

16. Japan's Ministry of Economy, Trade and Industry, "Future Supply and Demand Trends for Petrochemical Products in the World," October 2019, https://warp.da.ndl.go.jp/info:ndljp/pid/12685722/www.meti.go.jp/policy/mono_info_service/mono/chemistry/sekaijukyuudoukou201910.html.

17. Japan's Ministry of Economy, Trade and Industry, "Future Supply and Demand Trends for Petrochemical Products in the World."

18. Levi and Cullen, "Mapping Global Flows of Chemicals"; Michael Bender, "An Overview of Industrial Processes for the Production of Olefins—C4 Hydrocarbons," *ChemBioEng Reviews* 1, no. 4 (August 2014): 136–47, https://doi.org/10.1002/cben.201400016.

19. ResearchAndMarkets, "Global Carbon Black Industry Analysis 2017–2020 and Forecast to 2025—Top Companies Focusing on Innovating Carbon Black Production Technologies in an Effort to Comply with Global Sustainability Goals—ResearchAndMarkets.com," January 12, 2022, https://www.businesswire.com/news/home/20220112005648/en/.

20. Tayeb Benchaita, "Greenhouse Gas Emissions from New Petrochemical Plants: Background Information Paper for the Elaboration of Technical Notes and Guidelines for IDB Projects" (Tech. Note No. IDB-TN-562, Inter-American Development Bank, Washington, D.C., July 2013), https://publications.iadb.org/publications/english/document/Greenhouse-Gas-Emissions-from-New-Petrochemical-Plants-Background-Information-Paper-for-the-Elaboration-of-Technical-Notes-and-Guidelines-for-IDB-Projects.pdf.

21. International Energy Agency, *The Future of Petrochemicals*.

22. International Energy Agency, "World Energy Balances Data Service."

23. Levi and Cullen, "Mapping Global Flows of Chemicals."

24. Levi and Cullen, "Mapping Global Flows of Chemicals."

25. Levi and Cullen, "Mapping Global Flows of Chemicals."

26. Levi and Cullen, "Mapping Global Flows of Chemicals."

27. Tim Fitzgibbon, Theo Simons, Gustaw Szarek, and Sari Varpa, "Crude Oil to Chemicals: How Refineries Can Adapt," McKinsey & Company, June 30, 2022, https://www.mckinsey.com/industries/chemicals/our-insights/from-crude-oil-to-chemicals-how-refineries-can-adapt-to-shifting-demand.

28. Roland Geyer, Jenna R. Jambeck, and Kara Lavender Law, "Production, Use, and Fate of All Plastics Ever Made," *Science Advances* 3, no. 7 (July 1, 2017): e1700782, https://doi.org/10.1126/sciadv.1700782.

29. Geyer, Jambeck, and Law, "Production, Use, and Fate of All Plastics Ever Made."

30. Woods Hole Oceanographic Institution and National Oceanic and Atmospheric Administration, "Marine Debris Is Everyone's Problem," poster, accessed May 20, 2023, https://web.archive.org/web/20221209070608/https://www.whoi.edu/fileserver.do?id =107364&pt=2&p=88817; Ghada Atiwesh, Abanoub Mikhael, Christopher C. Parrish, Joseph Banoub, and Tuyet-Anh T. Le, "Environmental Impact of Bioplastic Use: A Review," *Heliyon* 7, no. 9 (September 2021): e07918, https://doi.org/10.1016/j.heliyon .2021.e07918.

31. Jan Zrimec, Mariia Kokina, Sara Jonasson, Francisco Zorrilla, and Aleksej Zelezniak, "Plastic-Degrading Potential Across the Global Microbiome Correlates with Recent Pollution Trends," *MBio* 12, no. 5 (October 26, 2021), https://doi.org/10.1128/mBio .02155-21.

32. International Energy Agency, *Energy Technology Perspectives 2020* (report, Internationl Energy Agency, Paris, September 2020), https://www.iea.org/reports/energy -technology-perspectives-2020.

33. Dana S. Marlin, Emeric Sarron, and Ómar Sigurbjörnsson, "Process Advantages of Direct CO_2 to Methanol Synthesis," *Frontiers in Chemistry* 6 (2018), https://doi.org /10.3389/fchem.2018.00446.

34. Teng Li, Tuiana Shoinkhorova, Jorge Gascon, and Javier Ruiz-Martínez, "Aromatics Production via Methanol-Mediated Transformation Routes," *ACS Catalysis* 11, no. 13 (July 2, 2021): 7780–7819, https://doi.org/10.1021/acscatal.1c01422.

35. Asociacion Petroquimica y Quimica Latinoamericana, *Brazil Petrochemicals and Chemicals 2017.*

36. Renewable Fuels Association, "Annual U.S. & World Fuel Ethanol Production," 2022, https://ethanolrfa.org/markets-and-statistics/annual-ethanol-production.

37. International Energy Agency, *The Future of Petrochemicals.*

38. U.S. Department of Energy, Office of Energy Efficiency & Renewable Energy, "Bioenergy Frequently Asked Questions," accessed May 20, 2023, https://www.energy.gov/eere /bioenergy/bioenergy-frequently-asked-questions.

39. International Energy Agency, "World Energy Balances Data Service."

40. International Energy Agency, *The Future of Petrochemicals.*

41. International Energy Agency, *The Future of Petrochemicals.*

42. International Energy Agency, "World Energy Balances Data Service."

43. SICCODE.com, "NAICS Code 325194—Cyclic Crude, Intermediate, and Gum and Wood Chemical Manufacturing," accessed May 20, 2023, https://siccode.com/naics -code/325194/cyclic-crude-intermediate-gum-wood-chemical-manufacturing.

44. Levi and Cullen, "Mapping Global Flows of Chemicals."

45. BASF, *Steam Cracker at BASF's Ludwigshafen Site*, October 31, 2014, photo, October 31, 2014, https://www.flickr.com/photos/basf/15970578176/; Heather Doyle, "US Ethane Cracker Construction Costs Rise a Further 1 percent in Q4 2016," *Reuters*, February 3, 2017, https:// www.reutersevents.com/downstream/supply-chain-logistics/us-ethane-cracker -construction-costs-rise-further-1-q4-2016.

46. Hydrocarbon Processing, "Accelerating Electrification with the 'Cracker of the Future' Consortium," *Hydrocarbon Processing*, September 30, 2021, https://www.hydrocarbonprocessing.com/news/2021/09/accelerating-electrification-with-the-cracker-of-the-future-consortium#x__ftn1.

47. Hydrocarbon Processing, "Accelerating Electrification with the 'Cracker of the Future' Consortium."

48. BASF, "BASF, SABIC and Linde Join Forces to Realize the World's First Electrically Heated Steam Cracker Furnace," March 24, 2021, https://www.basf.com/global/en/media/news-releases/2021/03/p-21-165.html.

49. Na Young Kang, Won Choon Choi, and Yong-Ki Park, "Emerging Catalytic Light Olefin Production Technologies," 2018, https://www.shokubai.org/tocat8/pdf/Invited/IC206.pdf.

50. National Energy Technology Laboratory, "Syngas Composition."

51. Arno de Klerk, "Engineering Evaluation of Direct Methane to Methanol Conversion," *Energy Science & Engineering* 3, no. 1 (2015): 60–70, https://doi.org/10.1002/ese3.51; International Renewable Energy Agency and Methanol Institute, *Innovation Outlook: Renewable Methanol*.

52. Arno de Klerk, "Engineering Evaluation of Direct Methane to Methanol Conversion."

53. BASF, "BASF Develops Process for Climate-Friendly Methanol," May 24, 2019, https://www.basf.com/global/en/media/news-releases/2019/05/p-19-218.html.

54. EnginZyme, "Our Technology," accessed March 2, 2021, https://enginzyme.com/technology/.

55. *IMicrobes*, Carbon Impact.Tech Lightning Talks (San Francisco, CA, 2019), https://www.youtube.com/watch?v=k4aoOrpLJnA.

56. Zymergen, "We Make Tomorrow," accessed March 2, 2021, https://www.zymergen.com/.

57. U.S. Environmental Protection Agency, *Global Non-CO_2 Greenhouse Gas Emission Projections & Mitigation Potential: 2015–2050* (report no. EPA-430-R-19-010, U.S. Environmental Protection Agency, Washington, D.C., October 2019), https://www.epa.gov/sites/default/files/2020-05/documents/epa_non-co2_greenhouse_gases_rpt-epa430r19010.pdf.

58. Xiaochi Zhou, Fletcher H. Passow, Joseph Rudek, Joseph C. von Fisher, Steven P. Hamburg, and John D. Albertson, "Estimation of Methane Emissions from the U.S. Ammonia Fertilizer Industry Using a Mobile Sensing Approach," ed. Detlev Helmig, *Elementa: Science of the Anthropocene* 7, no. 19 (May 28, 2019), https://doi.org/10.1525/elementa.358.

59. United Nations, "Amendment to the Montreal Protocol on Substances That Deplete the Ozone Layer: Kigali, 15 October 2016," February 9, 2021, https://treaties.un.org/Pages/ViewDetails.aspx?src=IND&mtdsg_no=XXVII-2-f&chapter=27&clang=_en.

60. U.S. Environmental Protection Agency, "Proposed Rule – Phasedown of Hydrofluorocarbons: Allowance Allocation Methodology for 2024 and Later Years," fact sheet, October, 2022, https://www.epa.gov/system/files/documents/2022-10/2024%20HFC%20Allocation%20Rule%20NPRM%20Draft%20Fact%20Sheet%20final.pdf.

61. U.S. Environmental Protection Agency, *Global Non-CO₂ Greenhouse Gas Emission Projections & Mitigation Potential: 2015–2050*; U.S. Environmental Protection Agency, "Fluorinated Greenhouse Gas Emissions and Supplies Reported to the GHGRP," Data and Tools, September 27, 2015, https://www.epa.gov/ghgreporting/fluorinated-greenhouse -gas-emissions-and-supplies-reported-ghgrp.

62. W. Goetzler, T. Sutherland, M. Rassi, and J. Burgos, "Research & Development Roadmap for Next-Generation Low Global Warming Potential Refrigerants" (Washington, D.C.: U.S. Department of Energy, November 2014), https://www.energy.gov/sites/prod /files/2014/12/f19/Refrigerants%20Roadmap%20Final%20Report%202014.pdf.

63. Scott C. Bartos and C. Shepherd Burton, "PFC, HFC, NF3, and SF6 Emissions from Semiconductor Manufacturing" (Intergovernmental Panel on Climate Change, 2000), https:// www.ipcc-nggip.iges.or.jp/public/gp/bgp/3_6_PFC_HFC_NF3_SF6_Semiconductor _Manufacturing.pdf.

64. European Semiconductor Industry Association, "Continued Access to HFC Compounds Is Essential for European Semiconductor Manufacturing," April 2013, https://www .eusemiconductors.eu/sites/default/files/uploads/ESIA_HFC_Position_F_Gas_Regulation _April_2013__Final.pdf.

65. Rong Xia, Sean Overa, and Feng Jiao, "Emerging Electrochemical Processes to Decarbonize the Chemical Industry," *JACS Au* 2, no. 5 (May 23, 2022): 1054–70, https://doi.org /10.1021/jacsau.2c00138.

66. Levi and Cullen, "Mapping Global Flows of Chemicals"; Shen Hong, "Polyamide & Intermediates Markets" (presented at the Synthetic Fibres Raw Materials Committee Meeting at APIC 2013, Taipei, Taiwan, May 10, 2013), https://web.archive.org/web /20170402045834/http://cpmaindia.com/pdf/apice2013_shen_hong.pdf.

67. American Chemical Society, "Molecule of the Week: Adipic Acid," February 9, 2015, https://www.acs.org/content/acs/en/molecule-of-the-week/archive/a/adipic-acid. html.

68. Stephen K. Ritter, "New Route to Adipic Acid Avoids Nitrous Oxide Production," *Chemical & Engineering News*, December 18, 2014, https://cen.acs.org/articles/92/i51 /New-Route-Adipic-Acid-Avoids.html.

69. A. Shimizu, K. Tanaka, and M. Fujimori, "Abatement Technologies for N₂O Emissions in the Adipic Acid Industry," *Chemosphere—Global Change Science*, 2, nos. 3–4 (July 1, 2000): 425–34, https://doi.org/10.1016/S1465-9972(00)00024-6.

70. Nitric Acid Climate Action Group, "Nitrous oxide emissions from nitric acid production," accessed June 27, 2023, https://www.nitricacidaction.org/transforming-the-sector /nitrous-oxide-emissions-from-nitric-acid-production/.

71. Martin Brudermüller, "Our Journey to Net Zero 2050" (presentation at BASF Capital Markets Day, Ludwigshafen, Germany, March 26, 2021), https://www.basf.com/global /documents/en/investor-relations/calendar-and-publications/calendar/2021/cmd /BASF_CMD-2021_Keynote-Presentation.pdf.

72. Zhou, Passow, Rudek, von Fisher, Hamburg, and Albertson, "Estimation of Methane Emissions from the U.S. Ammonia Fertilizer Industry Using a Mobile Sensing Approach"; Yuzhong Zhang, Ritesh Gautam, Sudhanshu Pandey, Mark Omara,

Joannes D. Maasakkers, Pankaj Sadavarte, David Lyon, et al., "Quantifying Methane Emissions from the Largest Oil-Producing Basin in the United States from Space," *Science Advances* 6, no. 17 (April 1, 2020), https://doi.org/10.1126/sciadv.aaz5120.

3. CEMENT AND CONCRETE

1. Global Cement and Concrete Association, "Global Cement and Concrete Industry Announces Roadmap to Achieve Groundbreaking 'Net Zero' CO_2 Emissions by 2050," October 12, 2021, https://gccassociation.org/news/global-cement-and-concrete-industry-announces-roadmap-to-achieve-groundbreaking-net-zero-co$_2$-emissions-by-2050/.
2. International Energy Agency and Cement Sustainability Initiative, *Technology Roadmap: Low-Carbon Transition in the Cement Industry* (technology report, Paris, April 6, 2018), https://iea.blob.core.windows.net/assets/cbaa3da1-fd61-4c2a-8719-31538f59b54f/TechnologyRoadmapLowCarbonTransitionintheCementIndustry.pdf.
3. Zhi Cao, Eric Masanet, Anupam Tiwari, and Sahil Akolawala, *Decarbonizing Concrete: Deep Decarbonization Pathways for the Cement and Concrete Cycle in the United States, India, and China* (report, Industrial Sustainability Analysis Laboratory, Northwestern University, Evanston, IL, March 2021), https://www.climateworks.org/wp-content/uploads/2021/03/Decarbonizing_Concrete.pdf.
4. National Minerals Information Center, U.S. Geological Survey, "Cement," in *Minerals Yearbook*, December 13, 2021, https://d9-wret.s3.us-west-2.amazonaws.com/assets/palladium/production/s3fs-public/media/files/myb1-2019-cemen-adv.xlsx.
5. International Energy Agency and Cement Sustainability Initiative, *Low-Carbon Transition in the Cement Industry.*
6. Portland Cement Association, "Cement Types," accessed May 22, 2023, https://www.cement.org/cement-concrete/concrete-materials/cement-types.
7. Global Cement and Concrete Association, "GNR 2.0—GCCA in Numbers," accessed May 22, 2023, https://gccassociation.org/sustainability-innovation/gnr-gcca-in-numbers/.
8. Johanna Lehne and Felix Preston, *Making Concrete Change: Innovation in Low-Carbon Cement and Concrete* (report, Chatham House, London, June 13, 2018), https://www.chathamhouse.org/2018/06/making-concrete-change-innovation-low-carbon-cement-and-concrete.
9. Portland Cement Association, "Cast-In-Place (CIP) Concrete," accessed July 1, 2023, https://www.cement.org/cement-concrete/cement-specific-materials/how-concrete-is-made.
10. Market Growth Reports, "Size and Share of Ready Mix Concrete Market by 2030," (press release, MarketWatch, May 13, 2023), https://www.marketwatch.com/press-release/size-and-share-of-ready-mix-concrete-market-by-2030-2023-05-15.
11. National Minerals Information Center, U.S. Geological Survey, "Cement."
12. Portland Cement Association, "How Cement Is Made," accessed May 22, 2023, https://www.cement.org/cement-concrete/how-cement-is-made.

13. Ernst Worrell and Christina Galitsky, *Energy Efficiency Improvement and Cost Saving Opportunities for Cement Making* (report, LBNL-54036-Revision, Lawrence Berkeley National Laboratory, Berkeley, March 2008), https://www.osti.gov/servlets/purl /927882.

14. Worrell and Galitsky, *Energy Efficiency Improvement and Cost Saving Opportunities for Cement Making.*

15. Global Cement and Concrete Association, "GNR 2.0—GCCA in Numbers."

16. Global Cement and Concrete Association, "GNR 2.0—GCCA in Numbers."

17. Worrell and Galitsky, *Energy Efficiency Improvement and Cost Saving Opportunities for Cement Making.*

18. AGICO, "Cement Rotary Kiln," accessed May 22, 2023, http://www.cementplantequipment.com/products/rotary-kiln/; Worrell and Galitsky, *Energy Efficiency Improvement and Cost Saving Opportunities for Cement Making.*

19. Worrell and Galitsky, *Energy Efficiency Improvement and Cost Saving Opportunities for Cement Making.*

20. Portland Cement Association, "How Cement Is Made."

21. International Energy Agency and Cement Sustainability Initiative, *Low-Carbon Transition in the Cement Industry.*

22. International Energy Agency and Cement Sustainability Initiative, *Low-Carbon Transition in the Cement Industry*; Cao, Masanet, Tiwari, and Akolawala, *Decarbonizing Concrete.*

23. Worrell and Galitsky, *Energy Efficiency Improvement and Cost Saving Opportunities for Cement Making.*

24. International Energy Agency and Cement Sustainability Initiative, *Low-Carbon Transition in the Cement Industry.*

25. International Energy Agency and Cement Sustainability Initiative, *Low-Carbon Transition in the Cement Industry.*; Worrell and Galitsky, *Energy Efficiency Improvement and Cost Saving Opportunities for Cement Making.*

26. International Energy Agency and Cement Sustainability Initiative, *Low-Carbon Transition in the Cement Industry.*

27. International Energy Agency and Cement Sustainability Initiative, *Low-Carbon Transition in the Cement Industry*; Lehne and Preston, "Making Concrete Change."

28. International Energy Agency and Cement Sustainability Initiative, *Low-Carbon Transition in the Cement Industry.*

29. Fengming Xi, Steven J. Davis, Philippe Ciais, Douglas Crawford-Brown, Dabo Guan, Claus Pade, Tiemao Shi, et al., "Substantial Global Carbon Uptake by Cement Carbonation," *Nature Geoscience* 9, no. 12 (December 2016): 880, https://doi.org/10.1038 /ngeo2840; Climate Watch, "Historical GHG Emissions," accessed May 22, 2023, https://www.climatewatchdata.org/ghg-emissions.

30. Ivan Janotka, Michal Bačuvčík, and Peter Paulík, "Low Carbonation of Concrete Found on 100-Year-Old Bridges," *Case Studies in Construction Materials* 8 (June 2018): 97–115, https://doi.org/10.1016/j.cscm.2017.12.006.

31. Cao, Masanet, Tiwari, and Akolawala, *Decarbonizing Concrete.*

32. A. Silva, R. Neves, and J. de Brito, "Statistical Modelling of Carbonation in Reinforced Concrete," *Cement and Concrete Composites* 50 (July 2014): 73–81, https://doi.org/10.1016/j.cemconcomp.2013.12.001.

33. Kim Basham, "Choices in Corrosion-Resistant Rebar," *Concrete Construction*, October 1, 1999, https://www.concreteconstruction.net/how-to/repair/choices-in-corrosion-resistant-rebar_o.

34. Global Cement and Concrete Association, "Global Cement and Concrete Industry Announces Roadmap to Achieve Groundbreaking 'Net Zero' CO_2 Emissions by 2050"; European Cement Association, "Cementing the European Green Deal," March 2020, https://cembureau.eu/media/kuxd32gi/cembureau-2050-roadmap_final-version_web.pdf.

35. International Energy Agency and Cement Sustainability Initiative, *Low-Carbon Transition in the Cement Industry*.

36. International Energy Agency and Cement Sustainability Initiative, *Low-Carbon Transition in the Cement Industry*; European Cement Research Academy, Cement Sustainability Initiative, ed., *Development of State of the Art Techniques in Cement Manufacturing: Trying to Look Ahead* (CSI/ECRA Technology Papers 2017, Duesseldorf, Geneva, March 20, 2017), https://www.wbcsd.org/contentwbc/download/3604/47080/1.

37. Lehne and Preston, *Making Concrete Change*.

38. Lehne and Preston, *Making Concrete Change*.

39. Lehne and Preston, *Making Concrete Change*.

40. Lehne and Preston, *Making Concrete Change*.

41. Ruben Snellings, "Assessing, Understanding and Unlocking Supplementary Cementitious Materials," *RILEM Technical Letters* 1 (August 16, 2016): 50–55, https://doi.org/10.21809/rilemtechlett.2016.12.

42. John L. Provis and Susan A. Bernal, "Geopolymers and Related Alkali-Activated Materials," *Annual Review of Materials Research* 44, no. 1 (2014): 299–327, https://doi.org/10.1146/annurev-matsci-070813-113515.

43. Lehne and Preston, *Making Concrete Change*.

44. Lehne and Preston, *Making Concrete Change*.

45. Cao, Masanet, Tiwari, and Akolawala, *Decarbonizing Concrete*.

46. Cao, Masanet, Tiwari, and Akolawala, *Decarbonizing Concrete*.

47. Cao, Masanet, Tiwari, and Akolawala, *Decarbonizing Concrete*.

48. Cao, Masanet, Tiwari, and Akolawala, *Decarbonizing Concrete*; Basham, "Choices in Corrosion-Resistant Rebar."

49. Nicholas DeChristofaro, telephone interview, August 22, 2018.

50. Cao, Masanet, Tiwari, and Akolawala, *Decarbonizing Concrete*.

51. Cao, Masanet, Tiwari, and Akolawala, *Decarbonizing Concrete*.

52. Sam A. Walling and John L. Provis, "Magnesia-Based Cements: A Journey of 150 Years, and Cements for the Future?," *Chemical Reviews* 116, no. 7 (March 22, 2016): 4170–4204, https://doi.org/10.1021/acs.chemrev.5b00463.

53. Sean Monkman and Mark MacDonald, "On Carbon Dioxide Utilization as a Means to Improve the Sustainability of Ready-Mixed Concrete," *Journal of Cleaner Production* 167 (November 20, 2017): 365–75, https://doi.org/10.1016/j.jclepro.2017.08.194.

54. Monkman and MacDonald, "On Carbon Dioxide Utilization as a Means to Improve the Sustainability of Ready-Mixed Concrete."

55. Mehrdad Mahoutian and Yixin Shao, "Production of Cement-Free Construction Blocks from Industry Wastes," *Journal of Cleaner Production* 137 (November 20, 2016): 1339–46, https://doi.org/10.1016/j.jclepro.2016.08.012.

56. Julian M. Allwood and Jonathan M. Cullen, *Sustainable Materials Without the Hot Air* (Cambridge, England: UIT Cambridge Ltd., 2015).

57. International Energy Agency and Cement Sustainability Initiative, *Low-Carbon Transition in the Cement Industry*; Cao, Masanet, Tiwari, and Akolawala, *Decarbonizing Concrete*.

58. International Energy Agency and Cement Sustainability Initiative, *Low-Carbon Transition in the Cement Industry*.

59. European Cement Research Academy, Cement Sustainability Initiative, ed., *Development of State of the Art Techniques in Cement Manufacturing*.

60. Cao, Masanet, Tiwari, and Akolawala, *Decarbonizing Concrete*.

61. European Cement Research Academy, Cement Sustainability Initiative, ed., *Development of State of the Art Techniques in Cement Manufacturing*.

62. European Cement Research Academy, Cement Sustainability Initiative, ed., *Development of State of the Art Techniques in Cement Manufacturing*.

63. European Cement Association, "Cementing the European Green Deal."

64. European Cement Research Academy, Cement Sustainability Initiative, ed., *Development of State of the Art Techniques in Cement Manufacturing*.

65. Bodil Wilhelmsson, Claes Kollberg, Johan Larsson, Jan Eriksson, and Magnus Eriksson, *CemZero* (Cementa and Vattenfall, December 17, 2018), https://www.cementa.se/sites /default/files/assets/document/65/de/final_cemzero_2018_public_version_2.0.pdf .pdf.

66. Leah D. Ellis, Andres F. Badel, Miki L. Chiang, Richard J.-Y. Park, and Yet-Ming Chiang, "Toward Electrochemical Synthesis of Cement—An Electrolyzer-Based Process for Decarbonating $CaCO_3$ While Producing Useful Gas Streams," *Proceedings of the National Academy of Sciences* 117, no. 23 (June 9, 2020): 12584–91, https://doi.org /10.1073/pnas.1821673116.

67. Cao, Masanet, Tiwari, and Akolawala, *Decarbonizing Concrete*.

68. Jan Skocek, Maciej Zajac, and Mohsen Ben Haha, "Carbon Capture and Utilization by Mineralization of Cement Pastes Derived from Recycled Concrete," *Scientific Reports* 10, no. 1 (March 27, 2020): 5614, https://doi.org/10.1038/s41598-020-62503-z.

69. Cambridge University, Department of Engineering, "Cambridge Engineers Invent World's First Zero Emissions Cement," news article, May 23, 2022, http://www.eng .cam.ac.uk/news/cambridge-engineers-invent-world-s-first-zero-emissions-cement.

70. George C. Wang, ed., "Ferrous Metal Production and Ferrous Slags," in *The Utilization of Slag in Civil Infrastructure Construction* (Cambridge: Woodhead, 2016), 9–33, https://doi.org/10.1016/B978-0-08-100381-7.00002-1.

71. Martin Verweij, "Terugwinnen van cement uit beton," *BETONIEK*, 2020, https://www .slimbreker.nl/downloads/2020-09%20-%20Betoniek%20September%202020%20 Recycling%20cement.pdf.

72. Cao, Masanet, Tiwari, and Akolawala, *Decarbonizing Concrete*.

73. Heidelberg Materials, "Carbon Capture and Storage (CCS)," accessed May 22, 2023, https://www.sement.heidelbergmaterials.no/en/CCSmaineng; Global CCS Institute, *Global Status of CCS 2020* (report, Global CCS Institute, Melbourne, Australia, 2020), https://www.globalccsinstitute.com/wp-content/uploads/2020/12/Global-Status-of -CCS-Report-2020_FINAL_December11.pdf.

4. ENERGY EFFICIENCY

1.   U.S. Department of Energy, "Energy Conservation Standards for Commercial and Industrial Electric Motors," Pub. L. No. 10 CFR 431, Subpart B, accessed May 23, 2023, https://www.energy.gov/sites/prod/files/2014/05/f15/electric_motors_ecs_final_rule.pdf.

2.   John W. Sutherland, David A. Dornfeld, and Barbara S. Linke, eds., *Energy Efficient Manufacturing: Theory and Applications* (Beverly, MA: Scrivener, 2018).

3.   International Energy Agency, *Energy Efficiency 2019* (report, International Energy Agency, Paris, revised November 2019), https://iea.blob.core.windows.net/assets/8441ab46 -9d86-47eb-b1fc-cb36fc3e7143/Energy_Efficiency_2019.pdf.

4.   U.S. Department of Energy, "Energy Efficiency Potential Studies Catalog," accessed May 23, 2023, https://www.energy.gov/eere/slsc/energy-efficiency-potential-studies-catalog.

5.   U.S. Department of Energy, "Industrial Energy Efficiency Potential Analysis," 2016, https://www.energy.gov/sites/prod/files/2017/04/f34/energy-savings-by-state-industrial -methodology.pdf.

6.   International Energy Agency, *Energy Efficiency 2018: Analysis and Outlooks to 2040*, (report, International Energy Agency, Paris, 2018), https://iea.blob.core.windows.net /assets/d0f81f5f-8f87-487e-a56b-8e0167d18c56/Market_Report_Series_Energy_Efficiency _2018.pdf.

7.   Sutherland, Dornfeld, and Linke, *Energy Efficient Manufacturing*.

8.   Sutherland, Dornfeld, and Linke, *Energy Efficient Manufacturing*.

9.   Sutherland, Dornfeld, and Linke, *Energy Efficient Manufacturing*.

10. Sutherland, Dornfeld, and Linke, *Energy Efficient Manufacturing*.

11. Christina Galitsky and Ernst Worrell, *Energy Efficiency Improvement and Cost Saving Opportunities for the Vehicle Assembly Industry* (report, LBNL-54036-Revision, Lawrence Berkeley National Laboratory, Berkeley, March 2008), https://www.osti.gov/servlets /purl/927881.

12. Galitsky and Worrell, *Energy Efficiency Improvement and Cost Saving Opportunities for the Vehicle Assembly Industry*"

13. Sutherland, Dornfeld, and Linke, *Energy Efficient Manufacturing*.

14. Ernst Worrell, Paul Blinde, Maarten Neelis, Eliane Blomen, and Eric Masanet, *Energy Efficiency Improvement and Cost Saving Opportunities for the U.S. Iron and Steel Industry: An ENERGY STAR® Guide for Energy and Plant Managers* (technical report, Lawrence Berkeley National Laboratory, Berkeley, October 2010), https://www.osti.gov /servlets/purl/1026806; U.S. Department of Energy, Advanced Manufacturing Office,

Improving Steam System Performance: A Sourcebook for Industry, Second Edition (U.S. Department of Energy, Washington, D.C., October 1, 2012), https://www.energy.gov/sites/prod/files/2014/05/f15/steamsourcebook.pdf.

15. International Energy Agency, ETSAP (Energy Technology Systems Analysis Program), "Industrial Combustion Boilers" (technology brief, International Energy Agency, Paris, May 2010), https://iea-etsap.org/E-TechDS/PDF/I01-ind_boilers-GS-AD-gct.pdf.

16. U.S. Department of Energy, Federal Emergency Management Program, "Purchasing Energy-Efficient Large Commercial Boilers," June 2020, https://www.energy.gov/eere/femp/purchasing-energy-efficient-large-commercial-boilers.

17. G. P. Sullivan, R. Pugh, A. P. Melendez, and W. D. Hunt, *Operations & Maintenance Best Practices: A Guide to Achieving Operational Efficiency* (report, U.S. Department of Energy, Federal Emergency Management Program, Washington, D.C., August 2010, https://www.energy.gov/sites/default/files/2020/04/f74/omguide_complete_w-eo-disclaimer.pdf.

18. Elorm Obotey Ezugbe and Sudesh Rathilal, "Membrane Technologies in Wastewater Treatment: A Review," *Membranes* 10, no. 5 (May 2020): 89, https://doi.org/10.3390/membranes10050089.

19. Miura Co., "Energy Saving by Multiple Installation System of High-Efficiency Small Once-Through Boilers and Energy Management System," accessed May 23, 2023, https://www.jase-w.eccj.or.jp/technologies/pdf/factory/F-36.pdf.

20. Worrell, Blinde, Neelis, Blomen, and Masanet, *Energy Efficiency Improvement and Cost Saving Opportunities for the U.S. Iron and Steel Industry*.

21. Galitsky and Worrell, *Energy Efficiency Improvement and Cost Saving Opportunities for the Vehicle Assembly Industry*.

22. Industrial Technologies Program, "Waste Heat Reduction and Recovery for Improving Furnace Efficiency, Productivity and Emissions Performance" (report no. DOE/GO-102004-1975, U.S. Department of Energy, Washington, D.C., November 2004), https://www.energy.gov/eere/amo/articles/waste-heat-reduction-and-recovery-improving-furnace-efficiency-productivity-and/.

23. Dennis Chojnacki and Curt Bermel, "GTI Super Boiler Technology," webcast slides, November 20, 2008, https://www1.eere.energy.gov/manufacturing/pdfs/webcast_2008-1120_super_boiler.pdf.

24. U.S. Department of Energy, *Industrial Heat Pumps for Steam and Fuel Savings*, (Best Practices Steam Technical Brief, U.S. Department of Energy, Washington, D.C., June 2003), https://www.energy.gov/sites/prod/files/2014/05/f15/heatpump.pdf.

25. Anton Firth, Bo Zhang, and Aidong Yang, "Quantification of Global Waste Heat and Its Environmental Effects," *Applied Energy* 235 (February 1, 2019): 1314–34, https://doi.org/10.1016/j.apenergy.2018.10.102.

26. Michael Papapetrou, George Kosmadakis, Andrea Cipollina, Umberto La Commare, and Giorgio Micale, "Industrial Waste Heat: Estimation of the Technically Available Resource in the EU per Industrial Sector, Temperature Level and Country," *Applied Thermal Engineering* 138 (June 25, 2018): 207–16, https://doi.org/10.1016/j.applthermaleng.2018.04.043.

27. Paul Otis, "CHP Industrial Bottoming and Topping Cycle with Energy Information Administration Survey Data" (discussion paper, U.S. Energy Information Administration, Washington, D.C., August 14, 2015), https://www.eia.gov/workingpapers/pdf/chp-Industrial_81415.pdf.

28. U.S. Department of Energy, "Overview of CHP Technologies" (Combined Heat and Power Technology Fact Sheet Series no. DOE/EE-1692, U.S. Department of Energy, Washington, D.C., November 2017), https://www.energy.gov/sites/default/files/2017/12/f46/CHP%20Overview-120817_compliant_0.pdf.

29. Otis, "CHP Industrial Bottoming and Topping Cycle with Energy Information Administration Survey Data."

30. U.S. Energy Information Administration, "Form EIA-860 Detailed Data with Previous Form Data (EIA-860A/860B)" (Washington, D.C., June 1, 2023), https://www.eia.gov/electricity/data/eia860/.

31. U.S. Department of Energy, *Combined Heat and Power (CHP) Technical Potential in the United States* (report no. DOE/EE-1328, U.S. Department of Energy, Washington, D.C., March 2016), https://www.energy.gov/sites/default/files/2016/04/f30/CHP%20Technical%20Potential%20Study%203-31-2016%20Final.pdf.

32. Colin McMillan, Carrie Schoeneberger, Jingyi Zhang, Parthiv Kurup, et al., *Opportunities for Solar Industrial Process Heat in the United States* (technical report no. NREL/TP-6A20-77760, U.S. National Renewable Energy Laboratory, U.S. Department of Energy, Washington, D.C., January 2021), https://www.nrel.gov/docs/fy21osti/77760.pdf.

33. McMillan, Schoeneberger, Zhang, Kurup, et al., *Opportunities for Solar Industrial Process Heat in the United States.*

34. Caleb Rockenbaugh, Jesse Dean, David Lovullo, Lars Lissell et al., *High Performance Flat Plate Solar Thermal Collector Evaluation*, (report for the General Services Administration by U.S. National Renewable Energy Laboratory, August 2016), https://www.nrel.gov/docs/fy16osti/66215.pdf.

35. McMillan, Schoeneberger, Zhang, Kurup, et al., *Opportunities for Solar Industrial Process Heat in the United States.*

36. Charles Kutscher, Frank Burkholder, and Kathleen Stynes, "Generation of a Parabolic Trough Collector Efficiency Curve from Separate Measurements of Outdoor Optical Efficiency and Indoor Receiver Heat Loss" (paper presented at SolarPACES 2010, Perpignan, France, 2010), https://www.nrel.gov/docs/fy11osti/49304.pdf.

37. Francisco José Sepúlveda, María Teresa Miranda, Irene Montero, José Ignacio Arranz, Francisco Javier Lozano, Manuel Matamoros, and Paloma Rodríguez, "Analysis of Potential Use of Linear Fresnel Collector for Direct Steam Generation in Industries of the Southwest of Europe," *Energies* 12, no. 21 (January 2019): 4049, https://doi.org/10.3390/en12214049.

38. Sepúlveda, Miranda, Montero, Arranz, et al.,, "Analysis of Potential Use of Linear Fresnel Collector for Direct Steam Generation in Industries of the Southwest of Europe."

39. McMillan, Schoeneberger, Zhang, Kurup, et al., *Opportunities for Solar Industrial Process Heat in the United States.*

40. Alicia Crespo, Camila Barreneche, Mercedes Ibarra, and Werner Platzer, "Latent Thermal Energy Storage for Solar Process Heat Applications at Medium-High Temperatures—A Review," *Solar Energy*, Thermal Energy Storage for Solar Applications, 192 (November 1, 2019): 3–34, https://doi.org/10.1016/j.solener.2018.06.101.

41. Sepúlveda, Miranda, Montero, Arranz, et al., "Analysis of Potential Use of Linear Fresnel Collector for Direct Steam Generation in Industries of the Southwest of Europe."

42. McMillan, Schoeneberger, Zhang, Kurup, et al., *Opportunities for Solar Industrial Process Heat in the United States.*

43. McMillan, Schoeneberger, Zhang, Kurup, et al., *Opportunities for Solar Industrial Process Heat in the United States.*

44. Sutherland, Dornfeld, and Linke, *Energy Efficient Manufacturing.*

45. U.S. Energy Information Administration, "2018 Manufacturing Energy Consumption Survey" (Washington, D.C., 2021), https://www.eia.gov/consumption/manufacturing/data/2018/.

46. Austin Weber, "Lights-Out Automation: Fact or Fiction?," *Assembly* magazine, May 9, 2019, https://www.assemblymag.com/articles/94982-lights-out-automation-fact-or-fiction?v=preview.

47. Weber, "Lights-Out Automation: Fact or Fiction?"

48. David Edwards, "Bosch Produces Its First Semiconductor Wafers Through 'Fully Automated' Fabrication Process," *Robotics & Automation News*, March 9, 2021, https://roboticsandautomationnews.com/2021/03/09/bosch-produces-its-first-semiconductor-wafers-through-fully-automated-fabrication-process/41272/; Drivers Jonas Deloitte, *Employment Densities Guide, 2nd Edition*, 2010, https://assets.publishing.service.gov.uk/government/uploads/system/uploads/attachment_data/file/378203/employ-den.pdf.

49. Sutherland, Dornfeld, and Linke, *Energy Efficient Manufacturing.*

50. Walmart Inc., "Walmart on Track to Reduce 1 Billion Metric Tons of Emissions from Global Supply Chains by 2030," news release, May 8, 2019, https://corporate.walmart.com/newsroom/2019/05/08/walmart-on-track-to-reduce-1-billion-metric-tons-of-emissions-from-global-supply-chains-by-2030.

51. Roland Stephen, Elizabeth Tennant, Christina Freyman, Jennifer Ozawa, John Chase, and Dan Querejazu, *Saving Energy, Building Skills: Industrial Assessment Centers Impact* (report, SRI, International, Menlo Park, CA, March 2015), https://iac.university/technicalDocs/Industrial%20Assessment%20Centers%20Impacts%20SRI%20International.pdf.

52. Anthony Wright, Michaela Martin, and Sachin Nimbalkar, *Results from the U.S. DOE 2008 Save Energy Now Assessment Initiative* (report no. ORNL/TM-2010/145, Oak Ridge National Laboratory, Oak Ridge, TN, July 2010), https://info.ornl.gov/sites/publications/files/Pub25190.pdf.

53. Christopher D. Watson, "U.S. Aluminum Manufacturing: Industry Trends and Sustainability" (report no. R47294, U.S. Congressional Research Service, Washington D.C., October 26, 2022), https://crsreports.congress.gov/product/pdf/R/R47294.

54. Ernst Worrell, John A Laitner, Michael Ruth, and Hodayah Finman, "Productivity Benefits of Industrial Energy Efficiency Measures," *Energy* 28, no. 11 (September 1, 2003): 1081–98, https://doi.org/10.1016/S0360-5442(03)00091-4.

55. Jeffrey Rissman, Chris Bataille, Eric Masanet, Nate Aden, William R. Morrow III, Nan Zhou, Neal Elliott, et al., "Technologies and Policies to Decarbonize Global Industry: Review and Assessment of Mitigation Drivers Through 2070," *Applied Energy* 266 (May 15, 2020): 114848, https://doi.org/10.1016/j.apenergy.2020.114848; Christopher H. Russell, *Multiple Benefits of Business-Sector Energy Efficiency: A Survey of Existing and Potential Measures* (research report, American Council for an Energy-Efficient Economy, Washington, D.C., January 6, 2015), https://aceee.org/research-report/ie1501.

56. Stephen, Tennant, Freyman, Ozawa, Chase, and Querejazu, *Saving Energy, Building Skills*.

57. International Organization for Standardization, "ISO 50001 Energy Management Systems" (Geneva, Switzerland, 2018), https://www.iso.org/files/live/sites/isoorg/files/store/en/PUB100400.pdf.

5. MATERIAL EFFICIENCY, MATERIAL SUBSTITUTION, AND CIRCULAR ECONOMY

1. Julian M. Allwood and Jonathan M. Cullen, *Sustainable Materials Without the Hot Air* (Cambridge, UK: UIT Cambridge Ltd., 2015).

2. Allwood and Cullen, *Sustainable Materials Without the Hot Air*.

3. Allwood and Cullen, *Sustainable Materials Without the Hot Air*.

4. Eric Beinhocker, *The Origin of Wealth: Evolution, Complexity, and the Radical Remaking of Economics* (Boston: Harvard Business School Press, 2007).

5. Carmen Krahe, Antonio Bräunche, Alexander Jacob, Nicole Stricker, and Gisela Lanza, "Deep Learning for Automated Product Design," in ed. Khumbulani Mpofu and Peter Butala, "Enhancing Design Through the 4th Industrial Revolution Thinking," special issue, *Procedia CIRP* 91 (January 2020): 3–8, https://doi.org/10.1016/j.procir.2020.01.135.

6. Kailun Feng, Weizhuo Lu, and Yaowu Wang, "Assessing Environmental Performance in Early Building Design Stage: An Integrated Parametric Design and Machine Learning Method," *Sustainable Cities and Society* 50 (October 2019): 101596, https://doi.org/10.1016/j.scs.2019.101596.

7. Formlabs, "Guide to 3D Printing Materials: Types, Applications, and Properties," accessed May 24, 2023, https://formlabs.com/blog/3d-printing-materials/.

8. GE, "Metal Powders for Additive Manufacturing," accessed May 24, 2023, https://www.ge.com/additive/additive-manufacturing/information/metal-additive-manufacturing-materials.

9. Formlabs, "Guide to 3D Printing Materials."

10. Ravi Toor, "The 3D Printing Waste Problem," *Filamentive* (blog), November 27, 2019, https://www.filamentive.com/the-3d-printing-waste-problem/.

11. AMFG, "Industrial Applications of 3D Printing: The Ultimate Guide," accessed May 24, 2023, https://amfg.ai/industrial-applications-of-3d-printing-the-ultimate-guide/.

12. Eric Masanet, Arman Shehabi, Nuoa Lei, Sarah Smith, and Jonathan Koomey, "Recalibrating Global Data Center Energy-Use Estimates," *Science* 367, no. 6481 (February 28, 2020): 984–86, https://www.science.org/doi/10.1126/science.aba3758.

13. Neville Millar, Julie E. Doll, and G. Philip Robertson, "Management of Nitrogen Fertilizer to Reduce Nitrous Oxide Emissions from Field Crops" (Climate Change and Agriculture Fact Sheet Series—MSU Extension Bulletin E3152, November 2014), https://www.canr.msu.edu/uploads/resources/pdfs/management_of_nitrogen_fertiler_(e3152).pdf.

14. ESN Smart Nitrogen, "Soil Testing Tips for The Perfect Fertilizer Application," *Smart Talk Blog*, accessed May 24, 2023, https://smartnitrogen.com/soil-testing-tips/.

15. Land Institute, "Perennial Grain Crop Development," accessed May 24, 2023, https://landinstitute.org/our-work/perennial-crops/; Angelo Eliades, "Perennial Plants and Permaculture," Permaculture Research Institute, June 6, 2012, https://www.permaculturenews.org/2012/06/06/perennial-plants-and-permaculture/.

16. Eliades, "Perennial Plants and Permaculture"; Land Institute, "Perennial Grain Crop Development."

17. Lloyd Alter, "What's the Difference Between All These Laminated Timbers?," *Treehugger*, updated October 7, 2019, https://www.treehugger.com/whats-difference-between-all-these-laminated-timbers-4858011; Kallesoe Machinery, "What Is the Difference Between CLT and Glulam?," accessed May 24, 2023, https://kallesoemachinery.com/the-green-products-of-the-future/what-is-the-difference-between-clt-and-glulam/.

18. Alter, "What's the Difference Between All These Laminated Timbers?"

19. Rameesha Sajwar, "This Sustainable Tower in Sweden Is Made Entirely Out of Timber," *Wonderful Engineering*, September 18, 2021, https://wonderfulengineering.com/this-sustainable-tower-in-sweden-is-made-entirely-out-of-timber/.

20. Niko Heeren, Christopher L. Mutel, Bernhard Steubing, York Ostermeyer, Holger Wallbaum, and Stefanie Hellweg, "Environmental Impact of Buildings—What Matters?," *Environmental Science & Technology* 49, no. 16 (August 18, 2015): 9832–41, https://doi.org/10.1021/acs.est.5b01735.

21. Chadwick Dearing Oliver, Nedal T. Nassar, Bruce R. Lippke, and James B. McCarter, "Carbon, Fossil Fuel, and Biodiversity Mitigation with Wood and Forests," *Journal of Sustainable Forestry* 33, no. 3 (April 3, 2014): 248–75, https://doi.org/10.1080/10549811.2013.839386.

22. UN Food and Agriculture Organization, "Global Forest Products Facts and Figures 2018," 2019, https://www.fao.org/3/ca7415en/ca7415en.pdf; Global Cement and Concrete Association, "Global Cement and Concrete Industry Announces Roadmap to Achieve Groundbreaking 'Net Zero' CO_2 Emissions by 2050," October 12, 2021, https://gccassociation.org/news/global-cement-and-concrete-industry-announces-roadmap-to-achieve-groundbreaking-net-zero-co$_2$-emissions-by-2050/.

23. Hannah Ritchie, "How Many People Does Synthetic Fertilizer Feed?," Our World in Data, November 7, 2017, https://ourworldindata.org/how-many-people-does-synthetic-fertilizer-feed.

24. Sarika Jain, David Newman, Ange Nizhou, Harmen Dekker, Pharoah Le Feuvre, Hannah Richter, et al., *Global Potential of Biogas* (report, World Biogas Association, London, June 2019), https://www.worldbiogasassociation.org/wp-content/uploads/2019/07/WBA-globalreport-56ppa4_digital.pdf.

25. U.S. Geological Survey, *Mineral Commodity Summaries 2022*, 2022, https://pubs.er.usgs.gov/publication/mcs2022.

26. U.S. Environmental Protection Agency, *Global Non-CO$_2$ Greenhouse Gas Emission Projections & Mitigation Potential: 2015–2050* (report no. EPA-430-R-19-010, U.S. Environmental Protection Agency, Washington, D.C., October 2019), https://www.epa.gov/sites/default/files/2020-05/documents/epa_non-co$_2$_greenhouse_gases_rpt-epa430r19010.pdf; Climate Watch, "Historical GHG Emissions," accessed May 22, 2023, https://www.climatewatchdata.org/ghg-emissions.

27. Jain, Newman, Nizhou, Dekker, Le Feuvre, Richter, et al., *Global Potential of Biogas*.

28. Nick Primmer and WBA Policy, Innovation and Technical Committee, *Biogas: Pathways to 2030* (report, World Biogas Association, London, March 2021), https://www.worldbiogasassociation.org/biogas-pathways-to-2030-report/.

29. Primmer and WBA Policy, Innovation and Technical Committee, *Biogas: Pathways to 2030*.

30. Jain, Newman, Nizhou, Dekker, Le Feuvre, Richter, et al., *Global Potential of Biogas*.

31. Tom Perkins, "'I Don't Know How We'll Survive': The Farmers Facing Ruin in America's 'Forever Chemicals' Crisis," *The Guardian*, March 22, 2022, https://www.theguardian.com/environment/2022/mar/22/i-dont-know-how-well-survive-the-farmers-facing-ruin-in-americas-forever-chemicals-crisis.

32. Jain, Newman, Nizhou, Dekker, Le Feuvre, Richter, et al., *Global Potential of Biogas*.

33. Allwood and Cullen, *Sustainable Materials Without the Hot Air*.

34. R. Přikryl, Á Török, M. Theodoridou, M. Gomez-Heras, and K. Miskovsky, "Geomaterials in Construction and Their Sustainability: Understanding Their Role in Modern Society," in *Sustainable Use of Traditional Geomaterials in Construction Practice*, ed. R. Přikryl, Á. Török, M. Gomez-Heras, K. Miskovsky, and M. Theodoridou (London: Geological Society, 2016), 1–22, https://pubs.geoscienceworld.org/gsl/books/book/2009/chapter-abstract/16290451/Geomaterials-in-construction-and-their?redirectedFrom=fulltext.

35. Allwood and Cullen, *Sustainable Materials Without the Hot Air*.

36. Ghada Atiwesh, Abanoub Mikhael, Christopher C. Parrish, Joseph Banoub, and Tuyet-Anh T. Le, "Environmental Impact of Bioplastic Use: A Review," *Heliyon* 7, no. 9 (September 1, 2021): e07918, https://doi.org/10.1016/j.heliyon.2021.e07918.

37. Atiwesh, Mikhael, Parrish, Banoub, and Le, "Environmental Impact of Bioplastic Use."

38. Clara Rosalía Álvarez-Chávez, Sally Edwards, Rafael Moure-Eraso, and Kenneth Geiser, "Sustainability of Bio-Based Plastics: General Comparative Analysis and Recommendations for Improvement," *Journal of Cleaner Production* 23, no. 1 (March 2012): 47–56, https://doi.org/10.1016/j.jclepro.2011.10.003.

39. Renee Cho, "The Truth About Bioplastics," Columbia University Climate School, December 13, 2017, https://news.climate.columbia.edu/2017/12/13/the-truth-about-bioplastics/.

40. A. Demetrious and E. Crossin, "Life Cycle Assessment of Paper and Plastic Packaging Waste in Landfill, Incineration, and Gasification-Pyrolysis," *Journal of Material Cycles and Waste Management* 21, no. 4 (2019): 850–60, https://doi.org/10.1007/s10163-019-00842-4.

41. Robert Kimmel, "Life Cycle Assessment of Grocery Bags in Common Use in the United States," (Clemson University, Environmental Studies 6, 2014), https://tigerprints.clemson.edu/cgi/viewcontent.cgi?article=1006&context=cudp_environment.

42. Allwood and Cullen, *Sustainable Materials Without the Hot Air*.

43. Allwood and Cullen, *Sustainable Materials Without the Hot Air*.

44. Gizmogrind, "What Happens to Phones That Are Traded In?," GizmoGrind, August 17, 2020, https://www.gizmogrind.com/blog/what-happens-phones-that-are-traded-in/.

45. Jim Motavalli, "Who Will Own the Cars That Drive Themselves?," *New York Times*, May 29, 2020, Business, https://www.nytimes.com/2020/05/29/business/ownership-autonomous-cars-coronavirus.html; Paul Barter, " 'Cars Are Parked 95 Percent of the Time'. Let's Check!," *Reinventing Parking* (blog), February 22, 2013, https://www.reinventingparking.org/2013/02/cars-are-parked-95-of-time-lets-check.html; U.S. Department of Transportation, Bureau of Transportation Statistics, *National Transportation Statistics*, accessed May 24, 2023, https://www.bts.gov/product/national-transportation-statistics.

46. U.S. Bureau of Labor Statistics, "American Time Use Survey," accessed May 24, 2023, https://www.bls.gov/tus/.

47. Allwood and Cullen, *Sustainable Materials Without the Hot Air*.

48. Urban Sustainability Directors Network, "Tool Lending Libraries," May 24, 2023, https://sustainableconsumption.usdn.org/initiatives-list/tool-lending-libraries.

49. Council for Textile Recycling, "The Facts About Textile Waste," infographic, accessed July 5, 2023, https://www.weardonaterecycle.org/images/textile-recycling-issues.png.

50. Council for Textile Recycling, "Action: Brands, Retailers, & Government," accessed May 24, 2023, http://www.weardonaterecycle.org/action/brands-retailers-govt.html.

51. Optoro, *Optoro Impact Report 2019*, (report, Optoro, Washington, D.C., 2020), https://info.optoro.com/hubfs/Optoro%202019%20Impact%20Report.pdf.

52. "What Retailers Like Amazon Do with Unsold Inventory," *CNBC*, December 14, 2019, https://youtu.be/AfDF3jQAzuk.

53. Optoro, *Optoro Impact Report 2019*.

54. "What Retailers Like Amazon Do with Unsold Inventory."

55. Optoro, *Optoro Impact Report 2019*.

56. Sophie Hirsh, "More and More Companies Are Launching Their Own Resell Programs, from IKEA to Lululemon," Green Matters, updated March 21, 2023, https://www.greenmatters.com/p/companies-own-buy-back-resell-programs.

57. Mister Jalopy, Phillip Rorrone, and Simon Hill, "The Maker's Bill of Rights," *Makezine.com*, 2005, https://cdn.makezine.com/make/MAKERS_RIGHTS.pdf.

58. U.S. Federal Trade Commission, *Nixing the Fix: An FTC Report to Congress on Repair Restrictions*" (report, U.S. Federal Trade Commission, Washington, D.C., May 2021), https://www.ftc.gov/system/files/documents/reports/nixing-fix-ftc-report-congress-repair-restrictions/nixing_the_fix_report_final_5521_630pm-508_002.pdf.

59. U.S. Federal Trade Commission, *Nixing the Fix*; Derrick Mead, "Design for Repair: Things Can Be Fixed," Lectorate Design, September 2, 2020, https://www.kabk.nl/en /lectorates/design/design-for-repair-things-can-be-fixed.

60. John Taaffe, "5 Factors of Machine Refurbishment," *Equipment Manager*, 2011.

61. James D. Abbey, Margaret G. Meloy, V. Daniel R. Guide, Jr., and Selin Atalay, "Remanufactured Products in Closed-Loop Supply Chains for Consumer Goods," *Production and Operations Management* 24, no. 3 (2015): 488–503, https://doi.org/10.1111/poms.12238.

62. Abbey, Meloy, Guide, and Atalay, "Remanufactured Products in Closed-Loop Supply Chains for Consumer Goods."

63. Abbey, Meloy, Guide, and Atalay, "Remanufactured Products in Closed-Loop Supply Chains for Consumer Goods."

64. Allwood and Cullen, *Sustainable Materials Without the Hot Air*.

65. European Cement Association, "Re-Use of Concrete," accessed May 24, 2023, https://www .cembureau.eu/media/rc3fihgd/cembureau-view-cement-sector-re-use-of-concrete .pdf; Allwood and Cullen, *Sustainable Materials Without the Hot Air*.

66. U.S. Green Building Council, *LEED v4 for Building Design and Construction*" updated July 25, 2019, https://www.usgbc.org/sites/default/files/LEED%20v4%20BDC_07.25.19_current.pdf.

67. Silpa Kaza, Lisa Yao, Perinaz Bhada-Tata, and Frank Van Woerden, *What a Waste 2.0: A Global Snapshot of Solid Waste Management to 2050* (Washington, D.C.: World Bank Group, 2018), https://openknowledge.worldbank.org/handle/10986/30317.

68. Piotr Dobrowolski, "Recycling in China: From Zero to Hero?," *Waste Management World*, April 20, 2021, https://waste-management-world.com/a/recycling-in-china-from-zero-to-hero.

69. Roland Geyer, Jenna R. Jambeck, and Kara Lavender Law, "Production, Use, and Fate of All Plastics Ever Made," *Science Advances* 3, no. 7 (July 19, 2017): e1700782, https://doi .org/10.1126/sciadv.1700782.

70. John Hocevar, "Circular Claims Fall Flat: Comprehensive U.S. Survey of Plastics Recyclability" (report, Greenpeace, Washington, D.C., February 18, 2020), https://www.greenpeace .org/usa/wp-content/uploads/2020/02/Greenpeace-Report-Circular-Claims-Fall-Flat.pdf.

71. Erin McCormick, Charlotte Simmonds, Jessica Glenza, and Katharine Gammon, "Americans' Plastic Recycling Is Dumped in Landfills, Investigation Shows," *The Guardian*, June 21, 2019, US news, https://www.theguardian.com/us-news/2019/jun/21/us-plastic -recycling-landfills.

72. Geyer, Jambeck, and Law, "Production, Use, and Fate of All Plastics Ever Made."

73. Mitch Jacoby, "Why Glass Recycling in the US Is Broken," *Chemical & Engineering News*, February 11, 2019, https://cen.acs.org/materials/inorganic-chemistry/glass-recycling-US -broken/97/i6.

74. Jacoby, "Why Glass Recycling in the US Is Broken."

6. ELECTRIFICATION

1. International Energy Agency, "World Energy Balances Data Service," updated April 2023, https://www.iea.org/data-and-statistics/data-product/world-energy-balances.

2. U.S. Energy Information Administration, "2018 Manufacturing Energy Consumption Survey—2018 MECS Survey Data," accessed May 25, 2023, https://www.eia.gov/consumption/manufacturing/data/2018/.

3. U.S. Energy Information Administration, "2018 Manufacturing Energy Consumption Survey."

4. U.S. Energy Information Administration, "2018 Manufacturing Energy Consumption Survey."

5. U.S. Energy Information Administration, "2018 Manufacturing Energy Consumption Survey."

6. International Energy Agency, "World Energy Balances Data Service."

7. U.S. Energy Information Administration, "2018 Manufacturing Energy Consumption Survey."

8. Donald W. Olson, "Graphite," in *2017 Minerals Yearbook* (U.S. (Washington, D.C.: Geological Survey, August 2020), https://d9-wret.s3.us-west-2.amazonaws.com/assets/palladium/production/atoms/files/myb1-2017-graph.pdf.

9. Albert V. Tamashausky, "Introduction to Synthetic Graphite" (Asbury, NJ: Asbury Carbons, 2006), https://asbury.com/media/1225/syntheticgraphiteparti.pdf.

10. U.S. Department of Energy, *Industrial Heat Pumps for Steam and Fuel Savings* (Best Practices Steam Technical Brief, U.S. Department of Energy, Washington, D.C., June 2003), https://www.energy.gov/sites/prod/files/2014/05/f15/heatpump.pdf.

11. Cordin Arpagaus, Frédéric Bless, Michael Uhlmann, Jürg Schiffmann, and Stefan Bertsch, "High Temperature Heat Pumps: Market Overview, State of the Art, Research Status, Refrigerants, and Application Potentials" (presented at 17th International Refrigeration and Air Conditioning Conference, Purdue University, West Lafayette, IN, 2018), paper 1876, https://docs.lib.purdue.edu/cgi/viewcontent.cgi?article=2875&context=iracc.

12. Union City Filament Corp., "About Nichrome Alloys," accessed May 25, 2023, https://ucfilament.com/materials/nichrome/.

13. Fred McLaughlin, "Understanding Tungsten Mesh Heating Elements," *Industrial Heating*, March 1, 2016, https://www.industrialheating.com/articles/95374-understanding-tungsten-mesh-heating-elements?v=preview.

14. Oxy-Gon Industries, "General Purpose Furnaces," accessed May 25, 2023, https://oxy-gon.com/product/the-oxy-gon-fc-series-general-purpose-ceramic-furnace/.

15. Valery Rudnev, Don Loveless, and Raymond L. Cook, "Theoretical Background," in *Handbook of Induction Heating*, 2nd ed. (Boca Raton, FL: CRC Press, 2017), https://www.routledge.com/Handbook-of-Induction-Heating/Rudnev-Loveless-Cook/p/book/9781138748743#.

16. Oscar Lucia, Pascal Maussion, Enrique J. Dede, and Jose Burdio, "Induction Heating Technology and Its Applications: Past Developments, Current Technology, and Future Challenges," *IEEE Transactions on Industrial Electronics* 61, no. 5 (May 2014): 2509–20, https://doi.org/10.1109/TIE.2013.2281162.

17. Robert Keshecki, "Better Productivity, Metal Quality w/Natural Induction Stirring," *Foundry Management & Technology*, January 21, 2010, https://www.foundrymag.com

/issues-and-ideas/article/21924831/better-productivity-metal-quality-wnatural-induction-stirring.

18. Lucia, Maussion, Dede, and Burdio, "Induction Heating Technology and Its Applications."

19. EUROfusion Consortium, "Top FAQ," accessed May 25, 2023, https://www.euro-fusion.org/faq/.

20. Ambrell Induction Heating Solutions, "What Is Induction Heating and How Do Induction Coils Work?," *AZo Materials*, January 27, 2015, https://www.azom.com/article.aspx?ArticleID=11659.

21. ENRX, "Induction Heating Applications," accessed May 25, 2023, https://www.efd-induction.com/en/induction-heating-applications.

22. Lucia, Maussion, Dede, and Burdio, "Induction Heating Technology and Its Applications."

23. Ambrell Induction Heating Solutions, "What Is Induction Heating and How Do Induction Coils Work?"

24. Radyne, "Susceptor Heating," accessed May 25, 2023, https://radyne.com/induction-heating-applications/susceptor-heating/.

25. *U.S. Steel's Electric Arc Furnace* (Fairfield, AL: AL.com, 2020), https://www.youtube.com/watch?v=8J3bMtX9Wqo&t=127s.

26. International Energy Agency, *Iron and Steel Technology Roadmap* (technology report, IEA, Paris, October 8, 2020, https://www.iea.org/reports/iron-and-steel-technology-roadmap.

27. U.S. Environmental Protection Agency, "11.4 Calcium Carbide Manufacturing Final Report," in *AP-42: Compilation of Air Emissions Factors* (Washington, D.C.: U.S. EPA, 1995), https://www.epa.gov/sites/production/files/2020-10/documents/c11s04.pdf; U.S. Environmental Protection Agency, "Elemental Phosphorus," 1994, https://archive.epa.gov/epawaste/nonhaz/industrial/special/web/pdf/id4-eph.pdf.

28. Materials Research Furnaces, "Large Bell Jar Arc Melt Furnace," accessed May 25, 2023, https://www.mrf-furnaces.com/PDF/MRF_ABJ900.pdf?o6fda8&o6fda8.

29. Bodil Wilhelmsson, Claes Kollberg, Johan Larsson, Jan Eriksson, and Magnus Eriksson, "CemZero: A Feasibility Study Evaluating Ways to Reach Sustainable Cement Production Via the Use of Electricity" (Cementa and Vattenfall, December 17, 2018), https://www.cementa.se/sites/default/files/assets/document/65/de/final_cemzero_2018_public_version_2.0.pdf.pdf.

30. Wilhelmsson, Kollberg, Larsson, Eriksson, and Eriksson, "CemZero."

31. Tara McHugh, "Radio Frequency Processing of Food," *Food Technology Magazine*, August 1, 2016, https://www.ift.org/news-and-publications/food-technology-magazine/issues/2016/august/columns/processing-radio-frequency-processing-of-food.

32. New Zealand Energy Efficiency and Conservation Authority, "Direct Process Heating: Microwave and Radio Frequency," 2019, https://genless.govt.nz/assets/Business-Resources/Direct-Process-Heating-microwave-radio-frequency.pdf; U.S. Department of Defense, "Compact and Efficient Magnetron Source for Continuous Wave Microwave Power Generation," December 10, 2019, https://www.sbir.gov/node/1654739.

33. McHugh, "Radio Frequency Processing of Food"; Sairem, "Microwave vs RF: Differences & Advantages," SAIREM, accessed May 25, 2023, https://www.sairem.com/microwave-vs-rf-differences-and-advantages/.

34. McHugh, "Radio Frequency Processing of Food."

35. Max Industrial Microwave, "Industrial Microwave Application," accessed May 25, 2023, https://www.maxindustrialmicrowave.com/application-t-11.html.

36. MOR Electric Heating Association, "Basic Information About Infrared (Radiant) Heating," https://www.infraredheaters.com/basic.html.

37. Marty Sawyer, "Is Infrared Right for Your Part?," *Process Heating*, August 4, 2020, https://www.process-heating.com/articles/93481-is-infrared-right-for-your-part?v=preview.

38. David Weisman, "Using Infrared Heating Effectively in Industrial Process Heating Applications," *Process Heating*, June 22, 2019, https://www.process-heating.com/articles/93079-using-infrared-heating-effectively-in-industrial-process-heating-applications?v=preview.

39. MOR Electric Heating Association, "Basic Information About Infrared (Radiant) Heating."

40. Jeff Hecht, "Laser," in *Encyclopedia Britannica*, updated May 18, 2023, https://www.britannica.com/technology/laser/Fundamental-principles.

41. Jeff Hecht, "Photonic Frontiers: High-Efficiency Optical Pumping: 'Going Green' Cranks Up the Laser Power," *Laser Focus World*, April 13, 2016, https://www.laserfocusworld.com/lasers-sources/article/16547048/photonic-frontiers-highefficiency-optical-pumping-going-green-cranks-up-the-laser-power.

42. Lawrence Livermore National Laboratory, "What Is the National Ignition Facility?," accessed May 25, 2023, https://lasers.llnl.gov/about/what-is-nif.

43. John DeLalio, "Electron Beam or Laser Beam Welding?," *The Fabricator*, August 2, 2016, https://www.thefabricator.com/thefabricator/article/laserwelding/electron-beam-or-laser-beam-welding-.

44. AMG Engineering, "EB: Electron Beam Melting," accessed May 25, 2023, https://www.ald-vt.com/portfolio/engineering/vacuum-metallurgy/electron-beam-melting-furnace-eb-melting/.

45. DeLalio, "Electron Beam or Laser Beam Welding?"

46. Julian Spector, "This Startup's Energy Storage Tech Is 'Essentially a Giant Toaster.'" Canary Media, April 13, 2022, https://www.canarymedia.com/articles/energy-storage/this-startups-energy-storage-tech-is-essentially-a-giant-toaster; Zhiwen Ma, Douglas Hofer, James Tallman, Ruichong Zhang, Aaron Morris, and Matthew Lambert, "Economic Long-Duration Electricity Storage Using Low-Cost Thermal Energy Storage and a High-Efficiency Power Cycle (ENDURING)" (PowerPoint presentation, DAYS Annual Meeting, March 2021), https://arpa-e.energy.gov/sites/default/files/2021-03/07%20Day1-Zhiwen%20Ma_NREL.pdf.

47. Julian Spector, "This Startup's Energy Storage Tech Is 'Essentially a Giant Toaster.'"

48. Julian Spector, "This Startup's Energy Storage Tech Is 'Essentially a Giant Toaster.'"

49. Jeffrey Rissman and Eric Gimon, "Industrial Thermal Batteries: Decarbonizing U.S. Industry While Supporting a High-Renewables Grid," report, Energy Innovation,

San Francisco, July 2023, https://energyinnovation.org/publication/thermal-batteries
-decarbonizing-u-s-industry-while-supporting-a-high-renewables-grid/.

50. Jeffrey Rissman and Eric Gimon, "Industrial Thermal Batteries."

51. Jeffrey Rissman and Eric Gimon, "Industrial Thermal Batteries." Veronica Henze,
"Lithium-Ion Battery Pack Prices Rise for First Time to an Average of $151/KWh,"
BloombergNEF, December 6, 2022, https://about.bnef.com/blog/lithium-ion-battery
-pack-prices-rise-for-first-time-to-an-average-of-151-kwh/.

52. Roberto Ponciroli, Haoyu Wang, Richard Vilim, Konor Frick, and Cristian Rabiti,
"Development of Energy Storage: Cost Models" (report no. ANL/NSE-21/13, Argonne
National Laboratory, Chicago, March 31, 2021), https://publications.anl.gov/anlpubs
/2021/04/167188.pdf.

53. Ramana G. Reddy, "Molten Salts: Thermal Energy Storage and Heat Transfer Media,"
Journal of Phase Equilibria and Diffusion 32, no. 4 (August 1, 2011): 269–70, https://doi.org
/10.1007/s11669-011-9904-z; Ponciroli, Wang, Vilim, Frick, and Rabiti, "Development
of Energy Storage."

54. Leah D. Ellis, Andres F. Badel, Miki L. Chiang, and Yet-Ming Chiang, "Toward Electrochemical Synthesis of Cement—An Electrolyzer-Based Process for Decarbonating
$CaCO_3$ While Producing Useful Gas Streams," *Proceedings of the National Academy
of Sciences* 117, no. 23 (September 16, 2020): 12584–91, https://doi.org/10.1073/pnas
.1821673116.

55. Permabond Engineering Adhesives, "Heat Cure Epoxy—Making Sure the Adhesive Is
Properly Cured," accessed May 24, 2023, https://www.permabond.com/resource-center
/heat-cure-epoxy-making-adhesive-properly-cured/.

56. U.S. Energy Information Administration, "Annual Energy Outlook 2020," January 29,
2020, https://www.eia.gov/outlooks/archive/aeo20/.

57. European Commission, "Dashboard for Energy Prices in the EU and Main Trading Partners," accessed May 25, 2023, https://energy.ec.europa.eu/data-and-analysis
/energy-prices-and-costs-europe/dashboard-energy-prices-eu-and-main-trading
-partners_en.

58. Steven R. Mickey, "Efficient Gas Heating of Industrial Furnaces," *Thermal Processing*,
January 20, 2017, https://thermalprocessing.com/efficient-gas-heating-of-industrial
-furnaces/.

59. United Nations Environment Programme, "Furnaces and Refractories," in *Energy Efficiency Guide for Industry in Asia*, 2006, http://www.moderneq.com/pdf/Refractories.pdf.

60. The Energy Research Institute (TERI), "Energy Efficiency Best Operating Practices
Guide for Foundries" (Coimbatore, India, October 2015), http://sameeeksha.org/brouchres
/BOP-Guide-Oct2015.pdf.

61. IEA-ETSAP (Energy Technology Systems Analysis Program), "Industrial Combustion
Boilers" (Technology Brief I01, International Energy Agency, Paris, May 2010), https://iea
-etsap.org/E-TechDS/PDF/I01-ind_boilers-GS-AD-gct.pdf.

62. U.S. Department of Energy, "Purchasing Energy-Efficient Large Commercial Boilers," updated September 2022, https://www.energy.gov/eere/femp/purchasing-energy
-efficient-large-commercial-boilers.

63. United Nations Industrial Development Organization, "Energy Efficiency Potentials in Industrial Steam Systems in China: Development of a Steam Systems Energy Efficiency Cost Curve " (report, UN Industrial Development Organization, Vienna, 2014), https:// www.unido.org/sites/default/files/2015-09/EE_Potentials_Steam_Systems_China__0.pdf.

64. Philip Sutter, "Heating Water by Direct Steam Injection," Chemical Processing, May 3, 2012, https://cdn.chemicalprocessing.com/files/base/ebm/chemicalprocessing/document /2022/08/1661893299229-heatingwaterbydirectsteaminjection.pdf.

65. U.S. Department of Energy, Advanced Manufacturing Office, *Improving Steam System Performance: A Sourcebook for Industry, Second Edition* (U.S. Department of Energy, Washington, D.C., October 2012), https://www.energy.gov/sites/prod/files/2014/05/f15 /steamsourcebook.pdf.

66. Craig Anderson, "Gas vs Electric Boilers: Pros, Cons, & Recommendations," Appliance Analysts, updated April 19, 2023, https://applianceanalysts.com/gas-vs-electric-boilers/.

67. IEA-ETSAP, "Industrial Combustion Boilers."

68. International Energy Agency, "World Energy Balances Data Service."

7. HYDROGEN AND OTHER RENEWABLE FUELS

1. National Grid PLC, "The Hydrogen Colour Spectrum," accessed May 26, 2023, https:// www.nationalgrid.com/stories/energy-explained/hydrogen-colour-spectrum.

2. Linde plc, "Industrial Gases: Hydrogen in Refining," accessed May 26, 2023, https://www .linde-gas.com/en/processes/petrochemical-processing-and-refining/hydrogen _applications_refineries/index.html.

3. International Energy Agency, "The Future of Hydrogen: Seizing today's opportunities," (report, Paris, France, June 2019), https://iea.blob.core.windows.net/assets/9e3a3493 -b9a6-4b7d-b499-7ca48e357561/The_Future_of_Hydrogen.pdf.

4. U.S. Department of Energy, Office of Energy Efficiency & Renewable Energy, "Hydrogen Production Processes," accessed May 26, 2023, https://www.energy.gov/eere/fuelcells /hydrogen-production-processes.

5. Pingping Sun and Amgad Elgowainy, "Updates of Hydrogen Production from SMR Process in GREET® 2019," Argonne National Laboratory, October 2019, https://greet.es .anl.gov/files/smr_h2_2019.

6. U.S. Department of Energy, Office of Energy Efficiency & Renewable Energy, "Hydrogen Production Processes."

7. National Energy Technology Laboratory, "Technologies for Hydrogen Production" in *Gasifipedia*, accessed May 26, 2023, https://www.netl.doe.gov/research/coal/energy -systems/gasification/gasifipedia/technologies-hydrogen; International Energy Agency, "The Future of Hydrogen."

8. International Energy Agency, "The Future of Hydrogen."

9. International Energy Agency, "The Future of Hydrogen."

10. International Energy Agency, *Energy Technology Perspectives 2020* (report, International energy Agency, Paris, September 2020), https://www.iea.org/reports/energy -technology-perspectives-2020.

11.   Kai Zeng and Dongke Zhang, "Recent Progress in Alkaline Water Electrolysis for Hydrogen Production and Applications," *Progress in Energy and Combustion Science* 36, no. 3 (June 2010): 307–26, https://doi.org/10.1016/j.pecs.2009.11.002; Marcelo Carmo, David L. Fritz, Jürgen Mergel, and Detlef Stolten, "A Comprehensive Review on PEM Water Electrolysis," *International Journal of Hydrogen Energy* 38, no. 12 (April 22, 2013): 4901–34, https://doi.org/10.1016/j.ijhydene.2013.01.151.

12.   International Energy Agency, "The Future of Hydrogen."

13.   Carmo, Fritz, Mergel, and Stolten, "A Comprehensive Review on PEM Water Electrolysis."

14.   Zeng and Zhang, "Recent Progress in Alkaline Water Electrolysis for Hydrogen Production and Applications."

15.   Carmo, Fritz, Mergel, and Stolten, "A Comprehensive Review on PEM Water Electrolysis"; International Energy Agency, "The Future of Hydrogen."

16.   International Energy Agency, "The Future of Hydrogen"; Carmo, Fritz, Mergel, and Stolten, "A Comprehensive Review on PEM Water Electrolysis."

17.   Carmo, Fritz, Mergel, and Stolten, "A Comprehensive Review on PEM Water Electrolysis."

18.   National Energy Technology Laboratory, "Technologies for Hydrogen Production."

19.   Carmo, Fritz, Mergel, and Stolten, "A Comprehensive Review on PEM Water Electrolysis."

20.   National Energy Technology Laboratory, "Technologies for Hydrogen Production."

21.   Pavlos Nikolaidis and Andreas Poullikkas, "A Comparative Overview of Hydrogen Production Processes," *Renewable and Sustainable Energy Reviews* 67 (January 2017): 597–611, https://doi.org/10.1016/j.rser.2016.09.044.

22.   Sebastian Timmerberg, Martin Kaltschmitt, and Matthias Finkbeiner, "Hydrogen and Hydrogen-Derived Fuels Through Methane Decomposition of Natural Gas—GHG Emissions and Costs," *Energy Conversion and Management: X* 7 (September 2020): 100043, https://doi.org/10.1016/j.ecmx.2020.100043.

23.   Timmerberg, Kaltschmitt, and Finkbeiner, "Hydrogen and Hydrogen-Derived Fuels Through Methane Decomposition of Natural Gas."

24.   Nikolaidis and Poullikkas, "A Comparative Overview of Hydrogen Production Processes."

25.   Amrith Ramkumar, "Big-Name Investors Pour Billions Into Clean Hydrogen Projects," *The Wall Street Journal*, July 14, 2022, https://webreprints.djreprints.com/2336619.html.

26.   National Energy Technology Laboratory, "Technologies for Hydrogen Production."

27.   Nikolaidis and Poullikkas, "A Comparative Overview of Hydrogen Production Processes."

28.   National Energy Technology Laboratory, "Technologies for Hydrogen Production."

29.   National Energy Technology Laboratory, "Technologies for Hydrogen Production"; Brian D. James, George N. Baum, Julie Perez, and Kevin N. Baum, *Technoeconomic Analysis of Photoelectrochemical (PEC) Hydrogen Production* (report, Directed Technologies Inc., Arlington, VA, December 2009), https://www.energy.gov/sites/default/files/2014/03/f12/pec_technoeconomic_analysis.pdf.

30.   National Energy Technology Laboratory, "Technologies for Hydrogen Production."

31.   National Energy Technology Laboratory, "Technologies for Hydrogen Production"; Nikolaidis and Poullikkas, "A Comparative Overview of Hydrogen Production Processes."

32.   International Energy Agency, "The Future of Hydrogen."

33.   International Energy Agency, "The Future of Hydrogen."

34.   International Energy Agency, "The Future of Hydrogen."

35.   Linde plc, "HYDROPRIME On-Site Hydrogen Generators," accessed May 16, 2023, https://www.linde-gas.com/en/products_and_supply/electronic_gases_and_chemicals /on_site_gas_generation/hydroprime-on-site-hydrogen-generation/index.html.

36.   Bioenergy International, "Norwegian Industry Group to Develop Hydrogen Hub Mo," *Bioenergy International*, June 3, 2020, https://bioenergyinternational.com/biogas /hydrogen-production-green-steel-mo-industrial-park.

37.   Kerstine Appunn, "Energy and Grid Companies Team Up for Hydrogen Project at German Coast," news release, *Clean Energy Wire*, March 25, 2021, https://www.cleanenergywire .org/news/energy-and-grid-companies-team-hydrogen-project-german-coast.

38.   M. Niermann, S. Drünert, M. Kaltschmitt, and K. Bonhoff, "Liquid Organic Hydrogen Carriers (LOHCs)—Techno-Economic Analysis of LOHCs in a Defined Process Chain," *Energy & Environmental Science* 12, no. 1 (2019): 290–307, https://doi.org/10.1039/C8EE02700E.

39.   Niermann, Drünert, Kaltschmitt, and Bonhoff, "Liquid Organic Hydrogen Carriers (LOHCs)."

40.   Niermann, Drünert, Kaltschmitt, and Bonhoff, "Liquid Organic Hydrogen Carriers (LOHCs)."

41.   Nicola Warwick, Paul Griffiths, James Keeble, Alexander Archibald, John Pyle, and Keith Shine, *Atmospheric Implications of Increased Hydrogen Use* (report, UK Department for Business, Energy, and Industrial Strategy, London, April 2022), https://assets .publishing.service.gov.uk/government/uploads/system/uploads/attachment_data/file /1067144/atmospheric-implications-of-increased-hydrogen-use.pdf.

42.   Warwick, Griffiths, Keeble, Archibald, Pyle, and Shine, *Atmospheric Implications of Increased Hydrogen Use*.

43.   U.S. Environmental Protection Agency, *Global Non-CO$_2$ Greenhouse Gas Emission Projections & Mitigation Potential: 2015–2050* (report no. EPA-430-R-19-010, U.S. Environmental Protection Agency, Washington, D.C., October 2019), https://www .epa.gov/sites/default/files/2020-05/documents/epa_non-co$_2$_greenhouse_gases_rpt -epa430r19010.pdf.

44.   Mehmet Salih Cellek and Ali Pınarbaşı, "Investigations on Performance and Emission Characteristics of an Industrial Low Swirl Burner While Burning Natural Gas, Methane, Hydrogen-Enriched Natural Gas and Hydrogen as Fuels," *International Journal of Hydrogen Energy* 43, no. 2 (January 11, 2018): 1194–1207, https://doi.org/10.1016/j .ijhydene.2017.05.107.

45.   M. Ayoub, C. Rottier, S. Carpentier, C. Villermaux, A. M. Boukhalfa, and D. Honoré, "An Experimental Study of Mild Flameless Combustion of Methane/Hydrogen Mixtures," in "III Iberian Symposium on Hydrogen, Fuel Cells and Advanced Batteries, HYCELTEC-2011," ed. Felix Barreras, Antonio Lozano, Luis Valiño, and Radu Mustata,

special issue, *International Journal of Hydrogen Energy* 37, no. 8 (April 2012): 6912–21, https://doi.org/10.1016/j.ijhydene.2012.01.018.

46. Hydrogen Tools, Pacific Northwest National Laboratory, "Hydrogen Compared with Other Fuels," accessed May 26, 2023, https://h2tools.org/bestpractices/hydrogen-compared -other-fuels.

47. Hydrogen Safety Panel, Pacific Northwest National Laboratory, *Hydrogen Equipment Certification Guide* (Pacific Northwest National Laboratory, Richland, WA, January 2017), https://h2tools.org/sites/default/files/Hydrogen%20Equipment%20Certification% 20Guide_Jan2017.pdf.

48. "Haber-Bosch Process," *Encyclopedia Britannica*, accessed May 26, 2023, https://www .britannica.com/technology/Haber-Bosch-process.

49. Collin Smith, Alfred K. Hill, and Laura Torrente-Murciano, "Current and Future Role of Haber-Bosch Ammonia in a Carbon-Free Energy Landscape," *Energy & Environmental Science* 13, no. 2 (2020): 331–44, https://doi.org/10.1039/C9EE02873K.

50. International Energy Agency, "The Future of Hydrogen."

51. Hideaki Kobayashi, Akihiro Hayakawa, K. D. Kunkuma A. Somarathne, and Ekenechukwu C. Okafor, "Science and Technology of Ammonia Combustion," *Proceedings of the Combustion Institute* 37, no. 1 (January 2019): 109–33, https://doi.org /10.1016/j.proci.2018.09.029.

52. Kobayashi, Hayakawa, Kunkuma, Somarathne, and Okafor, "Science and Technology of Ammonia Combustion."

53. S. Giddey, S. P. S. Badwal, C. Munnings, and M. Dolan, "Ammonia as a Renewable Energy Transportation Media," *ACS Sustainable Chemistry & Engineering* 5, no. 11 (November 6, 2017): 10231–39, https://doi.org/10.1021/acssuschemeng.7b02219.

54. International Renewable Energy Agency and Methanol Institute, *Innovation Outlook: Renewable Methanol* (International Renewable Energy Agency, Abu Dhabi, 2021), https://www.irena.org/-/media/Files/IRENA/Agency/Publication/2021/Jan/IRENA _Innovation_Renewable_Methanol_2021.pdf.

55. International Renewable Energy Agency and Methanol Institute, *Innovation Outlook: Renewable Methanol*.

56. National Energy Technology Laboratory, "Syngas Conversion to Methanol" in *Gasifipedia*, accessed May 16, 2023, https://www.netl.doe.gov/research/coal/energy-systems /gasification/gasifipedia/methanol; International Renewable Energy Agency and Methanol Institute, *Innovation Outlook: Renewable Methanol*.

57. International Renewable Energy Agency and Methanol Institute, *Innovation Outlook: Renewable Methanol*.

58. International Renewable Energy Agency and Methanol Institute, *Innovation Outlook: Renewable Methanol*.

59. International Renewable Energy Agency and Methanol Institute, *Innovation Outlook: Renewable Methanol*.

60. International Energy Agency, "The Future of Hydrogen."

61. Saheli Biswas, Aniruddha P. Kulkarni, Sarbjit Giddey, and Sankar Bhattacharya, "A Review on Synthesis of Methane as a Pathway for Renewable Energy Storage with a

Focus on Solid Oxide Electrolytic Cell-Based Processes," *Frontiers in Energy Research* 8 (September 8, 2020), https://doi.org/10.3389/fenrg.2020.570112.

62.   Environmental and Energy Study Institute, "Fact Sheet: Biogas: Converting Waste to Energy," October 3, 2017, https://www.eesi.org/papers/view/fact-sheet-biogasconverting -waste-to-energy.

63.   Nick Primmer and WBA Policy, Innovation and Technical Committee, *Biogas: Pathways to 2030* (report, World Biogas Association, London, March 2021), https://www .worldbiogasassociation.org/biogas-pathways-to-2030-report/; International Energy Agency, "World Energy Balances Data Service," updated April 2023, https://www.iea .org/data-and-statistics/data-product/world-energy-balances.

64.   Sarika Jain, David Newman, Ange Nizhou, Harmen Dekker, Pharoah Le Feuvre, Hannah Richter, et al., *Global Potential of Biogas* (report, World Biogas Association, London, June 2019), https://www.worldbiogasassociation.org/wp-content/uploads/2019/07/WBA -globalreport-56ppa4_digital.pdf.

65.   International Energy Agency, *Net Zero by 2050: A Roadmap for the Global Energy Sector* (report, International Energy Agency, Paris, May 2021), https://iea.blob.core.windows .net/assets/20959e2e-7ab8-4f2a-b1c6-4e63387f03a1/NetZeroby2050-ARoadmapfor theGlobalEnergySector_CORR.pdf.

66.   World Biogas Association, *Biogas: Pathways to 2030.*

67.   World Biogas Association, *Biogas: Pathways to 2030.*

68.   International Energy Agency, *Net Zero by 2050: A Roadmap for the Global Energy Sector.*

69.   Timur Gül, Laura Cozzi, and Petr Havlik, *What Does Net-Zero Emissions by 2050 Mean for Bioenergy and Land Use?* (report, International Energy Agency, Paris, May 31, 2021), https://www.iea.org/articles/what-does-net-zero-emissions-by-2050-mean-for-bioenergy -and-land-use; International Energy Agency, "World Energy Balances Data Service."

70.   H. Chum, A. Faaij, J. Moreira, G. Berndes, P. Dhamija, H. Dong, B. Gabrielle, et al., "Bioenergy," in *IPCC Special Report on Renewable Energy Sources and Climate Change Mitigation*, ed. O. Edenhofer, R. Pichs-Madruga, Y. Sokona, K. Seyboth, et al. (Cambridge: Cambridge University Press, 2011), https://www.ipcc.ch/site/assets/uploads/2018/03 /Chapter-2-Bioenergy-1.pdf.

71.   Chum, Faaij, Moreira, Berndes, Dhamija, Dong, Gabrielle, et al., "Bioenergy."

72.   Gül, Cozzi, and Havlik, *What Does Net-Zero Emissions by 2050 Mean for Bioenergy and Land Use?*

73.   Chum, Faaij, Moreira, Berndes, Dhamija, Dong, Gabrielle, et al., "Bioenergy."

74.   Chum, Faaij, Moreira, Berndes, Dhamija, Dong, Gabrielle, et al., "Bioenergy."

75.   Chum, Faaij, Moreira, Berndes, Dhamija, Dong, Gabrielle, et al., "Bioenergy."

76.   Harvard T. H. Chan School of Public Health, "Negative Impacts of Burning Natural Gas and Biomass Have Surpassed Coal Generation in Many States," May 5, 2021, https://www.hsph.harvard.edu/c-change/news/gas-biomass/.

77.   C. B. Oland, "Guide to Low-Emission Boiler and Combustion Equipment Selection" (publication no. ORNL/TM-2002/19, Oak Ridge National Laboratory, Oak Ridge, TN, April 2002), https://www.energy.gov/sites/prod/files/2014/05/f15/guide_low_emission.pdf.

78. Mark W. Rosegrant, Tingju Zhu, Siwa Msangi, and Timothy Sulser, "Global Scenarios for Biofuels: Impacts and Implications," *Review of Agricultural Economics* 30, no. 3 (2008): 495–505.

79. International Renewable Energy Agency, *Green Hydrogen Cost Reduction: Scaling Up Electrolysers to Meet the 1.5°C Climate Goal* (report, International Renewable Energy Agency, Abu Dhabi, 2020), https://irena.org/-/media/Files/IRENA /Agency/Publication/2020/Dec/IRENA_Green_hydrogen_cost_2020.pdf; International Renewable Energy Agency and Methanol Institute, *Innovation Outlook: Renewable Methanol.*

80. International Energy Agency, "World Energy Balances Data Service."

81. International Energy Agency, "World Energy Balances Data Service."

8. CARBON CAPTURE AND USE OR STORAGE

1. Global CCS Institute, *Global Status of CCS 2020* (report, Global CCS Institute, Melbourne, Australia, 2020), https://www.globalccsinstitute.com/wp-content/uploads/2020/12/Global -Status-of-CCS-Report-2020_FINAL_December11.pdf.

2. Global CCS Institute, *Global Status of CCS 2020.*

3. Linde plc, "Industrial Gases: Carbon Dioxide," accessed May 26, 2023, https://www .linde-gas.com/en/products_and_supply/gases_atmospheric/carbon_dioxide.html.

4. International Energy Agency, *Putting CO_2 to Use: Creating Value from Emissions* (report, International Energy Agency, Paris, September 2019), https://iea.blob.core .windows.net/assets/50652405-26db-4c41-82dc-c23657893059/Putting_CO_2_to_Use .pdf; Linde plc, "Atmospheric Gases," accessed May 26, 2023, https://www.linde-gas.com /en/products_and_supply/gases_atmospheric/index.html.

5. Jeffrey Rissman, Chris Bataille, Eric Masanet, Nate Aden, William R. Morrow, Nan Zhou, Neal Elliott, et al., "Technologies and Policies to Decarbonize Global Industry: Review and Assessment of Mitigation Drivers Through 2070," *Applied Energy* 266 (May 15, 2020): 114848, https://doi.org/10.1016/j.apenergy.2020.114848.

6. International Energy Agency, *CCUS in Clean Energy Transitions* (report, International Energy Agency, Paris, September 2020), https://www.iea.org/reports/ccus-in -clean-energy-transitions.

7. International Energy Agency, *Curtailing Methane Emissions from Fossil Fuel Operations* (report, International Energy Agency, Paris, October 2021), https://iea.blob.core .windows.net/assets/585b901a-e7d2-4bca-b477-e1baa14dde5c/CurtailingMethane EmissionsfromFossilFuelOperations.pdf; Climate Watch, "Historical GHG Emissions," accessed May 22, 2023, https://www.climatewatchdata.org.

8. European Environment Agency, *Air Pollution Impacts from Carbon Capture and Storage (CCS)* (EEA Technical Report no. 14/2011, Copenhagen, November 17, 2011), https:// www.eea.europa.eu/publications/carbon-capture-and-storage/at_download/file.

9. European Environment Agency, *Air Pollution Impacts from Carbon Capture and S torage (CCS).*

10. European Environment Agency, *Air Pollution Impacts from Carbon Capture and Storage (CCS)*.

11. European Environment Agency, *Air Pollution Impacts from Carbon Capture and Storage (CCS)*.

12. International Energy Agency, *CCUS in Clean Energy Transitions*.

13. International Energy Agency, *CCUS in Clean Energy Transitions*.

14. Joshua White and William Foxall, "Assessing Induced Seismicity Risk at CO_2 Storage Projects: Recent Progress and Remaining Challenges," *International Journal of Greenhouse Gas Control* 49 (June 2016): 413–24, https://doi.org/10.1016/j.ijggc.2016.03.021.

15. Lawrence Irlam, "Global Costs of Carbon Capture and Storage" (summary report, Global CCS Institute, Melbourne, Australia., June 2017), https://www.globalccsinstitute.com/archive/hub/publications/201688/global-ccs-cost-updatev4.pdf.

16. International Energy Agency, *CCUS in Clean Energy Transitions*.

17. National Energy Technology Laboratory, "Syngas Composition," in *Gasifipedia*, accessed May 26, 2023, https://netl.doe.gov/research/coal/energy-systems/gasification/gasifipedia/syngas-composition.

18. Xiaoxing Wang and Chunshan Song, "Carbon Capture from Flue Gas and the Atmosphere: A Perspective," *Frontiers in Energy Research* 8 (December 15, 2020): 265, https://doi.org/10.3389/fenrg.2020.560849.

19. Stephen A. Rackley, *Carbon Capture and Storage*, 2nd ed. (Oxford, UK: Butterworth-Heinemann, 2017).

20. Rackley, *Carbon Capture and Storage*.

21. Rackley, *Carbon Capture and Storage*.

22. Rackley, *Carbon Capture and Storage*.

23. Rackley, *Carbon Capture and Storage*.

24. Global CCS Institute, *Global Status of CCS 2020*.

25. U.S. Environmental Protection Agency, "5.3 Natural Gas Processing," in *AP-42: Compilation of Air Emissions Factors*, 5th ed. (Washington, D.C.: U.S. EPA, January 1995), https://www.epa.gov/sites/default/files/2020-09/documents/5.3_natural_gas_processing.pdf.

26. Rajab Khalilpour, Kathryn Mumford, Haibo Zhai, Ali Abbas, Geoff Stevens, and Edward S. Rubin, "Membrane-Based Carbon Capture from Flue Gas: A Review," in "Carbon Emissions Reduction: Policies, Technologies, Monitoring, Assessment and Modeling," ed. Donald Huisingh, Zhihua Zhang, John C. Moore, Qi Qiao, and Qi Li, special issue, *Journal of Cleaner Production* 103 (September 15, 2015): 286–300, https://doi.org/10.1016/j.jclepro.2014.10.050.

27. Dipak Sakaria, "Case Study: Al Reyadah CCUS Project" (PowerPoint presented at Carbon Sequestration Leadership Forum, May 2, 2017), https://www.cslforum.org/cslf/sites/default/files/documents/AbuDhabi2017/AbuDhabi17-TW-Sakaria-Session2.pdf.

28. Xiaoxing Wang and Chunshan Song, "Carbon Capture from Flue Gas and the Atmosphere: A Perspective," *Frontiers in Energy Research* 8 (December 15, 2020): 265, https://doi.org/10.3389/fenrg.2020.560849.

29. Rackley, *Carbon Capture and Storage*.

30. Rackley, *Carbon Capture and Storage*.
31. International Energy Agency, Technology Collaboration Program, "The CCS Project at Air Products' Port Arthur Hydrogen Production Facility," May 2018, https://ieaghg.org /publications/technical-reports/reports-list/9-technical-reports/956-2018-05-the-ccs -project-at-air-products-port-arthur-hydrogen-production-facility.
32. Rackley, *Carbon Capture and Storage*.
33. Rackley, *Carbon Capture and Storage*; International Energy Agency, *CCUS in Clean Energy Transitions*; Global CCS Institute, *Global Status of CCS 2020*.
34. Khalilpour, Mumford, Zhai, Abbas, Stevens, and Rubin, "Membrane-Based Carbon Capture from Flue Gas."
35. Rackley, *Carbon Capture and Storage*.
36. Rackley, *Carbon Capture and Storage*.
37. Wang and Song, "Carbon Capture from Flue Gas and the Atmosphere."
38. Rackley, *Carbon Capture and Storage*.
39. Elliott Levine and Keith Jamison, "Oxy-Fuel Firing for the Glass Industry: An Update on the Impact of This Successful Government-Industry Cooperative Effort," in *Proceedings of 2001 Summer Study on Energy Efficiency in Industry*, 2001, (Washington, D.C.: American Council for an Energy-Efficient Economy, 2001), https://www.aceee.org/files /proceedings/2001/data/papers/SS01_Panel1_Paper33.pdf.
40. Global CCS Institute, *Global Status of CCS 2020*.
41. Rackley, *Carbon Capture and Storage*.
42. Wang and Song, "Carbon Capture from Flue Gas and the Atmosphere."
43. Rackley, *Carbon Capture and Storage*.
44. Wang and Song, "Carbon Capture from Flue Gas and the Atmosphere."
45. Rackley, *Carbon Capture and Storage*.
46. Rackley, *Carbon Capture and Storage*.
47. Steven Jackson and Eivind Brodal, "Optimization of the Energy Consumption of a Carbon Capture and Sequestration Related Carbon Dioxide Compression Processes," *Energies* 12, no. 9 (January 2019): 1603, https://doi.org/10.3390/en12091603.
48. Jackson and Brodal, "Optimization of the Energy Consumption of a Carbon Capture and Sequestration Related Carbon Dioxide Compression Processes."
49. David Kearns, Harry Liu, and Chris Consoli, *Technology Readiness and Costs of CCS* (Global CCS Institute, Melbourne, Australia, March 2021), https://www.globalccsinstitute .com/wp-content/uploads/2021/03/Technology-Readiness-and-Costs-for-CCS-2021 -1.pdf.
50. Rackley, *Carbon Capture and Storage*.
51. Edward S. Rubin, John E. Davison, and Howard J. Herzog, "The Cost of CO_2 Capture and Storage," Special Issue Commemorating the 10th Year Anniversary of the Publication of the Intergovernmental Panel on Climate Change Special Report on CO_2 Capture and Storage, ed. J. Gale, J.C. Abanades, S. Bachu, and C. Jenkins, special issue, *International Journal of Greenhouse Gas Control*, 40 (September 2015): 378–400, https://doi.org/10.1016/j.ijggc.2015.05.018.
52. International Energy Agency, *CCUS in Clean Energy Transitions*.

53. Kearns, Liu, and Consoli, *Technology Readiness and Costs of CCS*.
54. Rackley, *Carbon Capture and Storage*.
55. Kearns, Liu, and Consoli, *Technology Readiness and Costs of CCS*.
56. International Energy Agency, *CCUS in Clean Energy Transitions;* Rackley, *Carbon Capture and Storage*.
57. Kearns, Liu, and Consoli, *Technology Readiness and Costs of CCS*. U.S. Department of Energy, "Enhanced Oil Recovery," accessed May 26, 2023, https://www.energy.gov/fe/science-innovation/oil-gas-research/enhanced-oil-recovery.
58. National Energy Technology Laboratory, *Carbon Dioxide Enhanced Oil Recovery* (U.S. Department of Energy, March 2010), https://www.netl.doe.gov/sites/default/files/netl-file/co₂_eor_primer.pdf.
59. National Energy Technology Laboratory, *Carbon Dioxide Enhanced Oil Recovery*.
60. Christophe McGlade, "Can CO_2-EOR Really Provide Carbon-Negative Oil?," International Energy Agency, April 11, 2019, https://www.iea.org/commentaries/can-co₂-eor-really-provide-carbon-negative-oil.
61. June Sekera and Andreas Lichtenberger, "Assessing Carbon Capture: Public Policy, Science, and Societal Need," *Biophysical Economics and Sustainability* 5, no. 3 (October 6, 2020): 14, https://doi.org/10.1007/s41247-020-00080-5.
62. Sekera and Lichtenberger, "Assessing Carbon Capture."
63. Kearns, Liu, and Consoli, *Technology Readiness and Costs of CCS*.
64. Rackley, *Carbon Capture and Storage*.
65. Kearns, Liu, and Consoli, *Technology Readiness and Costs of CCS*.
66. IPCC, *Carbon Dioxide Capture and Storage* (report, International Panel on Climate Change, Geneva, 2005), https://archive.ipcc.ch/report/srccs/.
67. IPCC, *Special Report: Global Warming of 1.5oC* (report, International Panel on Climate Change, Geneva, 2018), https://www.ipcc.ch/sr15/.
68. IPCC, *Special Report: Global Warming of 1.5 oC*.
69. IPCC, *Special Report: Global Warming of 1.5 oC*.
70. IPCC, *Special Report: Global Warming of 1.5 oC*.
71. Rackley, *Carbon Capture and Storage*.
72. Rackley, *Carbon Capture and Storage*.
73. Rackley, *Carbon Capture and Storage*.
74. Devin Coldewey, "44.01 Secures $5M to Turn Billions of Tons of Carbon Dioxide to Stone," *TechCrunch*, August 10, 2021, https://techcrunch.com/2021/08/10/44-01-secures-5m-to-turn-billions-of-tons-of-carbon-dioxide-to-stone/; Bioenergy International, "Blue Planet Systems Secures US$10 Million for Synthetic Limestone Tech," September 23, 2020, https://bioenergyinternational.com/technology-suppliers/blue-planet-systems-secures-us10-million-for-synthetic-limestone-tech.
75. Peter G. Levi and Jonathan M. Cullen, "Mapping Global Flows of Chemicals: From Fossil Fuel Feedstocks to Chemical Products," *Environmental Science & Technology* 52, no. 4 (January 24, 2018): 1725–34, https://doi.org/10.1021/acs.est.7b04573.
76. Alexander L. Brown, "The Decomposition Behavior of Thermoset Carbon Fiber Epoxy Composites in the Fire Environment," (Sandia National Labs report no.

SAND2013-1920C, submitted for Combustion Institute Joint US Sections Meeting May 19–22, 2013), https://www.osti.gov/servlets/purl/1115966; Sujit Das, "Life Cycle Assessment of Carbon Fiber-Reinforced Polymer Composites," *International Journal of Life Cycle Assessment* 16, no. 3 (March 1, 2011): 268–82, https://doi.org/10.1007/s11367-011-0264-z.

77. International Energy Agency, *Energy Technology Perspectives 2020* (report, International Energy Agency, Paris, September 2020), https://www.iea.org/reports/energy-technology-perspectives-2020; Niall Mac Dowell, Paul S. Fennell, Nilay Shah, and Geoffrey C. Maitland, "The Role of CO_2 Capture and Utilization in Mitigating Climate Change," *Nature Climate Change* 7, no. 4 (April 2017): 243–49, https://doi.org/10.1038/nclimate3231.

9. CARBON PRICING AND OTHER FINANCIAL POLICIES

1. Hal Harvey, Robbie Orvis, and Jeffrey Rissman, *Designing Climate Solutions: A Policy Guide for Low-Carbon Energy* (Washington, D.C.: Island Press, 2018).

2. Marc Hafstead, Susanne Brooks, Nathaniel Keohane, and Wesley Look, "Carbon Tax Adjustment Mechanisms (TAMs): How They Work and Lessons from Modeling" (Issue Brief 20-08, Resources for the Future, Washington, D.C., August 2020), https://media.rff.org/documents/IB_20-08_TAM.pdf.

3. World Bank, "State and Trends of Carbon Pricing 2021," May 25, 2021, https://openknowledge.worldbank.org/handle/10986/35620.

4. Metropolitan Planning Council, "Transit Has a Net Economic Benefit," accessed May 28, 2023, https://transitmeansbusiness.metroplanning.org/benefits/transit-has-a-net-economic-benefit.

5. Oxford Economics, *National & State Level Household Income Distributional Analysis of Baker-Shultz Carbon Dividends Plan* (report, Oxford Economics, New York, February 2021), https://clcouncil.org/reports/Oxford-household-income-distributional-analysis.pdf.

6. George P. Shultz and Ted Halstead, *The Dividend Advantage* (report, Climate Leadership Council, Washington, D.C., October 2018), https://clcouncil.org/media/The-Dividend-Advantage.pdf.

7. Shultz and Halstead, *The Dividend Advantage.*

8. Alex Brown, "Landmark Climate Policy Faces Growing Claims of Environmental Racism," Stateline, December 23, 2020, https://pew.org/3aASg3m.

9. Nathanael Johnson, "Cap and Trade-Offs," *Grist*, October 19, 2020, https://grist.org/climate/the-biggest-fight-over-cap-and-trade-isnt-about-what-you-think-it-is/.

10. Samuel Jonsson, Anders Ydstedt, and Elke Asen, "Looking Back on 30 Years of Carbon Taxes in Sweden," Tax Foundation, September 23, 2020, https://taxfoundation.org/sweden-carbon-tax-revenue-greenhouse-gas-emissions/.

11. California Air Resources Board, "Overview of ARB Emissions Trading Program," February 9, 2015, https://www.arb.ca.gov/cc/capandtrade/guidance/cap_trade_overview.pdf.

12. California Air Resources Board, "Overview of ARB Emissions Trading Program."

13. California Air Resources Board, "Overview of ARB Emissions Trading Program."

14. Emily Pontecorvo and Shannon Osaka, "California Is Banking on Forests to Reduce Emissions. What Happens When They Go Up in Smoke?," *Grist*, October 27, 2021, https://grist.org/wildfires/california-forests-carbon-offsets-reduce-emissions/.

15. Meredith Fowlie and Mar Reguant, "Challenges in the Measurement of Leakage Risk," *AEA Papers and Proceedings* 108 (May 2018): 124–29, https://doi.org/10.1257/pandp.20181087.

16. Frédéric Branger, Philippe Quirion, and Julien Chevallier, "Carbon Leakage and Competitiveness of Cement and Steel Industries Under the EU ETS: Much Ado About Nothing," *Energy Journal* 37, no. 3 (July 2017): 109–36, https://doi.org/10.5547/01956574.37.3.fbra.

17. Jeffrey Rissman, Chris Bataille, Eric Masanet, Nate Aden, William R. Morrow, Nan Zhou, Neal Elliott, et al., "Technologies and Policies to Decarbonize Global Industry: Review and Assessment of Mitigation Drivers #through 2070," *Applied Energy* 266 (May 15, 2020): 114848, https://doi.org/10.1016/j.apenergy.2020.114848.

18. European Commission, Directorate-General for Climate Action, E. Zelljadt, D. Phylipsen, J. Tröltzsch, et al., *Evaluation of the EU ETS Directive—Carried Out Within the Project "Support for the Review of the EU Emissions Trading System"* (European Commission, November 2015), https://op.europa.eu/en/publication-detail/-/publication/0478bafo-d6d4-11e5-8fea-01aa75ed71a1/language-en.

19. Ernst & Young, "European Parliament Adopts Carbon Legislation Package, Final Negotiations with EU Member State Representatives Expected Soon," June 23, 2022, https://www.ey.com/en_gl/tax-alerts/european-parliament-adopts-carbon-legislation-package-final-negotiations-with-eu-member-state-representatives-expected-soon.

20. Ernst & Young, "European Parliament Adopts Carbon Legislation Package."

21. OECD, *Green Investment Banks: Scaling Up Private Investment in Low-Carbon, Climate-Resilient Infrastructure* (report, OECD, Paris, 2016), https://www.oecd-ilibrary.org/finance-and-investment/green-investment-banks_9789264245129-en.

22. Coalition for Green Capital, "Our Impact," accessed May 28, 2023, http://coalitionforgreencapital.com/our-impact/.

23. Center for the New Energy Economy, Colorado State University, "Innovative Financing Programs," 2016, https://spotforcleanenergy.org/wp-content/uploads/2017/05/2669a69fc2a1888cb8f7c5caffbofbo6.pdf.

24. Connecticut Green Bank, "Societal Impact Report," 2022, https://www.ctgreenbank.com/wp-content/uploads/2022/09/FY12-FY22-CGB-ImpactReport-8242022.pdf.

25. Coalition for Green Capital, "Green Bank Techniques," accessed May 28, 2023, https://coalitionforgreencapital.com/what-is-a-green-bank/green-bank-techniques/.

26. Hallie Kennan, *Working Paper: State Green Banks for Clean Energy* (Energy Innovation LLC, San Francisco, January 2014), https://energyinnovation.org/wp-content/uploads/2014/06/WorkingPaper_StateGreenBanks.pdf.

27. Bryan Garcia, "Connecticut Green Bank," Bondlink, accessed May 28, 2023, https://www.ctgreenbankbonds.com/connecticut-green-bank-ct/i6126.

28. Kennan, *Working Paper: State Green Banks for Clean Energy.*

29. Coalition for Green Capital, *Green Banks in the United States: 2018 Annual Industry Report* (report, Coalition for Green Capital, Washington, D.C., May 2019), http://coalitionfor greencapital.com/wp-content/uploads/2019/07/GreenBanksintheUS-2018Annual IndustryReport.pdf.

30. Bipartisan Policy Center, "Reassessing Renewable Energy Subsidies Issue Brief," March 22, 2011, https://bipartisanpolicy.org/download/?file=/wp-content/uploads/2019/03/BPC _RE-Issue-Brief_3-22.pdf.

31. International Energy Agency, ETSAP (Energy Technology Systems Analysis Program), *Industrial Combustion Boilers* (technology brief, International Energy Agency, Paris, May 2010), https://iea-etsap.org/E-TechDS/PDF/I01-ind_boilers-GS-AD-gct.pdf.

32. German Federal Ministry for Economic Affairs and Climate, "What Actually Are Carbon Contracts for Difference?," December 18, 2020, https://www.bmwi-energiewende.de /EWD/Redaktion/EN/Newsletter/2020/11/Meldung/direkt-account.html.

33. Bioenergy International, "Swedish Energy Agency Awards Record Funding to HYBRIT," June 18, 2018, https://bioenergyinternational.com/research-development/swedish-energy -agency-awards-record-funding-to-hybrit.

34. China FAQs, World Resources Institute, "China's Ten Key Energy Efficiency Projects," November 12, 2009, http://neec.no/uploads/ChinaFAQs_Chinas_Ten_Key_Energy _Efficiency_Projects_.pdf.

35. Lee Beck, "The US Section 45Q Tax Credit for Carbon Oxide Sequestration: An Update" (brief, Global CCS Institute, Melbourne, Australia, April 2020), https://www .globalccsinstitute.com/wp-content/uploads/2020/04/45Q_Brief_in_template_LLB .pdf.

36. Sidley Austin LLP, "Inflation Reduction Act: Overview of Energy-Related Tax Provisions—An Energy Transition 'Game Changer,'" August 12, 2022, https://www.sidley .com/en/insights/newsupdates/2022/08/inflation-reduction-act-an-energy-transition -game-changer.

37. N.C. Clean Energy Technology Center, "Database of State Incentives for Renewables & Efficiency (DSIRE)," accessed May 28, 2023, https://www.dsireusa.org/.

38. European Automobile Manufacturers' Association, "CO_2-Based Motor Vehicle Taxes in the European Union," June 18, 2020, https://www.acea.auto/fact/overview-co$_2$-based -motor-vehicle-taxes-in-the-european-union/.

39. Yannick Monschauer and Sonja Kotin-Förster, "Bonus-Malus Vehicle Incentive System in France" fact sheet, European Climate Initiative, September 3, 2018, https://www.euki .de/wp-content/uploads/2018/09/fact-sheet-bonus-malus-vehicle-incentive-system -fr.pdf.

10. STANDARDS AND GREEN PUBLIC PROCUREMENT

1. U.S. Census Bureau, "Annual Survey of Manufactures 2019," June 29, 2021, https://www .census.gov/library/publications/2021/econ/e19-asm.html.

2. Dan Ariely, *Predictably Irrational: The Hidden Forces That Shape Our Decisions*, rev. and expanded ed. (New York: Harper Perennial, 2010).

3. U.S. Department of Energy, "Energy Conservation Standards for Commercial and Industrial Electric Motors," Pub. L. No. 10 CFR 431, Part I, "Summary of the Final Rule and Its Benefits," accessed May 28, 2023, https://www.energy.gov/sites/prod/files/2014/05/f15/electric_motors_ecs_final_rule.pdf.

4. European Council for an Energy Efficient Economy, "Ecodesign and Labelling," accessed May 28, 2023, https://www.eceee.org/ecodesign/.

5. Christian Egenhofer, Eleanor Drabik, Monica Alessi, and Vasileios Rizos, *Stakeholders' Views on the Ecodesign Directive: An Assessment of the Successes and Shortcomings* (research report no. 2018, CEPS Energy Climate House, Brussels, November 2, 2018), https://www.ceps.eu/wp-content/uploads/2018/03/RRNo2018_02_EcoDesignDirective.pdf.

6. Government of Canada, "Review of the Federal Output-Based Pricing System Regulations," February 12, 2021, https://www.canada.ca/en/environment-climate-change/services/climate-change/pricing-pollution-how-it-will-work/output-based-pricing-system/review.html.

7. Government of Ontario, *GHG Emissions Performance Standards and Methodology for the Determination of the Total Annual Emissions Limit*, July 2019, https://www.ontariocanada.com/registry/showAttachment.do?postingId=28727&attachmentId=41017.

8. Richard King, Jacob Sadikman, Evan Barz, and Bryan Salazar, "Details of Ontario's Transition to Emissions Performance Standards Program Released," Osler, *Canada Energy Transition Blog*, November 23, 2021, http://www.osler.com/en/blogs/energy/november-2021/details-of-ontario-s-transition-to-emissions-performance-standards-program-released.

9. Jane Nakano and Scott Kennedy, "China's New National Carbon Trading Market: Between Promise and Pessimism," Center for Strategic & International Studies, July 23, 2021, https://www.csis.org/analysis/chinas-new-national-carbon-trading-market-between-promise-and-pessimism.

10. U.S. Environmental Protection Agency, "ENERGY STAR® Unit Shipment and Market Penetration Report: Calendar Year 2020 Summary," 2021, https://www.energystar.gov/sites/default/files/asset/document/2020%20USD%20Summary%20Report_Lighting%20%20EVSE%20Update.pdf.

11. David Gerard and Lester B. Lave, "Implementing Technology-Forcing Policies: The 1970 Clean Air Act Amendments and the Introduction of Advanced Automotive Emissions Controls in the United States," *Technological Forecasting and Social Change* 72, no. 7 (September 2005): 761–78, https://doi.org/10.1016/j.techfore.2004.08.003.

12. Steven Skerlos, "CAFE Standards Create Profit Incentive for Larger Vehicles," news release, University of Michigan, December 7, 2011, https://news.umich.edu/cafe-standards-create-profit-incentive-for-larger-vehicles/.

13. Egenhofer, Drabik, Alessi, and Rizos, *Stakeholders' Views on the Ecodesign Directive: An Assessment of the Successes and Shortcomings*.

14. Hui He, "Credit Trading in the US Corporate Average Fuel Economy (CAFE) Standard," International Council on Clean Transportation, March 7, 2014, https://theicct .org/wp-content/uploads/2021/06/ICCTbriefing_CAFE-credits_20140307.pdf.

15. Deborah Sun, "South Korea Raises Renewables Standard," *Argus Blog*, December 28, 2021, https://www.argusmedia.com/en/news/2287102-south-korea-raises-renewables -standard.

16. Daniel Moran, Ali Hasanbeigi, and Cecilia Springer, "The Carbon Loophole in Climate Policy: Quantifying the Embedded Carbon in Traded Products" (report, Climate-Works Foundation, San Francisco, August 2018), https://www.bluegreenalliance.org /wp-content/uploads/2021/05/TheCarbonLoopholeinClimatePolicy-Final.pdf;Climate Watch, "Historical GHG Emissions," 2022, https://www.climatewatchdata.org.

17. UN Environment Programme, *Global Review of Sustainable Public Procurement 2017* (report, United Nations Environment Programme, Nairobi 2017), https://wedocs.unep .org/bitstream/handle/20.500.11822/20919/GlobalReview_Sust_Procurement.pdf ?sequence=1&isAllowed=y.

18. UN Environment Programme, *Global Review of Sustainable Public Procurement 2017*.

19. Ted Gayer, Austin Drukker, and Alexander Gold, "Tax-Exempt Municipal Bonds and the Financing of Professional Sports Stadiums" (report, Economic Studies, Brookings Institution, Washington, D.C., September 2016), https://www.brookings.edu/wp-content /uploads/2016/09/gayerdrukkergold_stadiumsubsidies_090816.pdf.

20. Good Jobs First, "Subsidy Tracker Megadeals," accessed May 28, 2023, https://subsidytracker .goodjobsfirst.org/megadeals.

21. UN Environment Programme, *Global Review of Sustainable Public Procurement 2017*.

22. Ali Hasanbeigi, Renilde Becqué, and Cecilia Springer, *Curbing Carbon from Consumption: The Role of Green Public Procurement* (report, Global Efficiency Intelligence, San Francisco, August 2019), https://www.bluegreenalliance.org/wp-content /uploads/2021/05/Green-Public-Procurement-Final-28Aug2019.pdf.

23. Hasanbeigi, Becqué, and Springer, *Curbing Carbon from Consumption*.

24. Hasanbeigi, Becqué, and Springer, *Curbing Carbon from Consumption*.

25. Hasanbeigi, Becqué, and Springer, *Curbing Carbon from Consumption*.

11. R&D, DISCLOSURE, LABELING, AND CIRCULAR ECONOMY POLICIES

1. Abby Monteil, "50 Inventions You Might Not Know Were Funded by the US Government," Stacker, December 9, 2020, https://stacker.com/stories/5483/50-inventions -you-might-not-know-were-funded-us-government; Peter L. Singer, *Federally Supported Innovations: 22 Examples of Major Technology Advances That Stem from Federal Research Support* (report, Information Technology & Innovation Foundation, Washington, D.C., February 2014), https://www2.itif.org/2014-federally-supported-innovations .pdf.

2. Geoffrey Jones and Loubna Bouamane, *"Power from Sunshine": A Business History of Solar Energy* (Working Paper 12-105, Harvard Business School, Cambridge, MA, May 25, 2012), https://www.hbs.edu/ris/Publication%20Files/12-105.pdf.

3. Jones and Bouamane, *"Power from Sunshine."*

4. U.S. Department of Energy, Office of Energy Efficiency & Renewable Energy, "Manufacturing Energy Bandwidth Studies," https://www.energy.gov/eere/iedo/manufacturing-energy-bandwidth-studies.

5. Jeffrey Rissman and Maxine Savitz, *Unleashing Private Sector Energy R&D: Insights from Interviews with 17 R&D Leaders* (AEIC Staff Report, American Energy Innovation Council, Washington, D.C., January 2013), https://bpcaeic.wpengine.com/wp-content/uploads/2013/01/Unleashing-Private-RD-Jan2013.pdf.

6. Rissman and Savitz, *Unleashing Private Sector Energy R&D.*

7. Fraunhofer-Gesellschaft, "Finances," accessed June 7, 2023, https://www.fraunhofer.de/en/about-fraunhofer/profile-structure/facts-and-figures/finances.html.

8. Fraunhofer-Gesellschaft, *Annual Report 2020: For a Secure Future: Resilience Through Innovation,* January 2021, https://www.archiv.fraunhofer.de/Fraunhofer_Annual_Report_2020/epaper/ausgabe.pdf.

9. U.S. Department of Commerce, National Institute of Standards and Technology, *Manufacturing USA: 2019/2020 Highlights Report,* February 5, 2021, https://nvlpubs.nist.gov/nistpubs/ams/NIST.AMS.600-6.pdf.

10. U.S. National Science Foundation, "National Patterns of R&D Resources: 2019–20 Data Update," February 22, 2022, https://ncses.nsf.gov/pubs/nsf22320; Rissman and Savitz, *Unleashing Private Sector Energy R&D.*

11. Carolyn Snyder, "Update on Industrial and Manufacturing Technology Programs at EERE: A Focus on Industrial Decarbonization" (ACEEE presentation, U.S. Department of Energy, Office of Energy Efficiency and Renewable Energy, September 14, 2022), https://www.energy.gov/eere/amo/events/update-industrial-and-manufacturing-technology-programs-eere-focus-industrial.

12. U.S. Bureau of Labor Statistics, "Consumer Expenditures Report 2019," December 2020, https://www.bls.gov/opub/reports/consumer-expenditures/2019/home.htm.

13. Snyder, "Update on Industrial and Manufacturing Technology Programs at EERE."

14. German Federal Ministry of Education and Research, "Education and Research in Figures 2022," 2022, https://www.datenportal.bmbf.de/portal/en/bildung_und_forschung_in_zahlen_2022.pdf.

15. Sustainable Development Technology Canada, *Poised for Growth: 2020–2021 Annual Report,* 2021, https://www.sdtc.ca/wp-content/uploads/2022/03/SDTC-Annual-Report-2020-2021-limited-accessibility-EN.pdf.

16. Adrian Cho, "Department of Energy's 'Mini–Manhattan Projects' for Key Energy Problems Wind Down," *Science,* August 11, 2021, https://www.science.org/content/article/department-energy-s-mini-manhattan-projects-key-energy-problems-wind-down.

17. Rissman and Savitz, *Unleashing Private Sector Energy R&D.*

18. Rissman and Savitz, *Unleashing Private Sector Energy R&D.*

19. Klaus Schwab, *The Global Competitiveness Report 2019* (Insight Report, World Economic Forum, Geneva, 2019), https://www3.weforum.org/docs/WEF_TheGlobal CompetitivenessReport2019.pdf.

20. Ellie Bothwell, "World University Rankings 2022: Saudi Arabia and Egypt Fastest Risers," Times Higher Education, September 2, 2021, https://www.timeshighereducation. com/news/world-university-rankings-2022-saudi-arabia-and-egypt-fastest-risers; Times Higher Education, "About the Times Higher Education World University Rankings," July 27, 2021, https://www.timeshighereducation.com/world-university-rankings /about-the-times-higher-education-world-university-rankings.

21. Rissman and Savitz, *Unleashing Private Sector Energy R&D.*

22. Government of Canada, "Federal Skilled Worker Program (Express Entry)—Six Selection Factors," modified May 26, 2023, https://www.canada.ca/en/immigration -refugees-citizenship/services/immigrate-canada/express-entry/eligibility/federal -skilled-workers/six-selection-factors-federal-skilled-workers.html.

23. Daniel Kim, "Canada Looked Upon As Leader When It Comes to Immigration and Settlement Policy," *TRIEC* (blog), March 28, 2018, https://triec.ca/canada-looked-upon -as-leader-when-it-comes-to-immigration-and-settlement-policy/; Rissman and Savitz, *Unleashing Private Sector Energy R&D.*

24. World Trade Organization, "Intellectual Property: Protection and Enforcement," accessed June 7, 2023, https://www.wto.org/english/thewto_e/whatis_e/tif_e/agrm7_e.htm.

25. Josh Landau, "Granted in 19 Hours," Patent Progress, March 6, 2018, https://www .patentprogress.org/2018/03/06/granted-19-hours/.

26. Patent Progress, "Too Many Patents," accessed June 7, 2023, https://www.patentprogress .org/systemic-problems/too-many-patents/.

27. Christina Mulligan and Timothy B. Lee, "Scaling the Patent System," *NYU Annual Survey of American Law* 68 (2012), https://papers.ssrn.com/abstract=2016968.

28. Executive Office of the President, "Patent Assertion and U.S. Innovation," June 2013, https://obamawhitehouse.archives.gov/sites/default/files/docs/patent_report.pdf.

29. Branka Vuleta, "25 Patent Litigation Statistics: High-Profile Feuds About Intellectual Property," updated May 20, 2023, https://legaljobs.io/blog/patent-litigation-statistics/; Executive Office of the President, "Patent Assertion and U.S. Innovation."

30. John Allison, Mark Lemley, and David Schwartz, "How Often Do Non-Practicing Entities Win Patent Suits?," *Berkeley Technology Law Journal* 32 (2017): 235–308.

31. Ronald Yu and Kenneth Yip, "New Changes, New Possibilities: China's Latest Patent Law Amendments," *GRUR International* 70, no. 5 (May 2021): 486–89, https://doi.org /10.1093/grurint/ikaa201.

32. United for Patent Reform, "Inter Partes Review," 2022, https://www.unitedforpatentre form.com/_files/ugd/6c49d6_22e40b364cf645879b9d8c155d75b578.pdf.

33. Yu and Yip, "New Changes, New Possibilities."

34. U.S. Federal Trade Commission, *Patent Assertion Entity Activity: An FTC Study*, October 2016, https://www.ftc.gov/system/files/documents/reports/patent-assertion-entity -activity-ftc-study/p131203_patent_assertion_entity_activity_an_ftc_study_0.pdf.

35. Electronic Frontier Foundation, "Legislative Solutions for Patent Reform," accessed June 7, 2023, https://www.eff.org/issues/legislative-solutions-patent-reform.

36. LOT Network, "How We Protect Members," accessed June 7, 2023, https://lotnet.com/how-we-protect-members/.

37. Raymond Millien, "Defensive Patent Pools: There Are Surprisingly Few Options," IPWatchdog, December 10, 2012, https://www.ipwatchdog.com/2012/12/10/defensive-patent-pools-there-are-surprisingly-few-options-2/id=31233/.

38. CDP, "WPP: A Renewable Transformation," accessed June 7, 2023, https://www.cdp.net/en/articles/companies/wpp-a-renewable-transformation.

39. CDP, "What We Do," 2022, https://www.cdp.net/en/info/about-us/what-we-do.

40. Task Force on Climate-Related Financial Disclosures, *Recommendations of the Task Force on Climate-Related Financial Disclosures*, June 2017, https://assets.bbhub.io/company/sites/60/2021/10/FINAL-2017-TCFD-Report.pdf.

41. Science Based Targets Initiative, "Sector Guidance," accessed June 7, 2023, https://sciencebasedtargets.org/sectors.

42. Science Based Targets Initiative, "Companies Taking Action," accessed June 7, 2023, https://sciencebasedtargets.org/companies-taking-action.

43. CDP, "What We Do."

44. UK Government, "UK to Enshrine Mandatory Climate Disclosures for Largest Companies in Law," press release, October 29, 2021, https://www.gov.uk/government/news/uk-to-enshrine-mandatory-climate-disclosures-for-largest-companies-in-law.

45. New Zealand Ministry for the Environment, "Mandatory Climate-Related Disclosures," updated January 18, 2023, https://environment.govt.nz/what-government-is-doing/areas-of-work/climate-change/mandatory-climate-related-financial-disclosures/.

46. Oliver Rae, "Japan's Mandatory Climate Risk Disclosures," *Sinai*, September 19, 2022, https://www.sinai.com/post/japans-mandatory-climate-risk-disclosures.

47. Matthew Triggs, Sarah Mishkin, and Thibault Meynier, "EU Finalizes ESG Reporting Rules with International Impacts," The Harvard Law School Forum on Corporate Governance, January 30, 2023, https://corpgov.law.harvard.edu/2023/01/30/eu-finalizes-esg-reporting-rules-with-international-impacts/.

48. Maxine Joselow and Douglas MacMillan, "The SEC Proposed a Landmark Climate Disclosure Rule. Here's What to Know," *Washington Post*, March 21, 2022, Business, https://www.washingtonpost.com/business/2022/03/21/sec-climate-change-rule/.

49. Lucy Atkinson, " 'Wild West' of Eco-Labels: Sustainability Claims Are Confusing Consumers," *The Guardian*, July 4, 2014, Guardian Sustainable Business, https://www.theguardian.com/sustainable-business/eco-labels-sustainability-trust-corporate-government.

50. U.S. Federal Trade Commission, *Nixing the Fix: An FTC Report to Congress on Repair Restrictions*, May 2021, https://www.ftc.gov/system/files/documents/reports/nixing-fix-ftc-report-congress-repair-restrictions/nixing_the_fix_report_final_5521_630pm-508_002.pdf.

51. U.S. Federal Trade Commission, *Nixing the Fix*.

52. Jason Koebler, "Biden Wants to Give Us the Right to Repair. Now What?," *Vice*, July 16, 2021, https://www.vice.com/en/article/4av7pd/biden-wants-to-give-us-the-right-to-repair-now-what.

53. Jean-Paul Ventere, Laeticia Vasseur, and Ernestas Oldyrevas, "The French Repair Index: Challenges and Opportunities" (webinar), Right to Repair Europe, February 3, 2021, https://repair.eu/news/the-french-repair-index-challenges-and-opportunities/.

54. OECD, *Extended Producer Responsibility: A Guidance Manual for Governments* (Paris: OECD Publishing, 2001), https://doi.org/10.1787/9789264189867-en.

55. Californians Against Waste, "How the California Bottle Bill Works," accessed June 7, 2023, https://www.cawrecycles.org/how-the-california-bottle-bill-works.

56. OECD, *Extended Producer Responsibility.*

57. National Conference of State Legislatures, "State Beverage Container Deposit Laws," March 13, 2020, https://www.ncsl.org/research/environment-and-natural-resources /state-beverage-container-laws.aspx.

58. Steffen Saecker and Leonie Willms, "Chemical Leasing of Solvents—A Sustainable Approach for Metal Cleaning" (prepared for Knowledge Collaboration & Learning for Sustainable Innovation ERSCP-EMSU conference, Delft, Netherlands, October 25-29, 2010), https://repository.tudelft.nl/islandora/object/uuid:0c2a5614-0488-45f7 -be3b-b9494b5c9e93/datastream/OBJ/download.

59. OECD, *Extended Producer Responsibility.*

60. State of California, "Plastic Minimum Content Standards (AB 793)," accessed June 7, 2023, https://calrecycle.ca.gov/bevcontainer/bevdistman/plasticcontent/.

61. Government of France, "*Loi du 10 février 2020 relative à la lutte contre le gaspillage et à l'économie circulaire,*" Vie publique, February 18, 2020, https://www.vie-publique.fr/loi /268681-loi-10-fevrier-2020-lutte-contre-le-gaspillage-et-economie-circulaire.

62. Government of France, "*Loi du 10 février 2020 relative à la lutte contre le gaspillage et à l'économie circulaire.*"

63. Natural Resources Council of Maine, "Extended Producer Responsibility for Packaging," 2021, https://www.nrcm.org/programs/sustainability/extended-producer-responsibility -packaging/.

64. Sustainable Packaging Coalition, *2020–2021 Centralized Study on Availability of Recycling,* 2021, https://sustainablepackaging.org/wp-content/uploads/2022/03/UPDATED -2020-21-Centralized-Study-on-Availability-of-Recycling-SPC-3-2022.pdf.

65. Sustainable Packaging Coalition, *2020–2021 Centralized Study on Availability of Recycling.*

66. Scott Mouw, *2020 State of Curbside Recycling Report* (Recycling Partnership, Washington, D.C., February 13, 2020), https://recyclingpartnership.org/wp-content/uploads /dlm_uploads/2020/02/2020-State-of-Curbside-Recycling.pdf.

67. Mouw, *2020 State of Curbside Recycling Report.*

68. Fengming Xi, Steven J. Davis, Philippe Ciais, Douglas Crawford-Brown, Dabo Guan, Claus Pade, Tiemao Shi, et al., "Substantial Global Carbon Uptake by Cement Carbonation," *Nature Geoscience* 9, no. 12 (December 2016): 880–83, https://doi.org/10.1038/ngeo2840; Yanfeng Qian, "China Must Replace Half Its Homes in 20 Years," *China Daily,* August 7, 2010, http://www.chinadaily.com.cn/bizchina/2010-08/07/content_11114619.htm.

69. World Economic Forum, *The Global Competitiveness Report 2019;* Viola Zhou, "Firms Punished for Cutting Corners on Chinese High-Speed Rail Line," *South China Morning*

Post, November 15, 2017, Politics, https://www.scmp.com/news/china/policies-politics /article/2119961/firms-punished-construction-work-chinese-high-speed.

70. Donald C. Clarke, "Full Private Land Ownership Returns to China's Cities," Chinese Law Prof Blog, April 15, 2017, https://lawprofessors.typepad.com/china_law_prof_blog /2017/04/full-private-land-ownership-returns-to-chinas-cities.html.

71. Wade Shepard, "Why China Is Building Disposable Cities," Vagabond Journey, February 4, 2016, https://www.vagabondjourney.com/why-china-is-building-disposable-cities/.

72. Fei Meng, "Review of China Building Longevity," email to author, April 27, 2022.

73. Ben Blanchard, "China's Forced Evictions Cause Instability," *Reuters*, March 28, 2010, World News, https://www.reuters.com/article/us-china-evictions-idUSTRE62R13U20100328.

12. EQUITY AND HUMAN DEVELOPMENT

1. World Bank, "World Development Indicators," updated May 12, 2023, https://datacatalog .worldbank.org/search/dataset/0037712.

2. United Nations, "Universal Declaration of Human Rights" (1948), https://www.un.org/en /about-us/universal-declaration-of-human-rights.

3. Hannah Ritchie, "Who Has Contributed Most to Global CO_2 Emissions?," Our World in Data, October 1, 2019, https://ourworldindata.org/contributed-most-global-co$_2$.

4. Daniel Moran, Ali Hasanbeigi, and Cecilia Springer, *The Carbon Loophole in Climate Policy: Quantifying the Embedded Carbon in Traded Products* (report ClimateWorks Foundation, San Francisco, August 2018), https://www.bluegreenalliance.org/wp-content /uploads/2021/05/TheCarbonLoopholeinClimatePolicy-Final.pdf.

5. Peng Yin, Michael Brauer, Aaron J. Cohen, Haidong Wang, Jie Li, Richard T. Burnett, Jeffrey D. Stanaway, et al., "The Effect of Air Pollution on Deaths, Disease Burden, and Life Expectancy Across China and Its Provinces, 1990–2017: An Analysis for the Global Burden of Disease Study 2017," *Lancet Planetary Health* 4, no. 9 (September 2020): e386–98, https://doi.org/10.1016/S2542-5196(20)30161-3; World Health Organization, "WHO Global Air Quality Guidelines: Particulate Matter (PM2.5 and PM10), Ozone, Nitrogen Dioxide, Sulfur Dioxide and Carbon Monoxide," September 22, 2021, https://www.who.int/publications/i/item/9789240034228.

6. World Bank, "World Development Indicators"; Yin, Brauer, Cohen, Wang, Li, Burnett, Stanaway, et al., "The Effect of Air Pollution on Deaths, Disease Burden, and Life Expectancy Across China and Its Provinces, 1990–2017."

7. Yin, Brauer, Cohen, Wang, Li, Burnett, Stanaway, et al., "The Effect of Air Pollution on Deaths, Disease Burden, and Life Expectancy Across China and Its Provinces, 1990–2017."

8. White House, "Fact Sheet: The United States and European Union to Negotiate World's First Carbon-Based Sectoral Arrangement on Steel and Aluminum Trade," October 31, 2021, https://www.whitehouse.gov/briefing-room/statements-releases/2021/10/31/fact -sheet-the-united-states-and-european-union-to-negotiate-worlds-first-carbon-based -sectoral-arrangement-on-steel-and-aluminum-trade/.

9. Africa Growth Initiative, *Foresight Africa: Top Priorities for the Continent 2020–2030* (report, Brookings Institution, Washington, D.C., 2020), https://www.brookings.edu/wp-content/uploads/2020/01/ForesightAfrica2020_20200110.pdf.

10. Stéphane Willems and Kevin Baumert, *Institutional Capacity and Climate Actions* (report, OECD, Paris, 2003), https://www.oecd.org/env/cc/21018790.pdf.

11. Duke Global Health Innovation Center, "Vaccine Manufacturing—The Murky Manufacturing Landscape," updated July 1, 2022, https://launchandscalefaster.org/covid-19/vaccinemanufacturing.

12. Achal Prabhala and Alain Alsalhani, "Pharmaceutical Manufacturers Across Asia, Africa and Latin America with the Technical Requirements and Quality Standards to Manufacture MRNA Vaccines," December 10, 2021, https://accessibsa.org/mrna/.

13. Pharmaceutical Research and Manufacturers of America, "PhRMA Statement on WTO TRIPS Intellectual Property Waiver," press release, May 5, 2021, https://phrma.org/Coronavirus/PhRMA-Statement-on-WTO-TRIPS-Intellectual-Property-Waiver.

14. Damian Garde, Helen Branswell, and Matthew Herper, "Waiver of Patent Rights on Covid-19 Vaccines, in near Term, May Be More Symbolic Than Substantive," *STAT*, May 6, 2021, https://www.statnews.com/2021/05/06/waiver-of-patent-rights-on-covid-19-vaccines-in-near-term-may-be-more-symbolic-than-substantive/.

15. Africa Growth Initiative, *Foresight Africa: Top Priorities for the Continent 2020–2030*.

16. UNICEF, "Secondary Education," June 2022, https://data.unicef.org/topic/education/secondary-education/.

17. Tamar Jacoby, "Why Germany Is So Much Better at Training Its Workers," *The Atlantic*, October 16, 2014, https://www.theatlantic.com/business/archive/2014/10/why-germany-is-so-much-better-at-training-its-workers/381550/.

18. Jacoby, "Why Germany Is So Much Better at Training Its Workers."

19. World Bank, "World Development Indicators."

20. Africa Growth Initiative, *Foresight Africa: Top Priorities for the Continent 2020–2030*.

21. Carol Jenkins, "Why STEM Needs Girls," Council on Foreign Relations, March 10, 2016, https://www.cfr.org/blog/why-stem-needs-girls.

22. UN Conference on Trade and Development, *World Investment Report 2021: Investing in Sustainable Recovery* (report, United Nations, New York, 2021), https://unctad.org/system/files/official-document/wir2021_en.pdf.

23. Climate Policy Initiative, *Global Landscape of Climate Finance 2021* (report, Climate Policy Initiative, December 2021), https://www.climatepolicyinitiative.org/wp-content/uploads/2021/10/Full-report-Global-Landscape-of-Climate-Finance-2021.pdf.

24. Climate Policy Initiative, *Global Landscape of Climate Finance 2021*.

25. OECD, "Aid (ODA) by Sector and Donor [DAC5]," accessed June 8, 2023, https://stats.oecd.org/Index.aspx?datasetcode=TABLE5.

26. UN Conference on Trade and Development, "Foreign Direct Investment: Inward and Outward Flows and Stock, Annual," accessed June 8, 2023, https://unctadstat.unctad.org/wds/TableViewer/tableView.aspx?ReportId=96740.

27. UN Conference on Trade and Development, *World Investment Report 2021*.

28. World Bank, "Gross Fixed Capital Formation, Private Sector (% of GDP)," accessed July 11, 2023, https://data.worldbank.org/indicator/NE.GDI.FPRV.ZS.

29. Ariane Volk, *Investing for Impact: The Global Impact Investing Market 2020* (report, International Finance Corporation, World Bank Group, Washington, D.C., 2021), https://www.ifc.org/wps/wcm/connect/365d09e3-e8d6-4da4-badb-741933e76f3b/2021 -Investing+for+Impact_FIN2.pdf?MOD=AJPERES&CVID=nL5SF6G.

30. Paul Boynton, "Sub-Saharan Africa's Struggle to Attract Impact Investment," *Financial Times*, August 28, 2019, https://www.ft.com/content/18752b94-c8d1-11e9-a1f4-3669401 ba76f.

31. Megan McHugh, Jiancheng Ye, Claude Maechling, and Jane Holl, "Anchor Businesses in the United States" (Northwestern University Feinberg School of Medicine, April 2020), https://www.feinberg.northwestern.edu/sites/health-outcomes/docs/anchors-report -april-2.pdf.

32. Economic Innovation Group, "Distressed Communities Index"—*The Spaces Between Us: The Evolution of American Communities in the New Century* (4th ed.) (report, October 2020), https://eig.org/wp-content/uploads/2020/10/EIG-2020-DCI-Report.pdf.

33. Economic Innovation Group, "Distressed Communities Index."

34. Richard Rothstein, *The Color of Law: A Forgotten History of How Our Government Segregated America* (New York: Liveright, 2017).

35. Nick Chiles, "Everyone Pays a Hefty Price for Segregation, Study Says," *NPR*, March 31, 2017, https://www.npr.org/sections/codeswitch/2017/03/31/522098019/everyone-pays-a -hefty-price-for-segregation-study-says; Ani Turner, "The Business Case for Racial Equity" (W. K. Kellogg Foundation, July 24, 2018), https://wkkf.issuelab.org/resource /business-case-for-racial-equity.html#download-options.

36. Economic Innovation Group, "Distressed Communities Index."

37. BlueGreen Alliance, "Solidarity for Climate Action," June 2019, http://www.bluegreenal liance.org/wp-content/uploads/2019/07/Solidarity-for-Climate-Action-vFINAL.pdf.

38. Suzanne Gamboa, Phil McCausland, Josh Lederman, and Ben Popken, "Bulldozed and Bisected: Highway Construction Built a Legacy of Inequality," NBC News, June 18, 2021, https://www.nbcnews.com/specials/america-highways-inequality/.

39. BlueGreen Alliance, "Manufacturing Investments to Build Back Better," October 2021, https://www.bluegreenalliance.org/wp-content/uploads/2021/10/BGA-MFG-Industrial -Factsheet_FINAL_102121.pdf.

40. Camilla Hodgson, "Risks to Global Supply Chains Rising as Climate Change Worsens, IPCC Warns," *Financial Times*, February 28, 2022, https://www.ft.com/content/83f0e5c3 -f399-444e-be46-23b3a7e33630.

41. Hodgson, "Risks to Global Supply Chains Rising as Climate Change Worsens, IPCC Warns."

42. BlueGreen Alliance, "Solidarity for Climate Action."

43. BlueGreen Alliance, "Solidarity for Climate Action."

44. Jonathan Weisman, "Manchin's Choice on Build Back Better: Mine Workers or Mine Owners," *New York Times*, January 10, 2022, U.S., https://www.nytimes.com/2022/01/10 /us/politics/manchin-coal-miners.html.

45. BlueGreen Alliance, "Solidarity for Climate Action."

46.   William Wilkes, Charlie Devereux, and Ewa Krukowska, "Populism and Protest Lurk Behind Europe's Dying Coal Mines," *Bloomberg*, August 30, 2019, https://www .bloomberg.com/news/features/2019-08-31/germany-election-dying-coal-mines-give -rise-to-populism-protest; University of Cambridge, "Former Coal Mining Communities Have Less Faith in Politics Than Other 'Left Behind' Areas," September 20, 2021, https://www.cam.ac.uk/research/news/former-coal-mining-communities-have-less -faith-in-politics-than-other-left-behind-areas.

47.   World Resources Institute, "Colorado, United States: State-Level Planning for a Just Transition from Coal," April 1, 2021, https://www.wri.org/update/colorado-united-states -state-level-planning-just-transition-coal.

48.   U.S. Federal Reserve Bank, "What Economic Goals Does the Federal Reserve Seek to Achieve Through Its Monetary Policy?," August 27, 2020, https://www.federalreserve .gov/faqs/what-economic-goals-does-federal-reserve-seek-to-achieve-through -monetary-policy.htm.

INDEX